The Complete Small Business Guide

■

SOURCES OF INFORMATION

FOR NEW AND SMALL BUSINESSES

Colin Barrow

BBC BOOKS

Published by BBC Books, an imprint of BBC Worldwide Publishing
BBC Worldwide Limited, Woodlands, 80 Wood Lane, London W12 0TT

First published in 1993
This updated and revised edition published in 1995
© Colin Barrow 1995
ISBN 0 563 37083 1

Designed by Ged Lennox
Set in Stone serif
Printed and bound in Great Britain by Clays Ltd, St Ives plc

Author's note

This is a reference book and is not intended to be read in its entirety. The reader will need to use the Contents list to focus attention on the areas of greatest interest (or importance) to him or her. The index lists organizations, books and publications and the topics referred to in the main text, complementing the Contents and extending the cross-referencing provided in the text.

Contents

SECTION 7

1 | *Why small firms matter, who starts them and why they often fail*

■ WHY SMALL FIRMS MATTER

Small businesses are a vital spark in the economy. Almost without exception throughout the 1980s and 90s countries have sought ways and means to stimulate an increase in the numbers of small firms starting up in the economy. Their reasons for this concern are included in the list that follows.

Responsiveness to change

Being small and having limited resources, small firms are at the mercy of market falls. When economic conditions change, so must they. Large firms are not so nimble and can often continue in a direction not signalled or required by the economy for some time before recognizing the need for change.

For example, during the 1970s in the United Kingdom, the corner food store was universally recognized as being on the way out. The graphs showed the number of outlets contracting sharply, being replaced by larger, less local and more efficient supermarkets. The major food retailers' vision was that virtually all purchasing would be confined to supermarkets and cash-and-carries on the edge of town. These arguments were supported by the increase in car and freezer ownership.

But suddenly during the late 1970s and 80s this trend was sharply reversed. Arguments abound as to its cause. Popular mythology suggests that an influx of Asians from such countries as Uganda altered the economic equilibrium with their willingness, desire and necessity to work long hours and their ability to draw exclusively on family and friends who were prepared to work for a low wage.

But the central fact remains. The market had wanted and needed a strong local food shopping network, but big business had misread the signals. With their strong resources and less than flexible attitudes, big firms had been able to continue pursuing a wrong-headed strategy for over a decade.

In the United States, for example, with its strong entrepreneurial bias, a quite different remedy was offered. When local shops were in danger of becoming uneconomic relative to larger competitors, they changed their format. They reduced their range to meet only major buying requirements, carrying only the top couple of brands of coffee, for example, rather than the eight to ten that supermarkets carry. They also varied opening hours. Business format franchises came into the market, simplifying and routinizing procedures and thus making it easier for new people to enter the market. The fastest-growing retailer in the United States over this period was the Seven Eleven Store – a franchise that closely responded to the changing economic conditions and improved the flow of food at economic prices.

The United Kingdom, on the other hand, still suffers from the effect of leaving food retailing in the hands of a few large multiples. For example, food costs more because the supermarkets have higher margins than retailers in most other European countries and the United States.

A major source of innovation

Small businesses play a crucial role in creating new technology and products. During the last few decades the roles of large and small businesses in the development of new technologies and products have differed substantially. Large organizations are more likely to be sources of 'process' innovation. When they do develop new products, these tend to emerge from incremented improvements or refinements. Small business is more likely to strive for the unexpected, 'leap-frog' product innovations.

Over 60% of the major inventions developed in the twentieth century were the work of independent inventors and small companies. So when you consider that small firms have historically accounted for only around 20% of output, it is clear that they are three times as 'effective' at innovating than larger firms. Examples of such inventions include the aeroplane, the helicopter, catalytic oil refining, oxygen steel-making, photocopying, the automatic transmission, power steering, air conditioning, the Polaroid camera, the zipper and dacron-polyester fibre.

More than half of today's inventors work outside the organized research groups of the corporate industrial laboratories. Independent inventors took out roughly 40% of the total patents in the United States over the past twenty years. Of the 60% of patents held by corporations, one-third came from corporate employees working outside corporate laboratories. Firms with fewer than 1,000 employees produced innovation at about a quarter of the cost of middle-sized (1,000-10,000 employees) firms, and at about one-twenty-fifth that of large (10,000 and over employees) firms.

Small firms seem to encourage innovation because less restrictive organization provides for more individual initiative. Four other reasons have been suggested. First, in a small technological firm, innovation is necessary to ensure survival, whereas the large firm tends simply to maintain its product market position. Second, managers of small technological companies (in which they often own a share) have more incentive to innovate. Third, large firms may prefer to hold technical improvements to a minimum for marketing reasons. Fourth, researchers and innovators in large firms tend to specialize; those in small firms tend to be technical generalists. Specialization can limit innovation;

the more knowledge a developer has to draw on, the more original the resulting innovation tends to be. The conclusion to be drawn is that small businesses are a substantial source of innovation and technical change, and that they make their contribution more efficiently and at lower cost than larger businesses.

Job creation

Until the mid-1970s popular mythology had it that big businesses created most new jobs. That view was first seriously challenged by Professor David L Birch of the Massachusetts Institute of Technology. His researchers disclosed that between 1969 and 1976 in the United States:

- Small businesses with 20 or fewer employees created 66% of all new jobs. In New England alone, such businesses created 99% of all new jobs.
- Mid-sized and big businesses created few new jobs.

These conclusions were based on a study of the data files of 5.6 million businesses. To quote Professor Birch, 'It appears that the smaller corporations are aggressively seeking out most new opportunities, while the larger ones are primarily redistributing their operations.' Another US study found that small, young high-technology businesses created new jobs at a much faster rate than older, larger businesses.

Recent studies in France have confirmed that small firms were net creators of jobs throughout the 1970s, roughly absorbing the reduction in large firms' employment. In the United Kingdom much the same job creation phenomenon has been seen, with firms employing fewer than 100 people increasing their share of employment at the expense of larger firms.

■ WHY DO PEOPLE WANT TO START A SMALL BUSINESS?

The stimulus for starting a business may come from having a brilliant idea, spotting a gap in the market or, as in the case of Tim Waterstone, getting fired. These ideas are explored further in Section 3. Whatever the reason, there are some common advantages and diasadvantages to starting up.

Advantages of running your own business

Few people get rich working for someone else. Running a business at least provides the opportunity to make more money, but whether you become wealthy depends very much on the success you make of it. If the business does well the founder can determine the amount of money he or she takes out as salary and can claim extra benefits on the firm (e.g. cars, pensions). Big businesses are only small businesses that succeed. If a business makes it to the big time the founder might consider going public, which will dramatically increase the value of shares, or may decide to sell out for a large profit and retire in luxury. More important than riches to many an entrepreneur, though, is the freedom which comes from being your own boss. Proprietors are totally independent and can plan the business and run it on a day-to-day basis in the way they want. It also gives them the opportunity to work in a field they really enjoy.

There are tax advantages too. Self-employed people have more allowances against income than employees. Directors of their own limited-liability companies, though, are not classified as self-employed for tax purposes, but the benefits they can take from the company frequently mitigate their tax bills.

Disadvantages

Running a business is much more risky than working for someone else. If the business fails you stand to lose far more than just your job. Not only will all your hard work have been to no avail, but you might suffer severe financial hardship if your business owes money since, as a self-employed person, you are personally liable to your debtors. This might mean selling your assets, including your home, and, at the worst, may result in bankruptcy. If you form a limited company your personal liability to creditors is limited to the value of the shares you hold – in theory. But, in practice, banks usually require a personal guarantee from the director(s) to secure an overdraft or loan for the business, which to some extent negates the benefits of limited-liability status.

You are totally responsible for the success or failure of your business. This can be very exhilarating, but it is, inevitably, very stressful: constant pressure and long hours are par for the course for most entrepreneurs. This can drastically affect your social and family life, also your health.

To give a flavour of what it's like being your own boss, here in their own words are selected comments from some small-business founders.

- It gives you a feeling of being totally in control of your own destiny which is very exciting.
- You feel totally productive. You use your own time as you wish to spend it. Often this means working all hours of the day, six days a week – permanently. But it isn't a grind if you're doing it for yourself.
- I have earned far more in personal reward than I have financial benefits. It has given me self-confidence which has made me calmer, less neurotic and more prepared to take risks than hitherto.
- No longer being involved in office politics has given me an enormous feeling of freedom.
- You get pleasure from the simplest things – just the fact that the office copier is working!
- The ability to buy more and better material possessions is irrelevant compared to the sense of achievement you feel.
- To begin with it's a very exciting feeling, you've stuck your flag in the sand. Then ... there is a deadly pause while you sit and wait for the business to pour in. The bank manager/your spouse is going berserk and you wonder why you've done it. If you're sensible, you ride out this period by concen-

trating on planning the business properly and making sure you've got your costings right.
- It's food for the soul.
- It's good fun.

But ...

- It's very lonely knowing you are totally responsible for the success or failure of the business.
- You have to be totally single-minded, which can make you appear selfish to family and friends. It bust up my marriage.
- You have to be prepared to turn your hand to anything that needs doing. A small firm can't afford all the back-up services – typing help, tea lady, mail boy – you might have become accustomed to as an employee.
- Some aspects of the work are unpleasant – e.g. cold-canvassing for clients, chasing up slow payers, and doing VAT returns.
- You must develop a strong sense of responsibility to your staff. You can't be cavalier with them, after all, their career and jobs are in your hands.
- You must be prepared to be ruthless, however friendly you are with staff or suppliers. If staff are no good you must fire them. If suppliers let you down get rid of them.
- It was a great relief going back to being an employee since I no longer had the burden of finding staff salaries each week.
- These days everyone is trying to live on credit so the biggest problem is cash flow.
- It's very terrifying at the beginning. You sit there waiting for the phone to ring and when it does you hope like hell it's a potential customer rather than someone you owe money to.
- The paperwork and form-filling is time-consuming and irritating. The Department of Employment returned a form to us because we omitted to indicate the type of business of a client even though the client was called the Bank of America!
- I find the responsibility a constant worry – it brings me out in cold sweats every night.

Despite the complaints most business owners are pleased to have gone on their own and would have no hesitation in starting up another business rather than work for someone else.

In 1991 some 800 independent profitable companies with turnover of less than £25 million were asked what motivated them to start up and run their own businesses (see Figure 1.1). The majority of the responses, 73.5%, had turnover between £1 million and £10 million. A massive 98% of respondents rated personal satisfaction from success as an important motivator, with 70% of these rating it very important. 88% rated 'ability to do things my own way' and 87% rated 'freedom to take a longer-term view' as important or very important, indicating that independence is a key motivator in entrepreneurs' minds.

Evidently, financial rewards register as an important motivator, but it is interesting to note that they are rated less highly than personal satisfaction, and only marginally more highly than independence. To assume, as some do, that owners of growing businesses are motivated purely by pecuniary gain is not only naive but also demonstrates a lack of understanding of entrepreneurs' personal goals.

Few were highly motivated by 'something to pass on to the children' – only 15% rated this as very important. Does the idea of a family company belong to the past?

Figure 1.1   Ranking of small-business motivation

Source: Coopers and Lybrand

What do you consider are your principal motivations in running your business?

1   Personal satisfaction from success
2   Capital growth
3   Income
4   Ability to do things my own way
5   Freedom to take a longer-term view
6   Personal wealth
7   Security
8   Funds for retirement
9   Something to pass on to the children

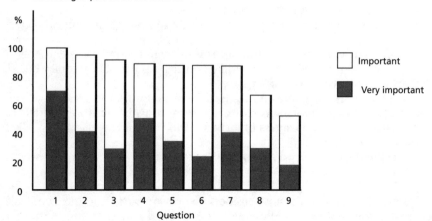

■ THE CHARACTERISTICS OF A SMALL-BUSINESS PERSON

To launch a new business successfully calls for a particular type of person. The business idea must also be right for the market and the timing must be spot on. The world of business failures is full of products that are ahead of their time.

The business founder is frequently seen as someone who is always bursting with new ideas, is highly enthusiastic, hyperactive and insatiably curious. But the more you try to create a picture of the typical small-business founder, the more elusive he or she becomes.

Peter Drucker, the international business guru, captured the problem clearly with this description.

Some are eccentrics, others painfully correct conformists; some are fat and some are lean; some are worriers, some relaxed; some drink quite heavily, others are total abstainers; some are men of great charm and warmth, some have no more personality than a frozen mackerel.

Many such efforts have been made to 'divine' the characteristics of those people who are best suited to become small-business proprietors. These efforts will no doubt continue, but it is unlikely they will be any more successful than prediction techniques are today.

The following fairly broad characteristics are generally accepted as being 'essential', but such evidence as there is to support this view is largely anecdotal.

Total commitment and hard work

Small-business founders have complete faith in their business idea. That's the only way they can convince all the doubters they are bound to meet on the way. They are usually single-minded and more than capable of putting in an eighteen-hour working day. This can put a strain on other relationships, so successful small-business founders usually involve their families and get them on their side too.

Small-business proprietors are also likely to put in many more hours at work than their employees. This is true for both male and female small-business people, although generally male proprietors do seem to work longer hours than their female equivalent. Running your own business is like being in a race with no tape – it just goes on like a 365-day-a-year marathon.

Acceptance of uncertainty

Managers in big business, on the other hand, tend to seek to minimize risk by delaying decisions until every possible fact is known. This response to uncertainty is one that challenges the need to operate in the unknown. There is a feeling that to work without all the facts is not prudent or desirable. Entrepreneurs, on the other hand, have known that by the time the fog of uncertainty has been completely lifted too many people will be able to spot the opportunity clearly. In point of fact an entrepreneur would usually be interested only in a decision that involved accepting a degree of uncertainty and would welcome, and on occasion even relish, that position.

Good health

Apart from being able to put in long days, the successful small-business owner needs to be on the spot to manage the firm every day. Owners are the essential lubricant that keeps the wheels of the small business turning. They have to turn their hands to anything that needs to be done to make the venture work, and they have to plug any gaps caused either by other people's sickness or the fact that they just can't afford to employ anyone else for that particular job. They themselves cannot afford the luxury of sick leave. Even a week or so's holiday would be viewed as something of a luxury in the early years of a business life.

Self-discipline

One of the most common pitfalls for the novice business man or woman is failing to recognize the difference between cash and profit. Cash can make people 'feel' wealthy and, if it results in a relaxed attitude to corporate status symbols such as cars and luxury office fittings, then failure is just around the corner.

The owner-manager needs strong personal discipline to keep him or herself and the business on the schedule the plan calls for. This is the drum beat that sets the timing for everything in the firm. Get that wrong and wrong signals are sent to every part of the business – both inside and out.

Originator/investor characteristics

Most people recognize innovation as the most distinctive trait of business founders. They tend to tackle the unknown; they do things in new and difficult ways; they weave old ideas into new patterns. But they go beyond innovation itself and carry their concept to market rather than remain in an ivory tower.

The high failure rate shows that small businesses are faced with many dangers. An essential characteristic of someone starting a business is a willingness to make decisions and to take risks. This does not mean gambling on hunches. It means carefully calculating the odds and deciding which risks to take and when to take them.

Small-business founders are rarely geniuses. There are nearly always other people in their business who have more competence, in one field, than they could ever aspire to. But they have a wide range of ability and willingness to turn their hands to anything that has to be done to make the venture succeed. They can usually make the product, market it and count the money, but above all they have the self-confidence that lets them move comfortably through uncharted waters.

Planner/organizer characteristics

Business founders need to be results-oriented. Successful people set themselves goals and get pleasure out of trying to achieve them. Once a goal has been reached, they have to get the next target in view as quickly as possible. This restlessness is very characteristic. Sir James Goldsmith is a classic example, moving the base of his business empire from the United Kingdom to France, then to the United States – and finally into pure cash, ahead of the 1987 stock market crash.

To succeed, the owner-manager needs both the ability and the willingness to make decisions – often involving unpleasant choices and always concerning matters of commercial life or death.

Unfortunately such decisions usually have to be taken without adequate information and without much 'professional' assistance. The ability to take irrevocable decisions on the basis of inadequate information is vital, and any tendency to procrastination will waste more time than any 'one-man band' has available.

Later on, when it becomes possible and appropriate to delegate decision-making, this situation will change. But in the early period the small-business owner's day is filled with large and small decisions.

■ WHY THINGS GO WRONG

Of the million new businesses born each year in the developed world, only half live as long as eighteen months and only one in five live as long as ten years. These dramatic figures are often quoted, but are nevertheless open to question. In fact no one has really defined failure. Many proprietors shut down because they are bored, can make more money elsewhere, have sold out to the competition, or have retired.

A recent UK study which confined itself to looking at businesses registered for VAT (i.e. had a turnover of around £25,000 or greater in 1990) came up with an interesting perspective on failure (see Figure 1.2). Only half the businesses superficially recorded as 'failures' in the United Kingdom's national statistics had actually ceased trading. Nearly a third had either changed their legal identity (i.e. become a company), or had been taken over by another business. However, the remaining fifth of small firms de-registered from VAT because they fell below the turnover threshold. (This is a sign that they are probably on their way to failure – but have not failed yet!)

Figure 1.2   Reasons for small firms 'failing'

Source: *Employment Gazette*, November 1990

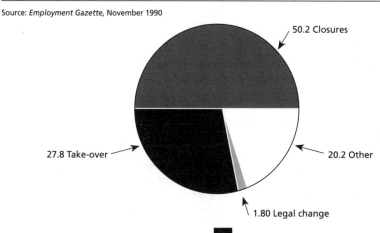

50.2 Closures

27.8 Take-over

20.2 Other

1.80 Legal change

The study concentrated on VAT returns as non-incorporated businesses do not file their accounts centrally. Of the firms that do fail, the biggest single reason is incompetence. Disaster overtakes few, except perhaps in the eyes of the proprietor. However you manage the statistics, many small businesses do go to the wall each year, which bears witness to the fact that running a business makes large demands, and that many people who start up are ill-equipped to do so. The highest risks are in the first few years.

Some of these budding entrepreneurs lose their life savings, others end up in endless debt. A fortunate few lose only their dignity and rise phoenix-like a few years later, using their experience as a base on which to build a successful venture.

Some academics believe the high failure rate is the price that has to be paid in order to produce a thriving new business sector – the survival of the fittest. There is no risk-free way to a profitable business but it is as well to know the dangers that lie ahead. New start-up businesses fail for the following basic reasons.

Nothing new to say

Many people starting up in business have no clear idea as to why people should buy from them rather than from existing suppliers of competitive products or services. Indeed, many budding entrepreneurs have little idea what governs their potential customers' purchase decisions. Trying to sell sausage to consumers who are preoccupied with buying sizzle is largely a waste of time.

case study

Tom Farmer, the son of a Leith shipping clerk who earned £5 a week, launched Kwik-Fit in 1971. By 1990 the company had a turnover of £200 million, made £40 million profit and employed 3,400 people by servicing 3.5 million cars a year.

Farmer founded the business out of a deep dissatisfaction with the level of service provided by garage servicing. No one ever called customers to tell them when their cars were ready, and the bills bore no relation to the original estimates. In his own words, the enduring philosophy behind his business, to which he ascribes its success, is, '100% customer satisfaction. Just giving service – phoning back in half an hour if you say you will, standing by promises – puts you miles ahead of anyone else in the field.'

case study

Shirt Point, started just before Christmas 1987, was the brainchild of ad-man Robert Barclay and his friend since primary school, art dealer Jeremy Wayne. 'We were having lunch eighteen months earlier and complaining about the hassle we had trying to get shirts done,' says Barclay, aged 29. 'High performers in the City, earning perhaps £100,000 a year and working from 7 a.m. until 7 p.m., still have to get up at the crack of dawn to iron a shirt.'

Their catchment area was initially restricted to the City and they laundered up to 1,000 shirts a week, charging £3.65 a piece. Hard-pressed brokers and bankers could take their *dirty laundry to the office, telephone Shirt Point, have it collected the same day and then returned, hand-finished with buttons sewn on and collar bones renewed where necessary, within forty-eight hours. This proved more attractive than the 'same day' service offered by dry-cleaner shops.*

These are two examples of new businesses that had something new to say and knew exactly who to say it to. If there is nothing unique about your product or service or the way in which you plan to do business, you must surely question why anyone would want to buy from you. It may only be that your opening hours are different, and that the customers feel that matters; or that you keep your promises while operating in a sector such as building, which is renowned for poor integrity. But you must have an edge that matters in the market.

Lack of expertise

Starting a business from scratch calls for remarkable versatility. The owner-manager types the invoices with one finger in the evenings, does the books at the weekend, sells on Monday, makes the goods from Tuesday and delivers when he or she can. People with a history in large firms sometimes find it difficult to become a jack of all trades.

Table 1.1 summarizes the findings of a Dun and Bradstreet study into the reasons for failure. Lack of experience, unbalanced experience or inexperience in the industry or trade accounts for most of the problems.

Table 1.1   Causes of business failure

Source: *The Business Failure Record* (New York: Dun and Bradstreet, Inc.)

% of business failures	Cause of failure	Explanation
44	Incompetence	Lack of fitness to run the business – physical, moral, or intellectual
17	Lack of managerial experience	Little, if any, experience managing employees and other resources before going into business
16	Unbalanced experience	Not well rounded in marketing, finance, purchasing and production
15	Inexperience in line	Little, if any, experience in the product or service before going into business
1	Neglect	Too little attention to the business, due to bad habits, poor health, or marital difficulties
1	Fraud or disaster	Fraud: misleading name, statements, premeditated overbuy, or irregular disposal of assets. Disaster: fire, flood, burglary, employees' fraud, or strike (some could have been provided against through insurance)
6	Unknown	

Nowhere does this lack of experience show up faster and with more disastrous results than during recessionary times. Lots of people are propelled into entrepreneurship through redundancy and others forsake their own industries believing that the best opportunities lie elsewhere. However, it is clear that the further you move away from what you know and understand, in terms of products or services and customers or markets, the less your chances of success are.

If you have nothing new to say then you are selling an existing product or service into an existing market. Here you end up in a price war. If you propose to sell a new product or service into a new market then the risks will in all probability exceed the potential reward.

The low-risk way in is to build on either your product (service) experience or your knowledge of the market. If you are more adventurous, you can increase the risk by moving away from one area of expertise while building on another, e.g. move into an unknown market with an existing product or service.

Bad timing

There is no doubt that small firms fare badly in recessions. It follows that if you can avoid starting up as the market is falling you will improve your chances of success.

The four distinct phases of short business cycles

Business activity moves in cycles – measured from peak to peak or from trough to trough. Four distinct phases can be seen in Figure 1.4. In the first part of the downturn after the peak in activity, growth is above trend (phase D1). The most depressed part of the cycle is reached in the second phase of the downturn (phase D2) as growth slips below trend. Growth may or may not be negative at this time, depending on how fierce the downturn is and on the rate of underlying growth. The upturn from trough to peak also has two phases when growth is first below trend (U1) and then above it (U2).

Figure 1.3   Small-business numbers

Source: Barclays, *Small Business Bulletin* (Issue 1, 1994)

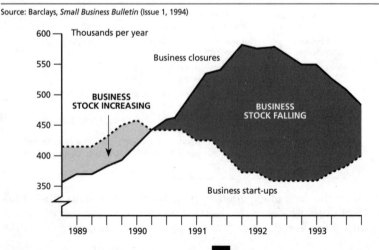

Figure 1.4 Textbook cycle

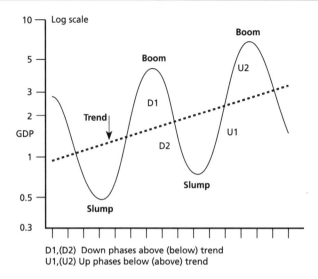

D1,(D2) Down phases above (below) trend
U1,(U2) Up phases below (above) trend

Since 1955, a peak year, there have been six complete business cycles – so a broad picture is beginning to appear. There is, for example, a clear difference between the almost clockwork cycles of the 1950s and the 1960s and those which happen after 1973. The earlier cycles were roughly symmetrical, lasting 4-5 years (Table 1.2). By contrast, the post-1973 world saw longer cycles – over nine years in the case of the post-1979 cycles – with much deeper troughs and, in 1988, a higher peak (Table 1.3).

Table 1.2 UK output cycle

Source: UK Output Statistics

Peak to peak		Trough to trough	
Period	*No. of quarters*	*Period*	*No. of quarters*
1955 Q3 – 1960 Q1	18	1958 Q2 – 1963 Q1	19
1960 Q1 – 1964 Q4	19	1963 Q1 – 1967 Q1	16
1964 Q4 – 1969 Q2	18	1967 Q1 – 1972 Q1	20
1969 Q2 – 1973 Q3	17	1972 Q1 – 1975 Q3	14
1973 Q3 – 1979 Q2	23	1975 Q3 – 1981 Q1	22
1979 Q2 – 1988 Q3	37	1981 Q1 – 1991 Q1	40
Average 1955-73	18	Average 1958-75	17.5
1955-88	22	1958-91	22

Table 1.3   Capacity utilization peaks and troughs*

Source: UK Output Statistics

Peaks	1955	1960	1964	1969	1973	1979	1988
%	81.7	81.5	81.7	81.7	82.0	79.8	83.7

Troughs	1958	1963	1967	1972	1975	1981
%	75.4	76.0	75.3	75.6	72.8	70.6

*Current activity rates in manufacturing as % of full plant capacity.

The major differences in timing are due to long upswings of the later cycles (Table 1.4). Down phases have been more even. The first part of the down phase – while growth is above trend – has typically lasted around a year. Another year usually goes by in the more depressed second phase of below-trend growth until the trough is reached. In the 1950s and 1960s cycles, the two up phases of first below-trend and then above-trend growth each lasted about a year. But in the post-1973 cycles, the upturns – especially in the above-trend phase – were far longer, some five years in the case of the 1980s second-phase recovery. The drawn-out nature of the 1980s upswing was a global event which led to a rash belief that the cycle had been abolished.

Table 1.4   Up and down phases

No. of quarters	D1	D2	U1	U2
Average 1957-1973	6.0	4.5	3.5	4.0
Average 1957-1989	5.5	4.0	4.5	7.5

D1, D2 – first and second down phases of cycle;
U1, U2 – first and second up phases of cycle (see Figure 1.4).

So when will cycles turn up?

If you accept the arguments above, the down phase of the business cycle lasts around two years, and a further year and a half is needed to get back on to the long-run growth trend. This is four years in all, which is very much the experience of the 1990-93 recession.

Spotting when the market will turn is notoriously tricky: every cycle is different because the experience gained in previous cycles is built in. The rule about business cycles is that all are recognizable except the current one – whatever the experts say.

Still, there are some forward indicators which signpost that an economic spring is on the way. Just as all industries don't go into a recession at the same time, they come out in a different order too. These differences make the horizon visible. Take a maker of bathroom fittings for example. The sellers of building plots, followed by the housebuilders, will all have nosedived before the bathroom fittings manufacturer begins to feel the pinch. After all, even without a sale, most housebuilders will still put a bathroom into a house. To spot the upturn, a bathroom fittings maker needs to look out for such things as changes in the volume of building land sales, or brick production.

Bricks are a useful pointer to the country's economic health generally. Redland Bricks has closed five of its 128 works since the end of 1989 because of the slump in the housing market. However, figures for 1993 show that brick stocks were diminishing and output was rising for the first time in two years.

Interest rates and inflation are not really indicators of stages in the business cycle. In fact, interest rates are usually used to try to push economic growth up or down according to the Government's current goals.

One of the most reliable forward indicators of a return to economic activity is when companies return to the market and start buying up small fry. This means that larger firms are gearing themselves up for growth and see target companies as representing good value for money. The point at which merger and acquisition activity stirs is usually the point when small-firm insolvencies and liquidations have reached a peak.

There is one further aspect of timing that makes small firms more vulnerable than they need be. As many products and services have an element of seasonality about them, it follows that sales demand varies over the year: more toys are sold at Christmas than at any other time, and fewer sausages and more ice-creams are sold in the summer.

It follows that you need to take account of seasonality as well as the economic cycle if you want to survive. But it may not always be in your interest to start-up in your high season – if your systems are unproven, taking on lots of orders may only lead to an army of dissatisfied customers.

The Channel Tunnel, for example, having missed its spring 1994 opening date, elected for a low-risk start-up strategy. It did not try to open up for full business in the peak summer months. Rather, the plan was to 'invite' suppliers, journalists and some key market influencers to try out the service over the summer months, and open up to the public later in the year, when demand is lower – and the systems would have been fully tested.

At a more modest level, how many new restaurants have you been to that appear to have opened too early? Meals are late, due to equipment failures, and service is badly provided by untrained staff. Unhappy customers, on average, tell 15 other people of their bad experiences. For a restaurant, reliant heavily on word of mouth, the effect can be disastrous.

Cash crisis

Too few small businesses prepare a cash-flow forecast at the outset and maintain a permanent one-year projection as they start to trade. Received wisdom is that all forecasts are wrong so why bother making them? Paradoxically it is exactly because events are so unpredictable that cash-flow projections are essential. The aim in the cash-flow forecast is to make a realistic and prudent estimate of the likely timing of cash moving in and out of your business. This will allow you to anticipate potential danger points when you could run out of cash, and so be able to build in a margin of safety.

The forecast will also let you see how much money you are likely to need overall to get started. If the forecast shows you need more money than you have or are prepared or able to raise, then you can do something about it before you start out. For example you could postpone purchasing a car, computer or a fax and beg or borrow a desk and chair.

Further factors can contribute to the cash crisis.

Underestimating the start-up time

There's often a great deal to do before the customers come along – premises to be found and fitted out, equipment and stock to be bought. This all has to be done before any cash can start to come in, as opposed to just go out. Estimate how long you think it will take, double it and add on a bit more. Unfortunately entrepreneurs, being optimists, usually believe only the rosiest projections.

Consequences of early growth

Many people think their problems are over once customers start to roll in – but they may have only just begun. A business changes its shape and size very rapidly in its early days. As sales grow, ever increasing sums of cash are needed to fuel that growth. And the danger is overtrading, i.e. growing faster than cash resources allow.

Mistaking cash for profit

The cash that flows into the business hasn't had any of the automatic deductions knocked off it as has a pay cheque from an employer. Too often entrepreneurs yield to the temptation to use this cash to maintain their living standards, and when the bills come in – from the suppliers, for National Insurance, for VAT – they can't pay them. The Inland Revenue and Customs and Excise put more businesses into liquidation than anyone else.

Wrong location

Where you conduct your business and how much rent you pay are vital. Don't be tempted to take premises just because the rent is cheap – no customers may pass that way. Equally, don't take on an expensive high street site if your business turnover is unlikely to cover the costs. Your initial market research should help you identify a suitable location.

Falling out

Hidden in all of the reasons why small firms fail is the failure of relationships between business partners.

If the business is going to have any chance of success, it is essential that the partners trust each other and can work together harmoniously. Also, since you and your partner(s) have unlimited financial credibility for the firm, if things go wrong – regardless of whose fault it is – creditors can claim the personal possessions of each and every partner. A partnership is therefore almost as close a relationship as a marriage. So the choice of partner must be made with as much care as selecting a wife or husband.

If you are considering a partnership, ask yourself first if you have the right temperament to be a partner. Some people are too individual to be able to cope with pooling their ideas and resources on an equal footing, as the case that follows illustrates.

Case study

Within a year of taking a partner, Eric O'Keefe opted out of the highly successful Spanish bar he had painstakingly set up and nurtured for seven years. He took the partner because he needed finance to expand but Eric couldn't tolerate what he saw as the partner's 'interference' with the way the bar was run. He now admits – with hindsight – that the partner was perfectly entitled to express his views on what had, after all, become a joint project. Eric agrees that his personality was the problem. 'I'm better off on my own,' he admits and, perhaps equally significantly, 'Alcohol always causes personality clashes but it's the only business I would contemplate working in.'

There are no hard and fast rules about selecting a partner, but the most successful partnerships do seem to be those where the partners have known each other for some time – either as friends or business associates – and where they have complementary skills and personalities. One partner, for instance, might be a technical person who looks after the manufacturing side of the operation while the other is good at dealing with people and looks after sales, or an 'ideas' person who can often be successfully teamed with a down-to-earth practical man or woman who can implement the ideas.

If your spouse is your proposed business partner, then the problems can be greatly magnified. In this case you really do need to be sure that there is a separate and valuable role for each partner to fill – and that someone is the boss. Fifty-fifty partnerships are rarely successful: hard decisions are often avoided, as they cannot be 'forced' through the legal structure. (See Section 7 for more information on Partnerships.)

No management accounts

Alongside the sharp rise in new 'entrepreneurs' has come an urgent requirement to become financially literate, an essential prerequisite to raising finance and using it wisely. Further pressure for awareness of matters financial has been applied by the Insolvency Act, making it an offence for directors to continue trading once they know – or should have known – their business is in trouble.

A heavy fog seems to descend as soon as anyone approaches the financial management field for the first time. Whether running or setting up a business, getting a first taste of responsibility for accounts or taking a business course, the first steps towards an understanding of finance are the most difficult. The consequences of failing to understand business finance are not the same for everyone. The student simply fails an exam, while the businessman all too often loses his business, and the executive gets fired. Competition is generally greater today and the margin for mistakes smaller.

Poor financial control is a major contribution to business failure. People running small businesses frequently leave financial questions to their accountants to sort out at the year end. They often have the mistaken belief that keeping the books is an activity quite divorced from the 'real' task of getting customers or making products.

By the time the first set of figures is prepared (a year or so late) most small businesses are already too far down the road to financial failure to be saved. The final accounts become all too final and a good business proposition has been ruined by financial illiteracy. The few businessmen who do ask the way, perhaps of an accountant or bank manager, often do not understand the terms being used to explain the situation.

There is an urgent need for those starting up and running small firms to become financially literate and to operate using monthly budgets and actual trading results comparisons from the outset. Only in this way can problems be identified quickly, more profitable opportunities exploited and loss-making activities eliminated.

No business plan

Perhaps the most important step in launching any new venture or expanding an existing one is the construction of a business plan. Such a plan must include your goals for the enterprise, both short and long term; a description of the products or services you will offer and the market opportunities you have anticipated for them; and finally, an explanation of the resources and means you will employ to achieve your goals in the face of likely competition.

Preparing a comprehensive business plan along these lines takes time and effort. In our experience at Cranfield on our new enterprise programmes, anything between 200 and 400 man hours is needed, depending on the nature of your business and how much data you have already gathered. Not surprisingly fewer than one in five new businesses prepares a business plan at the outset.

Less than 50% of firms employing up to 20 people have a current business plan. However, it has to be remembered that most new ventures fail. Preparing a business plan is essential if you are both to crystallize and focus your ideas, and test your resolve about entering or expanding your business. Once completed, your business plan will serve as a blueprint to follow which, like any map, improves the user's chances of reaching the destination. Section 11 gives detailed guidance on preparing viable business plans.

Getting the money right

Some 60% of the UK's small firms were funded exclusively by overdraft as they went into the last recession (1990-92). Overdraft is a form of money which is repayable on demand. As such, it is not appropriate as a way to fund the long term needs of business. A comparison would be a private individual choosing to finance the purchase of a house on overdraft rather than on a mortgage.

When bankers get the jitters, as they almost always do in recessions, they call in overdrafts, sometimes irrespective of the underlying performance of the firm itself.

case STUDY

Ted Bryant's Surrey and Hants (S & H) Financial Services Company went into liquidation at the beginning of 1991 and he was declared bankrupt on 2 April 1991. Like many others in the financial services business he lived a high life in 1980s and then lost it all.

Bryant had an overdraft limit of £100,000, but ran it up to £220,000 to enable him to open new branches. One of those was tied to Colonial Mutual, a life assurance company, which had agreed to clear S & H's overdraft with the bank. The bank manager was enthusiastic about the deal, and agreed to give Bryant a working overdraft of £50,000 to continue his business. However, the week that Bryant paid in the last cheque to clear the £220,000 overdraft the bank 'pulled the rug' and immediately bounced four cheques and withdrew the £50,000 trading facility which the company had already partly spent.

But even when a bank doesn't actually pull the rug from under your feet, it can quickly remind you that an overdraft is repayable on demand and subject to constant and sometimes expensive reviews.

case STUDY

The Brass Tacks publishing company started up in 1986, founded by five directors with about £30,000 of mostly borrowed money and bank lending of £70,000 under the Guaranteed Loans Scheme.

The company's first venture, The Mortgage Magazine *(now called* What Mortgage*) soon had sales of £45,000 a month and made a modest profit. Somewhat ambitiously Brass Tacks launched two magazines in its second year of trading and by April 1989, turnover hit £700,000 and profits were encouraging. Against this background the company launched* Stately Home; *the magazine was not a success and with the recession looming Brass Tacks saw its bottom line plummet. The founders held a crisis meeting in April 1990 and made substantial redundancies, shut or sold two titles and offered themselves to all and sundry as contract publishers.*

To tide the company over until its new strategies bore fruit, the directors asked their bankers to provide a 40% increase in the overdraft. They were met with a £4,000 bill for a special audit, a 10% cut in facility and a request for personal guarantees. The company's accountants introduced Brass Tacks to another bank which provided the necessary cash, but insisted on personal guarantees. Within 18 months the company was making six-figure profits – no thanks to their original bankers.

In Germany, for example, only 14% of small firms are financed exclusively by overdraft. The majority have long-term loans, often at fixed interest rates.

Overdraft interests can fluctuate rapidly and what seemed a small sum of money one year can prove crippling the next.

Small firms need a financial strategy, not just an overdraft. You need a judicious mixture of long-term loans, leasing and hire purchase finance, factoring (see Section 6), grants, your own money, retained profits, money from other investors, either your family or some other business angel – and then use overdraft finance to even out the cash-flow peaks and troughs. Overdraft should never be allowed to form the financial core of your business – if it does, you are closer to the roulette wheel than the stockmarket.

■ GETTING IT RIGHT

All this implies that in order to keep out of the failure statistics it is vital for the owner or manager of a new or small business to be better informed.

There are now thousands of organizations and even more publications that can provide the much-needed information for small business. Many of these organizations have only recently come into being, and many are still in a state of flux. There has been a parallel growth in other organizations, some shaping their policies to recognize the needs of small ventures, and others being wholly new activities. So 'entrepreneurs' have plenty of help to turn to and evidence is beginning to emerge that those who take this advice improve their chances of survival significantly. They very often do not know where that help is, or just how much it can do for them. The rest of this book is a guide to these organizations and their services, and the important directories, books and periodicals that will provide up-to-date information on each main topic. Enough information is generally included to allow a choice of service and organization, or of publications to find and read. The decision to include or exclude an entry is based on two criteria. Does the organization (or directory) provide either a service or information of specific help to a new or small business? Would the entry simply extend the reader's choice without necessarily extending the possible reward?

2 | *Sources of direct help and advice*

Each year over 1 million people use the services of a small-business advisory organization. Most are simple telephone enquiries but others involve face-to-face counselling sessions – perhaps to help raise money or to cope with an in-depth tax problem. There are now several hundred organizations specifically concerned with providing help, advice and resources (including finance) for small businesses and those starting them. For the most part, these services are provided free or at a very low cost, at least at the outset. In order to give a better understanding of their nature and purpose it will help to look at them in six groups: National Agencies, Local Enterprise Agencies, Training and Enterprise Councils, Property Services, Enterprise Zones and Small-Business Associations.

■ NATIONAL AGENCIES

Although all the agencies and advisory services have their roots in the local community, the direct initiative for starting them often came from a central body. These bodies are in the forefront of these initiatives.

The Department of Trade and Industry (DTI)

What help does the DTI give to small firms?

The DTI's Enterprise Initiative aims to enhance the competitiveness of established firms, particularly in manufacturing, by promoting best management practice and by providing practical help and guidance in several areas such as strategic management advice, exports and regional development.

The Enterprise Initiative includes financial support for consultancy projects in order to encourage the use of outside expertise as a regular part of management strategy. Consultancy help is available to most independent firms or groups with fewer than 500 employees. The projects cover the six key management areas of quality, design, marketing, manufacturing and service systems, financial and management information systems, and business planning.

Since its introduction in January 1988 the scheme has been a great success. Over 130,000 applications have been received and some 60,000 projects have been completed.

Total net expenditure to date is £300 million. An evaluation has found that

70% of firms began to reap clear commercial benefits within a year of their consultancy project and expected to recover their costs within three years.

With effect from 24 March 1993 the DTI has met half the cost of consultancy in Assisted Areas and Urban Programme Areas and one-third elsewhere. Lower subsidy rates will enable the continuing process of creating a self-sustaining market for consultancy among small and medium-sized businesses. This scheme is being phased out during 1995 and a new package of support including a new diagnostic service, a consultancy brokerage scheme, new consultancy services and technology advice will be phased in alongside the Consultancy Scheme from 1995 onwards to ensure a smooth transition to the new arrangements. This comprehensive range of local services, contracted through Training and Enterprise Councils (TECs) and delivered by TECs and Business Links, will provide high quality support for business, be suited to business needs and make cost-effective use of public funds.

The consultancy scheme is complemented by the DTI's 'Managing in the 90s' programme, which offers information and advice on the key management skills of quality, manufacturing, purchasing and supply, marketing, design and successful product development. The programme also focuses on the need to innovate and to manage the resulting need for change.

The network of (TECs) offers a wide range of provision to assist small companies at different stages of development. This includes information, counselling, advice, consultancy and training in business skills. The DTI contracts with TECs for the delivery of these services.

Business Link. A key aim of Business Link is to eliminate customer confusion caused by the current profusion of agencies and services. Customers must be able to access the full range of existing business support services through a single local point. They must be confident that they will receive high quality help which is independent and directly relevant to their needs.

Each centre will need the active commitment of all the major providers of business support services in its area. Those areas which are able to draw together a strong and enduring partnership will be in the strongest position to offer a 'new deal' for local business, in which the clutter of the past is replaced by a coherent, user-friendly, and credible framework for business support. Each centre should also seek to involve other local bodies and local businesses in its activities.

Drawing on the involvement and knowledge of local business people, the business plan for each centre should set out the plans for meeting the business support needs of the area which it will serve.

Each centre will need to provide a service to firms of widely differing sizes and to those who wish to start new businesses. Current services are directed mainly towards helping very small firms and those who wish to start-up in business. However, in terms of helping to lay the foundations for future growth, it is particularly important to help those firms which are passing through the transition from the 'owner-manager' to the 'team-managed' stage of development. It will be important to continue to help start-ups and small firms generally. The future development of services must reflect the needs of the large number of existing companies which wish to grow.

The DTI supports the Development Plan of the Association of British Chambers of Commerce to establish a strong and more comprehensive chamber network. Chambers are important sources of business support to small firms and are key partners in Business Link.

New Government regional offices as from April 1994 and a new Single Regeneration Budget have brought a more coherent approach to support for regeneration, economic development and industrial competitiveness. Such increased co-ordination should be of particular benefit to small firms.

The Small Firms Merit Award for Research and Technology (SMART) is an annual competition for individuals or businesses employing fewer than 50 people, offering phased financial support towards the development of new technology projects with a good prospect of commercial success. The maximum grant is £45,000 for Stage 1 and £60,000 for Stage 2. Over 1,000 projects have now been supported.

Support for Products Under Research (SPUR) provides help to smaller independent companies of up to 500 employees for the development of new products or processes which can demonstrate a significant technological advance. The scheme provides a fixed grant of 30% of eligible costs where the need for Government support is established, up to a maximum of £150,000. A further one-year programme for SPUR, from April 1994, was approved by the European Commission. (Note: the new programme as from April was open to companies with up to 250 employees rather than 500.)

The Technical Action Line, run by certain Regional Technology Centres or similar organizations, is designed to help small firms solve immediate problems concerned with the application and use of technology. It enables them to have easy access to experienced trouble-shooters, who provide a quick problem-solving service at a subsidized cost. The scheme has been extended in the same regions as an interim measure while Business Links are being established.

The Teaching Company Scheme (TCS) aims to strengthen the competitiveness and wealth creation of the UK by the stimulation of innovation in industry through collaborative partnerships between academia and industry. TCS involves young graduates working in companies for two years on technology transfer projects jointly supervised by academics and industrialists. Over 60% of companies currently participating in TCS are SMEs (Small and Medium-Sized Enterprises). SMEs contribute 30% of the direct costs of a programme and large companies up to 70% of the costs. TCS is delivered on behalf of the sponsoring departments and research councils by the Teaching Company Directorate through its team of regional consultants. There are about 500 live programmes at any one time involving over 80 universities. All grant money from the sponsors is channelled through the Research Grant mechanism of the Science and Education Research Council (SERC) to the universities who are grant holders for the programmes.

The Senior Academics in Industry Scheme (SAIS) has a mission similar to TCS but involves senior and experienced academic staff undertaking strategic new technology projects in UK industry for up to six months; 75% of SAIS projects will be in SMEs. The DTI's financial contribution to each project is paid to the university. The SAIS is delivered on behalf of the DTI by the Teaching Company Directorate.

The Shell Technology Enterprise Programme (STEP) places undergraduates for eight weeks during their final summer vacation to work on technology, science or engineering projects identified by small and medium-sized firms. The main aim of the programme is to encourage undergraduates to consider careers in SMEs and encourage SMEs to consider employing graduates. DTI support has enabled the expansion of STEP, which is administered by consultants on behalf of Shell UK's Enterprise Unit.

Regional Enterprise Grants are aimed at smaller businesses and are available for both investment (RIG) and innovation (RIN). Grants for investment projects are available if the project is to take place in a Development Area or designated localities affected by colliery closure. They are available in most manufacturing and some service sectors and the DTI will pay 15% of the expenditure on fixed assets in the project, up to a maximum of £15,000. Firms must employ fewer than 25 people. Grants for innovation projects are available for projects taking place in a Development, Intermediate, Objective 2, Task Force or City Challenge Area, designated localities affected by colliery closure, or certain Scottish urban areas, which lead to the development and introduction of new products and processes. The DTI will pay up to 50% of the eligible costs, up to a maximum grant of £25,000. Firms must employ fewer than 50 people. The Regional Enterprise Grants scheme became part of the Single Regeneration Budget administered by the DoE on 1 April 1994.

Regional Selective Assistance (RSA) is available to all manufacturing industries, except those where special European Community sectoral restrictions apply, and to some service sector industries, to encourage sound investment in the Assisted Areas (AAs). The scheme is open to businesses of all sizes whose projects will either create or safeguard employment in the AAs. Eligible projects must conform to strict scheme criteria, which include additionality (i.e. proving the need for the grant support) and viability. There must also be some regional or national economic benefit. Grants are negotiated as the minimum necessary for the project to proceed.

The Small Firms Loan Guarantee Scheme helps small firms with viable business proposals obtain finance where conventional loans are not available because of lack of security or track record. The Scheme provides banks and other financial institutions with a government guarantee of 70% on loans of up to £100,000. The guarantee increases to 85% for established small firms or in Inner City Task Force and City Challenge Areas. The loan maximum is £250,000 for established small firms.

Five **informal investment** demonstration projects are being run by TECs in partnership with other local agencies with the aim of bringing together potential investors and entrepreneurs looking for investment.

Overseas Trade Services offer a wide range of help, advice and financial assistance to firms involved in exporting for Britain. The services are, however, particularly targeted at smaller firms, especially those new to, or inexperienced in, exporting.

What publicity material is available?
Small Firms Division is responsible for a number of free publications designed to help small businesses. These provide an overview of help and advice available to small businesses from Government departments, TECs, Local Enterprise Agencies and other sources. They also give brief details of services and programmes available with the aim of helping businesses survive and grow.

Titles include:

- *Tendering for Government Contracts* – advice for small firms on how to get business from Government departments (PL 823).
- *Your Guide to Help for Small Firms* – general information and sources of help (PL 889).
- *Making the Cash Flow* – advice on late payment of bills (PL 954F).
- *Finance without Debt* – a guide to sources of venture capital (revised November 1993).
- *Loan Guarantee Scheme* – helps small firms to obtain finance by providing a Government guarantee.
- *Increasing the Supply of Informal Equity Capital* – a guide to setting up a business introduction service.

These can be ordered from: DTI Small Firms Publications, PO Box 1143, London W3 8EQ.

DTI Regional Office contacts

DTI East
Building A, The Westbrook Centre, Milton Road, Cambridge, CB4 1YG. Contact: J McConnell (Tel: 01223 346 701); S Ellis (Tel: 01223 346 703).

DTI East Midlands
Severns House, 20 Middle Pavement, Nottingham NG1 7DW. Contact: A Beale (Tel: 0115 9596 461); R Newell (Tel: 0115 9596 304).

DTI North East
Stanegate House, 2 Groat Market,
Newcastle-upon-Tyne, NE1 1YN.
Contact: R Cordiner (Tel: 0191 235
7285); R Flood (Tel: 0191 235 7227).

DTI North West (Liverpool)
Graeme House, Derby Square,
Liverpool, L2 7UP. Contact:
R Smith (Tel: 0151 224 6366).

DTI North West (Manchester)
Sunley Tower, Piccadilly Plaza,
Manchester, M1 4BA. Contact:
P Shilliday (Tel: 0161 838 5025);
J Ray (Tel: 0161 838 5027).

DTI South East (London)
Bridge Place, 88/89 Eccleston Square,
London, SW1V 1PT. Contact:
A Ferries (Tel: 0171 215 0577).

DTI South East (Reading)
40 Caversham Road, Reading, RG1

7EB. Contact: N Robinson
(Tel: 01734 395 631).

DTI South East (Reigate)
Douglas House, London Road,
Reigate, RH2 9QP. Contact:
K Edgington (Tel: 01737 226 905).

DTI South West
The Pithay, Bristol, BS1 2PB. Contact:
I Morris (Tel: 0117 9308 403);
R Punchard (Tel: 0117 9308 453).

DTI West Midlands
77 Paradise Circus, Queensway,
Birmingham, B1 2DT. Contact:
D Mahoney (Tel: 0121 212 5144);
F Birkett (Tel: 0121 212 5158).

DTI Yorkshire and Humberside
25 Queen Street, Leeds LS1 2TW.
Contact:
J Colclough (Tel: 0113 2338 205);
T Smith (Tel: 0113 2338 356).

Business Link Directory
Aylesbury: Unit 1, Gatehouse Way,
Aylesbury, Buckinghamshire HP19
3XU (Tel: 01296 392288;
Fax: 01296 434142)
Barnsley: Burleigh Court, Burleigh
Street, Barnsley, S70 1XY
(Tel: 01226 771000.
Fax: 01226 752000)
Birmingham: Harbourne Road,
Birmingham, B15 3DH
(Tel: 0121 60708090;
Fax: 0121 6079 8999)
Coalville (North West Leicestershire):
Unit 5 The Courtyard, Whitwick
Business Park, Stenson Road,
Coalville, Leicestershire, LE67 3FA
(Tel: 01530 810470;
Fax: 01530 510452)
Chester and Ellesmere Port: Hilliards
Court Business Centre, Chester

Business Park, Wrexham Road,
Chester, CH4 9QP (Tel: 01244
674111;
Fax: 01244 674333)
Congleton: Riverside Mountbatten
Way, Congleton, CW12 1DY
(Tel: 01260 294500;
Fax: 01260 294501)
Crewe: Electra House, Crewe Business
Park, Crewe, CW1 1YZ
(Tel: 01270 504700;
Fax: 01270 504701)
Derby: Rose Hill Business Centre,
Normanton Road, Derby, DE23 6US
(Tel: 01332 298123;
Fax: 01332 298345)
Doncaster: White Rose Way, Hyde
Park, Doncaster, DN4 5ND
(Tel: 01302 761000;
Fax: 01302 739999)

■

Dorset: Newfields Business Park, Stinsford Road, Nuffield Trading Estate, Poole, BH17 7NF (Tel: 0345 448844; Fax: 01202 448838)
Dudley: Dudley Court South, Waterfront East, Level Street, Brierley Hill, Dudley, DY5 1XN (Tel: 01384 868000; Fax: 01384 868400)
East Manchester: 49 Whitworth Street, Openshaw, Manchester, M11 7BZ (Tel 0161 2374000; Fax: 0161 3210695)
Gateshead: West Street, Gateshead, Tyne & Wear, NE8 1BH (Tel: 0191 4775544; Fax: 0191 4774650)
Hereford: Crossway House, Holmer Lane, Hereford, HR4 9SS (Tel: 01432 356699; Fax: 01432 274499)
Hertfordshire: Grosvenor Road, St Albans, Herts, AL1 3AW (Tel: 01727 813400; Fax: 01727 813443)
Hinckley: Druid Street, Hinckley, Leicestershire, LE10 1QH (Tel: 01455 891848; Fax: 01455 891923)
Leicester: York Street, Leicester, LE1 5TS (Tel 0116 2559944; Fax: 0116 2553470)
Leominster (Hereford & Worcester): Corn Square, Leominster, Herefordshire, HR6 8LR (Tel: 01568 616344; Fax: 01568 616355)
Lincolnshire: Welton House, Greetwell Road, Lincoln, LN2 4UU (Tel: 01522 574000; Fax: 01522 574005)
Macclesfield: Dukes Court, Mill Street, Macclesfield, SK11 6NN (Tel: 01625 664455; Fax: 01625 664401)
Malvern: Brunel House, Portland Road, Malvern, Worcestershire, WR14 2TB (Tel: 01684 567070; Fax: 01684 567080)
Manchester: Churchgate House, Oxford Street, Manchester, M60 7HJ (Tel: 0161 237 4000; Fax: 0161 237 4040)
Newcastle: Anderson House, Market Street, Newcastle Upon Tyne, NE1 6XA (Tel: 0191 2305989; Fax: 0191 2305517)
North Tyneside: Howard House, Saville Street, North Shields, Tyne & Wear, NE30 1NT (Tel: 0191 2964477; Fax: 0191 2964499)
Pershore: Council Offices, Civic Centre, Pershore, Worcestershire, WR10 1PT (Tel: 01386 555577; Fax: 01386 555588)
Redruth (West Cornwall): Redruth, Cornwall, TR15 1SS (Tel: 01209 314555; Fax: 01209 314442)
Ross-on-Wye: The Swan, High Street, Herefordshire, HR9 5HL (Tel: 01989 769744; Fax: 01432 274499)
Runcorn: Church Street, Runcorn, WA7 1LD (Tel 01928 563037; Fax: 01928 580711)
Salford: Business Link House, Unit 8a, Winders Way, Salford, M6 6BU (Tel: 0161 742 4413; Fax: 0161 742 4401)
Slough: Commerce House, 6 Bath Road, Slough, Berkshire, SL1 3SB (Tel: 01753 512288; Fax: 01753 533523)
Southern Derbyshire: New Enterprise House, St Helen's Street, Derby, DE1 3GY (Tel: 01332 327071; Fax: 01332 299736)
South Tyneside: c/o TEDCO, Eldon Street, South Shields, Tyne & Wear, NE33 5JE (Tel: 0191 4554300;

Fax: 0191 4277561)
Swadlincote: 48 Grove Street,
Derbyshire, DE11 5DD
(Tel: 01283 551324;
Fax: 01283 552566)
Tameside: Business Development
Centre, Windmill Lane, Denton, Manchester, M24 3YA
(Tel: 0161 337 4200;
Fax: 0161 343 7367)
Telford: Trevithick House, Unit B1
Stafford Park 4, Telford, TF3 3BA
(Tel: 0345 543210;
Fax: 01952 208208)
Thames Valley: Wesley Gate, Queen's
Road, Reading, Berkshire, RG1 4AP
(Tel: 01734 512288;
Fax: 01734 569024)
Trafford Park: Lloyd House, 3rd
Avenue, Trafford Park, Manchester,
M17 1BL (Tel: 0161 848 4300;
Fax: 0161 848 4313)
Tyneside: Tyneside TEC, Moongate
House, 5th Avenue Business Park,

Team Valley Trading Estate,
Gateshead, NE11 0HF
(Tel: 0191 491 6161; Fax: 091 491
6199)
Walsall: Walsall Chamber of
Commerce, Ward Street, Walsall, WS1
2AG (Tel: 01922 721777;
Fax: 01922 647359)
Widnes: Halton Business Forum,
Victoria Square, Widnes, Cheshire,
WA8 7QZ (Tel: 0151 420 9420;
Fax: 0151 423 2749)
Wigan (Metropolitan): Buckingham
Row, North Way, Wigan, WN1 1XX
(Tel: 01942 324547;
Fax: 01942 821410)
Wirral: Egerton House, Tower Road,
Birkenhead, Wirral, L41 1FN
(Tel: 0151 650 6900;
Fax: 0151 650 0101)
Worcester: Commerce House, The
Moors, Worcester, WR1 3EE
(Tel: 01905 22877;
Fax: 01905 22878)

Rural Development Commission (RDC)

The Rural Development Commission was created in 1988 by bringing together into a single organization the long-established Development Commission and its agency CoSIRA (Council for Small Industries in Rural Areas). The Commission's Business Service now provides the services previously provided by CoSIRA.

The RDC exists to advise Government on all matters concerning the people and communities in the rural parts of England, and to use its resources to create or maintain stable and prosperous communities in villages and country towns. The Commission is therefore concerned with jobs and housing, communications and transport, and services and facilities from health and information to village halls and village shops. To achieve its objective, the Commission works closely with local authorities, community councils and other bodies.

To assist job creation the Commission finances English Estates to build small factories and workshops in rural areas which are sold or rented to people who want to start up or expand their own businesses. In the designated Rural Development Areas nearly 2,800 of these small industrial units have been built and numbers are increasing.

The RDC's Advisory Service, based at 31 offices all over rural England, provides business and technical advice and skill training to help small businesses employing fewer than 20 people to prosper. Currently some 50,000 small rural businesses are in touch with the Service and many have enjoyed a friendly relationship with the Business Adviser for their county over a number of years.

In response to your enquiry a Business Adviser – the local representative – will arrange to meet you. Whether you are an established business or a new starter, the Business Adviser will be able to answer or find the answers to many of the questions you may want to ask. The first meeting is almost always free. Thereafter the rate is £70 per half-day.

Their services cover:

- Business planning and management
- Business development
- Financial planning
- Raising finance
- Marketing and sales advice
- Productivity and manufacturing efficiency
- Quality Assurance BS5750 accreditation
- COSHH assessments
- Planning and building advice
- Business and technical training.

Finance

Rural Development normally expects the major part of funding for small businesses to be arranged with a bank, or other commercial lending source. However, Rural Development has its own limited loan fund which can be used in appropriate cases to finance part of the cost of the project, up to a maximum of £75,000. Repayment may be between 2 and 20 years according to the type of loan. Management accountants are available to assist with the preparation of a case to support an application for a loan.

Rural Development has agreements with major banks which provide favourable terms for client businesses and opportunities for joint lending by the Commission and the bank.

Grants

Grants are not generally available for rural businesses; however, in certain circumstances the Commission does make grants to help a business convert redundant rural buildings. The rate of grant will not normally exceed 25% of the eligible costs, up to a maximum of £62,500.

Who is eligible?

If you live in the country or in a country town in England with fewer than 10,000 inhabitants the Business Service is available to help you to start up, run or expand your business. Normally Rural Development helps manufacturing and service industries. Agriculture, horticulture and the professions are excluded but non-agricultural businesses on the farm are eligible for assistance. Any firm with fewer than 20 skilled employees can ask for Rural Development help.

Training for the owners and employees of rural businesses is available at Technical and Agricultural Colleges, and through local courses organized by the

RDC. The subjects covered range from business management topics to manual skill training (both modern and traditional). The RDC and the ATB can arrange training in selected subjects on the employer's premises. The agenda provides a wide range of business management training courses, including financial and human resource planning, work methods and total quality management. The RDC offers training and advice in such areas as environmental protection and enhancement; the recognition, creation and management of wildlife and landscape features; and the presentation of such features for public enjoyment.

RDC NETS and open courses

The New Entrants Training Scheme (NETS) is run by the RDC and is designed to help small rural firms by providing supported training in a range of craft skills. These include thatching, saddlery, upholstery, forgework, furniture making and restoration, wheelwrighting and woodworking machinery. In addition, a wide range of open courses are run to give extra task-related training at more advanced levels.

Tourism

A range of short training courses and distance-learning programmes are available for those operating a rural enterprise who want to develop their existing knowledge and skills. There are also a number of training programmes aimed at those who are planning to start a tourism or leisure business, or are thinking of diversifying into tourism from agriculture. These courses cover all aspects of running a rural tourism enterprise, including development, marketing and management skills.

RDC offices
Head office
11 Cowley Street, London SW1P 3NA (071 276 6969) or 141 Castle Street, Salisbury, Wiltshire SP1 3TP (0722 336255)

The RDC has regional, area and county offices (which sometimes overlap within a region).

North region
Regional office: Morton Road, Yarm Road Industrial Estate, Darlington, Co. Durham DL1 4PT (Tel: 01325 384100).

Area office for North East (Cleveland, Durham, Northumberland, Tyne and Wear): as regional (Tel: 01325 487123).

County offices
Cleveland: as area.
Durham: as area.
Northumberland: Unit 11, White-house Centre, Stannington, Morpeth, Northumberland NE61 6AW (Tel: 01670 7889017).
Tyne and Wear: as area.
Area office for Humberside and Yorkshire: William House, Shipton Road, Skelton, York YO3 6XW (Tel: 01904 646866).

County offices
Humberside:
14 Market Place, Howden, Goole, North Humberside DN14 7BJ (Tel: 01430 431138).

Yorkshire – South: as Humberside.
Yorkshire – North and West: William House, Shipton Road, Skelton, York YO3 6XW (Tel: 01904 646866/7).

South region
Regional office: 141 Castle Street, Salisbury, Wiltshire SP1 3TP (Tel: 01722 336255).
Area office for South East (Berkshire, Buckinghamshire, Hampshire, Isle of Wight, Kent, Oxfordshire, Surrey, East and West Sussex): 141 Castle Street, Salisbury, Wiltshire SP1 3TP (Tel: 01722 336255).

County offices
Berkshire: as Oxfordshire.
Buckinghamshire: as Oxfordshire.
Hampshire: Barton Farm, Andover Road, Winchester, Hampshire SO22 6AX (Tel: 01962 880503).
Isle of Wight: 6–7 Town Lane, Newport, Isle of Wight PO30 1JU (Tel: 01983 528019).
Kent: 8 Romney Place, Maidstone, Kent ME15 6LE (Tel: 01622 765222).
Oxfordshire: The Maltings, St John's Road, Wallingford, Oxfordshire OX10 9BZ (Tel: 01491 835523).
Surrey and East and West Sussex: as Kent.

Area office for South Central (Avon, Dorset, Somerset, Wiltshire): 3 Chartfield House, Castle Street, Taunton, Somerset TA1 4AS (Tel: 01823 247161).

County offices
Avon: as area (Tel: 01823 276905).
Dorset: Wing D, Government Buildings, Prince of Wales Road, Dorchester, Dorset DT1 1QJ (Tel: 01305 268558).

Somerset: as area (Tel: 01823 276905).
Wiltshire: as regional.

Area office for South West (Cornwall and Isles of Scilly, Devon): 27 Victoria Park Road, Exeter, Devon EX2 4NT (Tel: 01392 421245).

County offices
Cornwall and Isles of Scilly: 2nd Floor, Highshore House, New Bridge Street, Truro, Cornwall TR1 2AA (Tel: 01872 73531).
Devon: as area (Tel: 01392 52616).

East region
Regional office: 18 Market Place, Bingham, Nottingham NG13 8AP (Tel: 01949 837268).

Area office for East Midlands (Derbyshire, Leicestershire, Lincolnshire, Nottinghamshire): as regional (Tel: 01949 839222).

County offices
Derbyshire: De Bradelie House, Chapel Street, Belper, Derbyshire DE5 1AR (Tel: 01773 828485).
Leicestershire: as regional (Tel: 01949 839222).
Lincolnshire: 6 Mill House, Carre Street, Sleaford, Lincolnshire NG34 7TW (Tel: 01529 306001).
Nottinghamshire: as regional (Tel: 01949 839222).

Area office for Bedfordshire, Cambridgeshire, Essex, Hertfordshire, Norfolk, Northamptonshire, Suffolk: Lees Smith House, 12 Looms Lane, Bury St Edmunds, Suffolk IP33 1HE (Tel: 01284 701743).
County offices
Bedfordshire: Agriculture House,

55 Goldington Road, Bedford MK40 3LU (Tel: 01234 261381).
Cambridgeshire: as Bedfordshire.
Essex: as regional.
Hertfordshire: as Bedfordshire.
Norfolk: 13 Unthank Road, Norwich, Norfolk NR2 2PA (Tel: 01603 624498).
Northamptonshire: as Bedfordshire.
Suffolk: as area.

West region
Regional office: The Old School House, 108 Welsh Row, Nantwich, Cheshire CW5 5EY (Tel: 01270 610080).

Area office for North West (Cheshire, Cumbria, Lancashire): Haweswater Road, Penrith, Cumbria CA11 7EH (Tel: 01768 65752).

County offices
Cheshire: Leachfield Estate, Green Lane West, Garstang, Preston, Lancashire PR3 1NJ

(Tel: 01995 604117).
Cumbria: as area.
Lancashire: as Cheshire.

Area office for West Midlands (Gloucestershire, Hereford and Worcester, Shropshire, Staffordshire, Warwickshire): Strickland House, The Lawns, Park Street, Wellington, Telford, Shropshire TF1 3BX (Tel: 01952 247161).

County offices
Gloucestershire: 32 Church Street, Malvern, Hereford and Worcester WR14 2AZ (Tel: 01684 564506/564784).
Hereford and Worcester: as Gloucestershire.
Shropshire: as area.
Staffordshire: as area.
Warwickshire: National Rural Enterprise Centre, Stoneleigh Park, Warwickshire CV8 2RR (Tel: 01203 696982).

British Coal Enterprise

The National Coal Board set up British Coal Enterprise to increase job prospects and regenerate prosperity in coal-mining areas. Help from British Coal Enterprise is not limited to British Coal employees, but the projects which it supports must result in permanent jobs being created in mining areas.

They can help almost anyone who has a proposal that will create real, new, permanent jobs in mining areas: from a one-man operation to big business – even international companies looking to expand and/or locate their operations in the coalfield areas of the UK. The three major criteria are:

■ New permanent jobs must be created.
■ The project must be located in an area associated with coal-mining.
■ The project must be financially viable.

British Coal Enterprise can help in four main ways.

Advice and guidance
They know the coalfield areas, the advisers, the business people, the financiers, the government bodies and the local councils in and around them extremely

well. Positive links have been forged with Enterprise Agencies and Training and Enterprise Councils (TECs) and they have encouraged the establishment of Managed Workshops in all coalfield areas.

Finance
Enterprise financial help is usually provided in the form of a loan. The amount of loan would, normally, be geared to the job-creating element of the project (usually based on a figure of up to £5,000 for each new job created) and would normally not exceed 25% of the total financial requirement of the project. Their loans can be arranged relatively quickly, at favourable rates of interest, with few formalities, and, for smaller loans, usually without security. For example, they guarantee a decision on loans up to £50,000 in 21 days. Loans up to £1 million are available and Equity Investments up to £250,000 can be made. In addition to providing their own loans, they can help put you in touch with other sources, e.g. Department of Trade and Industry grants, local authorities, financial institutions, the private sector, the EC and Enterprise Agencies. A business plan is required to support any request for financial support.

Premises
They can help find suitable properties in coalfield areas for sale or rent – at competitive prices. In some coalfield areas, buildings no longer needed by the coal industry may be available, and they are also prepared to consider helping with the erection of new buildings in such coal-mining areas for particular businesses. A number of ex-NCB premises and other buildings have been converted into Managed Workshops with great success, and this programme is continuing. A Managed Workshop provides smaller businesses and start-ups with workspace on an easy-in, easy-out basis at reasonable rentals and also provides on-site business advice, secretarial, reception, copying and other shared services.

Liaison with other forms and sources of help and advice
British Coal Enterprise offers contacts with sources of other financial help, business advice, local expertise and government aid. By helping to cut through some of the red tape, Enterprise can save time, energy and money in relation to your business proposal.

They can also help to identify and co-ordinate retraining programmes for those ex-employees leaving coal-mining and seeking work in new companies.

British Coal Enterprise has a head office and seven regional offices responsible for activities in their localities.

Head office
British Coal Enterprise Ltd, Edwinstowe House, Edwinstowe, Mansfield, Nottinghamshire NG21 9PR (Tel: 01623 826833; Fax: 01623 826800).

Regional contact points
Scotland (coalfield areas):
British Coal Enterprise Ltd, Suite 1, Alloa Business Centre, The Whins, Alloa FK10 3SA (Tel: 01259 218021).

Western (coalfield areas of North West England, North Wales, Staffordshire, Shropshire and West Midlands – excluding Coventry): British Coal Enterprise Ltd, 622 Westbrook Centre, Westbrook, Warrington WA5 5UH (Tel: 01925 417388).
South Wales: British Coal Enterprise Ltd, Eastmoors Road, The Docks, Cardiff CF1 5EE (Tel: 01222 462667).
North East (coalfield areas of Northumberland, Tyne and Wear, and Durham): British Coal Enterprise Ltd, GEAR House, Saltmeadows Road, Gateshead, Tyne and Wear NE8 3AH

(Tel: 0191 490 0866).
Yorkshire: British Coal Enterprise Ltd, Carcroft Enterprise Park, Station Road, Carcroft, Doncaster DN6 8DD (Tel: 01302 727228).
Midlands (Nottinghamshire and the coalfield areas of Derbyshire, Leicestershire and Warwickshire): British Coal Enterprise Ltd, Eastwood Hall, Eastwood, Nottinghamshire NG16 3EB (Tel: 01773 531313).
British Coal Enterprise Ltd, Enterprise House, Ashby Road, Coalville, Leicestershire LE6 2LA (Tel: 01530 813143).

URBED (Urban and Economic Development) Ltd

3/7 Stamford Street, London SE1 9NT
(Tel: 0171 928 9515; Fax: 0171 261 1015)

This non-profit-making company was established in 1976 with a grant from one of the Sainsbury Charitable Trusts in order to 'find practical solutions to the problems of regenerating run-down areas and creating new work'.

It has carried out a series of research studies in a cross-section of inner-city areas, which have enabled URBED to develop a unique understanding of local economies, the needs of small firms, and the problems of under-utilized resources in inner-city areas.

Their services include the establishment of workshops, working communities, small-enterprise centres, industrial associations, small-business clubs and local enterprise trusts. Through research into demand, case studies of successful conversions, feasibility studies and promotion material, the company has encouraged the conversion of redundant buildings into premises for small firms and has become involved in property finance.

It provides consultancy services for a range of clients, including local and public authorities and government departments. URBED's training initiatives include a ten-day business start-up course, 'Getting Going', which is run three times a year and is free to most participants in central London.

Tourist Boards

The English Tourist Board does not have a grant-aiding capacity. However, it offers a comprehensive business advice service through a network of Regional Tourist Boards. This is targeted at small businesses both from a start-up situation and a business development point of view. They also produce a number of

Development Guides aimed at particular tourism products. These include:
- Starting a Bed and Breakfast Business
- Starting a Self-Catering Business
- Starting a Caravan Business.

For information contact the appropriate Tourist Board, address given below.

English Tourist Board
Thames Tower, Blacks Road,
Hammersmith, London W6 9E1 (Tel:
0171 846 9000).

Regional Tourist Boards
Cumbria Tourist Board: Ashleigh,
Holly Road, Windermere, Cumbria
LA23 2AQ (Tel: 015394 44444).
East Anglia Tourist Board
(Cambridgeshire, Essex, Norfolk,
Suffolk): Toppesfield Hall, Hadleigh,
Suffolk IP7 5DN
(Tel: 01473 822922).
East Midlands Tourist Board
(Derbyshire, Leicestershire,
Lincolnshire, Northamptonshire, Not-
tinghamshire): Exchequergate,
Lincoln LN2 1PZ
(Tel: 01522 531521).
Heart of England Tourist Board
(Gloucestershire, Hereford and
Worcester, Shropshire, Staffordshire,
Warwickshire, West Midlands):
Woodside, Larkhill Road, Worcester
WR5 2EF (Tel: 01905 763436).
London Tourist Board: 26 Grosvenor
Gardens, London SW1W 0DU
(Tel: 0171 730 3450).
Northumbria Tourist Board
(Cleveland, Durham, Northumber-
land, Tyne and Wear): Aykley Heads,
Durham DH1 5UX
(Tel: 0191 384 6905).
North West Tourist Board (Cheshire,
Greater Manchester, Lancashire,
Merseyside, High Peak District of Der-
byshire): The Last Drop Village,

Bromley Cross, Bolton, Lancashire
BL7 9PZ (Tel: 01204 591511).
South East England Tourist Board
(East Sussex, Kent, Surrey, West
Sussex): 1 Warwick Park, Tunbridge
Wells, Kent TN2 5TU
(Tel: 01892 540766).
Southern Tourist Board (Eastern
Dorset, Northern Dorset, Hampshire,
Isle of Wight): 40 Chamberlayne
Road, Eastleigh, Hampshire SO5 5JH
(Tel: 01703 620006).
Thames and Chilterns Tourist Board
(Bedfordshire, Berkshire,
Buckinghamshire, Hertfordshire,
Oxfordshire): The Mount House,
Church Green, Witney,
Oxfordshire OX8 6DZ
(Tel: 01993 778800).
West Country Tourist Board (Avon,
Cornwall, Devon, Somerset,
Isles of Scilly): 60 St David's Hill,
Exeter EX4 4SY (Tel: 01392 76351).
Yorkshire and Humberside Tourist
Board (North, South and West
Yorkshire, Humberside):
312 Tadcaster Road, York, Yorkshire
YO2 2HF (Tel: 01904 707961).
Welsh Tourist Board: Brunel House, 2
Fitzalen Road, Cardiff CF2 1UY (Tel:
01222 499909).
Scottish Tourist Board: 23 Ravelston
Terrace, Edinburgh EH4 3EH
(Tel: 0131 332 2433).
Northern Ireland Tourist Board: River
House, 48 High Street,
Belfast BT1 2DS (Tel: 01232 231221).

Task Force

An initiative launched by the Department of Trade and Industry in 1986 and expanded to:

■ encourage and facilitate enterprise by local people through the provision of enterprise training and financial and managerial assistance;

■ provide more jobs for local people by identifying and removing impediments to their recruitment by local employers, and by encouraging local enterprise development;

■ improve the employability of local people, including those about to enter the labour market, by training programmes aimed at specific employment opportunities or identified gaps in the labour market;

■ support initiatives designed to improve the environment, the provision of community services and to reduce the level of crime where these can be linked to the reintegration of local people into local economic activity.

How to use the scheme

Unless you have an enquiry about Task Forces in general you should approach each directly, as each has its own distinctive programme.

The work of the Task Forces varies a lot from year to year and from place to place. A very detailed literature pack is available from the central contact point:

Inner Cities Central Unit, Department of Trade and Industry, Ashdown House, 123 Victoria Street, London SW1E 6RB (Tel: 0171 215 6703; Fax: 0171 215 6055).

Schemes in operation include the following:

■ **Birmingham (East)** operates a small grant scheme for new or small firms in its area. It is devoting most of its efforts to improving training opportunities for its residents.

■ **Bristol** has supported an employment centre, which gives local residents information about job and training opportunities and offers companies in the area a source of new recruits; a small business centre which provides accommodation and service to new firms; customized pre-recruitment training and a technology centre which offers free training opportunities in commercial computer skills.

■ **Hartlepool** supports customized training and runs an enterprise loans and grants fund.

■ **London (North Peckham)** supports the Peckham Enterprise Centre, a one-stop source of advice for new and small businesses. It has supported the creation of managed workspace and encouraged work experience in schools and high-tech training.

■ **Middlesbrough** runs a customized training scheme which provides workers trained in the skills needed by specific companies, and has been supporting initiatives designed to reduce crime. It also runs a loans and grants scheme.

■ **Rochdale** runs a small loans fund and provides financial support to the Prince's Youth Business Trust to give bursaries in its areas. Like Middlesbrough, it is supporting customized training and crime prevention projects.

Task Force offices

Birmingham: Unit 10, Saltley Trading Estate, Birmingham B8 1BL (Tel: 0121 326 7005; Fax: 0121 328 4933).
Bradford: 2 Legrams Terrace, Fieldhead Business Centre, Lister Hills Road, Bradford BD7 1LN (Tel: 01274 725656; Fax: 01274 723020).
Bristol: 212 Lawrence Hill, Bristol BS5 0DR (Tel: 0117 9550205; Fax: 0117 9557825).
Coventry (Foleshill and Hillfields): Barclays Community Enterprise Centre, 12 Victoria Street, Hillfields, Coventry CV1 5LZ (Tel: 01203 631855; Fax: 01203 223017).
Derby: 33 Leopold Street, Derby DE1 2HF (Tel: 01332 298800; Fax: 01332 384228).
Hull: Room 220, Strand House, Leonard Street, Hull, HU3 1SA (Tel: 01482 23939; Fax: 01482 29656).
Liverpool (Granby/Toxteth): 129b Lodge Lane, Toxteth, Liverpool L8 0QF (Tel: 0151 734 5289; Fax: 0151 734 4181).

London area
Deptford: Unit 1, City Link Court, 471–473 New Cross Road, London SE14 6TA (Tel: 0181 694 9276; Fax: 0181 694 9314).
Hackney: Studio 2, Hackney Business Centre, 277 Mare Street, Hackney, London E8 1EB (Tel: 0181 533 5501/1885; Fax: 0181 986 4309).
North Peckham: 2nd Floor, 72 Rye Lane, Peckham, London SE15 5DQ (Tel: 0171 358 9018; Fax: 0171 358 9770).
West London: 2 Acklam Road, London W10 5QZ (Tel: 0181 960 8455; Fax: 0181 960 7264).
Manchester (Moss Side and Hulme): 21–25 Parisian Way, Moss Side District Centre, Moss Lane East, Moss Side, Manchester M15 5NQ (Tel: 0161 226 8899; Fax: 0161 226 3215).
Middlesbrough: Southlands Centre, Ormesby Road, Priestfields, Middlesbrough TS3 0HB (Tel: 01642 300420; Fax: 01642 300422).
Nottingham: 2–4 Radford Road, Hyson Green, Nottingham NG7 5FS (Tel: 0115 9421565; Fax: 0115 9421566).
South Tyneside: V11–V15 Commercial House, Commercial Road, South Shields, Tyne and Wear NE33 2RW (Tel: 0191 455 4300; Fax: 0191 427 7504).
Wirral: 20–22 Woodside Business Park, Woodside, Birkenhead, Wirral L41 1EH (Tel: 0151 650 1699; Fax: 0151 650 1054).

British Steel (Industry) Ltd

This company, a subsidiary of British Steel plc, helps new and growing businesses in 19 traditional steel industry areas in England, Scotland and Wales. Its objective is to help to put back long-term jobs into places where British Steel has discontinued or substantially reduced its activities.

The company has two main programmes of assistance for providing direct help to businesses, finance and premises.

Finance

The company provides loans, share capital or packages of both in amounts of between £10,000 and £150,000 and is one of the very few sources of share capital in such small amounts. In some circumstances up to £25,000 can be lent on an unsecured basis; and the company also provides loans linked to a share option. BS(I) concentrates its resources on businesses likely to make real contributions to the local economies of its areas. For this reason, the company provides finance mainly for manufacturing businesses, and for those engaged in providing services to the manufacturing sector.

Premises

BS(I) also provides workspace for small businesses with growth potential. These units range in size from a few hundred to a few thousand square feet and occupation is by tenancy-at-will or short-term lease arrangement. There are units suitable for light industrial activities at all locations, and there is also office accommodation available at some.

Contacts

Businesses seeking finance should contact the appropriate BS(I) Regional Office in the first instance. Those seeking premises should get in touch with the appropriate Workshop Manager.

Scotland (for Lanarkshire, SE Glasgow and Garnock Valley areas)
BS(I) Regional Office for Scotland: Grovewood Business Centre, Strathclyde Business Park, Bellshill, Lanarkshire ML4 3NQ
(Tel: 01698 845045).
Contact: John Fairlie.
Brown Street Business Units, Brown Street, Coatbridge, Lanarkshire ML5 4AS (Tel: 01236 423384).
Contact: Frances Sunderland.
Clyde Workshops, Fullerton Road, Glasgow G32 8YL
(Tel: 0141 641 4972).
Contact: Margaret Goode.
Coatbank Business Units, Coatbank Way, Coatbridge, Lanarkshire ML5 3AG (Tel: 01236 423384).
Contact: Frances Sunderland.
Grovewood Business Centre and Units, Strathclyde Business Park, Bellshill, Lanarkshire ML4 3NQ
(Tel: 01698 845123).

Contact: Stewart Morrison.
North of England (for West Cumbria, Derwentside, Hartlepool and Teesside areas)
BS(I) Regional Office for North of England: Cleveland House, 7 Woodlands Road, Middlesbrough TS1 3BH (Tel: 01642 244633).
Contact: Adrian Lewis.
Hartlepool Workshops, Usworth Road Industrial Estate, Usworth Road, Hartlepool, Cleveland TS25 1PD (Tel: 01429 265128).
Contact: Barbara Elsdon.

Yorkshire and Humberside (for South Humber, Rotherham, Sheffield, also Corby and Dudley areas)
BS(I) Regional Office for Yorkshire and Humberside: Bridge House, Bridge Street, Sheffield S3 8NS
(Tel: 0114 2700933).
Contact: Stuart Green.
Normanby Park Workshops,

Normanby Road, Scunthorpe, South Humberside DN15 8QZ (Tel: 01724 849457). Contact: Sue Wells.

Wales (for Deeside, Llanelli, Merthyr, Blaenau Gwent, West Glamorgan, South Glamorgan and South Gwent areas)
BS(I) Regional Office for Wales: Lewis Road, East Moors, Cardiff CF1 5EJ (Tel: 01222 471122). Contact: David Hughes.
Cardiff Workshops, Lewis Road, East Moors, Cardiff CF1 5EJ (Tel: 01222 471122). Contact: Alan Henderson.
Port Talbot Workshops, Addison Road, Port Talbot, West Glamorgan SA12 6HZ (Tel: 01639 887171). Contact: Ivor Vincent.

General enquiries
BS(I) London Office, Canterbury House, 2–6 Sydenham Road, Croydon, CR9 2LJ (Tel: 0181 686 2311). Contact: John Northcott.

Crafts Council

(England and Wales)

Setting-up Scheme
The Council offers grants to enable craftspeople to establish workshops of their own. The majority go to people who have completed a recognized form of training, but those without formal training whose work is of a high standard may also apply.

The grant has two parts, one for maintenance, the other for equipment. The maximum maintenance grant is £2,500 over 12 months, designed to cover the cost of materials, overheads, running and servicing equipment and general subsistence. The equipment grant covers up to 50% of the cost of buying new or second-hand equipment in good condition, up to a maximum cost of £10,000. Contact: Crafts Council, 44a Pentonville Road, Islington, London N1 9BY (Tel: 0171 278 7700; Fax: 0171 837 6891).

How to apply
Application forms are available from the Council.

Grants for projects and exhibitions
The Council aims to extend understanding and appreciation of contemporary crafts through support of projects or events which are of national significance.

Projects
The current priority areas for funding are:
■ projects to develop critical writing about the crafts;
■ projects to develop crafts which are perceived as requiring particular help – current priorities are lettering, calligraphy and fine metalwork;
■ research or pilot projects which look at the uses of new technology in craft production;

- research of pilot projects which encourage craftspeople in undertaking large-scale commissions (however, the cost of craft commissions is specifically excluded);
- national conferences which contribute to an understanding and appreciation of the crafts, enhance debate on key issues or encourage innovation;
- research or pilot projects to develop initiatives in all sectors of education in the crafts;
- research or pilot projects which pioneer new methods of widening access, develop appreciation and understanding of the crafts or improve professional practice.

Exhibitions
The current priority areas for funding are:
- exhibitions which illustrate or explore themes and debates about current craft practice, which may include major retrospective exhibitions of influential craftspeople;
- exhibitions which place contemporary craft work in a historical and/or international context, which may include exhibitions of work from other countries;
- exhibitions which examine contemporary craft work in relationship to other arts disciplines;
- exhibitions which explore cultural diversity, including developing an understanding of historical and contemporary non-European influences on contemporary craft work.

Grants range from a minimum of £1,000 to £20,000.

Regional Enterprise Boards
Most of these were created by the now abolished Metropolitan County Councils. For the most part they have survived, raising finance from private sector sources and directing it towards helping the larger new enterprise to develop.

Addresses, contacts and information on Enterprise Boards are available from the Centre for Local Economic Strategies, Ground Floor, Barclay House, Whitworth Street West, Manchester M1 5NG (Tel: 0161 236 7036; Fax: 0161 236 1891).

Centre Points outside England
The following agencies and organizations provide advisory services and assistance to new and small businesses outside England.

Scotland
Since April 1991, the structure of support for business in Scotland has been radically changed. Two new organizations were established – Scottish Enterprise and Highlands and Islands Enterprise – which took over the functions of

the two existing development agencies (the Scottish Development Agency and the Highlands and Islands Development Board) and those of the Training Agency as well. However, the first line of contact with the business community is a new network of Local Enterprise Companies – which are loosely based on the Scottish equivalent of Training and Enterprise Councils in the rest of Great Britain. Local Enterprise Companies are allowed considerable discretion over the support they offer. Each company is trying out new ways of delivering support within a very broad framework set by Scottish Enterprise and Highlands and Islands Enterprise.

You can expect, however, that Local Enterprise Companies will have more to offer than their English counterparts. They are in a position to offer access to capital resources in a way that their English counterparts cannot.

Highlands and Islands Enterprise indicates in its brochure that financial support remains available for investment in most branches of the economy – manufacturing, agriculture and fisheries, tourism and some service industries – but it does not set out the terms under which support will be available.

For firms operating in Scotland, the first point of contact is the nearest Local Enterprise Company. For companies elsewhere but thinking of relocating to Scotland, the contact point is a new organization, 'Locate in Scotland', which can be found at 17/19 Cockspur Street, London SW1Y 5BL (Tel: 0171 839 2117) or 120 Bothwell Street, Glasgow G2 7JP (Tel: 0141 248 2700).

Locate in Scotland aims to provide a 'one-stop shop' for firms considering a location in Scotland. It aims to answer all the enquiries by inward investors covering finance, site location, premises, manpower, communications and telecommunications, local sources of component supplies and the physical environment. In some cases, it can provide government support directly.

Local Enterprise Companies

Local Enterprise Companies are now your first point of contact if you are looking for any form of support for your business.

Scottish Enterprise

Aberdeen: Grampian Enterprise Ltd, 27 Albyn Place, Aberdeen AB1 1YL (Tel: 01224 211500; Fax: 01224 213417).

Clydebank: Dunbartonshire Enterprise, Spectrum House, Clydebank Business Park, Clydebank G81 2DR (Tel: 0141 951 2121; Fax: 0141 951 1907).

Dumfries: Dumfries and Galloway Enterprise, Cairnsmore House, Bankend Road, Dumfries DG1 4TA (Tel: 01387 54444; Fax: 01387 51650).

Dundee: Scottish Enterprise Tayside, Enterprise House, 45 North Lindsay Street, Dundee DD1 1NT (Tel: 01382 23100; Fax: 01382 201319).

Edinburgh: Lothian and Edinburgh Enterprise Ltd, Apex House, 99 Haymarket Terrace, Edinburgh EH12 5HD (Tel: 0131 313 4000; Fax: 0131 313 4231).

Elgin: Moray, Badenoch and Strathspey Enterprise, Elgin Business Centre, Maisondieu Road, Elgin IV30 1RH (Tel: 01343 550567;

Fax: 01343 550678).
Galashiels: Scottish Borders
Enterprise, Bridge Street,
Galashiels TD1 2SW
(Tel: 01896 58991; Fax: 01896 58625).
Glasgow: Glasgow Development
Agency, Atrium Court, 50 Waterloo
Street, Glasgow G2 6HQ
(Tel: 0141 204 1111;
Fax: 0141 248 1600).
Glenrothes: Fife Enterprise,
Huntsman's House, 33 Cadham
Centre, Glenrothes KY7 6RU (Tel:
01592 621000; Fax: 01592 742609).
Kilmarnock: Enterprise Ayrshire,
17/19 Hill Street, Kilmarnock,
Ayrshire KA3 1HA
(Tel: 01563 26623;
Fax: 01563 43636).
Motherwell: Lanarkshire Develop-
ment Agency, 166 Park Street,
Motherwell ML1 1PF
(Tel: 01698 745454;
Fax: 01698 51989).
Paisley: Renfrewshire Enterprise,
25–29 Causeyside Street, Paisley PA1
1UL (Tel: 0141 848 0101;
Fax: 0141 848 6930).
Stirling: Forth Valley Enterprise,
Laurel House, Laurelhill Business
Park, Stirling FK7 9JQ
(Tel: 01786 451919;
Fax: 01786 478123).

Highlands and Islands Enterprise
Argyll: Argyll and the Islands
Enterprise, Stag Chambers, Lorne
Street, Lochgilphead, Argyll PA31 8LU
(Tel: 01546 2281).
4 George Street, Oban, Argyll

PA34 5RX (Tel: 01631 66368).
7a Alexandra Parade, Dunoon,
Argyll PA23 8AB (Tel: 01369 2023).
Caithness: Caithness and Sutherland
Enterprise, 2 Princes Street,
Thurso, Caithness KW14 7BQ
(Tel: 01847 66115).
Inverness: Inverness and Nairn Enter-
prise, 4th Floor, Metropolitan House,
31–33 High Street, Inverness IV1 1RX
(Tel: 01463 713504).
Lochaber Limited, 5 Cameron
Square, Fort William PH33 6AJ (Tel:
01397 704326/702160).
Orkney Islands: Orkney Enterprise,
1 Castle Street, Kirkwall, KW15 1HD
(Tel: 01856 4638).
Ross and Cromarty: Ross and Cro-
marty Enterprise, 62 High Street,
Invergordon, Ross and Cromarty IV18
9DH (Tel: 01349 853666).
Shetland Islands: Shetland Enterprise,
Bank Lane, Lerwick,
Shetland ZE1 0DS (Tel: 01595 3177).
Skye: Skye and Lochalsh Enterprise,
Bridge Road, Portree, Isle of Skye IV51
9ER (Tel: 01478 2841).
Speyside: Moray, Badenoch and
Strathspey Enterprise, Elgin Business
Centre, Elgin IV30 1RH
(Tel: 01343 550567) (lies partly in
Scottish Enterprise area)
The Square, Grantown-on-Spey
PH26 3HF (Tel: 01479 3288).
Western Isles: Western Isles Enter-
prise, 16 South Beach, Stornoway, Isle
of Lewis PA87 2BE (Tel: 01851
703625/703905).
Balivanich, Benbecula PA88 5LA
(Tel: 01870 602646).

Wales

In Wales two organizations, the Welsh Development Agency (WDA) and the Development Board for Rural Wales (DBRW), both provide help to small and medium-sized businesses as well as to inward investors.

The WDA concentrates on the largely urbanized area of South Wales and the DBRW covers the rest of Wales which is more rural.

The Welsh Development Agency

The WDA operates a wide range of services for small and medium-sized businesses. These include Eurolink, which helps companies find suitable partners in Europe, and the Welsh Euro Information Centre (WEIC), which offers a fast efficient information service keeping local firms abreast of European legislation and business opportunities.the Technology Marketing Division helps with product acquisition, market development and commercial exploitation of R and D.

The WDA can provide low-interest loans, and equity funds for a wide variety of purposes. A number of land and property based schemes are also operated, including a Rural Buildings Conversion Grant, and a Valley Enterprise loan scheme to purchase property in formal coal areas. The WDA offices are:

Head office

The Welsh Development Agency, QED Centre, Main Avenue, Treforest Industrial Estate, Pontypridd, Mid Glamorgan CF37 5YL (Tel: 01443 841345; Fax: 01443 841393).

WDA regional offices

North East Wales: Wrexham Industrial Estate, Wrexham, Clwyd LL13 9UF (Tel: 01978 661011; Fax: 01978 661007).
North West Wales: Llys-y-Bont, Parc Menai, Bangor, Gwynedd LL57 4BN (Tel: 01248 670076; Fax: 01248 671197).
West Wales: Cillefwr Industrial Estate, Johnstown, Carmarthen, Dyfed SA31 3RB (Tel: 01267 235642; Fax: 01267 236642).
South Wales (West): Coronet Way, Enterprise Park, Morriston, Swansea SA6 8RH (Tel: 01792 790000;

Fax: 01792 702000).
South Wales Valleys: Business Centre, Triangle Business Park, Pentrebach, Merthyr Tydfil, Mid Glamorgan CF48 4YB (Tel: 01685 722177; Fax: 01685 359884).
South Wales (East): as head office.
Business Services Division
   Pearl House, Greyfriars Road, Cardiff CF1 3XX (Tel: 01222 222666; Fax: 01222 345615).
   QED Centre, Main Avenue, Treforest Industrial Estate, Pontypridd, Mid Glamorgan CF37 5YL (Tel: 01443 841404; Fax: 01443 841393).

Development Board for Rural Wales

The DBRW – Ladywell House, Newtown, Powys SY16 1JB (Tel: 01686 626965; Fax: 01686 622499) – carries out a broadly similar role to the WDA, with greater emphasis on agriculture and tourism.

For example their Rural small loans provide unsecured loans of between £1,000 and £10,000 for firms employing fewer than 10 people. Secured loans up to £75,000 are also available for firms employing up to 20 skilled people.

There is a 12-month repayment moratorium on such loans.

Northern Ireland

LEDU (the Local Enterprise Development Unit) is the small-business agency for Northern Ireland. It aims to strengthen the Northern Ireland economy by encouraging enterprise and stimulating improvements in the competitiveness of new and existing business within defined markets. To achieve this, LEDU offers a suite of programmes which cater for clients at each of the four stages of business development: pre-start, start-up, established and growth.

Pre-start

LEDU provides a range of initiatives for those who are not yet ready to start up in business but who wish to learn more about enterprise. Much of this activity is carried out through the Northern Ireland enterprise network and in particular local Enterprise Agencies. Initiatives to increase 'Business Awareness' include 'ideas-generation' workshops, special 'target programmes', 'self-assessment' seminars and LEDU's Student Information Pack.

Start-up

'Business Start' is the centrepiece of a graduated start-up support programme for those entering self-employment for the first time. The support offered includes business advice, enterprise training, on-going counselling and financial support.

A start-up package of assistance is also available for new businesses with employees and will be related to the needs of the business, whether servicing the local market or selling outside Northern Ireland.

Established

'Business Advance' provides a comprehensive range of support to help established businesses become more competitive, get involved in exporting and plan for future success and growth. Established businesses have a key role to play in the future of the Northern Ireland economy. They may be consolidating, or growing in the Northern Ireland market, but their long-term success depends on increasing competitiveness and developing export opportunities.

The 'Business Advance' programme of assistance can help established businesses plan for a successful and profitable future. Operated through LEDU's six regional offices, it includes a business analysis, business improvement plan and use of LEDU's General Services and Advisory Business Consultancy scheme.

Growth

'Business Growth' is for those businesses already actively selling their products/services outside Northern Ireland and who are capable of, and committed to, significantly expanding their activities in export markets as the vehicle for future profitable growth.

The 'Business Growth' programme enables such businesses to undertake a business analysis to identify and agree with LEDU their strengths, weaknesses and barriers to growth. Support is then available to address weaknesses, improve competitiveness and prepare for, and implement, strategic plans for accelerated growth in export markets.

LEDU head office
Local Enterprise Development Unit
(LEDU), LEDU House, Upper Gal-
wally, Belfast BT8 4TB
(Tel: 01232 491031;
Fax: 01232 691432).

LEDU regional offices
North Western: 13 Shipquay Street,
Londonderry, Belfast BT48 6DJ
(Tel: 01504 267257).
North Eastern: Clarence House, 86

Mill Street, Ballymena BT43 5AF
(Tel: 01266 49215).
Southern: 6–7 The Mall, Bewry BT34
1BX (Tel: 01693 62955).
Western: 15–17 High Street, Omagh
BT2 8DT (Tel: 01662 245763).
Belfast: 25–27 Franklin Street, Belfast
BT2 8DT (Tel: 01232 242582).
South Eastern: 43–45 Frances Street,
Newtownards BT23 3DX
(Tel: 01247 813880).

The Irish Republic

(Note: All phone numbers are as from Ireland. Add international code from
outside.) Ireland is rich in schemes and organizations whose job it is to encourage people to start up and develop a business.

Industrial Development Agency (IDA)

The IDA offers grants, advice and other assistance. Once an application is under
consideration, certain factors are taken into account to decide the suitability of
the project for funding. They also have a bearing on the amount and composi-
tion of the grant aid. These factors include the resources available to promote
the project, its commercial viability, the economic benefits to the national
economy, and the need for financial assistance.

The Small Business Programme, which has evolved through various forms
since the 1950s, is one IDA support scheme most suited to start-up companies.
At present grants of up to £425,000 can be attained under this programme,
which is ideally suited to manufacturing start-up and Irish international traded
service companies. Another scheme of interest is the Enterprise Development
Programme. This seeks to attract senior managers from existing jobs to join
with others to create high-potential companies. Under these programmes the
assistance offered varies according to the need of the new company but can
include the following:

- employment grants of up to £5,000 per person for new start-up companies
  employing up to 15 people;
- capital grants for machinery and buildings;
- leasing grants for machinery;
- rent subsidies of up to 45% for five years' rental;
- loan guarantees to cover loans raised to finance asset investment or
  working capital.

In addition to grant-aiding, the IDA also helps entrepreneurs in research.
This grant may cover up to 50% of the cost of investigating the feasibility of a

new business, including market research, salaries and prototypes.

To fulfil the criteria, manufacturing companies must:

- be an individual, community group or company;
- be investigating a new manufacturing product or process;
- apply before beginning the study;
- carry out most of the work in the Republic of Ireland;
- not repeat work that has previously produced negative results (whether carried out by applicant or someone else);
- not seek aid from any other State body for the expenditure incurred in this project.

Feasibility study grants are also available for international services projects. If your study is in an area already known to have over-capacity, you are unlikely to be given a grant.

Eligible studies include:

- market research;
- preparation of costings and financial projections;
- assessment of manufacturing processes;
- assessment of suitable plant, equipment etc;
- sourcing of raw materials;
- negotiation with potential joint venture partners;
- negotiation of manufacturing licences.

The feasibility grant will agree costs under a number of headings – for example, travel, market research or prototyping. The amount of grant aid is limited to the amount agreed under each heading.

If you spend more than anticipated, you will not get grant aid on the excess. And you cannot transfer savings under one heading to offset overspending elsewhere. Therefore, in making your application, it is essential that:

- your estimates are accurate;
- you justify each item of expenditure;
- you include some margin, in case your estimates are cut back in arriving at the amount to be grant-aided – though don't be too greedy or you may lose out on the grant altogether.

The format suggested for your application is:

- Information on promoter
  promoter's name
  address
  present position
  qualifications
  work history
  background
  business objectives (if existing company)
- Details of project to be examined
  products
  customer/markets

if exports are proposed, are they necessary for profitability initially?
competitors
relevance of product to company's existing business (where applicable)
estimated size of investment (including working capital)
estimated employment
promoter's capital availability
the critical issues for the project (e.g. technical development and performance; obtaining planning permission; finding equity partners)

- Present status of project, including work carried out to date
- For each separate stage of the study, details of:
  work to be done
  by whom/time involved/cost and details of travel and other
  special expenditures
- Where consultants will be involved, the name of the consultant (get a few quotations), the exact work to be undertaken, standard costs per week and number of weeks, and any special expenses agreed
- For prototype expenditure, the number of units proposed, the material and labour cost per unit and a justification of the number of units
- Details of any export market research to be carried out.

The grant is considered under two headings – home market research and export market research. When setting out the order in which the study will be undertaken, it is important to label these two stages carefully (if they both apply), with sub-stages within these clearly indicated.

If your application is accepted (this can take up to two months, during which you cannot proceed with your study), you will receive a letter of offer. Read this carefully. Query any parts of it that you do not understand. It will be against this document, not your original application, that your expenditure will be checked before any grants are paid out to you. Make sure that you know what the terms of the grant aid are and keep to them. Be sure to sign and return the letter of offer within the time period indicated, otherwise the grant aid may lapse.

Contact:

IDA Regional Office Enterprise Centre, North Mall, Cork (Tel: 0121 397711; Fax: 0121 395393).
IDA regional offices Co. Kerry: 57 High Street, Killarney, Co. Kerry (Tel: 0164 34133; Fax: 0164 34135).
Donegal: Portland House, Port Road, Letterkenny, Co. Donegal (Tel: 0174 21155; Fax: 0174 21424).
Dublin/East: Wilton Park House, Wilton Place, Dublin 2

(Tel: 011 668 6633; Fax: 011 660 5095).
Midlands: Auburn, Dublin Road, Athlone, Co. Westmeath (Tel: 01902 72695; Fax: 01902 74516).
North West: Finisklin Industrial Estate, Sligo (Tel: 0171 61311; Fax: 0171 61896).
North East: Finnabair Industrial Estate, Dundalk, Co. Louth

(Tel: 0142 31261/39031;
Fax: 0142 39034).
South West: Industry House, Rossa
Avenue, Bishopstown, Co. Cork
(Tel: 0121 343555;
Fax: 0121 343444).

South East: IDA Industrial Estate,
Cork Road, Waterford
(Tel: 0151 72911; Fax: 0151 72719).
West: IDA Industrial Estate, Mervue,
Galway (Tel: 0191 51111;
Fax: 0191 51515).

County enterprise boards

The restructuring of national industrial policy has led to the introduction of county enterprise boards to replace county development teams. The new boards have a wide brief, spanning manufacturing, tourism, agriculture and infrastructure. These changes reflect the government's plan to expand county and local community-based enterprise initiative and to place a particular emphasis on establishing new businesses. This support will take the form of providing necessary financial, technical and professional support.

A fund of £12 million was made available for start-up and small businesses, to be channelled through the new enterprise boards. A special emphasis will be placed on new companies with fewer than a dozen employees, and on local community development and education. With this in mind, proposals involving grant support over £50,000, or projects with investment costs over £100,000, will not normally be considered.

Grant levels are determined at a maximum of 50% of the cost of capital and other investment or £50,000, whichever is less. Grants for preparing feasibility study/business plans are awarded up to a maximum of 75% of the cost, subject to an overall limit of £5,000.

Assistance is based on several criteria:

■ A market exists for the product or service to be produced.
■ There is adequate finance available to fund the project.
■ There is management and technical capacity to implement the proposed project.

For more information, contact the Department of Enterprise and Employment at Kildare Street, Dublin 2 (Tel: 011 661 4444; Fax: 011 676 2654) or local county councils in the Irish Republic.

Shannon Development

This is the agency responsible for economic development in the mid-west region, which comprises Limerick, Clare, north Kerry, north Tipperary and south-west Offaly.

The following grants are administered by Shannon Development (see later in this chapter) in the Shannon region:

■ Employment grants: to companies planning to start up or to increase employment. Grants range between £4,000 (for projects with fewer than 15 employees) and £9,000 (for projects with more than 15 employees) per new job created, depending on the industrial sector involved. Half is paid on recruitment, the balance after six months' employment.

■ Feasibility grants: to encourage companies to investigate new products or processes. Grants of up to 50% of eligible expenditure (e.g. salaries, travel costs, development of product prototypes, consultants' fees etc) are available up to a maximum of £15,000 per study.

■ Capital grants: on plant and equipment (Note: projects may receive one grant type only – either employment grants or capital grants).

■ Rent subsidies: typically in the range 25% to 40%.

■ Interest subsidies and/or loan guarantees: available, in exceptional cases, in lieu of capital grants on new loans for fixed asset investments.

■ Product and process development grants: jointly administered by the Shannon Development and EOLAS (the Irish Science and Technology Agency), these grants are available to enable companies to acquire new technology and/or products. Grants of up to 50% are available for new product research. Grants of up to 30% are available for process research.

■ Management development programme: to assist firms to strengthen their management capabilities and structures, a modular series of management development programmes is available. The modules focus on:
  – record and management information systems (MIS) – £2,000 maximum grant for setting up records and implementing an MIS.
  – business planning – £2,100 maximum grant for implementing a business plan and monitoring its achievement.
  – strategic planning – £4,100 maximum grant for strategic planning.
  – strengthening the management team – £15,000 maximum a year for two years for strengthening the management team.

■ Training grants: grants of up to 100% of the agreed cost are available for operatives in significant start-up projects, for small manufacturers (planning to employ more than 15 people) which can demonstrate that they have the ambition and the opportunity to grow in terms of staff numbers.

■ Enterprise Development Programme: offers the same range of incentives for new projects as already listed. The programme is aimed at experienced managers, academics and professionals who have the necessary experience and qualifications to establish and run a substantial successful new business.

■ Mentor programme: links small businesses with experienced business people who are willing to act as mentors on a short-term basis, to assist the businesses identify and overcome the problems and obstacles that limit their ability to grow. Mentors are not professional business consultants. They neither become actively involved in day-to-day management nor assume the role of an executive in the business. Mentors help to identify and solve problems in the following areas:
  – general management
  – corporate organization
  – strategic planning
  – financial structuring
  – production planning
  – marketing

■ Technology transfer: by twinning each regional IDA office with an overseas IDA office, the IDA can help companies find partners for joint ventures, licensing agreements and technology transfers. Under this scheme, grants of up to 50% are available for technology acquisition.

Contact Shannon Development offices:

Town Centre, Shannon, Co. Clare
(Tel: 0161 361555;
Fax: 0161 361903).
The Innovation Centre, National
Technological Park, Castletroy,
Limerick (Tel: 0161 338177;
Fax: 0161 338065).
Clare Business Centre, Francis Street,
Ennis, Co. Clare
(Tel: 0165 20165/20166;
Fax: 0165 21234).
The Granary, Michael Street,

Limerick (Tel: 0161 410777;
Fax: 0161 315634).
Silverline Building, Connolly Street,
Nenagh, Co. Tipperary
(Tel: 0167 32100; Fax: 0167 33418).
Brendan Street, Birr, Co. Offaly
(Tel: 01509 20440;
Fax: 01509 20660).
Ashe Memorial Hall, Denny Street,
Tralee, Co. Kerry (Tel: 0166 24988;
Fax: 0166 24267).

Udaras na Gaeltachta

Udaras aims to establish and develop job-creating industries and services in the Gaeltacht regions of Donegal, Mayo, Galway, Kerry, Cork, Waterford and Meath. Udaras has schemes and incentives to help small and medium-sized enterprises raise money and obtain grants in these areas.

The following grants are available:

■ Employment grants: rates vary from £3,000 to £9,000, according to skill level and industrial sector. Half of the employment grant is paid when the job is created; the balance is paid when the job has been in existence for six months.

■ Capital grants: in the case of certain food/fish processing or aqua-culture projects, assistance from the European Community's Fisheries Fund may be obtained up to a level of 50% investment in fish-processing and 40% in aqua-culture projects. In such cases, a capital grant of up to 25% may be approved by Udaras in addition to amounts from the Fisheries Fund.

■ Interest subsidy: may be paid to small industry projects where the total grant aid is less than £100,000. It applies to agreed-term loan borrowings of up to £20,000. Under this scheme, 100% of interest is subsidized in year one, 75% in year two, 50% in year three and 25% in year four.

■ Rent subsidy: up to 40% (or 60% in exceptional cases) may be paid in respect of an industrial premises for a period of up to ten years. This subsidy may be applied either to a premises leased from Udaras, if such is available, or to a premises leased privately.

■ Feasibility study grants: at a rate of up to 50% (maximum grant £5,000) are available in certain cases.

■ Research and development grants: payable in respect of approved projects relating to product or process development. Grants of 50% of research costs up to a maximum of £100,000 or 60% of the total research outlay on direct material and labour, consultants, overheads, research and development and buildings and equipment may be provided.

■ Training grants: can cover up to 100% of agreed training costs and be paid in conjunction with employment grants.

■ Technology acquisition grants: towards the cost of a licence, technical consultants, salaries, R and D costs etc. The technology must be capable of being produced in the State and must be innovative in relation to the company's existing level of technology.

Udaras also provides non-financial incentives, such as advice and consultation on legal documentation.

Contact Udaras na Gaeltachta offices:

Na Forbacha, Galway
(Tel: 0191 92011; Fax: 0191 92037).
Teach IPC, Shelbourne Road,
Ballsbridge, Baile, Atha Cliath 4
(Tel: 011 660 7888;
Fax: 011 668 6030).
Na Doiri Beaga, Co. Dhun na nGall
(Tel: 0175 31200/31479;

Fax: 0175 31319).
An Daingean, Co. Chiarrai
(Tel: 0166 51658/51417;
Fax: 0166 51788).
Sraid na mBearaice, Beal an Mhuirthead, Co. Mhaigh Eo
(Tel: 011 097 01418;
Fax: 0197 82179).

Factory or office space

For many new companies, finding relatively inexpensive accommodation is a very important way of controlling costs.

Assistance of this nature is provided by the IDA which from time to time makes workspace units available. These units may be up to 1,000 square metres in size but smaller 'incubator' units are usually provided for start-up projects. A range of back-up and secretarial services is usually available on site. Contact local IDA office (numbers given earlier, page 47).

Enterprise training schemes

In addition to providing practical advice and information, the national training and employment authority offers courses to help individuals secure employment, including those developing their own businesses.

FAS (the Irish training body) also provides a recruitment service by advertising for employees in its local offices throughout the country. In addition, it advertises vacancies on RTE's Aertel service and matches available jobs with people on the Live Register. These services are provided free of charge.

Shannon Development runs an imaginative 'Training the Entrepreneurs' programme. Run part-time over five months, it seeks to build teams of experienced executives to the point where they can start a business of their own. The programme costs around £1,000 and up to 30 people are taken on each year. People returning to Ireland from the UK have found this programme invaluable. Contact: Gerry Glynn on 061 338177.

The Project/Product Development Centre in Dublin also runs a start-up programme, this time for graduates. This practical programme lasts for one year and attracts a modest grant. Participants research their market, develop prototypes and are introduced to mentors who can help progress their idea. A business plan has to be produced. A number of people eventually start-up in the building where the programme is run from, in Dublin. Contact: Margaret Wheelan on 011 661 1910.

Information and advice

A number of centres throughout the country provide would-be entrepreneurs with start-up advice, ranging from general business and financial information to practical assistance in setting up your business.

Although in operation less than two years, the Mentor programme has proved to be one of the most effective schemes run by the IDA. Mentor offers start-up businesses expert advice from recognized industry figures. The service is not a consultancy but provides entrepreneurs with the opportunity to talk to highly experienced operators in their field. Programmes last 10 days.

Small Business Information Centre

Wilton Park House, Wilton Place, Dublin 2 (Tel: 011 660 2244; Fax: 011 660 5095): a source of advice for people who want to start their own manufacturing business. The Centre focuses on:
- finance and general business information
- IDA incentive packages for small business
- role of other State agencies.

Each IDA office has a Small Business Information Centre. Entrepreneurs who wish to discuss their planned business venture must fill out a questionnaire, to which IDA specialists will respond. A public phone information line is provided to help with queries on the questionnaire.

Crafts Council of Ireland

The IDA's Small Business Programme co-operates with the Crafts Council of Ireland (CCI), Powerscourt Townhouse, South William Street, Dublin 2 (Tel: 011 679 7368; Fax: 011 679 9197), to advise and help craft business.

The CCI's brief covers marketing and design aspects. It is independent, though funded by the IDA. It disseminates information and co-ordinates the efforts of the local craft associations and craftspersons. It has no funding to disburse grants. However, the IDA often seeks the advice of the CCI before offering a grant to a craft-based company.

National Microelectronics Research Centre (NMRC)

The NMRC, Lee Maltings, University College, Cork (Tel: 0121 276871; Fax: 0121 270271), has advanced facilities for designing, fabricating, and testing integrated circuits.

The NMRC plays a major role in keeping Irish graduates abreast of new scientific and technological developments and, at the same time, stimulates the creative application of new ideas and discoveries among Irish companies. The NMRC trains Irish graduates in the in-depth specialisms required by the electronics engineers of the future. It is also fostering a closer relationship between the electronics laboratory and industry.

Business Innovation Centres (BICs): based in Dublin (Tel: 011 671 3111), Cork (Tel: 0121 509044), Limerick (Tel: 0161 338177) and Galway (Tel: 0191 67974). Backed by the EC and the Government, the BICs are private limited companies which provide access to sources of seed and early-stage venture capital. Consultancy support and advice are provided in addition to practical support for entrepreneurs seeking to set up a business. A small fee is charged for these services, including a percentage fee where BIC finds equity capital for a business.

Other options for sources of start-up finance
Aside from the financial packages offered by the banks, there are limited options available to entrepreneurs seeking to raise capital to finance a new business.

One option is seed capital which can be obtained at the **Business Innovation Fund**, Merrion Square, Dublin 2. Available nationally, it is funded by a mix of institutional and private investors.

The fund offers seed capital of between £25,000 and £75,000 for start-ups and young businesses seeking development capital, in return for a minority share in the company.

Certain criteria exist to restrict investment to the start-up stage of business in order to promote employment, growth and export potential. The criteria include:

■ no more than 10 employees;
■ annual turnover of less than £75,000;
■ paid-up share capital of less than £1,150,000
■ significant future growth potential.

Contact: Karl Schutte (Tel: 011 661 2419).

Inner City Enterprise deals exclusively with start-up companies in Dublin's inner-city area. Under the chairmanship of Mark Hely-Hutchinson, the organization is funded from private sources. It provides hands-on business advice and support by identifying likely pitfalls and requirements that the new business will encounter. It appoints a business adviser, can assist in formulating a business plan, and places a Voluntary Business Advisory Panel (consisting of successful business people) at the disposal of each project.

In 1993, a loan fund was introduced which provides loans up to a maximum of £5,000 at a fixed 5% interest rate, payable over three years. A rent subsidy up to a maximum of £2,000 is also available. Contact: Eamonn Brady (Tel: 011 364073).

The Smurfit Job Creation Enterprise Fund aims to assist job creation by providing capital in new or established businesses. This is done by means of minority equity investments. The fund also offers the management expertise of a team of professional managers to assist the new business. New companies with a well-researched business proposal, intending to create at least 10 new jobs, can seek finance from £100,000 to £500,000. Contact: Gert Kealey (Tel: 011 478 4091).

EOLAS

EOLAS, the Irish Science and Technology Agency, Glasnevin, Dublin 9 (Tel: 011 370 101; Fax: 011 379 620), is the State agency responsible for the development, application and promotion of science and technology. It stimulates the Irish economy through programmes of investment in science and technology, carried out in industry, third-level colleges and in other specialized research centres. In addition, EOLAS provides a range of technical and consultancy service to Irish industry. These, combined with the investment programmes, are aimed at raising the level of technological competence and competitiveness in Irish industry.

The National Standards Authority of Ireland (NSAI) is a division of EOLAS and, in consultation with industry sectors, it develops and publishes standards to meet increasingly stringent market requirements for quality, design, personnel and safety of products.

EOLAS operates a number of programmes of particular relevance to new and existing small firms.

The National Technology Audit Programme is designed to assist companies assess the current status of their technology and identify how it can be improved to reduce costs and increase competitiveness.

The average cost of a technology audit is £4,000. The audit is grant-aided by EOLAS, through the Department of Enterprise and Employment, reducing the net cost to a small company to approximately £1,000. Small and medium indigenous companies with a definite product range are eligible.

The Technology Management Programme offers grant assistance to companies that wish to employ an experienced technical person.

A salary supplement over three years is available (50% of salary up to £10,000 in year one, £5,000 in year two and £2,500 in year three), plus an additional £5,000 for technical consultancy.

The TechStart Programme offers grant assistance to companies that take on a technically qualified graduate to carry out an agreed work programme. A salary support of £5,000 for a degree holder (£4,500 for a diploma holder) is paid for one year, plus an additional £2,000 for external consultancy. Small Irish-owned companies with little or no technical capability but with potential to develop are eligible.

EOLAS scheme for assistance with inventions

EOLAS can offer to fund a patent programme for an invention, covering 100% of the patent costs, subject to agreement with the inventor on a division of royalties resulting from the sales of the patented product or process. Where a patent programme is being funded, EOLAS will normally also assist with legal fees associated with drawing up licensing agreements. Inventions developed by industry, private individuals, government-sponsored research, universities or colleges are eligible.

EOLAS has a network of eight regional offices nationwide – in Dublin, Cork, Waterford, Athlone, Limerick, Sligo, Dundalk and Galway – serving Irish-based industry and acting as a gateway to a wide range of technical support, information and development services in Ireland and overseas.

National Microelectronics Application Centre

The National Microelectronics Application Centre (MAC) – the University of Limerick, Plassey, Limerick (Tel: 0161 333644) – is sponsored by Shannon Development, the University of Limerick, the IDA and the National Board for Science and Technology (NBST).

MAC's primary activity is the contract development of new and improved electronic, software, telematic and information products and processes for Irish entrepreneurs and industry. If your idea falls into one of these categories, MAC can help you identify, select, and develop your product in the following ways.

■ Discussing your market opportunity, concept, product, process or service idea with you. MAC can give you a good idea of what technology is appropriate and whether it is possible at the price, size and time that the market will require. These sessions are confidential, free and without obligation.

■ Doing an on-line search of world databases to identify whether a similar product exists anywhere else, to identify potential competitors, and to identify whether there are technologies that might lead to a competing product by the time you get to market with your product. This usually costs no more than a few hundred pounds.

■ Conceiving, designing and building a working prototype of your product or system, as part of a feasibility study.

■ Developing and building production prototypes, as part of your main development stage, which is usually grant-aided. This involves designing for manufacture, sourcing appropriate state-of-the-art components to give you a competitive edge, adhering to standards and regulations, avoiding electro-magnetic interference etc.

MAC normally works on fixed-price contracts to agreed schedules, so the entrepreneur's exposure is defined and can be budgeted exactly to the grant application. However, MAC is willing to consider any arrangement that makes commercial sense for both MAC and the entrepreneur.

Small Firms Association

The Small Firms Association (SFA) – Confederation House, Kildare Street,

Dublin 2 (Tel: 011 877 9801; Fax: 011 677 7823) – is the sole representative voice of small and medium-sized firms in Ireland and, as such, is regularly consulted by Government departments and the State development agencies on matters that have an impact on small firms. The SFA is an independent, non-party political body, financed entirely by voluntary membership subscriptions.

The SFA's primary objective is to promote the profitable development of small business. The SFA develops public awareness of the vital role of small business to national economic development through press, radio, TV and public meetings. The association aims to improve the competitiveness of Irish industry *vis-à-vis* trading competitors by providing advice, assistance and information on developments that may affect its members at national, European and international levels.

Specifically, the SFA provides its members with practical advice and assistance on a range of crucial issues:

- liaison with Government departments and State agencies
- industrial development policy
- national legislation
- EEC directives
- taxation – local and national
- company law
- economics
- roads and infrastructure
- supply of materials and services
- foreign trade
- industrial grants and taxation incentives
- patents, trade marks and licensing.

The SFA holds regional Management Development Workshops for small and medium-sized firms on a regular basis. Its publications include:

- *A Comprehensive Guide to Government and EC Support Programmes*
- *EC Budget Lines of Use to Small and Medium-sized Industries*
- *A Guide to Employment and Social Obligations and Procedures.*

First Step

First Step – Jefferson House, Eglinton Road, Donnybrook, Dublin 4 (Tel: 011 260 0988; Fax: 011 260 0989) – was set up in 1990 by Mrs Norma Smurfit, who brought together prominent members of the Irish business community to harness the goodwill of the private sector. First Step works through existing community enterprise groups, and in parallel with State support agencies, without any committees or bureaucratic structures. If a project has the potential to create more jobs in disadvantaged areas and an examination of it reveals no basic flaw, the entrepreneur may subsequently be given financial and/or practical assistance.

First Step can provide seed funding for projects or people with no security. It can make grants towards prototype development or feasibility studies. First Step has a panel of successful business people prepared to give some free time to a young enterprise in the critical start-up years.

First Step's project funding comes entirely from the private sector both at home and abroad. First Step uses this fund to trigger other available resources, whether from the State or the European Commission. All funds given for projects go 100% to those projects, without any deduction for administration.

First Step is designed to support projects where the promoters come from socio-economically disadvantaged backgrounds. Project promoters must demonstrate that they have been unsuccessful in raising the necessary finance from commercial sources. First Step is not an alternative to commercial bank finance, but rather a lender of last resort. Contact: Pat Kearney.

The Liffey Trust

The Liffey Trust – 117–126 Upper Sheriff Street, Dublin 1 (Tel: 011 364651; Fax: 011 364818) – was founded in 1984, and is a voluntary, non-political, non-profit-making organization devoted to job creation in Ireland. It receives no State aid and relies for its funding on private companies and individuals, on raffles and functions, and on promotions of various sorts.

The Trust believes that bureaucracy hinders the setting up and development of new enterprises and endeavours to eliminate the obstacles that prevent would-be entrepreneurs from getting started. It has helped 150 different businesses to date and has the largest enterprise centre in Europe funded without State aid.

The Liffey Trust provides the following services to start-up businesses:

- preparation of business plans, feasibility studies and grant applications, free of charge
- advice on ways and means of raising finance
- guidance on setting up accounting and control systems
- provision of Model Rules, free of charge, for co-operatives
- free management consultancy for the first year
- free marketing consultancy for the first year
- organizing combined marketing of products
- provision of working space in Dublin with free or reduced rent for new businesses while they are getting established
- taking care of the bureaucratic procedures to help a new business:
  - decide its legal structure
  - become registered
  - obtain a VAT number
  - register for PAYE and PRSI
  - obtain sub-contract numbers
- explanations of the many different kinds of grants available.

There are no charges for the Liffey Trust consultancy services, either before or after the business is in operation. The Trust does charge for rented space – this amounts to two-thirds of commercial rates.

The Bolton Trust

The Bolton Trust – Pigeon House Road, Ringsend, Dublin 4 (Tel: 011 668 7155;

Fax: 011 668 7945) – runs the Powerhouse, which has almost 6,000 square feet of lettable office space to accommodate enterprises. The monthly rental for desk space is £43.33. Office rental rates vary with room size between £90 to £322 per month. The charge is inclusive of building services.

Powerhouse is unique among enterprise centres in that a full-time Enterprise Development Manager is employed. The role of the Manager is to advise and work with companies to help them succeed. In addition, the resources of the Bolton Trust, namely 400 lecturers from the Dublin Institute of Technology colleges (Bolton Street, Kevin Street, the College of Marketing and Design, the College of Commerce at Rathmines, the College of Catering at Cathal Brugha Street and the College of Music), can be called upon to assist in a company's development.

Powerhouse also provides reception secretarial services, telephone service, typing, desk-top publishing, mailshots, photocopying, business address, security cards and electricity heating – all priced on a usage basis.

Some other useful contacts

- AIB Bank Enterprise Development Bureau, Bankcentre, Ballsbridge, Dublin 4 (Tel: 011 660 0311; Fax: 011 668 2508). Contact: John Kelly.
- AIB Venture Capital Centre, Jefferson House, Eglinton Road, Dublin 4 (Tel: 011 260 0966; Fax: 011 260 0538). Contact: Billy Morgan.
- Arthur Andersen & Co, Chartered Accountants, Andersen House, Harbourmaster Place, Dublin 1 (Tel: 011 670 1000; Fax: 011 670 1010).
- Bank of Ireland Enterprise Support Unit, Head Office, Lower Baggot Street, Dublin 2 (Tel: 011 661 5933; Fax: 011 676 3493).
- Business Expansion Scheme, The Secretariat of Taxes, Office of the Revenue Commissioners, Dublin Castle, Dublin 2 (Tel: 011 679 2777; Fax: 011 679 9287).
- Business Incubation Centre, Ossory Road, North Strand, Dublin 3 (Tel: 011 363994; Fax: 011 363997). Contact: Rory O'Meara.
- Business Information Centre,

Central Library, Ilac Centre, Henry Street, Dublin 1 (Tel: 011 873 3996; Fax: 011 872 1451).
- Business Innovation Fund, Karl Schutte, 40 Merrion Square, Dublin 2 (Tel: 011 661 2419; Fax: 011 661 2473).
- Carey O'Connor, Chartered Accountants, 1 Drinan Street, Sullivan's Quay, Cork (Tel: 0121 961122; Fax: 0121 962480).
- Central Statistics Office, St Stephen's Green House, Earlsfort Terrace, Dublin 2 (Tel: 011 676 7531; Fax: 011 668 2221).
- Centre for Co-operative Studies, University College Cork, Western Road, Cork (Tel: 0121 276871).
- The Chambers of Commerce of Ireland, 22 Merrion Square, Dublin 2 (Tel: 011 661 2888; Fax: 011 661 2811).
- Chartered Association of Certified Accountants, 9 Leeson Park, Dublin 6 (Tel: 011 963260).
- Co-operative Development Society, 29 Dame Street, Dublin 2 (Tel: 011

677 0045).
■ Coopers & Lybrand, Chartered
Accountants, Fitzwilton House,
Wilton Place, Dublin 2
(Tel: 011 661 0333;
Fax: 011 660 1782).
■ Deloitte & Touche, Chartered
Accountants, Earlsfort Terrace,
Dublin 2 (Tel: 011 661 8311;
Fax: 011 675 6622).
■ Department of Finance,
Government Buildings, Merrion
Street, Dublin 2 (Tel: 011 676 7571;
Fax: 011 678 9936).
■ Department of Labour, Davitt
House, Mespil Road, Dublin 4
(Tel: 011 676 5861,
Fax: 011 660 3210).
■ Development Capital
Corporation, DCC House, Stilorgan,
Co. Dublin (Tel: 011 283 1011;
Fax: 011 283 1017).
■ Ernst & Young, Chartered Accoun-
tants, Harcourt Centre, Harcourt
Street, Dublin 2 (Tel: 011 475 0555).
■ European Business Institute, 11 Ely
Place, Dublin 2
(Tel: 011 676 8804;
Fax: 011 676 8805).
■ European Commission, 39
Molesworth Street, Dublin 2
(Tel: 011 671 2244;
Fax: 011 671 2657).
■ Irish Productivity Centre, 35
Shelbourne Road, Dublin 4
(Tel: 011 668 6244;
Fax: 011 668 6525).
■ Irish Quality Association, Merrion
Hall, Strand Road, Sandymount,

Dublin 4 (Tel: 011 695255;
Fax: 011 695820).
■ KPMG Stokes Kennedy Crowley,
Chartered Accountants, 1 Stokes
Place, St Stephens Green, Dublin 2
(Tel: 011 708 1000;
Fax: 011 708 1122).
■ National Food Centre, Dunisea,
Castleknock, Dublin 15
(Tel: 011 383222; Fax: 011 383684).
■ National Irish Bank Ltd, 7/8
Wilton Terrace, Dublin 2
(Tel: 011 878 5066;
Fax: 011 878 5949).
■ NISO (National Industrial Safety
Organization) Davitt House,
Mespil Road, Dublin 4
(Tel: 011 676 5861;
Fax: 011 660 3210).
■ NSAI (National Standards Author-
ity of Ireland), Glasnevin, Dublin 9
(Tel: 011 370101; Fax: 011 379620).
■ Patents Office, 45 Merrion Square,
Dublin 2 (Tel: 011 661 4144;
Fax: 011 676 0416).
■ Registrar of Friendly Societies, Ship
Street Gate, Dublin Castle,
Dublin 2 (Tel: 011 661 4333).
■ Registry of Business Names,
Lower Castle Yard, Dame Street,
Dublin 2 (Tel: 011 661 4222).
■ Revenue Commissioners, Dublin
Castle, Dublin 2 (Tel: 011 679 2777).
■ Revenue Commissioners, VAT
Branch, Castle House, South Great
George's Street, Dublin 2
(Tel: 011 679 2777;
Fax: 011 671 8653).

■ LOCAL ENTERPRISE AGENCIES

Local Enterprise Agencies or Trusts have been formed in about 400 places up
and down the UK. Some have been in existence for nearly two decades. The
great majority were formed in the last decade. They have in common the objectives of encouraging new and small businesses to start up in a particular area,

and of helping businesses in their area to survive and prosper.

These agencies are usually run by a small staff (the largest has over 30 people, but the average is a handful) who can call on the wealth of expertise within the organizations sponsoring the agency. Many hundreds of organizations have sponsored one or more Enterprise Agency. Sponsors include: local government; chambers of commerce; universities and colleges; industrial and commercial companies, both large and not so large; banks and merchant banks; accountancy firms; newspapers and television companies; insurance companies; and building societies. Moreover, organizations such as HM Dockyards, the Port of London Authority and the General and Municipal Workers' Union have played significant roles in the launching of Local Enterprise Agencies.

The services provided by sponsoring bodies to the agencies include: financial support towards running costs; office and workshop space; secretarial and administrative services; management and commercial advice; training facilities and resources; literature production and dissemination (including the use of advertising media); desk or field research; board representation; and help with forming and developing policy.

A rather smaller number of organizations second staff to help in the day-to-day running of the Enterprise Agency. These are very often specialists from banking or the property world, or experienced managers within big companies. There are even a few academics returning a step closer to the commercial world. These advisers are an important resource within the agency, but the sponsoring company is amply rewarded. For example, a secondee from a major clearing bank will see more new business proposals in a week at an Enterprise Agency than he may see in a year at a small local branch. At the end of his year's secondment he will be a seasoned campaigner and probably a better judge of a good proposal.

The scope of activities of each agency is broadly similar. Many provide small workshops and office premises; run business advice clinics to help people to find money and other resources. Courses on marketing, on exporting, bookkeeping, tax and employing people are run by agencies, usually through their links with local colleges.

Some agencies are particularly skilled in the Investors in People area (see Training and Enterprise Councils page 80), or in Quality Standards such as BS5750. Others may be a part of the Local Initiative Networking Company (see Raising the Money, Chapter 6), or operate a Women's Enterprise Centre.

If you are actively considering starting up a business or are experiencing problems with your existing business, then you would certainly be well advised to contact your nearest Enterprise Agency. If they cannot help or answer your questions they will almost certainly know who can.

England

Accrington: Hyndburn Enterprise Trust Ltd, Suites 4/5/6 Arcade Offices, Church Street, Accrington BB5 2EH. Tel: 01254 390000; Fax: 01254 398985.
Contact: Aileen Evans
Aldershot: Blackwater Valley Enterprise Trust, Princes Gardens, High Street, Aldershot GU11 1BJ. Tel: 01252 319272; Fax: 01252 319384.
Contact: Walter Oakey
Ashford: Enterprise Ashford Ltd, The Enterprise Centre, Old Railway Works, Newtown Road, Ashford, Kent TN24 0PD.
Tel: 01233 630307; Fax: 01233 625687.
Contact: Alan Duncan
Banbury: North Oxfordshire Business Venture Ltd, 2nd Floor, Globe House, Calthorpe Street, Banbury, Oxon OX16 8EX.
Tel: 01295 267900.
Contact: Tim Nattrass
Barnard Castle: Teesdale Enterprise Agency, 39 Galgate, Barnard Castle, Co. Durham DL12 8EJ.
Tel: 01833 31851.
Contact: Kenneth Lee
Barnsley: Barnsley Enterprise Centre, The Enterprise Centre, 1 Pontefract Road, Barnsley, South Yorkshire S71 1AJ.
Tel: 01226 774000; Fax: 01226 774099.
Contact: John Price
Barnstaple: The North Devon Enterprise Agency Ltd, Yelland Centre, West Yelland, Barnstaple, North Devon EX31 3EZ.
Tel: 01271 861215.
Contact: Tony Jennings
Barrow-in-Furness: Furness Enterprise Ltd, Trinity Enterprise Centre, Furness Business Park, Ironworks Road, Barrow-in-Furness, Cumbria LA14 2PN.
Tel: 01229 822132; Fax: 01229 813504.
Contact: John Barker
Basildon: Basildon and District Local Enterprise Agency Ltd, c/o Samson House Ltd, Unit 16, Arterial Road, Laindon, Basildon, Essex SS15 6DR. Tel: 01268 410400.
Contact: Dennis Pigden
Basingstoke: Basingstoke and Andover Enterprise Centre, 75 Church Street, Basingstoke, Hampshire RG21 1QT.
Tel: 01256 54041; Fax: 01256 476040.
Contact: Colin Close
Bath: Bath Enterprise Ltd, Green Park Station, Green Park Road, Bath BA1 1JB. Tel: 01225 338383; Fax: 01225 443220.
Contact: Roger Williams
Batley: Kirklees and Wakefield Venture Trust, Kirklees Enterprise Agency, Unit 6, Batley Enterprise Centre, 513 Batley Road, Batley WF17 8JY. Tel: 01924 420302; Fax: 01924 424863.
Contact: Christine Tolson
Bedale: Hambleton and Richmondshire Business Enterprise Centre, Enterprise House, Bridge Street, Bedale DL8 2AD.
Tel: 01677 423737; Fax: 01677 424174.
Contact: James Brown
Bedlington: South East Northumberland Enterprise Trust (SENET), 20 School Road, Bedlington Station, Northumberland NE22 7JB.
Tel: 01670 828686.
Contact: Thomas Dean
Bedminster: Hebron House Enterprise, Hebron House, Sion

Road, Bedminster, Bristol BS9 3BD.
Tel: 0117 9637634;
Fax: 0117 9631770.
Contact: Susan Lowman
Birmingham: Birmingham Venture,
Chamber of Commerce House,
75 Harborne Road, Edgbaston,
Birmingham B15 3DH.
Tel: 0121 454 6171;
Fax: 0121 455 8670.
Contact: Derek Bullivant
– Black Business in Birmingham,
15 The Square, 111 Broad Street,
Birmingham B15 1AS.
Tel: 0121 631 2860;
Fax: 0121 643 1843.
Contact: Olufemi Kolade
Bishop Auckland: Wear Valley
Enterprise Agency Ltd, Auckland
New Business Centre, Bishop
Auckland, Co. Durham DL14 9TX.
Tel: 01388 450505;
Fax: 01388 601516.
Contact: Peter Gawthrop
Blackburn: Blackburn and District
Enterprise Trust Ltd, 14
Richmond Terrace, Blackburn,
Lancashire BB1 7BH.
Tel: 01254 664747;
Fax: 01254 55465.
Contact: Ken Whittaker
Blackpool: Blackpool and Fylde
Business Agency Ltd, 20 Queen
Street, Blackpool FY1 1PD.
Tel: 01253 294929.
Contact: Dennis Scheib
Bolton: Bolton Business Ventures
Ltd, 46 Lower Bridgeman Street,
Bolton BL2 1DG. Tel: 01204 391400;
Fax: 01204 380076.
Contact: Paul Davidson
Bootle: South Sefton Enterprise
Agency, South Sefton Business
Centre, Canal Street, Bootle,
Merseyside L20 8AH. Tel:
051 933 0024; Fax: 0151 933 8974.

Contact: Colleen Bold
Bradford: Bradford Enterprise
Agency, Commerce House, 24
Kirkgate, Bradford, West
Yorkshire BD1 1QB.
Tel: 01274 734359.
Contact: John Smith
Braintree: Braintree District
Enterprise Agency Ltd, Town
Hall Centre, Braintree, Essex CM7
6YG. Tel: 01376 328221;
Fax: 01376 328221.
Contact: Brian Palmer
Brentwood: Brentwood Enterprise
Agency Ltd, Brentwood Training
Centre, Essex Way, Warley,
Brentwood, Essex CM13 3AX.
Tel: 01277 213405;
Fax: 01277 201391.
Contact: James Campbell
Bridgwater: Sedgemoor District Enter-
prise Centre, West Quay Business
Centre, 12–14 West Quay,
Bridgwater, Somerset TA6 3HW. Tel:
01278 452978;
Fax: 01278 453058.
Contact: Ian Billinge
Brighton: Brighton and Hove
Business Enterprise Agency,
23 Old Steine, Brighton, East
Sussex BN1 1EL. Tel: 01273 688882;
Fax: 01273 604023.
Contact: Michael Hogg
Bristol: Bristol and Avon Enterprise
Agency, The Coach House, 2 Upper
York Street, Bristol BS2 8QN.
Tel: 0117 9272222;
Fax: 0117 9445661
Contact: Keith Oxtoby
– Bristol Black Business Association, 9
Lower Ashley Road, St Agnes, Bristol
BS2 9QA.
Tel: 0117 9550916/35;
Fax: 0117 9350654.
Contact: Dennis de' Cordova
Brixton: South London Business

Initiative, Brixton Small Business Centre, 444 Brixton Road, London SW9 8EJ.Tel: 0171 274 4000; Fax: 0171 274 8921. Contact: Dr Walter Baker MBE
Bromley: Bromley Enterprise Agency Trust Ltd, 7 Palace Grove, Bromley, Kent BR1 3HA. Tel: 0181 290 6568; Fax: 0181 313 1925. Contact: Colin Parham
Burnley: Burnley Enterprise Trust Ltd, Burnley Business Centre, Bank Parade, Burnley, Lancashire BB11 1UQ. Tel: 01282 411320; Fax: 01282 830577. Contact: Michael Green
Burton: Burton Enterprise Agency Ltd, Suites 15/17, Imex Business Park, Shobnall Road, Burton upon Trent, Staffs DE14 2AU. Tel: 01283 37151; Fax: 01283 37130. Contact: Peter St John-Harris
Bury: Bury Partnership, Business Centre, Kay Street, Bury BL9 6BU. Tel: 0161 763 1781. Contact: John Weir
Bury St Edmunds: Mid Anglian Enterprise Agency Ltd, 9 Whiting Street, Bury St Edmunds, Suffolk IP33 1NX. Tel: 01284 760206; Fax: 01284 767157. Contact: Albert Cook
Camborne: West Cornwall Enterprise Trust, Lloyds Bank Chambers, Market Square, Camborne, Cornwall TR14 8JT. Tel: 01209 714914; Fax: 01209 717355. Contact: R N Smith
Cambridge: Cambridge Enterprise Agency Ltd, 71a Lensfield Road, Cambridge CB2 1EN. Tel: 01223 323553; Fax: 01223 323553. Contact: Malcolm Watson
Camden: Camden Enterprise Agency,

57 Pratt Street, Camden Town, London NW1 0DP. Tel: 0171 482 2128; Fax: 0171 485 7624. Contact: Jane Howden
Cannock: Cannock and Burntwood Enterprise Agency, Cannock, 80 High Green, Cannock, Staffs WS11 1BE. Tel: 01543 571978. Contact: A Hulbert
Canterbury: The Enterprise Agency of East Kent, 45 North Lane, Canterbury, Kent CT2 7EF. Tel: 01227 470234; Fax: 01227 472665. Contact: Wynford Jones
Carlisle: Business Initiatives Carlisle, The Enterprise Centre, James Street, Carlisle CA2 5BB. Tel: 01228 34120; Fax: 01228 514484. Contact: Bruce Clarke
Chelmsford: Chelmsford Enterprise Agency, Unit 3 Robjohns House, Navigation Road, Chelmsford, Essex CM2 6ND. Tel: 01245 496712. Contact: Patricia Gard
– Essex Business Centre, Church Street, Chelmsford, Essex CM1 1NH. Tel: 01245 283030; Fax: 01245 492486. Contact: Alan Menzies
Chester: Chester and Ellesmere Port Enterprise Agency Ltd, Chester Enterprise Centre, Hoole Bridge, Chester CH2 3NE. Tel: 01244 311474; Fax: 01244 310690. Contact: Richard Holt
Chesterfield: North Derbyshire Enterprise Agency, Enterprise House, 123 Saltergate, Chesterfield, Derbyshire S40 1NH. Tel: 01246 207379; Fax: 01246 232497. Contact: Michael Horner

Chester-Le-Street: Chester-le-Street and City of Durham, Newcastle Road, Chester-le-Street, County Durham DH3 3TS. Tel: 0191 389 2648; Fax: 0191 387 1684. Contact: Ronald Batty

Chichester: Downs Enterprise Agency Ltd, St James Training Centre, St Pancras, Chichester, West Sussex PO19 4NN. Tel: 01243 778077; Fax: 01243 774471. Contact: Tom Tyrwhitt Drake

Chippenham: North Wiltshire Enterprise, 3/4 New Road, Chippenham, Wiltshire SN15 1EJ. Tel: 01249 659275; Fax: 01249 659275. Contact: Jean Archer

Chorley: Chorley Local Enterprise Agency Ltd, 2 Southport Road, Chorley PR7 1LD. Tel: 01257 266166; Fax: 01257 241766. Contact: Susan Mann

Clacton-On-Sea: Enterprise Tendring Ltd, 27a Pier Avenue, Clacton-on-Sea, Essex CO15 1QE. Tel: 01255 421225. Contact: Christine Curry

Clitheroe: Ribble Valley Enterprise Agency Ltd, Bank House, York Street, Clitheroe BB7 2DL. Tel: 01200 22110; Fax: 01200 442626. Contact: Aileen Evans

Colchester: Colchester Business Enterprise Agency Ltd, 154 Magdalen Street, Colchester, Essex CO1 2JX. Tel: 01206 48833; Fax: 01206 574343. Contact: Graeme Garden

Consett: Derwentside Industrial Development Agency, Berry Edge Road, Consett, Co. Durham DH8 5EU. Tel: 01207 509124. Contact: Eddie Hutchinson

Coventry: Coventry Business . Centre Ltd, Christchurch House, Greyfriars Lane, Coventry, West Midlands CV1 2GY. Tel: 01203 552781; Fax: 01203 227486. Contact: John Gibney

Crawley: Crawley and Central Sussex Enterprise Agency Ltd, 6 Spencers Road, Crawley, West Sussex RH11 7DA. Tel: 01293 538670; Fax: 01293 538654. Contact: Sean Haimes

Crewe: South Cheshire Opportunity for Private Enterprise (SCOPE), Scope House, Weston Road, Crewe, Cheshire CW1 1DD. Tel: 01270 589569; Fax: 01270 582506. Contact: Cheryl Johnson

Cricklewood: Brent Business Venture Ltd, 177a Cricklewood Broadway, London NW2 3HT. Tel: 0181 450 6270; Fax: 0181 452 1882. Contact: Clair Ferguson

Croydon: Croydon Business Venture, Acorn House, 74–94 Cherry Orchard Road, Croydon, Surrey CR0 6BA. Tel: 0181 681 8339; Fax: 0181 680 1996. Contact: Sydney Laurence

Darlington: Darlington Business Venture, 4 Woodland Road, Darlington, Co. Durham DL3 7PJ. Tel: 01325 480891; Fax: 01325 467926. Contact: Alan Coultas

Deptford: Deptford Enterprise Agency, 146 Deptford High St, London SE8 3PQ. Tel: 0181 692 9204; Fax: 0181 694 9320. Contact: Joe Greenland

Derby: Derby and Derbyshire
Business Venture, Derven House,
32 Friar Gate, Derby DE1 1BX.
Tel: 01332 360345;
Fax: 01332 290880.
Contact: Emanuel Gatt
Doncaster: DonBAC The Doncaster
Enterprise Agency, 19/21 Hallgate,
Doncaster DN1 3NA.
Tel: 01302 340320;
Fax: 01302 344740.
Contact: Brian Crangle
Dudley: Dudley Business Venture,
Stanton House, 10 Castle St,
Dudley, West Midlands DY1 1LQ.
Tel: 01384 231283;
Fax: 01384 459997.
Contact: Derek Brind
East Barnet: The Barnet Enterprise
Trust, Enterprise House, St Wilfrid's
Road, East Barnet, Hertfordshire EN4
9SB. Tel: 0181 447 0110;
Fax: 0181 447 0432.
Contact: Peter Lovell
Eastbourne: Eastbourne and District
Enterprise Agency Ltd, Minster
House, Business Development
Centre, York Road, Eastbourne,
East Sussex BN21 4ST.
Tel: 01323 644470;
Fax: 01323 412470.
Contact: George Collier
Easton: East Bristol Enterprise
Agency, 42 Chelsea Road, Easton,
Bristol BS5 6AF. Tel: 0117 9554812;
Fax: 0117 9558101.
Contact: Viv Rayner
Edmonton: Enfield Enterprise
Agency, 2/3 Knights Chambers,
32 South Mall, Edmonton Green,
London N9 0TL. Tel: 0181 807 5333;
Fax: 0181 807 2801.
Contact: John Lindsay
Exeter: Business Enterprise Exeter, 39
Marsh Green Road, Marsh Barton,
Exeter, Devon EX2 8PN.

Tel: 01392 56060;
Fax: 01392 413538.
Contact: Mike Lillywhite
Finsbury Park: North London
Business Development Agency,
35/37 Blackstock Road, Finsbury
Park, London N4 2JF.
Tel: 0171 359 7405;
Fax: 0171 354 5643.
Contact: Emmanuel Cotter
Fleetwood: Wyre Business Agency Ltd,
Rees House, Burn Hall Estate, Fleet-
wood Road North,
Fleetwood, Lancashire FY7 8RS.
Tel: 01253 828265;
Fax: 01253 862001.
Contact: Clive Greaney
Folkestone: Shepway Business
Advisory Panel Ltd, 34 Bouverie
Square, Folkestone, Kent CT20 1BA.
Tel: 01303 259162;
Fax: 01303 258556.
Contact: Peter Patten
Frome: Fame Serving Business,
Vallis House, Robins Lane, Frome,
Somerset BA11 3EG.
Tel: 01373 452000.
Contact: Martin Knights
Gateshead: Design Works, William
Street, Felling, Gateshead NE10 0JP.
Tel: 0191 495 0066;
Fax: 0191 495 3207.
Contact: Richard Clark
Gillingham: Medway Enterprise
Agency Ltd, Unit 1, Sabre Court,
Valentine Close, Gillingham
Business Park, Gillingham, Kent
ME8 0RW. Tel: 01634 366565;
Fax: 01634 362828.
Contact: Linda Wolk
Gloucester: Gloucestershire Enterprise
Agency, Enterprise
House, 19–21 Brunswick Road,
Gloucester GL1 1HG.
Tel: 01452 501411;
Fax: 01452 305664.

Contact: Mike Blackie
Grantham: South Lincolnshire Enterprise Agency, Station Road (East), Grantham, Lincolnshire NG31 6HX. Tel: 01476 68970; Fax: 01476 75758.
Contact: Jacqueline Smith
Gravesend: Gravesham Enterprise Agency, The Maltings Enterprise Centre Ltd, Lower Higham Road, Gravesend, Kent DA12 2LY.
Tel: 01474 327118; Fax: 01474 335884.
Contact: Michael Fitzpatrick
Grays: Thurrock Local Enterprise Agency, 1 New Road, Grays, Essex RM17 6NY. Tel: 01375 374362.
Contact: John Harrington
Great Yarmouth: Great Yarmouth Business Advisory Service Ltd, Queens Road Business Centre, Queens Road, Great Yarmouth NR30 3HT. Tel: 01493 850204.
Contact: John Jennings
Greenhithe: North West Kent Enterprise Agency Ltd, Kestner Engineering Works, Station Road, Greenhithe, Kent DA9 9NG.
Tel: 01322 381885; Fax: 01322 381851.
Contact: Julia Fitzpatrick
Grimsby: Grimsby and Cleethorpes Area Enterprise Agency Ltd, 10–14 Hainton Avenue, Grimsby, South Humberside DN32 9BB.
Tel: 01472 241869; Fax: 01472 353902.
Contact: Mike Tink
Hackney: Hackney Business Venture, 277 Mare Street, Hackney, London E8 1HB. Tel: 0181 533 4599; Fax: 0181 533 6996.
Contact: Sally Johnson
Halifax: Calderdale Business Advice Centre, OP56, Dean Clough Industrial Park, Halifax, West Yorkshire HX3 5AX.
Tel: 01422 345631; Fax: 01422 361507.
Contact: Arthur Stonebridge
Hammersmith: Hammersmith and Fulham Business Resources Ltd, The Lilla Huset, 191 Talgarth Road, London W6 8BJ. Tel: 0181 748 3352; Fax: 0181 748 1813.
Contact: Barbara Hamilton
Harlow: Harlow Enterprise Agency Ltd, 19 The Rows, The High, Harlow, Essex CM20 1DD.
Tel: 01992 503456; Fax: 01992 503088.
Contact: David Matthews
Harrow: Harrow Enterprise Agency, Enterprise House, 297 Pinner Road, Harrow HA1 4HS.
Tel: 0181 427 6188; Fax: 0181 861 5709.
Contact: David Hill
Hartcliffe: Hartcliffe and Withywood Ventures Ltd, HWV Block, Bishport Avenue, Hartcliffe, Bristol BS13 0RL. Tel: 0117 9784865; Fax: 0117 9465602.
Contact: Pat Mundy
Hartlepool: Hartlepool Enterprise Agency Ltd, Suite 2, Municipal Buildings, Church Square, Hartlepool, Cleveland TS24 7ER.
Tel: 01429 221216.
Contact: Ian Robertson
– Hartlepool New Development Support Ltd, Suite 6–7, Municipal Buildings, Church Square, Hartlepool TS24 7ER. Tel: 01429 867100; Fax: 01429 864496.
Contact: Ronald Preece
Hastings: Hastings Business Venture Ltd, 18 Cornwallis Gardens, Hastings, East Sussex TN34 1LP.
Tel: 01424 433333; Fax: 01424 433714.

Contact: Ian McCullagh
Hemel Hempstead: Dacorum
Enterprise Agency Ltd, 83 Marlowes,
Hemel Hempstead, Herts HP1 1LF.
Tel: 01442 232333.
Contact: Dion Wilson
Hillingdon: Hillingdon Enterprise
Agency, 400a Long Lane, Hillingdon,
Middlesex UB10 9PG.
Tel: 01895 273433;
Fax: 01895 259119.
Contact: Alan Lane
Honiton: East Devon Small Industries
Group, 115 Border Road, Heathpark,
Honiton, Devon EX14 8BT. Tel:
01404 41806;
Fax: 01404 46865.
Contact: Geoffrey Hulley
Hounslow: West London Enterprise
Agency Ltd, 94 High Street,
Hounslow, Middlesex TW3 1NH.
Tel: 0181 570 3269;
Fax: 0181 577 9428.
Contact: Allan Bosson
Hull: Orchard Park and North Hull
Enterprises Ltd, Dane Park Road,
Orchard Park, Hull HU6 9AR.
Tel: 01482 806952;
Fax: 01482 806700.
Contact: Robert Edmondson
– Hull Area Business Advice
Centre Ltd, 34–38 Beverley Rd,
Hull, North Humberside HU1 1YE.
Tel: 01482 27266;
Fax: 01482 587780.
Contact: Derek Bell
Huntingdon: Huntingdonshire .
Enterprise Agency Ltd, 49 High
Street, Huntingdon, Cambs E18 6AQ.
Tel: 01480 450028;
Fax: 01480 455710.
Contact: David McDonnell
Ipswich: Ipswich Enterprise
Agency (IPSENTA), The Suffolk
Enterprise Centre, Russell Road,
Ipswich, Suffolk IP1 2DE.

Tel: 01473 259832;
Fax: 01473 252489.
Contact: Mervyn A W James
Islington: Manor Gardens
Enterprise Centre Ltd, 10–18
Manor Gardens, Islington, London
N7 6JY. Tel: 0171 272 8944;
Fax: 0171 272 9160.
Contact: Patrick Quarry
Kendal: Cumbria Rural Enterprise
Agency, Unit 1, Lake District
Business Park, Mintbridge Road,
Kendal, Cumbria LA9 6LZ.
Tel: 01539 726624;
Fax: 01539 730928.
Contact: Nick Jepps
Kensington: Portobello Trust,
14 Conlan Street, London
W10 5AR. Tel: 0181 969 4562;
Fax: 0181 968 3660.
Contact: Neil Johnston
Kettering: Kettering Business Venture
Trust, Venture House,
4 Robinson Way, Telford Way
Industrial Estate, Kettering
NN6 8PP. Tel: 01536 513840;
Fax: 01536 523209.
Contact: Edward George
King's Lynn: West Norfolk
Enterprise Agency Trust Ltd,
Enterprise Works, Bergen Way,
King's Lynn, Norfolk PE30 2JR.
Tel: 01553 764127;
Fax: 01553 768267.
Contact: Peter Bargh
Kingsbridge: South Hams Agency
for Rural Development, Tindle
Centre, King's Arms Passage,
Fore Street, Devon TQ7 1AB.
Tel: 01548 856850;
Fax: 01548 857755.
Contact: Suzanne Massingham
Knowsley: Knowsley Business
Resource Centre, Admin Building,
Admin Road, Knowsley Industrial
Park, Kirkby, Knowsley L33 7TX.

Tel: 0151 548 3245;
Fax: 0151 548 4423.
Contact: Lyndon R Symonds
Lancaster: Business for Lancaster Ltd,
St Leonard's House, St Leonardgate,
Lancaster, Lancashire LA1 1NN. Tel:
01524 66222.
Contact: Elizabeth Horsley
Launceston: Enterprise Tamar Ltd,
National School, St Thomas Road,
Launceston, Cornwall PL15 8BU.
Tel: 01566 775632;
Fax: 01566 775632.
Contact: David Stanbury
Leamington Spa: Warwickshire
Enterprise Agency Ltd, The
Business Centre, 3rd Floor,
William House, Clarendon Court,
The Parade, Leamington Spa
CV32 4DG. Tel: 01926 433344;
Fax: 01926 431711.
Contact: Denis Malone
Leeds: Leeds Business Venture,
1st Floor, County House, 82
Vicar Lane, Leeds LS1 7JH.
Tel: 0113 2446474;
Fax: 0113 2452365.
Contact: E Vevers
Letchworth: Letchworth Business
Centre, Avenue One, Business
Park, Letchworth Garden City,
Hertfordshire SG6 2HB.
Tel: 01462 678272;
Fax: 01462 481677.
Contact: Sue Cheshire
Lincoln: Lincoln Enterprise
Agency, Innovation Centre,
West Yard, Ropewalk, Lincoln
LN6 7DQ. Tel: 01522 540775.
Contact: Denis Wilson
Liverpool: Into Business Ltd,
Brunswick Small Business Centre,
Brunswick Business Park, Liverpool L3
4BD. Tel: 0151 709 2375;
Fax: 0151 709 9867.
Contact: James Duffy

– Business in Liverpool Ltd,
Merseyside Innovation Centre, 31
Mount Pleasant, Liverpool L3 5TF.
Tel: 0151 709 1231.
Contact: Allan Cooper
London: London Enterprise Agency,
4 Snow Hill, London EC1A 2BS.
Tel: 0171 236 3000;
Fax: 0171 329 0226.
Contact: Brian Wright
Loughton: Forest Enterprise Agency
Trust Ltd, Feat House, Rear of
Swimming Pool, Traps Hill,
Loughton, Essex IG10 1SZ.
Tel: 0181 508 7435.
Contact: Robert Vice
Lowestoft: Lowestoft Enterprise
Trust Ltd, Waveney Business
Development Centre, 40 Gordon
Road, Lowestoft, Suffolk NR32 1NL.
Tel: 01502 563286;
Fax: 01502 501215.
Contact: Iris Shuttleworth
Luton: BECENTA Bedfordshire
Enterprise Agency, The Business
Centre, Kimpton Road, Luton,
Bedfordshire LU2 0LB.
Tel: 01582 452288;
Fax: 01582 419422.
Contact: Derek Upcott
Maidstone: Maidstone Enterprise
Agency, Enterprise Centre, Wren
House, 64 Lower Stone Street,
Maidstone, Kent ME15 6NA.
Tel: 01622 675547;
Fax: 01622 662756.
Contact: Geoff McCue
Manchester: Manchester Business
Venture, c/o Manchester Chamber
of Commerce and Industry,
Churchgate House, 56 Oxford St,
Manchester M60 7HJ.
Tel: 0161 236 0153;
Fax: 0161 236 4160.
Contact: Martin Singer
Mansfield: Mansfield Sutton and

Kirkby Enterprise Partnership, The Old Town Hall, Market Place, Mansfield, Nottinghamshire NG18 1HX. Tel: 01623 21773; Fax: 01623 648579.
Contact: Bernard Wale
March: Fens Business Enterprise Trust Ltd (FENBET), Fenland Business Centre, Longhill Road, March, Cambridgeshire PE15 0BJ. Tel: 01354 660900; Fax: 01354 660021.
Contact: Stuart Hamilton
Middlesbrough: Cleveland Business Development Agency, New Exchange Buildings, Queens Square, Middlesbrough, Cleveland TS2 1AA. Tel: 01642 231389; Fax: 01642 251698.
Contact: Eric Sugden
Milton Keynes: Milton Keynes Business Venture, Medina House, 314 Silbury Boulevard, Central Milton Keynes, Bucks MK9 2AE. Tel: 01908 660044; Fax: 01908 233087.
Contact: Colin Offor
Minehead: West Somerset Enterprise Agency, Vennland Centre, Ponsford Road, Minehead, Somerset TA24 5DX. Tel: 01643 707500; Fax: 01643 704500.
Contact: Gill Howard
Morden: Merton Enterprise Agency, 12th Floor, Civic Centre, London Road, Morden, Surrey SM4 5DX. Tel: 0181 545 3067; Fax: 0181 543 6085.
Contact: Harry Corben
Morpeth: Northumberland Business Centre, Southgate, Morpeth, Northumberland NE61 2EH. Tel: 01670 533933; Fax: 01670 510878.
Contact: Graham Adams
Moss Side: Agency for Economic

Development, 44 Moss Lane West, Moss Side, Manchester M15 5PD. Tel: 0161 226 9434; Fax: 0161 226 9437.
Contact: Volney Harris
Newark: Newark Enterprise Trust, The Firs, 67 London Road, Newark, Nottinghamshire NG24 1RZ. Tel: 01636 640666; Fax: 01636 605558.
Contact: Brian Tindale
Newcastle: Tyne and Wear Enterprise Trust Ltd, Portman House, Portman Road, Newcastle upon Tyne NE2 1AQ. Tel: 0191 261 4838; Fax: 0191 261 4108.
Contact: Alan Arthur
– Project North East, Hawthorn House, Forth Banks, Newcastle upon Tyne NE1 3SG. Tel: 0191 261 7856; Fax: 0191 261 1910.
Contact: David Irwin
Newport: Isle of Wight Enterprise . Agency Ltd, 6 Town Lane, Newport, Isle of Wight PO30 1JU. Tel: 01983 529120.
Contact: John Wolfenden
Newton Abbot: Teignbridge Enterprise Agency, The Tindle Centre, St Marychurch Road, Newton Abbot, Devon TQ12 4UQ. Tel: 01626 67534; Fax: 01626 332591.
Contact: Leslie Saye
Newton Aycliffe: The Development Agency of Sedgefield District (SASDA), Bede House, St Cuthbert's Way, Aycliffe Industrial Estate, Newton Aycliffe, Co. Durham DL5 6DX. Tel: 01325 307270; Fax: 01325 307226.
Contact: John William Robson
Northampton: Northamptonshire Enterprise Agency Ltd, Royal Pavilion, Summerhouse Pavilions, Summerhouse Road, Moulton Park,

Northampton NN3 6BJ. Tel: 01604
671400; Fax: 01604 790835.
Contact: Allan Matthews
Norwich: Norwich Enterprise
Agency Trust, 112 Barrack St,
Norwich, Norfolk NR1 3TX.
Tel: 01603 613023.
Contact: Peter Smith
Nottingham: Nottinghamshire
Business Venture, Business
Information and Advice Centre,
309 Haydn Road, Sherwood,
Nottingham NG5 1DG.
Tel: 0115 9691151;
Fax: 0115 9856612.
Contact: Gordon Mackenzie
– First Enterprise Business Agency,
88/90 Radford Road, Nottingham
NG7 5FU. Tel: 0115 9423772;
Fax: 0115 9421504.
Contact: Jonathon Olaofe
Oldham: Oldham Enterprise
Agency, The Meridian Centre, King
Street, Oldham, Lancashire OL8 1EZ.
Tel: 0161 6651225;
Fax: 0161 6272252.
Contact: Ed Stacey
Ormskirk: West Lancashire
Enterprise Trust Ltd, The Malt
House, 48 Southport Road, Ormskirk,
Lancashire L39 1OR.
Tel: 01695 575488.
Contact: Graham Looker
Oxford: Thames Business Advice
Centre, Seacourt Tower, West Way,
Oxford OX2 0JP. Tel: 01865 249279;
Fax: 01865 792269.
Contact: Kim Hills Spedding
Paignton: Torbay Enterprise Agency,
Brunel Business Centre, Torquay
Road, Paignton, Devon TQ3 2AH. Tel:
01803 666662;
Fax: 01803 666664.
Contact: M Wortley
Pendle: Pendle Enterprise Trust, .
16 Carr Road, Nelson, Lancashire BB9

7JS. Tel: 01282 698001;
Fax: 01282 611634.
Contact: Ronald Morrish
Peterborough: Peterborough
Enterprise Programme, Winchester
Place, 80 Thorpe Road, Peterborough
PE3 6HZ. Tel: 01733 310159.
Contact: Paul Child
Peterlee: East Durham Development
Agency, 4th Floor, Lee House,
Peterlee, Co. Durham SR8 1BB.
Tel: 0191 586 3366;
Fax: 0191 518 0332.
Contact: Ken Greenfield
Plymouth: Enterprise Plymouth Ltd,
City Business Park, Stoke, Plymouth
PL3 4BB. Tel: 01752 569211;
Fax: 01752 605250.
Contact: Andrew Ashley
Poole: Dorset Enterprise Agency,
1 Britannia Road, Parkstone,
Poole, Dorset BH14 8AZ.
Tel: 01202 748333;
Fax: 01202 737275.
Contact: Peter Johnson
Portsmouth: South East
Hampshire Enterprise Agencies,
27 Guildhall Walk, Portsmouth
PO1 2RY. Tel: 01705 833321;
Fax: 01705 873711.
Contact: Tim Austin
Potters Bar: Hertsmere Enterprise
Agency, The Enterprise Centre,
Cranborne Road, Potters Bar,
Herts EN6 3DQ.
Tel: 01707 660270.
Contact: John Farnsworth
– Welwyn and Hatfield Enterprise
Agency Ltd, The Enterprise Centre,
Cranborne Road, Potters Bar, Herts
EN6 3DQ. Tel: 01707 664169.
Contact: Kenneth Sumeray
Preston: Preston Business Venture
Ltd, Premier House, Church Street,
Preston, Lancashire PR1 3BQ.
Tel: 01772 825723;

Fax: 01772 563942.
Contact: Susan Watkinson
– South Ribble Business Venture Ltd,
Leyland Daf Spurrier Gatehouse, Centurion Way, Farington, Leyland,
Preston, Lancashire PR5 2GR.
Tel: 01772 422242;
Fax: 01772 623446.
Contact: Ron Gates
Reading: Berkshire and Southern
Buckinghamshire Enterprise
Agency, 7–11 Station Road,
Reading, Berkshire RG1 1LG.
Tel: 01734 585715;
Fax: 01734 566884.
Contact: John Hiscocks
Redditch: Redditch Enterprise Agency
Ltd, Rubicon Centre,
17 Broad Ground Road, Lakeside,
Redditch, Worcestershire B98 8YP.
Tel: 01527 501122;
Fax: 01527 25942.
Contact: Peter Blacklock
Rochdale: Rochdale Enterprise Group,
Generation Centre, Dane Street,
Rochdale, Lancs OL12 6XB.
Tel: 01706 356250;
Fax: 01706 41811.
Contact: Bruce Harris
Romford: North East Thames
Business Advisory Centre,
Marshalls Chambers, 80a South
Street, Romford, Essex RM1 1RP.
Tel: 01708 766438;
Fax: 01708 731101.
Contact: Ulrik Middelboe
Rossendale: Rossendale Enterprise
Trust, 29 Kay Street, Rawtenstall,
Rossendale, Lancashire BB4 7LS.
Tel: 01706 229838;
Fax: 01706 210691.
Contact: Joyce Livesey
Rotherham: Rotherham Enterprise
Agency Ltd, 10 Church Street,
Rotherham, South Yorkshire
S60 1PD. Tel: 01709 823590;

Fax: 01709 836094.
Contact: John Clayton
Runcorn: Business Link Ltd,
62 Church Street, Runcorn, Cheshire
WA7 1LD. Tel: 01928 563037;
Fax: 01928 580711.
Contact: Alan Griffiths
Sale: Trafford Business Venture, 3rd
Floor, Acre House, Town Square, Sale
M33 1XZ.
Tel: 0161 905 2950;
Fax: 0161 976 6110.
Contact: Stephen Conroy
Salford: Salford 100 Venture,
Stamford House, 361 Chapel
Street, Salford, Manchester
M3 5JY. Tel: 0161 835 1166;
Fax: 0161 833 9674.
Contact: Michael Finnie
Salisbury: South Wiltshire Enterprise
Agency, 22 Bedwin Street, Salisbury,
Wiltshire SP6 3UT.
Tel: 01722 411052;
Fax: 01722 422003.
Contact: Richard James
Sandwell: Sandwell Enterprise Ltd,
Sandwell Business Advice Centre, Victoria Street, West Bromwich, Sandwell
B70 8ET.
Tel: 0121 500 5412;
Fax: 0121 553 3079.
Contact: Alfred Woodhouse
Scarborough: Scarborough
Enterprise Agency, The Sitwell
Centre, Sitwell Street, Scarborough,
North Yorkshire YO12 5EX.
Tel: 01723 354454;
Fax: 01723 363633.
Contact: Brian Wood
Sheffield: Sheffield Enterprise Agency
Ltd, 23 Shepherd St, Sheffield, South
Yorkshire S3 7BA. Tel: 0114 2755721;
Fax: 0114 2754784.
Contact: Ian Cruddas
Sittingbourne: Swale Enterprise
Agency, Broad Oak Enterprise

Village, Broad Oak Road,
Sittingbourne, Kent ME9 8AQ.
Tel: 01795 427623;
Fax: 01795 429572.
Contact: Jenny Aldridge
Skipton: Dales Enterprise Agency Ltd,
21/23 High Street, Gargrave, Skipton,
North Yorkshire BD23 3RP.
Tel: 01756 748194;
Fax: 01756 748195.
Contact: Peter Goulden
Solihull: Solihull Business
Enterprise Ltd, 142 Lode Lane,
Solihull, West Midlands B91 2HP.
Tel: 0121 704 1456;
Fax: 0121 711 1051.
Contact: Fred Smallman
South Humber: South Humber
Business Advice Centre Ltd,
7 Market Place, Brigg, South
Humberside DN20 8HA.
Tel: 01652 657637;
Fax: 01652 657955.
Contact: Derek Marshall
South Tyneside: The Tyneside
Economic Development Co Ltd,
Business Enterprise Centre, Eldon
Street, South Shields, Tyne and Wear
NE33 5JR. Tel: 0191 455 4300;
Fax: 0191 455 1847.
Contact: Anthony Tompkins
Southall: Enterprise Ealing Ltd,
Windmill Business Centre, 2–4
Windmill Lane, Southall,
Middlesex UB2 4NJ.
Tel: 0181 843 1188;
Fax: 0181 571 2998.
Contact: Jenny Evans
Southampton: Southampton
Enterprise Agency, Solent Business
Centre, Millbrook Road West,
Southampton, Hants SO1 0HW.
Tel: 01703 788088;
Fax: 01703 704046.
Contact: Barrie Levy
Southend: Southend Enterprise

Agency, 845 London Road, Westcliff
on Sea, Essex SS0 9SZ.
Tel: 01702 471118;
Fax: 01702 470598.
Contact: Sylvia Vincent
Southend-on-Sea: South East Essex
Business Enterprise Agency, 362
Chartwell Square, Southend-on-Sea,
Essex SS2 5SP. Tel: 01702 464443.
Contact: Terry Pasmore
Southport: Southport Marketing
and Enterprise Bureau, Gordon
House, Leicester Street, Southport,
Merseyside PR9 0ER.
Tel: 01704 544173;
Fax: 01704 539396.
Contact: Neil Annandale
St Albans: St Albans Enterprise
Agency Ltd, Unit 6G, The St Albans
Enterprise Centre, Long Spring,
Porters Wood, St Albans,
Hertfordshire AL3 6EN.
Tel: 01727 8837760.
Contact: Kenneth Hughesman
St Austell: Restormel Local
Enterprise Trust Ltd, Westhaul
Park, Par Moor Road, St Austell, Corn-
wall PL25 3RF.
Tel: 01726 813079;
Fax: 01726 814251.
Contact: Murray Gowan
St Helens: The Community of
St Helens Trust, Business
Development Centre, St Helens
Technology Campus, Waterside,
St Helens, Merseyside WA9 1UB.
Tel: 01744 453989;
Fax: 01744 453993.
Contact: Brian Andrews
St Peter Port: Guernsey Enterprise
Agency, States Arcade, Market Square,
St Peter Port, Guernsey, Channel
Islands GY1 1HD.
Tel: 01481 710043;
Fax: 01481 710755.
Contact: Meg Heyworth

Stafford: Stafford Enterprise Ltd, 23A Gaolgate Street, Stafford ST16 2NT. Tel: 01785 57057; Fax: 01785 225070. Contact: Douglas Marston – Staffordshire Development Association, The Business Advice Centre, Shire Hall, Market Street, Stafford ST16 2LQ. Tel: 01785 277370; Fax: 01785 21528. Contact: Ian Cass

Stevenage: Stevenage Business Initiative, Business and Technology Centre, Bessemer Drive, Stevenage, Herts SG1 2DX, Tel: 01438 315733; Fax: 01438 310001. Contact: Roy Pride

Stockport: Stockport Business Venture, Errwood Park House, Crossley Road, Heaton Chapel, Stockport SK4 5BH. Tel: 0161 432 3770. Contact: Bill Hurren

Stoke-on-Trent: North Staffordshire and District Business Initiative, Commerce House, Festival Park, Etruria, Stoke-on-Trent ST1 5BE. Tel: 01782 279013. Contact: Wanda Ford

Surrey Docks: Docklands Enterprise Centre, 11 Marshalsea Road, London SE1 1EP. Tel: 0171 357 7581; Fax: 0171 357 7890. Contact: Raymond Hook

Sutton: Sutton Enterprise Agency, 11 Lower Road, Sutton, Surrey SM1 4QJ.Tel: 0181 643 9430; Fax: 0181 643 3880. Contact: John Wren

Swindon: Great Western Enterprise Ltd, Great Western Business Centre, Emlyn Square, Swindon, Wiltshire SN1 5BP. Tel: 01793 488088; Fax: 01793 485186. Contact: Norman Hayes

Tameside: Tameside Business Advice Service, Charlestown Industrial Estate, Turner St, Ashton-under-Lyne, Tameside, Lancashire OL6 8NS. Tel: 0161 339 8960; Fax: 0161 343 7367. Contact: Kenneth Ackroyd

Taunton: Taunton District Enterprise Centre, 23 High St, Taunton, Somerset TA1 3PJ. Tel: 01823 336600; Fax: 01823 338245. Contact: Chris Clarke

Telford: Shropshire Enterprise Trust Ltd, Business Development Centre, Stafford Park 4, Telford, Shropshire TF3 3BA. Tel: 01952 290782/3/4; Fax: 01952 290753. Contact: Ernie Houghton MBE

Tiverton: Mid Devon Enterprise Agency, The Factory, Tiverton Devon EX16 5LL. Tel: 01884 255629; Fax: 01884 243031. Contact: Michael Dunk

Tonbridge: Great Weald Enterprise Agency, Peach Hall, Trench Road, Tonbridge, Kent TN10 3HA. Tel: 01732 360133; Fax: 01732 360133. Contact: Janet Sergison

Tower Hamlets: East London Small Business Centre Ltd, 76 Wentworth Street, London E1 7SE. Tel: 0171 377 8821; Fax: 0171 375 1415. Contact: Mike King

Trowbridge: West Wiltshire Enterprise, Business Development Centre, College Road, Trowbridge, Wiltshire BA14 0ER. Tel: 01225 774222; Fax: 01225 774018. Contact: Norman Pierce

Twickenham: Richmond upon Thames Enterprise Agency, 55 Heath Road, Twickenham, Middlesex TW1 4AW. Tel: 0181 891 3742. Contact: Paul Turrell
Walsall: Walsall Enterprise Agency Ltd, 139–144 Lichfield Street, Walsall, West Midlands WS1 1SE. Tel: 01922 646614. Contact: Peter O'Brien
Wandsworth: Wandsworth Enterprise Agency, 4th Floor, Woburn House, 155–159 Falcon Road, London SW11 2PD.
Tel: 0171 924 2811;
Fax: 0171 978 5593.
Contact: Alex Amponsah
Warrington: Warrington Business Venture, Warrington Business Park, Long Lane, Warrington, Cheshire WA2 8TX.
Tel: 01925 33309;
Fax: 01925 414059.
Contact: Peter Robinson
Watford: Watford Enterprise Agency, The Enterprise Centre, Cranborne Road, Potters Bar, Hertfordshire EN6 3DQ.
Tel: 01707 664169.
Contact: Kenneth Sumeray
Westminster: Westminster Enterprise Agency, 69/71 Praed Street, Paddington, London W2 1NS. Tel: 0171 706 4266.
Contact: John Skinner
Weston-super-Mare: Weston and Woodspring Enterprise Agency, Elizabeth House, 30/32 Boulevard, Weston-super-Mare, Avon BS23 1NF.
Tel: 01934 418118;
Fax: 01934 629541.
Contact: Angela Hicks
Whitby: Whitby and District Business Development Agency Ltd, St Hilda's Business Centre, The

Ropery, Whitby, North Yorkshire YO22 4ET. Tel: 01947 600827;
Fax: 01947 821307.
Contact: Peter Noble
Wigan: Wigan and District Chamber of Commerce, Buckingham Row, Northway, Wigan WN1 1XX.
Tel: 01942 324547;
Fax: 01942 821410.
Contact: Geoff Birkett
Winsford: Vale Royal Enterprise Agency, Verdin Exchange, High Street, Winsford, Cheshire CW7 2AN. Tel: 01606 861300;
Fax: 01606 861465.
Contact: Lisa Pritchard
Woking: Surrey Business Enterprise Agency Ltd, 19A High Street, Woking, Surrey GU21 1BW,
Tel: 01483 728434;
Fax: 01483 751147.
Contact: Michael Instone
Wolverhampton: Wolverhampton Enterprise Ltd, Lich Chambers, Exchange Street, Wolverhampton WV1 1TS. Tel: 01902 312095;
Fax: 01902 714476.
Contact: Fred Pickerill
Workington: West Cumbria Partnership, Thirlmere Building, 50 Lakes Road, Derwent Howe, Workington, Cumbria CA14 3YP.
Tel: 01900 65656; Fax: 01900 67587.
Contact: Barbara Stephens
Worksop: Bassetlaw Enterprise Agency, 96 Bridge Street, Worksop, Nottinghamshire S80 1AJ.
Tel: 01909 487344;
Fax: 01909 479710
Contact: Bob Cutts
Worthing: West Sussex Area Enterprise Centre Ltd, 69a Chapel Road, Worthing, West Sussex BN11 1HR. Tel: 01903 231499;
Fax: 01903 238051.
Contact: Brenda McCurdie

Yeovil: South Somerset and West Dorset Enterprise Agency, Unit 4, Yeovil Business Centre, Hounstone Business Park, Yeovil, Somerset BA22 8WA. Tel: 01935 79813; Fax: 01935 78550. Contact: Richard Tracey
York: York Enterprise Ltd, York Enterprise Centre, 1 Davygate, York YO1 2QE. Tel: 01904 646803; Fax: 01904 670216. Contact: Jenny Saben
– The Young Business Project, The Fishergate Centre, 4 Fishergate, York YO1 4AB. Tel: 01904 610045. Contact: Simon Daubeney
– Vale of York Small Business Association Ltd, 1 Davygate, York YO1 2QE. Tel: 01904 641401; Fax: 01904 670216 Contact: Jenny Saben

Wales

Aberdare: MADE and EDP Ltd, Gadlys Enterprise Centre, Gadlys, Aberdare, Mid Glamorgan CF44 8DL. Tel: 01685 882515; Fax: 01685 882806. Contact: J Alan Jones
Ammanford: Dinefwr Enterprise . Company, Betws Park Workshops, Park Street, Ammanford, Dyfed SA18 2ET. Tel: 01269 596655; Fax: 01269 596428. Contact: Bill Bishop
Bangor: Antur Menai, Llys y Bont, Parc Menai, Bangor, Gwynedd LL57 4BN. Tel: 01248 670627; Fax: 01248 670112. Contact: Peter McOwan
Bridgend: Enterprise Taff Ely Ogwr Partnership Ltd, Enterprise Centre, Brynn Road, Tondu, Bridgend, Mid Glamorgan CF32 9BS. Tel: 01656 724414;

Fax: 01656 721163. Contact: Gareth Bray
Cardiff: Cardiff and Vale Enterprise, 127 Bute Street, Cardiff CF1 5LE. Tel: 01222 494411; Fax: 01222 481623. Contact: Peter Fortune
– Innovation Wales (SEWBIC) Ltd, Cardiff Business Technology Centre, Senghennydd Road, Cardiff CF2 4AY. Tel: 01222 667041; Fax: 01222 373436. Contact: Douglas Hampson
Castle Newydd Emlyn: Antur Teifi, Parc Busnes, Aberarard, Castle Newydd Emlyn, Dyfed SA38 9DB. Tel: 01239 710238; Fax: 01239 710358. Contact: Wynfford James
Deeside: Deeside Enterprise Trust Ltd, Deeside Enterprise Centre, Rowleys Drive, Shotton, Deeside, Clwyd CH5 1PP. Tel: 01244 830003; Fax: 01244 830032. Contact: Mike Eden
Holywell: Delyn Business Partnership, Greenfield Business Centre, Greenfield, Holywell, Clwyd CH8 7QB. Tel: 01352 711747; Fax: 01352 711156. Contact: Brian Scoffield
Llanelli: Llanelli Enterprise Company, 100 Trostre Road, Llanelli, Dyfed SA15 2EA. Tel: 01554 772122; Fax: 01544 777755. Contact: Tony Giles
Milford Haven: Pembrokeshire Business Initiative, Milford Haven Business Centre, Havens Head Business Park, The Docks, Milford Haven SA73 3LD. Tel: 01646 695300; Fax: 01646 697806. Contact: Richard Packman
Neath: Neath Development Partnership, 7 Water Street, Neath,

West Glamorgan SA11 3EP.
Tel: 01639 634111;
Fax: 01639 630139.
Contact: Eamonn Kinsella
Newport: Newport and Gwent
Enterprise, Enterprise Way, Off Bolt
Street, Newport, Gwent, NP9 2AQ.
Tel: 01633 254041;
Fax: 01633 215774.
Contact: Alan Prosper
Penrhyndeudraeth: Antur Dwyryd,
Osmond Terrace, Penrhyndeudraeth,
Gwynedd LL48 6PA.
Tel: 01766 771345;
Fax: 01766 771396.
Contact: Dafydd Wyn Jones
Rhondda: Rhondda Development
Agency, RDA Enterprise Centre,
Caemawr Industrial Estate, Treorchy,
Rhondda CF42 6EJ.
Tel: 01443 440720;
Fax: 01443 437875.
Contact: John Hitchen
Ruthin: Clwydfro Enterprise Agency,
Llysfasi, Ruthin, Clwyd LL15 2LB.
Tel: 01978 790414;
Fax: 01978 790420.
Contact: Arwyn Jones
Swansea: West Glamorgan
Enterprise Trust, Pontardulais
Workshops, Tyn-y-Bonau Road,
Pontardulais, Swansea SA4 1RS.
Tel: 01792 885197;
Fax: 01792 885119.
Contact: Tony Morgan
Wrexham: Bersham Enterprise,
Bersham Enterprise Centre, Plas
Grono Road, Rhostyllen, Wrexham
LL14 4ED. Tel: 01978 352614;
Fax: 01978 290952.
Contact: Morag Murphy

Northern Ireland

Ballymena: Ballymena Business
Development Centre, Galgorm

Industrial Estate, Fenaghy Rd,
Ballymena, Co. Antrim.
Tel: 01266 658618;
Fax: 01266 630830.
Contact: Ian Niblock
Ballymoney: North Antrim Develop-
ment, 2 Riada Avenue, Garryduff
Road, Ballymoney, Co. Antrim BT53
7LH. Tel: 012656 66133;
Fax: 012656 65019.
Contact: Francis Henderson
Bangor: North Down Development
Organization Ltd, Enterprise House,
2/4 Balloo Avenue, Balloo Industrial
Estate, Bangor, Co. Down BT19 7QT.
Tel: 01247 271525;
Fax: 01247 270080.
Contact: Lynne Vance
Belfast: Action Resource Centre,
103/107 York Street, Belfast,
BT15 1AB. Tel: 01232 328000;
Fax: 01232 439666.
Contact: William McKay
– Business Incubation Systems Ltd,
Brookfield Business Centre, 333
Crumlin Road, Belfast BT14 7EA. Tel:
01232 745241;
Fax: 01232 748025.
Contact: Shane Wolsey
– Townsend Enterprise Park Ltd,
Townsend Street, Belfast BT13 2ES.
Tel: 01232 894500;
Fax: 01232 854502.
Contact: Colleen Miller
– Westlink Enterprise Centre, 30–50
Distillery Street, Belfast BT12 5BJ.
Tel: 01232 331549;
Fax: 01232 330803.
Contact: Kevin McGlennon
Craigavon: Craigavon Industrial
Development Organization,
Craigavon Enterprise Centre,
Carn Industrial Area, Portadown,
Craigavon, Co. Armagh BT63 5RH.
Tel: 01762 333393;
Fax: 01762 350390.

Contact: Jim Smith
Derry City: Eurocentre West Ltd,
Pennyburn Industrial Estate,
Buncrana Road, Derry City,
BT48 0LU. Tel: 01504 364015;
Fax: 01504 266032.
Contact: Denis Feeney
Downpatrick: Jobspace (NI) Ltd,
45 Saul Road, Downpatrick, Co.
Down BT30 6PA. Tel: 01396 616416;
Fax: 01396 616419.
Contact: Joe McCoubrey
Draperstown: Workspace
(Draperstown) Ltd, 5/7 Tobermore
Road, Draperstown, Derry BT45 7AF.
Tel: 01648 28113;
Fax: 01648 28975.
Contact: Patsy McShane
Dungannon: Dungannon Enterprise
Centre, 2 Coalisland Road,
Dungannon, Co. Tyrone
BT71 6JT. Tel: 018687 23489;
Fax: 018687 52200.
Contact: Brian MacAuley
Dungiven: Glenshane Community
Development Ltd, Glenshane
Enterprise Centre, 414a Ballyquin
Road, Dungiven BT47 4NQ.
Tel: 015047 42494;
Fax: 015047 42393.
Contact: John McNicholl
Dunmurry: Glenwood Enterprises
Ltd, Springbank Industrial Estate,
Pembroke Loop Road, Dunmurry,
Belfast BT17 0QL.
Tel: 01232 610311;
Fax: 01232 600929.
Contact: J J Grugan
Enniskillen: Fermanagh Enterprise
Ltd, Enniskillen Enterprise Centre,
Down Street, Enniskillen,
Co. Fermanagh. Tel: 01365 323117;
Fax: 01365 327878.
Contact: John Treacy
Lisburn: Lisburn Enterprise
Organization Ltd, Enterprise

Crescent, Ballinderry Road, Lisburn,
Co. Antrim BT28 2SA.
Tel: 01846 661160;
Fax: 01846 603084.
Contact: Niamh Goggin
Newry: Newry and Mourne Enterprise
Agency, Enterprise House, Win Business Park, Canal Quay,
Newry, Co. Down BT35 6PH.
Tel: 01693 67011;
Fax: 01693 61316.
Contact: Margaret Andrews
Newtownards: Ards Small Business
Centre Ltd, Jubilee Road,
Newtownards, Co. Down B23 4YH.
Tel: 01247 819787;
Fax: 01247 820625.
Contact: Trevor Topping
Omagh: Omagh Enterprise Co Ltd,
Omagh Business Complex, Gortrush
Industrial Estate, Derry Road, Omagh,
Co. Tyrone BT78 5LS.
Tel: 01662 249494;
Fax: 01662 249451.
Contact: Brian McGrath

Scotland

Aberdeen: Aberdeen Enterprise Trust,
6 Albyn Grove, Aberdeen AB1 6SQ.
Tel: 01224 582599;
Fax: 01224 584488.
Contact: Ian Grant
Aboyne: Kincardine and Deeside
Enterprise Trust Ltd, Unit 1, Aboyne
Business Centre, Huntly Road,
Aboyne, Aberdeenshire AB34 5HE.
Tel: 013398 87222;
Fax: 013398 85271.
Contact: Bill Marshall
Alloa: Alloa Clackmannan Enterprise,
Alloa Business Centre, Alloa FK10
3SA. Tel: 01259 721454;
Fax: 01259 217303.
Contact: Alan Stewart
Argyll: North Argyll Development

Agency, 4 George Street, Oban, Argyll PA34 5RX.Tel: 01631 66368; Fax: 01631 64710. Contact: Malcolm Michie
Ayr: Ayr Locality Enterprise Resource Trust (ALERT), Ayr Business Centre, 16 Smith Street, Ayr KA7 1TD. Tel: 01292 264181; Fax: 01292 262944. Contact: Bill Dunn
Bathgate: West Lothian Enterprise Ltd, 19 North Bridge Street, Bathgate, West Lothian EH48 4PJ. Tel: 01506 634024; Fax: 01506 54289. Contact: William V R Percy
Campbeltown: Campbeltown and Kintyre Enterprise Trust Ltd, Hazelburn Business Park, Millknowe, Campbeltown, Argyll PA29 6XD. Tel: 01586 552246; Fax: 01586 554168. Contact: Peter McKinlay
Clydebank: Clydebank Economic Development Company Ltd, Phoenix House, 7 South Avenue, Clydebank Business Park, Clydebank G81 2LG. Tel: 0141 951 1131; Fax: 0141 952 0312. Contact: Alastair Muir
Coatbridge: Monklands Enterprise Development Company, Units 10 and 32, Coatbridge Business Centre, 204 Main Street, Coatbridge, Lanarkshire ML5 3RD. Tel: 01236 423281; Fax: 01236 440569. Contact: Ian Russell
Cumnock: Cumnock and Doon Enterprise Trust, Enterprise Centre, Caponacre Industrial Estate, Cumnock, Ayrshire KA18 1SH. Tel: 01290 421159; Fax: 01290 425533. Contact: Colin Williamson
Dalkeith: Midlothian Enterprise Trust,

29a Eskbank Road, Dalkeith, Midlothian EH22 1HJ. Tel: 0131 654 1234; Fax: 0131 660 4057. Contact: Gregor Murray
Dumbarton: Dumbarton District Enterprise Trust, 2/2 Vale of Leven Industrial Estate, Dumbarton G82 3PD. Tel: 01389 750005; Fax: 01389 755424. Contact: Charles Shanlin
Dundee: Dundee Enterprise Trust, Dudhope Castle, Barrack Road, Dundee DD3 6HF. Tel: 01382 26002; Fax: 01382 21314. Contact: David Morrison
Dunoon: The Cowal Enterprise Trust, 24 Argyll Street, Dunoon PA23 7HJ. Tel: 01369 2023; Fax: 01369 5517. Contact: Ian McRae
East Kilbride: East Kilbride Business Centre, PO Box 1, 4 Platthorn Road, East Kilbride, G74 1NW. Tel: 013552 38456; Fax: 013352 30600. Contact: Linda McDowall
Edinburgh: Edinburgh Old Town Renewal Trust, 8 Advocates Close, 357 High Street, Edinburgh EH1 1PS. Tel: 0131 225 8818; Fax: 0131 225 8636. Contact: Jim Johnson
– The Capital Enterprise Trust, Allander House, 141 Leith Walk, Edinburgh EH6 8NQ. Tel: 0131 553 5566; Fax: 0131 555 2354. Contact: Trevor Slater
Elgin: Moray Enterprise Trust, Units 14–17 Elgin Business Centre, Maisondieu Road, Elgin, Moray IV30 1RH. Tel: 01343 548391; Fax: 01343 541020. Contact: Ron Taylor

Fife: North East Fife Enterprise Trust, 3 Riverside Court, Cupar, Fife KY15 5JY. Tel: 01334 56360;
Fax: 01334 53111.
Contact: Richard Henning
– South Fife Enterprise Trust, 6 Main Street, Crossgates, Fife KY4 8AJ.
Tel: 01383 515053.
Contact: David Blues
Glasgow: The Barras Enterprise Trust, The Barras Centre, Unit 1, 54 Carlton Entry, Glasgow G40 2SB.
Tel: 0141 552 7258;
Fax: 0141 552 4164.
Contact: James McMorrow
– East End Executive (Glasgow) Ltd, Unit C8, Building 5, Templeton Business Centre, 62 Templeton Street, Glasgow G40 1DA. Tel: 0141 554 8656;
Fax: 0141 556 1977.
Contact: John Kilpatrick
– Glasgow North Ltd, St Rollox House, 130 Springburn Road, Glasgow G21 1YA.
Tel: 0141 552 5413;
Fax: 0141 552 0886.
Contact: Francis Lyons
– Glasgow Opportunities, 7 West George Street, Glasgow G2 1EQ.
Tel: 0141 221 0955.
Contact: Agnes Samuel
Glenrothes: Glenrothes Enterprise Trust, Unit 6, Pentland Court, Saltire Centre, Glenrothes, Fife KY6 2DA.
Tel: 01592 630595;
Fax: 01592 630195.
Contact: Arthur Stutt
Grangemouth: Falkirk Enterprise Action Trust, Newhouse Business Park, Newhouse Road, Grangemouth FK3 8LL Tel: 01324 665500;
Fax: 01324 474418.
Contact: John Hoggan
Greenock: Inverclyde Enterprise Trust, 64–66 West Blackhall Street,
Greenock PA15 1XG.
Tel: 01475 892191;
Fax: 01475 84071.
Contact: James Barr
Hamilton: Hamilton Enterprise Development Company, Barncluith Business Centre, Townhead Street, Hamilton ML3 7DP.
Tel: 01698 429425;
Fax: 01698 891916.
Contact: Ronald Smith
Inverness: Highland Opportunity Ltd, Development Department, Regional Buildings, Glenurquhart Road, Inverness IV3 5NX.
Tel: 01463 702000;
Fax: 01463 710848.
Contact: Hugh Black
Inverurie: Gordon Enterprise Trust, Business Development Centre, Thainstone Agricultural Centre, Thainstone, Inverurie, Aberdeenshire AB51 9WU.
Tel: 01467 621166;
Fax: 01467 621919.
Contact: Jackie Hall
Kilbirnie: Garnock Valley Development Executive Ltd, 44 Main Street, Kilbirnie, Ayrshire KA25 7BY. Tel: 01505 685455;
Fax: 01505 684256.
Contact: Johan Madsen
Kilmarnock: Kilmarnock Venture Enterprise Trust, Royal Bank Buildings, 1 The Cross, Kilmarnock KA1 1LS. Tel: 01563 44602;
Fax: 01563 27900.
Contact: Gordon Rutherford
Kilsyth: Cumbernauld and Kilsyth Enterprise Trust, 10–14 Market Street, Kilsyth G65 0BD.
Tel: 01236 825500;
Fax: 01236 826500.
Contact: Alicia Bruce
Kirkintilloch: Strathkelvin Enterprise Trust, Southbank House, Southbank Business Park, Kirkintilloch G66 1XQ.

Tel: 0141 777 7171;
Fax: 0141 776 5331.
Contact: Andrew Thomson
Lanark: Clydesdale Development
Company, Clydesdale Business
Centre, 129 Hyndford Road, Lanark
ML11 9AU. Tel: 01555 665064;
Fax: 01555 665733.
Contact: Christopher Travis
Leven: Enterprise Levenmouth Ltd,
Levenmouth Business Centre,
Riverside Road, Leven, Fife KY8 4LT.
Tel: 01333 421112;
Fax: 01333 425244.
Contact: McLaren Young
Motherwell: Motherwell Enterprise
Development Company, 364 Brandon
Street, Motherwell ML1 1XA. Tel:
01698 269333;
Fax: 01698 264386.
Contact: James Hope
Newton Stewart: Wigtown Rural
Development Company, Royal Bank
Building, 44 Victoria Street, Newton
Stewart, Wigtownshire DG8 6BT.
Tel: 01671 403434;
Fax: 01671 403579.
Contact: Elaine Marr
Paisley: Paisley and Renfrew

Enterprise Trust, 27a Blackhall
Street, Paisley PA1 1TD.
Tel: 0141 889 0010;
Fax: 0141 848 7355.
Contact: David Logan
Perth: Perthshire Enterprise
Company, 1 High Street, Perth
PH1 2SY. Tel: 01738 29114;
Fax: 01738 34998.
Contact: Robert Main
Pitlochry: Highland Perthshire
Development Company Ltd,
21 Bonnethill Road, Pitlochry,
Perthshire PH16 5BS.
Tel: 01796 472697;
Fax: 01796 473902.
Contact: Gil Orr
Stevenston: Asset Trust Ltd, The APL
Centre, Stevenston Industrial Estate,
Stevenston, Ayrshire
KA20 3LR. Tel: 01294 61555;
Fax: 01294 605260.
Contact: Cairns Campbell
Stirling: Stirling Enterprise Trust, John
Player Building,
Players Road, Stirling FK7 7RP.
Tel: 01786 463416;
Fax: 01786 479611.
Contact: Derek Gavin

■ TRAINING AND ENTERPRISE COUNCILS (TECS)

Training and Enterprise Councils (TECs) – and their Scottish counterparts, Local
Enterprise Companies – have been established with five major principles in
mind:

- They are locally based so that national programmes can be adapted to local
  circumstances.
- They are employer-led, on the assumption that it is employers who are best
  placed to identify skills needs and to ensure that the quality and quantity
  of training available meets them.
- They are focused, i.e. they bring together the various interests involved in
  training and enterprise development.
- They are given incentives, through operating contracts, to perform well.
- They are intended to be enterprising: to develop their own ideas on what
  needs to be done and how to do it, i.e. they are not bound by the national
  rules governing the Training Agency.

Each TEC has to develop a business plan which sets objectives for its area, describes the economic and social conditions prevailing there in the national and the international context, identifies priorities for training and enterprise support, and sets out the activities which the TEC intends to carry through. These are public documents, so anyone can see what each TEC plans to do.

The TECs are the channels for the main training programmes, i.e. Youth Training and Employment Training, as well as the Enterprise Allowance and the advisory services of the Small Firms Service. The latter two services have been subsumed, and relabelled by TECs. As each TEC develops its own policies, their precise nature or method of delivery will vary from area to area and, if you contact your local TEC, you may well find that the names they use to describe their activities do not match up with nationally used descriptions. Furthermore, each TEC receives an allocation specifically to develop its own initiatives and each is encouraged to raise money from local business sources to develop its activities in ways that it chooses. Each TEC therefore is likely to have some schemes of support unique to it.

Another area of activity is the promotion of education and business links. Every town in the area is to have such a link, based on local action groups. A flavour of the type of activities on offer by TECs is as follows:

Business Advisory Services (BAS)

An information and counselling service to help small and growing businesses.

- A helpline provides a free enquiry service offering a useful source of business information. The service enables companies to get in touch quickly with contacts in central and local government, professional bodies etc.
- A confidential counselling service offers businesses a wealth of practical knowledge and experience across the spectrum of business and management disciplines. The first three consultations are free, with a modest charge for subsequent sessions.
- Leaflets and brochures are available, giving a comprehensive explanation of the services.
- Access to the Business Advisory Service is via a free business helpline.

Business Start-Up Programme

This programme is designed to help and support individuals to start and develop their own businesses successfully – from the initial concept stage through to business planning and up to the end of the first year's trading. The programme comprises three phases.

- Phase 1 is an introduction to running a business.
- Phase 2 provides training and assistance on how to plan and run a business.
- Phase 3 offers practical help and free counselling and, depending on eligibility, a Business Start-Up Grant may be available during the first year of trading. Further counselling is available free of charge from counsellors once the grant ceases.

A support training pack is available for business starters.
Contact: Ring Free on 0800 252713.

Business Development Consultancy Programme

Administered by the TEC to help companies with up to 500 employees effectively manage change and development which will allow businesses to maximize markets and exploit new ones.
■ Provides financial assistance for consultative and training help.
■ Any firm that employs between 10 and 500 people and has an existing management team may apply.
■ TEC will normally contribute 50% of the cost of the project, maximum contribution £15,000. In some circumstances this may be increased.

Business Focus

This initiative is directly targeted at providing help to small and medium-sized companies to grow or maintain current levels of growth.
■ The programme offers immediate help in a simple, direct and effective way combining professional advice with financial assistance to soundly based businesses with growth potential.
■ Areas where assistance may be needed are wide ranging, from a specific manufacturing problem to marketing, business planning or cash-flow dilemmas.
■ Access to the programme is primarily by referral from the company's bank, accountant or solicitor.

Management Extension Programme (MEP)

MEP aims to assist developing enterprises by providing experienced managers on a temporary basis to work with the existing company team.
■ Managers work with a host company on a particular project of importance to that company. Projects usually last for approximately 20 weeks.
■ Applicants must be under 60 years of age and unemployed when entering the programme.

Graduate Gateway Programme (GGP)

GGP aims to provide unemployed graduates with training and project-related work experience with local companies and organizations.
■ Participants must be unemployed on entry to the programme. Each programme lasts up to 16 weeks.
■ Entrants are typically graduates from any discipline and up to 30 years of age; equivalent qualifications are also accepted.
■ Participants enhance their knowledge and skills, as well as their awareness of the operation and career prospects within local businesses and organizations.

Business Angels

Five TECs are piloting a Department of Employment project to match individual investors with small and medium-sized businesses requiring financial assistance/venture capital.

■ The Business Angels project is of particular benefit to businesses in the early stages of development, or those seeking to expand, through the input of risk capital.

Investors in People (London East TEC)

An initiative to help organizations improve performance through a practical, planned approach to setting and communicating business goals and developing people to meet them, with TEC-funded expertise/financial assistance.

■ Participating businesses work towards the achievement of a new National Standard for Effective Investment in People. This is done by training their staff, at all levels, to their full potential to meet business objectives and effectiveness.

Business Relocation Service (Devon and Cornwall)

A service offered by the TEC to companies looking to locate/relocate to Devon and Cornwall.

■ The TEC can provide a relevant analysis of the local labour market.
■ The TEC will work with the company to analyse precise staffing and skills needs.
■ The TEC, working with the company, will design and manage a tailor-made recruitment/training package.
■ Financial assistance towards training costs will be discussed as part of the package on an individual company basis.
■ The TEC will provide information on local training and business support services.

TEC Development Fund (South Thames TEC)

This fund is used to finance solutions to employers' training needs.

■ The TEC will fund up to 50% of the cost of developing and piloting new training provision or a new way of delivering training to meet the changing demands of employers.

The TEC will consider funding projects that clearly demonstrate:

■ work towards National Vocational Qualification (NVQs);
■ good collaboration between employers with a common training problem;
■ that the training developed will continue beyond the development stage;
■ that the proposed activities are new, innovative and achievable;
■ substantial employer support.

Second Step (Devon and Cornwall)

This programme has been devised to assist the sole trader and self-employed business person to take on their first employee.
- There is confidential advice available to help with planning, expansion, recruitment and training involved with employing.
- There is financial assistance towards pay for the new employee.
- A training grant is available for use by the employee, employer or both, whichever is most beneficial to the company.
- Direct help and assistance with the paperwork required for employment.
- Assistance in selecting, interviewing and recruiting a suitable employee.

Superstart

This encourages the set-up of team-run businesses. It aims to help people who have the ambition and drive to start manufacturing or technology based businesses, but may lack one or more ingredients in the field of business knowledge and experience to have the confidence to go it alone.

Open Learning

Open Learning allows people to learn at a time, place and pace that suits them. Some TECs have demonstration centres and libraries containing books, audio tapes, videos, computer based training or interactive videos. Specialist staff are on hand to help and advise.

Europe

TECs act as a conduit for European funding for a wide variety of purposes, from child-minding to training in design skills. They also assist small firms to assess how the Single European Market affects them and how to identify and exploit opportunities.

As well as having their own schemes many TECs also help small firms develop in collaboration with others. For example, participants of the Business Growth Programme run at Cranfield University Business School have received financial help to enable them to attend from Avon TEC, Aztec, Bedfordshire TEC, CAMBSTEC, Gloucestershire TEC, Greater Nottingham TEC, Norfolk and Waveney TEC, North London TEC and South Thames TEC.

TEC contact points

Eastern region
Bedfordshire: Bedfordshire TEC, Woburn Court, 2 Railton Road, Woburn Road Industrial Estate, Kempston, Beds MK42 7PN (Tel:01234 843100;

Fax: 01234 843211).
Cambridgeshire: Cambstec, Units 2–3, Trust Court, Chivers Way, The Vision Park, Histon, Cambridge CB4 4PW (Tel: 01223 235633/5; Fax: 01223 235631/2).

Essex: Essex TEC, Hedgerows Business Park, Colchester Road, Chelmsford CM2 5PB (Tel: 01245 450123; Fax: 01245 451430).

Hertfordshire: Hertfordshire TEC, New Barnes Mill, Cotton Mill Lane, St Albans, Herts AL1 2HA (Tel: 01727 852313; Fax: 01727 841449).

Norfolk/Waveney: Norfolk and Waveney TEC, Partnership House, Unit 10, Norwich Business Park, Whiting Road, Norwich NR4 6DJ (Tel: 01603 763812; Fax: 01603 763813).

Greater Peterborough: Greater Peterborough TEC, Unit 4, Blenheim Court, Peppercorn Close, off The Lincoln Road, Peterborough PE1 2DU (Tel: 01733 890808; Fax: 01733 890809).

Suffolk: Suffolk TEC, 2nd Floor, Crown House, Crown Street, Ipswich IP1 3HS (Tel: 01473 218951; Fax: 01473 231776).

East Midlands region

North Derbyshire: North Derbyshire TEC, Block C, St Mary's Court, St Mary's Gate, Chesterfield S41 7TD (Tel: 01246 551158; Fax: 01246 238489).

South Derbyshire: Southern Derbyshire TEC, St Helen's Court, St Helen's Street, Derby DE1 3GY (Tel: 01332 290550; Fax: 01332 292188).

Leicestershire: Leicestershire TEC, Meridian East, Meridian Business Park, Leicester LE5 2WZ (Tel: 0116 2651515; Fax: 0116 2651503).

Lincolnshire: Lincolnshire TEC, Beech House, Witham Park, Waterside South, Lincoln LN5 7JH

(Tel: 01522 567765; Fax: 01522 510534).

West Midlands region

Birmingham: Birmingham TEC, Chaplin Court, 80 Hurst Street, Birmingham B5 4TG (Tel: 0121 622 4419; Fax: 0121 622 1600).

Northamptonshire: Northamptonshire TEC, Royal Pavilion, Summerhouse Pavilions, Summerhouse Road, Moulton Park, Northampton NN3 6BJ (Tel: 01604 671200; Fax: 01604 670362).

Greater Nottingham: Greater Nottingham TEC, Marina Road, Castle Marina Park, Nottingham NG7 3TW (Tel: 0115 9413313; Fax: 0115 9484589).

North Nottinghamshire: North Nottinghamshire TEC, 1st Floor, Block C, Edwinstowe House, High Street, Edwinstowe, Mansfield, Notts NG21 9PR (Tel: 01623 824624; Fax: 01623 824070).

Central England

Central England TEC, The Oaks, Clewes Road, Redditch B98 7ST (Tel: 01527 545415; Fax: 01527 543032).

Coventry/Warwickshire: Coventry and Warwickshire TEC, Brandon Court, Progress Way, Coventry CV3 2TE (Tel: 01203 635666; Fax: 01203 450242).

Dudley: Dudley TEC, Dudley Court South, Waterfront East, Level Street, Brierley Hill, West Midlands DY5 1XN (Tel: 01384 485000; Fax: 01384 483399).

Hereford and Worcester: HAWTEC, Haswell House, St Nicholas Street, Worcester WR1 1UW

(Tel: 01905 723200;
Fax: 01905 613338).
Sandwell: Sandwell TEC, 1st Floor,
Kingston House, 438/450 High Street,
West Bromwich, West Midlands B70
9LD (Tel: 0121 525 4242;
Fax: 0121 525 4250).
Shropshire: Shropshire TEC, 2nd
Floor, Hazledine House, Central
Square, Telford TF3 4JJ
(Tel: 01952 291471;
Fax: 01952 291437).
Staffordshire: Staffordshire TEC,
Festival Way, Festival Park,
Stoke on Trent ST1 5TQ
(Tel: 01782 202733;
Fax: 01782 286215).
Walsall: Walsall TEC, 5th Floor,
Townend House, Townend Square,
Walsall WS1 1NS (Tel: 01922 32332;
Fax: 01922 33011).
Wolverhampton: Wolverhampton
TEC, Pendeford Business Park,
Wobaston Road, Wolverhampton
WV9 5HA (Tel: 01902 397787;
Fax: 01902 397786).

London region
Bromley: SOLOTEC, Lancaster House,
7 Elmfield Road, Bromley, Kent BR1
1LT (Tel: 0181 313 9232; Fax: 0181
313 9245).
Central London: CENTEC, 12
Grosvenor Crescent, London SW1X
7EE (Tel: 0171 411 3500;
Fax: 0171 411 3555).
City and Inner London North:
CILNTEC, 80 Great Eastern Street,
London EC2A 3DP
(Tel: 0171 324 2424;
Fax: 0171 324 2400).
East London: London East TEC, City-
side House, 40 Adler Street,
London E1 1EE (Tel: 0171 377 1866;
Fax: 0171 377 8003).
Kingston/Merton/Wandsworth:

AZTEC, Manorgate House, 2 Manor-
gate Road, Kingston-upon-Thames
KT2 7AL (Tel: 0181 547 3934;
Fax: 0181 547 3884).
North London: North London TEC,
Dumayne House, 1 Fox Lane,
Palmers Green, London N13 4AB (Tel:
0171 447 9422;
Fax: 0171 882 5931).
North West London: North West
London TEC, Kirkfield House,
118–120 Station Road, Harrow,
Middlesex HA1 2RL
(Tel: 0171 424 8866;
Fax: 0171 424 2240).
South Thames: South Thames TEC,
200 Great Dover Street, London
SE1 4YB (Tel: 0171 403 1990;
Fax: 0171 378 1590).
West London: West London TEC,
Sovereign Court, 15–21 Staines Road,
Hounslow, Middlesex TW3 3HA (Tel:
0181 577 1010;
Fax: 0181 570 9969).

Northern region
County Durham: County Durham
TEC, Valley Street North, Darlington
DL1 1TJ (Tel: 01325 351166;
Fax: 01325 381362).
Northumberland: Northumberland
TEC, Suite 2, Craster Court, Manor
Walk Shopping Centre, Cramlington
NE23 6XX (Tel: 01670 713303;
Fax: 01670 713323).
Teesside: Teesside TEC, Training and
Enterprise House, 2 Queens Square,
Middlesbrough, Cleveland TS2 1AA
(Tel: 01642 231023;
Fax: 01642 232480).
Tyneside: Tyneside TEC, Moongate
House, 5th Avenue Business Park,
Team Valley Trading Estate,
Gateshead NE11 0HF
(Tel: 0191 487 5599;
Fax: 0191 482 6519).

Wearside: Wearside TEC, Derwent House, New Town Centre, Washington NE38 7ST (Tel: 0191 416 6161; Fax: 0191 415 1093).

North West
(Greater Manchester) region
Bolton/Bury: Bolton/Bury TEC, Clive House, Clive Street, Bolton BL1 1ET (Tel: 01204 397350; Fax: 01204 363212).
South and East Cheshire: South and East Cheshire TEC, PO Box 37, Middlewich Industrial and Business Park, Dalton Way, Middlewich, Cheshire CW10 0HU (Tel: 01606 737009; Fax: 01606 737022).
Manchester: Manchester TEC, Boulton House, 17–21 Chorlton Street, Manchester M1 3HY (Tel: 0161 236 7222; Fax: 0161 236 8878).
Oldham: Oldham TEC, Meridian Centre, King Street, Oldham OL1 1EZ (Tel: 0161 620 0006; Fax: 0161 620 0030).
Rochdale: Rochdale TEC, St James Place, 160–162 Yorkshire Street, Rochdale OL16 2DL (Tel: 01706 44909; Fax: 01706 49979).
Stockport/High Peak: Stockport/ High Peak TEC, 1 St Peter's Square, Stockport SK1 1NN (Tel: 0161 477 8830; Fax: 0161 480 7243).
Wigan: METROTEC (Wigan) Ltd, Buckingham Row, Northway, Wigan WN1 1XX (Tel: 01942 36312; Fax: 01942 821410).

North West region
North and Mid Cheshire: NORMID TEC, Spencer House, Dewhurst Road,
Birchwood, Warrington WA3 7PP (Tel: 01925 826515; Fax: 01925 820215).
Chester/Ellesmere Port/Wirral: CEWTEC, Block 4, Woodside Business Park, Birkenhead, Wirral L41 1EH (Tel: 0151 650 0555; Fax: 0151 650 07777).
Cumbria: Cumbria TEC, Venture House, Regents Court, Guard Street, Workington, Cumbria CA14 4EW (Tel: 01900 66991; Fax: 01900 604027).
East Lancashire: Red Rose Court, Petre Road, Clayton Business Park, Clayton-le-Moors, Accrington, Lancs BB5 5JR (Tel: 01254 301333; Fax: 01254 399090).
West Lancashire: LAWTEC (Lancashire Area West), 4th Floor, Duchy House, 96 Lancaster Road, Preston PR1 1HE (Tel: 01772 200035; Fax: 01772 54801).
Merseyside: Merseyside TEC, 3rd Floor, Tithebarn House, Tithebarn Street, Liverpool L2 2NZ (Tel: 0151 236 0026; Fax: 0151 236 4013).
St Helens: QUALITEC (St Helens) Ltd, 7 Waterside Court, Technology Campus, St Helens, Merseyside WA9 1VE (Tel: 01744 24433; Fax: 01744 453030).

South East region
Hampshire: Hampshire TEC, 25 Thackeray Mall, Fareham, Hants PO16 0PQ (Tel: 01329 230099; Fax: 01329 237733).
Heart of England: Heart of England TEC, 26/27 The Quadrant, Abingdon Science Park, Off Barton Lane, Abingdon OX14 3YS (Tel: 01235 553249; Fax: 01235 555706).

Isle of Wight: Wight Training and Enterprise, Mill Court, Furrlongs, Newport, Isle of Wight PO30 2AA (Tel: 01983 822818; Fax: 01983 527063).

Kent: Kent TEC, 5th Floor, Mountbatten House, 28 Military Road, Chatham, Kent ME4 4JE (Tel: 01634 844411; Fax: 01634 830991).

Milton Keynes/North Bucks: Milton Keynes and North Bucks TEC, Old Market Halls, Creed Street, Wolverton, Milton Keynes MK12 5LY (Tel: 01908 222555; Fax: 01908 222839).

Surrey: Surrey TEC, Technology House, 48–54 Goldsworth Road, Woking, Surrey GU21 1LE (Tel: 01483 728190; Fax: 01483 755259).

Sussex: Sussex TEC, 2nd Floor, Electrowatt House, North Street, Horsham RH12 1RS (Tel: 01403 271471; Fax: 01403 272082).

Thames Valley Enterprise: Thames Valley Enterprise, 6th Floor, Kings Point, 120 Kings Road, Reading RG1 3BZ (Tel: 01734 568156; Fax: 01734 567908).

South West region

Avon: Avon TEC, PO Box 164, St Lawrence House, 29–31 Broad Street, Bristol BS99 7HR (Tel: 0117 9277116; Fax: 0117 9226664).

Devon and Cornwall: Devon and Cornwall TEC, Foliot House, Brooklands, Budshead Road, Crownhill, Plymouth PL6 5XR (Tel: 01752 767929; Fax: 01752 770925).

Dorset: Dorset TEC, 25 Oxford Road, Bournemouth BH8 8EY (Tel: 01202 299284; Fax: 01202 299457).

Gloucestershire: Gloucestershire TEC, Conway House, 33–35 Worcester Street, Gloucester GL1 3AJ (Tel: 01452 524488; Fax: 01452 307144).

Somerset: Somerset TEC, Crescent House, 3–7 The Mount, Taunton TA1 3TT (Tel: 01823 259121; Fax: 01823 256174).

Wiltshire: Wiltshire TEC, The Bora Building, Westlea Campus,Westlea Down, Swindon SN5 7EZ (Tel: 01793 513644; Fax: 01793 542006).

Yorkshire and Humberside Region

Barnsley/Doncaster: Barnsley/Doncaster TEC, Conference Centre, Eldon Street, Barnsley S70 2TN (Tel: 01226 248088; Fax: 01226 291625).

Bradford and District: Bradford and District TEC, Fountain Hall, Fountain Street, Bradford BD1 3RA (Tel: 01274 723711; Fax: 01274 370980).

Calderdale/Kirklees: Calderdale and Kirklees TEC, Park View House, Woodvale Office Park, Woodvale Road, Brighouse HD6 4AB (Tel: 01484 400770; Fax: 01484 400672).

Humberside: Humberside TEC, The Maltings, Silvester Square, Silvester Street, Hull HU1 3HL (Tel: 01482 226491; Fax: 01482 213206).

Leeds: Leeds TEC, Belgrave Hall, Belgrave Street, Leeds LS2 8DD (Tel: 0113 2347666; Fax: 0113 2438126).

Rotherham: Rotherham TEC, Moorgate House, Moorgate Road, Rotherham S60 2EN

(Tel: 01709 830511;
Fax: 01709 362519).
Sheffield: Sheffield TEC, St Mary's
Court, 55 St Mary's Road, Sheffield S2
4AQ (Tel: 0114 2701911;
Fax: 0114 2752634).
Wakefield: Wakefield TEC, Grove
Hall, 60 College Grove Road,
Wakefield WF1 3RN
(Tel: 01924 299907;
Fax: 01924 201837).
North Yorkshire: North Yorkshire
TEC, TEC House, 7 Pioneer Business
Park, Amy Johnson Way, Clifton
Moorgate, York YO3 8TN
(Tel: 01904 691939;
Fax: 01904 690411).

Wales
Mid Glamorgan: Mid Glamorgan
TEC, Unit 17–20, Centre Court, Main
Avenue, Treforest Industrial Estate,
Pontypridd CF37 5YL
(Tel: 01443 841594;
Fax: 01443 841578).
South Glamorgan: South Glamorgan
TEC, 3–7 Drakes Walk, Waterfront

2000, Atlantic Wharf, Cardiff CF1
5AN (Tel: 01222 451000;
Fax: 01222 450424).
Gwent: Gwent TEC, Glyndwr House,
Unit B2, Cleppa Park, Newport,
Gwent NP9 1YE (Tel: 01633 817777;
Fax: 01633 810980).
North East Wales: North East Wales
TEC, Wynnstay Block, Hightown Bar-
racks, Kingsmill Road, Wrexham,
Clwyd LL13 8BH
(Tel: 01978 290049;
Fax: 01978 290061).
North West Wales: TARGED: North
West Wales TEC, Llys Brittania,
Parc Menai, Bangor, Gwynedd LL57
4BN (Tel: 01248 671444;
Fax: 01248 670889).
Powys: Powys TEC, 1st Floor, St
David's House, Newtown, Powys SY16
1RB (Tel: 01686 622494;
Fax: 01686 622716).
West Wales: West Wales TEC,
Orchard House, Orchard Street,
Swansea SA1 5DJ
(Tel: 01792 460355;
Fax: 01792 456341).

■ PROPERTY SERVICES

Finding suitable premises is one of the main problems encountered by many people starting up a new business. Apart from availability, these problems include finding somewhere the appropriate size, in the right location, on a flexible lease, with the services already connected.

An added bonus would be shared secretarial, telex, fax and book-keeping facilities – on site.

Public sector

English Estates: This is the trading name of the English Industrial Estates Corporation, a statutory body which develops and markets industrial and commercial property in England. The Welsh and Scottish Enterprise Agencies and the Local Enterprise Development Unit in Northern Ireland carry out a similar role in their respective countries. Their principal services include the provision of:

■ Beehive Workshops, who operate small workshop units from 500 sq ft, let with full services on simple tenancy agreements at attractive weekly rentals.

- Larger factories for manufacturing, service, warehousing or distribution based companies.
- Purpose-built units for high-technology use, near to universities.
- A full professional design and build service for individual or specific property needs.
- A business support service for small and medium-sized businesses who are tenants or prospective tenants. Advice is given on all aspects of running a business, including start-up, expansion, marketing, finance and grants.

Further information can be obtained from any of the offices below or, if outside England, from one of the agencies above.

London: London Industrial plc, Magenta House, Whitechapel Road, London E1 1DV (Tel: 0171 247 7614).
Rest of the country: English Estates, St George's House, Kingsway, Team Valley, Gateshead, Tyne and Wear NE11 0NA (Tel: 0191 487 8941).

Private sector

A growing number of organizations specialize in providing small office and workshop facilities, usually with shared services such as telex and fax, and sometimes with business advisory services. Sizes of units range from 100 sq ft up to 200,000 +; costs are from £1.50 up to £20 per sq ft. Most units are let on licences rather than a lease and some have a restriction on how long you can stay in them. Some of these are listed below.

England

Barnsley: Barnsley Enterprise Centre, 1 Pontefract Road, Barnsley S71 1AJ (Tel: 01226 733291 x 154). Contact: Mr A Johnson.
Bedford: Enterprise House, Old Ford End Road, Bedford MK40 4PH (Tel: 01234 327422). Contact: George Clarke.
Birmingham: Birmingham New Enterprise Workshops, 272 Montgomery Street, Sparkbrook, Birmingham B7 5RD (Tel: 0121 773 2224). Contact: A R Isherwood.
Blackburn: Blackburn Business Development Centre, Eanam Wharf, Blackburn Waterside, Blackburn BB1 5BL (Tel: 01254 56557). Contact: Mr Edworthy.

Blackpool: Blackpool Enterprise Centre, 20 Queen Street, Blackpool FY1 1PD (Tel: 01253 295929). Contact: Michael McDade.
Bolton: Bolton Business Centre, 46 Lower Bridgeman Street, Bolton BL2 1DG (Tel: 01204 392292). Contact: Paul Davidson.
Bradford: Robin Enterprise Centre, Robin Mills, Leeds Road, Bradford BD10 9TE (Tel: 01274 612561). Contact: Andrew Idle.
Bristol: Avondale Workshops, Woodland Way, Kingswood, Bristol BS15 1QH (Tel: 0117 9603871). Contact: Linda Searle.
Burton-on-Trent: Bretby Business Park, Ashby Road, Stanhope Bretby, Burton-on-Trent, Staffs DE15 0QD (Tel: 01283 5505000).

Contact: Vince Moran.
Bury: Bury Business Centre, Kay
Street, Bury BL9 6BD
(Tel: 0161 705 1878).
Contact: Eric Shipperbottom.
Cannock: Cannock Community
Enterprise Workspace, 75 Market
Street, Hednesford, Cannock
WS12 5AD (Tel: 01543 871049).
Contact: Norma Gethin.
Chester: Chester Enterprise Centre,
Hoole Bridge, Chester CH2 3NE
(Tel: 01244 311474).
Contact: Richard Holt.
Chesterfield: Bolsover Enterprise Park,
PO Box 10, Station Road,
Bolsover, Chesterfield S44 6BH,
Derbyshire (Tel: 01246 823030).
Contact: Mr T G Robinson. **Cirences-
ter:** Cirencester Workshops and
Niccol Centre, Brewery Court,
Cirencester, Glos GL7 1JH (Tel: 01285
651566).
Contact: Jennie Aylen.
Cleethorpes: Enterprise Workshop,
Jackson Place, Wilton Rd Industrial
Estate, Poplar Rd, Humberston,
Cleethorpes DN36 4AS
(Tel: 01472 200200 x 2219). Contact:
Peter Heinzman.
Cleveland: South Bank Business
Centre, Normansby Road, Cleveland
TS6 6RS (Tel: 01642 456282). Contact:
Ron Harrison.
Cornwall: Caradon Business Centre,
Enterprise House, Liskeard Enterprise
Centre, Station Road, Liskeard
PL14 4BT (Tel: 01579 44433).
Contact: Mary Gleeson.
Coventry: Enterprise Centre, Little
Heath Industrial Estate, Old Church
Road, Coventry CV6 7NB
(Tel: 01203 667701).
Contact: Les Gow.
Crewe: Scope House, Weston Road,
Crewe CW1 1DD

(Tel: 01270 589569).
Contact: Cheryl Johnson.
Cumbria: Blencathra Workshops,
Threlkeld Quarry, Threlkeld,
Keswick CA12 4TT
(Tel: 01768 779779).
Contact: Ray Patterson.
Cumbria: Cleator Moor Business
Centre, Cleator Moor Workspace,
Cragg Road, Cleator Moor CA25 5PT
(Tel: 01946 813555).
Contact: John Mann
Dartford: Coldart Business Centre,
3 King Edward Avenue, Dartford
DA21 2HZ (Tel: 01322 291451).
Contact: Michael Fitzpatrick.
Derby: Derwent Business Centre,
Clarke Street, Derby, DE1 2BV
(Tel: 01332 298788).
Contact: Peter Silvester.
Devon: Brunel Centre, 160A Torquay
Road, Paignton TQ3 2AH (Tel: 01803
666662).
Contact: M Wortley.
Doncaster: Acorn Workspace, Carcroft
Enterprise Park, Station Road, Car-
croft, Doncaster DN6 8DD (Tel: 01302
330802).
Contact: Joe Armishaw.
Dorset: Dorset Business Centre,
27 Dawkins Road, Hamworthy, Poole
BH15 4JY (Tel: 01202 681182).
Contact: P J Hayes.
Durham: Auckland New Business
Centre, St Helens Auckland Trading
Estate, Bishop Auckland, Co. Durham
DL14 9TX
(Tel: 01388 450505).
Contact: Joan Dawson.
East Sussex: Robert Tressell Work-
shops, Station Yard, Devonshire Road,
Hastings TN34 1NF
(Tel: 01424 722213).
Contact: Julia Robinson.
Ellesmere Port: Canalbridge
Enterprise Centre, Meadow Lane,

Ellesmere Port L65 4EH
(Tel: 0151 355 0013).
Contact: Laurie O'Neill.
Essex: Braintree Youth Enterprise
Centre, Black Notley Hospital,
Black Notley, Braintree CM7 8PN (Tel:
01376 550218).
Contact: Tony Woollett.
Gateshead: Blaydon Business Centre,
Cowen Road, Blaydon, Gateshead
NE21 5TW (Tel: 0191 414 7575).
Contact: Tony Church.
Grantham: Old Malt House, Spring
Gardens, off London Road,
Grantham NG31 6JP
(Tel: 01476 68970).
Contact: Jacqueline Smith.
Grimsby: New Enterprise Centre, King
Edward Street, Grimsby
DN31 3JH (Tel: 01472 351402).
Contact: Peter Vickers.
Halifax: Calderdale Business Park,
Club Lane, Ovenden, Halifax HX2
8DB (Tel: 01422 358171).
Contact: David Wood.
Hampshire: Liss Business Centre,
Station Road, Liss GU33 7AW
(Tel: 01730 892669).
Contact: Alex Addison.
Harrogate: Claro Court Business
Centre, Claro Road, Harrogate HG1
4BA (Tel: 01423 527827).
Contact: Jennifer Reffitt.
Hartlepool: Hartlepool Workshops,
Sandgate Industrial Estate,
Mainsforth Terrace, Cleveland, Hartle-
pool TS25 1UB
(Tel: 01492 235648).
Contact: Barbara Elsdon.
Hertfordshire: St Albans Enterprise
Centre, Unit 6G, Long Spring,
Porters Wood, St Albans AL3 6EN
(Tel: 01727 37760).
Contact: K J Hughesman.
Hinckley: Hinckley Workspace Ltd,
Unit 2B, Southfield Road,

Hinckley, Leicestershire LE10 1UB
(Tel: 01455 633666).
Contact: Andrew Kimberley.
Hull: Business Centre, Guildhall Road,
Hull HU1 1HJ
(Tel: 01482 593866).
Contact: John Bradshaw.
Kent: Broad Oak Enterprise Village,
Broad Oak Road, Sittingbourne
ME9 8AQ (Tel: 01795 477311).
Contact: E R Crawford.
King's Lynn: Enterprise Works, North
Lynn Industrial Estate,
Bergen Way, King's Lynn PE30 2JR
(Tel: 01553 760431).
Contact: Andrew Ramsey.
Leeds: Chapeltown and Harehills
Enterprises Ltd, CHEL House,
26 Roundhay Road, Chapeltown,
Leeds LS7 4AB (Tel: 0113 2425996).
Contact: Ravinder Singh Ghir. **Leices-
ter:** Leicester Enterprise Workshop, 76
Linden Street,
Leicester LE5 5EE
(Tel: 0116 2734165).
Contact: Geoff Clark-Monks.
Lincoln: Lincoln Innovation Centre,
West Yard, Rope Walk, Lincoln LN6
7DQ (Tel: 01522 540775).
Contact: D Wilson.
Liverpool: Gardners Row Business
Centre, Gardners Row, Liverpool
L3 6JE (Tel: 0151 207 5555). Contact:
Alan Jones.
London: Acton Business Centre,
School Rd, Acton, London NW10 6TD
(Tel: 0171 377 1154).
Contact: Harry Platt.
London: Barley Mow Workspace,
10 Barley Mow Passage, Chiswick,
London W4 4PH
(Tel: 0181 994 6477).
Contact: Netia Livingstone.
London: Bootstrap Services, The Print
House, 18 Ashwin Street,
Hackney, London E8 3DL

(Tel: 0171 254 0775).
Contact: Julie Townsend.
London: Business Centre, 758–760
Great Cambridge Road, Enfield,
Middlesex EN1 3RN
(Tel: 0181 367 7676).
Contact: Brian Quarm.
London: Buspace Studios, Conlan
Street, Notting Hill, London
W10 5AR (Tel: 0181 968 1119).
Contact: Aileen Hamilton-Farey.
London: Docklands Enterprise Centre,
11 Marshalsea Road, London SE1 1EP
(Tel: 0171 367 7581). Contact: Denis
Brookes.
London: Enterprise House, St Wilfrid's
Road, East Barnet,
Hertfordshire EN4 9SB
(Tel: 0181 447 1000).
Contact: Peter Lovell.
London: Five Dryden Street,
5 Dryden Street, Covent Garden,
London WC2E 9NW
(Tel: 0171 240 2430).
Contact: Jenny Coleman.
London: Hackney Business Centre,
277 Mare Street, Hackney, London E8
1HB (Tel: 0181 533 4599). Contact:
Paul Chaplin.
London: Kilburn Grange Workshop,
Kingsgate Workshops, 110–116 Kings-
gate Road, Kilburn, London NW6 2J9
(Tel: 0171 328 7878).
Contact: H Wright.
London: Manor Gardens Enterprise
Centre, 10/18 Manor Gardens,
Holloway, London N7 6JY
(Tel: 0171 272 8944).
Contact: Patrick Quarry.
London: Mercury Asset Management
Youth Enterprise Centre, 8 Nursery
Road, London SW9 8BP
(Tel: 0171 738 7707).
Contact: Tim Blackler.
London: Shakespeare Commercial
Centre, 25a Coldharbour Lane,

Brixton, London SE9 8RR
(Tel: 0171 274 7511).
Contact: Alan Dinsdale.
London: Spitalfields Small Business
Association, 170 Brick Lane,
London E1 6R (Tel: 0171 247 1960).
Contact: Kay Jordan.
London: St John's Studios, Church
Road, Richmond, London TW9 2QA
(Tel: 0181 948 5322).
Contact: R E Bicknell.
London: Stratford Workshops,
Unit 136, Burford Road, Stratford,
London E15 2SD
(Tel: 0181 519 3646).
Contact: June Dyke.
London: Tottenham Enterprise
Centre, 560–568 High Road,
Tottenham, London N17 9TA
(Tel: 0171 721 7200).
Contact: Debbie Essien.
London: Ventura House, 176–184
Acre Lane, London SW2 5UL
(Tel: 0171 733 7010).
Contact: Mrs Blackburn.
Loughborough: Loughborough
Centenary Workspace, Little Moor
Lane, Loughborough, Leicestershire
LE11 1SF (Tel: 01509 262249).
Contact: Tim Bacon.
Macclesfield: Compass Crown Centre,
Bond Street, Macclesfield SK11 6QT
(Tel: 01625 619177). Contact: Chris
Holland.
Manchester: Cariocca Managed Work-
shop Complex, 2 Hellidon Close,
Ardwick, Manchester
M12 4AH (Tel: 0161 273 6605).
Contact: S Buther.
Mansfield: Mansfield, Sutton and
Kirby Enterprise Partnership,
The Old Town Hall, Market Place,
Mansfield, Nottinghamshire
NG18 1HX (Tel: 01623 656432).
Contact: Peter Slack.
Middlesbrough: Cleveland Business

Centre, 1 Watson Street,
Middlesbrough TS1 2RQ
(Tel: 01642 232353).
Contact: Mrs K Turner.
Milton Keynes: Denbigh House,
Denbigh Road, Bletchley, Milton
Keynes, Bucks MK1 1YP
(Tel: 01908 368071).
Contact: D F Strachan.
Newark: Newark Enterprise
Workshops, c/o Newark Storage Ltd,
Bowbridge Road, Newark,
Nottinghamshire NG24 4QE
(Tel: 01636 76675).
Contact: C J Vallance.
Newcastle upon Tyne: Byker Business
Development Centre, Albion Row,
Byker, Newcastle upon Tyne NE6 1LQ
(Tel: 0191 276 4244).
Contact: Robert Dolman.
Northumberland: Blyth Valley
Venture Workshops, Plessey Road,
Newsham, Blyth, Northumberland
NE22 7JB (Tel: 01670 828686).
Contact: Peter Grant.
Nottingham: Nottingham Advanced
Business Centre, City House, Maid
Marion Way, Nottingham NG1 6BH
(Tel: 0115 9412334).
Contact: Resham Aujla.
Nuneaton: Centenary Business
Centre, Hammond Close,
Attleborough Fields, Nuneaton CV11
6RY (Tel: 01203 641399). Contact:
Robert Craig.
Oxford: Circus Workshops,
38 Cowley Road, Oxford OX4 1HZ
(Tel: 01865 722184).
Contact: Bob Valentine.
Peterborough: Peterborough
Workspace, 28/29 Maxwell Road,
Woodston, Peterborough,
Cambridgeshire PE2 0JE
(Tel: 01733 390707).
Contact: Rodney Britten.
Plymouth: City Business Park,

Enterprise House, Somerset Place,
Stoke, Plymouth PL13 4BB
(Tel: 01752 605645).
Contact: Philip Allbutt.
Pontefract: Westfield Resource and
Enterprise Centre, Westfield Lane,
South Elmsall, Pontefract WF9 2PU
(Tel: 01977 45141).
Contact: Tony Palmer.
Portsmouth: Portsmouth Enterprise
Centre, Quartermaine Road,
Portsmouth PO3 5QT
(Tel: 01705 661598).
Contact: J Barton.
Preston: Riversway Managed
Workshops, off Chain Caul Way,
Leeward Road, Ashton, Preston
PR2 2YL (Tel: 01772 729991).
Contact: E Gleeson.
Redditch: Greenlands Business
Centre, Studley Road, Studley,
Redditch, Worcs B98 7HD (Tel: 01527
517165).
Contact: Linda Allan.
Rochdale: Enterprise Generation
Centre, Dane Street, Rochdale
OL12 6XB (Tel: 01706 344031).
Contact: R A Brierly.
Rotherham: Bolton Road Managed
Workshops, Bolton Road, Wath upon
Dearne, Rotherham S63 7JY (Tel:
01709 526498).
Contact: Peter Lawrence.
Sandwell: Brook Street Business
Centre, Brook Street, Tipton, Sandwell
DY4 9DD
(Tel: 0121 522 3920).
Contact: Peter Rudolf.
Scarborough: Sitwell Centre, Sitwell
Street, Scarborough YO12 5EX
(Tel: 01723 354454).
Contact: Brian Wood.
Scunthorpe: Normanby Park
Workshops, Normanby Road,
Scunthorpe DN15 8QZ
(Tel: 01724 849457).

Contact: Alan Henderson.
Sheffield: Aizlewood Business Centre, Aizlewood's Mill, Nursery Street, Sheffield S3 8GG (Tel: 0114 2823123). Contact: Michael Sharpe.
St Helens: Bold Business Centre, Bold Lane, Sutton, St Helens WA9 4TX (Tel: 01925 220484). Contact: Bill Shepherd.
Stoke-on-Trent: Stoke-on-Trent Enterprise Centre, Bedford Street, Shelton, Stoke-on-Trent ST1 4PZ (Tel: 01782 273366). Contact: Neil Davies.
Suffolk: Suffolk Enterprise Centre, Russell Road, Ipswich IP1 2DE (Tel: 01473 288000). Contact: Chris Betson.
Sunderland: Pallion Residents Enterprises, Enterprise House, Pallion Industrial Estate, Roper Street, Sunderland SR4 6SN (Tel: 0191 510 9292). Contact: G Robson.
Surrey: Acorn House, 74–94 Cherry Orchard Road, Croydon CR0 6BA (Tel: 0181 681 8339). Contact: David Nash.
Sussex: Tindle Enterprise Centre, 86 Gloucester Road, Brighton BN1 6HF (Tel: 01273 688882). Contact: Mike Fradin.
Swindon: Kentwood Business Centre, 112/118 Crickdale Road, Gorse Hill, Swindon SN2 6AG (Tel: 01793 5135575). Contact: Irene Ettel.
Tamworth: Tamworth Starter Enterprise Centre, Amington Industrial Estate, 17 Sandy Way, Tamworth B77 1NR (Tel: 01872 50812). Contact: Marlene Ryall.
Telford: Telford Industrial Centre, Stafford Park 4, Telford TF3 3BA

(Tel: 01952 290769). Contact: David Chiva.
Wellingborough: Dennington New Business Centre, Dennington Estate, Everitt Close, Wellingborough, Northamptonshire NN8 2QE (Tel: 01933 440448). Contact: Rachel Mallows.
Wolverhampton: Wolverhampton Media Centre, Chubb Building, Long Street, Wolverhampton B3 1QA (Tel: 0121 233 2660). Contact: Peter White.
York: Fishergate Centre, 4 Fishergate, York YO1 4AB (Tel: 01904 610045). Contact: Bob Moore.

Scotland
Aberdeen: Aberdeen Managed Workspaces, 56–64 Frederick Street, Aberdeen AB2 1HY (Tel: 01224 633823). Contact: Rona Benzie.
Alloa: Alloa Business Centre, The Whins, Whins Road, Alloa FK10 3SA (Tel: 01259 217466). Contact: Alan Stewart.
Ayrshire: Highhouse Industrial Estate, Barony Road, Authinleck, Ayrshire KA18 1SH (Tel: 01290 421159). Contact: David Duncanson.
Coatbridge: Coatbridge Workshops, Coatbank Way, Coatbridge ML5 3AG (Tel: 01236 423384). Contact: Frances Sunderland.
Dundee: Blackness Trading Precinct and North Tay Complex, Meadow Mill, Blackness Trading Precinct, West Hendersons Wynd, Dundee DD1 5BY (Tel: 01382 26001). Contact: Mary Core.
Edinburgh: City Business Venture, Palmerston House, Torphichen Street, Edinburgh CH12 5AV

(Tel: 0131 228 6555).
Contact: Brian Crawley.
Fife: Kirkcaldy Enterprise Centre,
Mitchelson Industrial Estate,
Mitchelson Drive, Kirkcaldy, Fife KY1
3NF (Tel: 01592 55101).
Contact: Charles Wilson.
Glasgow: Greater Easterhouse
Managed Workspace, 19 Blairtum-
mock Road, Easterhouse, Glasgow
G33 4AN (Tel: 0141 774 8989).
Contact: W M Craw.
Isle of Skye: Ardelve Industrial Estate,
c/o Elgin Hostel, Portree,
Isle of Skye IV51 9BT
(Tel: 01478 612477).
Contact: Catriona MacLean.
Midlothian: Stoneyburn Workshops,
The Old Primary School, 4 Main
Street, Stoneyburn EH47 8AP
(Tel: 01501 62263).
Contact: Jack O'Hare.
Stirling: Stirling University Innova-
tion Park, Scottish Metropolitan
Alpha Centre, Innovation Park,
Stirling FK9 4NF (Tel: 01786 70080).
Contact: Stewart Cameron.
Strathclyde: Barrowfield Workspace
Ltd, 170 Stamford Street, Glasgow,
Strathclyde G40 3QY
(Tel: 0141 556 2731).
Contact: Ian Holmes.
West Calder: West Calder Workspace,
Society Place, West Calder EH55 8EA
(Tel: 01506 871222). Contact: Ian
Gould.

Wales
Bangor: Menai Enterprise and
Technology Centre, Deiniol Road,
Bangor, Gwynedd LL57 2UP
(Tel: 01248 354103).
Contact: Dafydd Jones.
Deeside: Deeside Enterprise Centre,
Rowley's Drive, Shotton,
Deeside CH5 1PP

(Tel: 01244 830003).
Contact: Sally Gosmore.
Dyfed: Betws Park Workshop, Park
Street, Betws, Ammanford, Dyfed
SA18 2ET (Tel: 01269 596237).
Contact: Mary James.
Gwent: Blaina Enterprise Centre, Unit
31, Rising Sun Industrial Estate,
Blaina NP3 3JW
(Tel: 01495 291911).
Contact: Irene Thomas.
Llanelli: Llanelli Enterprise
Workshop, 100 Trostre Road,
Llanelli, Dyfed SA15 2EΛ
(Tel: 01554 772122).
Contact: Tony Giles.
Merthyr Tydfil: Dowlais Enterprise
Centre, Cowlais, Merthyr Tydfil,
Mid Glamorgan CF48 2SR
(Tel: 01685 722497).
Contact: Patricia Jones.
Pembrokeshire: Taf and Cleddau
Rural Initiative, The Old School,
Narbeth SA67 8DU
(Tel: 01834 860965).
Contact: David John.
Rhyll: Clywd Coast YEC Ltd, 84
Marsh Road, Morfa Clywd, Rhyll LL18
2AF (Tel: 01745 330777). Contact:
Colin Gent.
Swansea: Abernant Centre for
Enterprise, Rhyd-y-Fro, Pontardwe,
Swansea SA8 4TY
(Tel: 01269 823840).
Contact: Steve Harford.
West Glamorgan: Crynant Business
Park, Treforgan Colliery, Dulais
Valley, Neath, West Glamorgan SA10
6RP (Tel: 01792 817368).
Contact: Gethlin Jones.
Wrexham: Bersham Enterprises, Plas
Grono Road, Rhostyllewn,
Wrexham, Clwyd LL14 4EG
(Tel: 01978 352614).
Contact: Morag Murphy.

∎ ENTERPRISE ZONES

Twenty-five Enterprise Zones have been defined within some inner cities and other neglected urban black spots. The zones can give new businesses substantial financial benefits as well as freedom from control. In this way business both inside the zones and on the perimeter will be strengthened. The zones are not aimed exclusively at small or new firms, but nevertheless they provide an attractive commercial inducement to locate in them.

The first zone to become operational was in the lower Swansea Valley in June 1981, and the last was North West Kent. The facilities, grants and other assistance available within each zone are comprehensively described in a booklet available from: The Department of the Environment, Room P2/155C, 2 Marsham Street, London SW1P 3EB (Tel: 0171 476 4468).

Local contact points

England

Dudley (Round Oak): Economic Development Unit, Dudley Metropolitan Borough Council, Dudley, West Midlands DY1 1HF (Tel: 01384 456000).

Glanford: Glanford Borough Council, Council Offices, Station Road, Brigg, South Humberside DN20 8EG (Tel: 01652 652441).

Middlesbrough: Enterprise Zone Office, Vancouver House, Gurney Street, Middlesbrough, Cleveland TS1 1QP (Tel: 01642 222279).

North-East Lancashire: Burnley Borough Council,Town Hall, Burnley BB11 1JA (Tel: 01282 425011).

– Pendle Borough Council, Town Hall, Nelson, Lancs BB9 7LG (Tel: 01282 67131).

– Rossendale Borough Council, Leisure and Industrial Development Office, 41/45 Kay Street, Rawtenstall, Rossendale, Lancs BB4 7LS (Tel: 01706 217777).

North West Kent: North Kent Enterprise Office, Civic Centre, Strood, Rochester, Kent ME2 4AW (Tel: 01634 732716).

Rotherham: Department of Planning, Rotherham MBC, Norfolk House,

Walker Place, Rotherham S60 1QT (Tel: 01709 372099).

Scunthorpe: Scunthorpe Borough Council, Civic Centre, Ashby Road, Scunthorpe, South Humberside DN16 1AB (Tel: 01724 280444).

Sunderland: Tyne and Wear Development Corporation, Scotswood House, Newcastle Business Park, Newcastle NE4 7YL (Tel: 0191 226 1234).

– Sunderland City Council, Civic Centre, Burdon Road, Sunderland SR2 7DN (Tel: 0191 567 6161).

Telford: Enterprise Zone Manager, Telford Development Corporation, Priorslee, Telford, Shropshire TF2 9NT (Tel: 01952 613131).

Wellingborough: Director of Development, Wellingborough Council, Council Offices, Tithe Barn Road, Wellingborough, Northants NN8 1BN (Tel: 01933 228885).

Wakefield: Planning Department, Wakefield MDC, Newton Bar, Wakefield, West Yorkshire WF1 2TT (Tel: 01924 290900).

Workington: Enterprise Zone Manager, Allerdale District Council, Holmewood, Cockermouth, Cumbria CA13 0DW (Tel: 01900 604351).

Wales
Delyn: Delyn Borough Council, Enterprise House, Aber Park, Flint, Clwyd CH6 5BD (Tel: 013526 62345).
Lower Swansea Valley: Director of Development, The Guildhall, Swansea SA1 4PH (Tel: 01792 302748).
Milford Haven: South Pembrokeshire District Council, Pier House, Pier Road, Pembroke Dock, Pembrokeshire SA72 6TR (Tel: 01646 684914).

Scotland
Inverclyde: Inverclyde District Council, Municipal Buildings, Clyde Square, Greenock PA15 1LY (Tel: 01475 724400).
Invergordon: Highlands and Islands Enterprise, 62 High Street, Invergordon IV18 0DH (Tel: 01349 853666).
Tayside (Arbroath): Director of Planning, Angus District Council, County Buildings, Forfar DD8 3LG (Tel: 01307 65101).
Tayside (Dundee): Dundee District Council, 7/21 Castle Street, Dundee DD1 3AA (Tel: 01382 23141).

Northern Ireland
Londonderry: Londonderry Enterprise Zone Office, The Richmond Chambers, The Diamond, Londonderry BT48 6HN (Tel: 01504 263992).

Freeports

A half-hearted attempt by the Government in 1984 to emulate the entrepreneurial havens of the Far East. Three of the six UK freeports are based on airports (Belfast, Prestwick, Birmingham) and three on seaports (Liverpool, Cardiff and Southampton).

The freeports allow users to process, store and manufacture goods, entering them without paying customs duties and local taxes. Goods can then be exported without duties being paid. This has obvious cash-flow advantages to anyone involved in the re-export field.

In the Far East, however, freeports also have a gamut of fiscal and financial incentives such as tax holidays of between five and ten years, generous depreciation allowances, and exemption from wage and welfare laws. So Hong Kong, Singapore and South Korea can relax for the moment at least.

Urban Development Corporations

These started in the north with the Merseyside Development Corporation in 1981. These were followed by Trafford Park, Teesside and Tyne and Wear. In 1988 four more were launched, covering Bristol, Leeds, Central Manchester and Sheffield. Each has a budget in excess of tens of millions and is responsible for securing the economic regeneration of their area, and to encourage commercial development.

■ SMALL-BUSINESS ASSOCIATIONS

Association of British Chambers of Commerce, 9 Tufton Street, London SW1T 3QB (Tel: 0171 222 1555). A co-ordinating body for chambers of commerce, which play an increasing role in providing information and help for existing businesses. They have been a major force in the launching of many of the most prominent and effective Enterprise Agencies. They have also sponsored many local new business competitions. They are a very important source of information, advice and help for new and small businesses. (They should be listed in your telephone directory.)

Association of Independent Businesses, 26 Addison Place, London W11 4RZ (Tel: 0171 371 1299; Fax: 0171 602 1922). This was established in 1968 to promote the cause of the smaller business. The aim of the Association is to remove discrimination against independent businesses in existing and proposed legislation, and so it maintains close contact with both Whitehall and Westminster. Its small national office staff has a limited capacity to answer members' queries on typical problems that face independent businesses, such as legal, accounting, insurance, taxation and European matters. They can also signpost enquirers to other useful sources of advice. It has 12,000 members.

Confederation of British Industry (CBI), Centre Point, 103 New Oxford Street, London WC1A 1DU (Tel: 0171 379 7400). The Council carries out research and publishes papers concerning the needs of business in general. Through this work they set out to influence government policy towards small business and government-sponsored activity in this field.

The Federation of Self-Employed and Small Businesses Ltd, 32 Orchard Road, Lytham St Annes, Lancashire FY8 1NY (Tel: 01253 720911; Fax: 01253 714651). The Federation is a campaigning pressure group in business to promote and protect the interests of all who are either self-employed or who own or are directors of small businesses. Formed in 1974, it now has some 60,000 members in 222 branches throughout the UK. The Federation has the funds to take major test cases of importance to small business through the expensive legal process leading to the House of Lords (or European Court of Human Rights). They have been particularly effective in taxation and VAT matters. Among other benefits, members are covered by a legal expenses compensation cover scheme. The cover includes:

■ VAT tribunal representation and costs up to £50,000 per case to appeal in VAT disputes

■ Defence of health and safety prosecutions, covering costs of prosecution under the Health and Safety at Work Act, 1974

■ In-depth investigation cover to meet accountants' fees in helping to deal with Inland Revenue investigation

■ Industrial Tribunal Compensation Awards to meet unfair dismissal awards. (This is supported by a telephone legal advice service)

Full annual membership costs £80 for sole traders and up to £520 to those employing over 100.

The Forum of Private Business Ltd, Ruskin Chambers, Drury Lane, Knutsford, Cheshire WA16 6HA (Tel: 01565 4467; Fax: 01565 650059). This is a non-profit-making organization with the objectives of promoting and preserving a system of free competitive enterprise in the UK, and also of giving private people a greater voice in the legislations that affect their business. The Forum researches and distributes a Referendum nine times a year, keeping members informed and asking their views on a number of topical and important business issues. It makes Government aware of these views both directly and by various public relations activities. The Forum also plays a role by initiating training programmes in schools and colleges to show the importance of free enterprise in our society. The Forum has 20,500 members.

The Home Office Club (HOC). The HOC is for people who want to concentrate on doing what they're best at, promoting and managing their own business. It exists to provide help and commercial advantage for all those working from home, as well as the opportunity to join forthcoming networking forums. A team of professional advisers is on hand to help members swiftly resolve most business problems over the phone. For the price of a phone call, you can get immediate assistance on a broad range of important everyday issues.

- **PC Online:** offers user-friendly support for most hardware and software, from technicians with at least three years' experience in handling IBM or other PC helplines.
- **LegalCall:** where calls are answered by a team of lawyers and trained advisers who can help with contracts, consumer legislation, company formation, insurance and so on.
- **DebtCall:** experts will advise you on handling creditors, financial planning, negotiating payment terms etc.
- **HomeCall:** is there to assist in the event of a domestic emergency by sourcing reliable, cost-checked and approved repair solutions for the home or 'home office'.
- **Discount Intelligence:** a sophisticated new database, updated daily by experienced purchasing managers, will give you well-researched and independent advice on where to buy computer hardware etc, at the best price.
- VAT and Tax advice is also available to registered members during office hours.

HOC has negotiated special and exclusive rates for members on many essential business products and services. The club has arranged these preferential terms with companies such as IBM, DHL, CityLink, BDO Binder Hamlyn, Office World, Dun & Bradstreet and Telecom Security among others.

The annual subscription charge for membership of the HOC is £59. To find out more, call 0502 511922, or fax 0502 511923, or write to The Home Office Club, Freepost, Lowestoft NR32 3BR.

The Institute of Directors, 116 Pall Mall, London SW1Y 5ED (Tel: 0171 839 1233). The Institute represents the interests both of the directors of large companies and owner-directors of smaller ones. In particular, it has a service for putting those looking for funds or other resources in touch with those with funds to invest.

The Institute of Small Business Affairs, PO Box 152, Leeds LS3 1TL (Tel: 0113 2832600; Fax: 0113 2833227). This is the leading forum for bringing together researchers, trainers, advisers and policy-makers. The Institute provides a focal point in the UK for interested parties involved with small businesses to meet and facilitate ideas and, most importantly, to create change.

Ismaili Business Information Centre (IBIC), 1 Cromwell Gardens, London SW7 2SL (Tel: 0171 581 2071; Fax: 0171 589 3246). This was founded in 1976 as a non-profit-making organization to aid the thousands of Ismaili Asians expelled from Uganda by Idi Amin. Since then the 10,000-strong UK Ismaili community, with IBIC's assistance, have formed 650 enterprises including stores, hotels, travel agencies and software houses, initially creating more than 2,000 jobs. IBIC's most important contribution, apart from counselling and advice, has been the introduction of a loan guarantee programme run in conjunction with Lloyds Bank, said to be a forerunner of the Government's Loan Guarantee Scheme.

National Forum of Small Business Clubs, PO Box 21, Hyde, Cheshire SK14 1HA (Tel: 0161 268 0085). Contact: Richard Nash. The Forum maintains liaison with about 120 business clubs across the country, and can put you in contact with your nearest one.

The Small Business Bureau, Curzon House, Church Road, Windlesham, Surrey GU20 6BH (Tel: 01276 452010; Fax: 01276 451607). Formed in 1976, the Bureau aims to serve the needs of the small business community. Membership costs about £60 per annum and gives you access to its advisory service and a copy of its monthly newspaper *Small Business* which has a circulation of 22,000. It also represents the small business point of view to Government, organizes trade delegations and provides European opportunities through its involvement with EMSU (the European Medium and Small Business Union).

Stoy Centre for Family Business, 8 Baker Street, London W1M 1DA (Tel: 0171 486 5888; Fax: 0171 487 3686). The Stoy Centre for Family Business is an organization dedicated to protecting and enhancing the interests of its members. The Centre has evolved out of the interest and expertise of Stoy Hayward. Because family businesses can face more complex issues than other companies, the Centre's activities are directed to these special needs, including:

- succession planning
- personal and corporate taxation
- training for the next generation

- retirement planning and finance
- developing a family constitution
- communications.

Other services to members include:
- invitations to VIP lunches with leading politicians or opinion-formers
- a quarterly newsletter targeted at family businesses giving you information on all the latest developments.

The annual fee is £120 + VAT.

Trade Associations, to be found through the Directory of British Associations, available in the reference section of your local library. Most business fields have a trade association, such as the Brewers' Society, the Federation of Fish Friers, or the Booksellers' Association. They are a useful source of help and advice to potential new entrants to their trade. This directory lists all such associations.

Women's business associations and sources of information One in four of the self-employed in the UK are women, and the numbers are growing. Over the past ten years over 350,000 more women have started up a business. Apart from all the business associations that are open to all entrepreneurs, those (and the publications) that follow are aimed specifically at women.

British Association of Women Entrepreneurs, 8 Eyre Court, London NW8 9TT (Tel: 0171 722 0192). A network support and information group of women running their own business. Affiliated to the World Association of Women Entrepreneurs.

Sandwell Women's Enterprise Development Agency (SWEDA), Unit Buildings, 54 Bratt Street, West Bromwich, West Midlands B70 8RD (Tel: 0121 525 2558). SWEDA provides business advice, training and support services for women wishing to become self-employed and those already in business. The Agency provides one-stop business support, counselling, information and training for women, and co-ordinates local women's business networks. Childcare facilities and a crèche are provided free of charge. SWEDA conducts outreach work, targeting black and Asian women and women on a low income for whom self-employment is a feasible option.

The Sandwell Women's Business Club meets on the last Thursday in the month at SWEDA's premises. It provides an informal setting for women to meet, exchange views and ideas and keep up-to-date with business matters.

Women into Business, c/o Small Business Bureau. Launched in October 1986 as a self-help and lobbying network with the following aims:
- To give successful businesswomen a higher national profile and greater visibility so as to publicize and acknowledge their achievements and con-

tributions to the economy.

■ To set up a counselling service by businesswomen for businesswomen whereby senior successful entrepreneurs who are aware of and sympathetic to the unique problems facing businesswomen will counsel and assist smaller businesswomen as well as potential entrepreneurs.

■ To ensure that Government policies encourage women to set up in business. Also that they recognize the significant contribution that they make to the small-business sector.

It has a bi-monthly newsletter, runs a counselling service and organizes teach-ins and seminars.

Women Returners' Network, Euston House, 81–103 Euston Road, London NW1 2ET (Tel: 0171 388 3111; Fax: 0171 387 7324). Provides a network, training and advice to women planning to return to work.

United Kingdom Federation of Business and Professional Women, 23 Ansdell Street, London W8 5BN (Tel: 0171 938 1729; Fax: 0171 938 2037). Founded in 1938, the Association has 6,000 members. It is a networking organization which encourages women to maximize their potential through confidence-building and training.

Publications
Business Matters for Women, by Joyce O'Connor and Helen Ruddle, published by Attic Press 1990, price £4.95.
Springboard: Women's Development Workbook, by Liz Willis and Jenny Daisley, published by the Hawthorn Press 1992, price £19.20.

3 | *Business opportunities*

Every business begins with an idea. It may be an entirely new product or service. It might be a new way of marketing existing products. The entrepreneur might offer a product or service in an area where it was previously unavailable, or else might find a way of being better, cheaper or faster than the competition.

Good business ideas often come from personal experience. Anita Roddick, founder of the Body Shop, used to travel widely and noticed that in developing countries people used natural beauty preparations, like cocoa butter to protect the skin. Back in Sussex, she tried to buy natural oils and creams and found that they could only be bought in huge quantities. She did some research and found that many other people would be interested in buying natural, cruelty-free products if they were available at a good price. So she began investigating possible suppliers. She was beginning to realize the potential of her idea.

For Anita Roddick, the research not only supported her original idea, but helped it develop. Initial research is crucial if a business is to succeed. Research the market, survey the competition, take a half-day stand at an exhibition or a street market. Above all, talk to people.

You need to see evidence that there's a real chance for this product or service. A real market, real customers, something genuinely different about it.

So how do you come up with a genuinely different business idea? You may have a blinding flash of inspiration. Or you may have to go looking for ideas: there are many out there, waiting to be recognized. Here are some of the ways people find them.

A gap in the market

Speak Easy Tele-language is a company which specializes in teaching modern European languages over the phone. It is run by 29-year-old Karine Hetherington, who got the idea for it while she was teaching English in Paris.

'I noticed that a lot of the language schools gave lessons over the telephone. It seemed like such a simple but effective idea. Clients could learn on a one-to-one basis, at a time convenient to them, and also without having to travel to lessons. People are also a lot less self-conscious when there's a telephone between themselves and the teacher.'

When she came back to Britain, she was amazed to find the same technique wasn't used here, and three and a half years on, her own business is booming. The company employs more than 20 language teachers and is looking to increase that number. 'The demand has been phenomenal, far greater than I ever anticipated,' she says. 'It's been extremely hard work and pretty nerve-racking at times, but definitely worth it.'

case

David Sinclair, 24, runs a fast-food bagel company. David's idea was sparked during an overseas trip: 'In 1988 I was backpacking my way round America on Greyhound buses,' he says. 'At one station in Vermont I saw a huge queue at what turned out to be a bagel stand. I'd hardly ever heard of bagels even though they were sold all over the States.'

When he returned home he discovered that bagels were only sold as fast food in a handful of outlets: 'They were very much a Jewish secret.'

He took advice from the Graduate Enterprise Programme run by the Cranfield School of Management, and now eight bagel shops exist and more are due to open. 'I can see a time when there's a shop selling bagels in every high street,' says David Sinclair.

case

Roger Freebody, managing director of Trees Unlimited, took the traditional approach to artificial Christmas trees and turned it on its head. His central idea was to escape from old-fashioned manufacturing-led tradition and to innovate and try new marketing approaches, such as offering a choice of colours. While Porth Textiles, Britain's then largest manufacturer of decorations, garlands and plastic trees, was collapsing with debts of £8 million, Freebody and his colleagues launched Trees Unlimited on the back of a whole new range of coloured trees from brown to pink. Their success is proof that Christmas trees do not have to be green.

case

For Tim Waterstone the basic concept of his bookshop chain, Waterstone's, came from wandering around Manhattan bookshops on his frequent solo trips to the United States. They were brilliant places: lively and consumer-led with huge stocks, accessible staff and long opening hours. He felt there was a gap in the market for a similar bookshop in Britain, but at the time did nothing about it. Sometimes, even when you have recognized a new way to get into an old business, there is not sufficient impetus to get going.

But once Tim Waterstone was made redundant, a trip to the dole office acted as a catalyst. It was the most horrific experience of his life. Not waiting for his turn, he rushed out and sat in his car. Instead of trying to get a new job, he formulated the Waterstone's concept. High street banks turned him down. He then went to a finance house and struck lucky. He pledged his house and committed £6,000 savings and £10,000 borrowed from his father-in-law, raising the rest through the Government's Loan Guarantee Scheme.

Three months later, the first Waterstone's opened. Based on a simple store plan an art student sketched out for £25, Waterstone filled the shop with the type of books that appeal to book lovers, not best-seller buyers. Late hours, Sunday trading (where possible) and bonus schemes for the staff led to dazzling sales. Within eight years, Waterstone's had some 40 shops employing 500 people with a turnover of £35 million plus. He sold the business out to WH Smith for nearly £60 million and was invited to stay on and run it – less than a decade after his dole queue experience.

Inventions

Inventions can be categorized as completely new ways of doing things. But a successful invention does not come out of thin air. It answers a need in the market and must be patented and properly marketed to earn the inventor large rewards. For example, the Black and Decker 'Workmate' has been extremely successful. It is an innovative and practical portable workbench which came on the market at the same time as DIY was gaining popularity in the UK, and, as a patented design, it has brought its inventor a substantial sum.

Sadly, most inventors are not so successful. In fact fewer than 1% of all patents filed return anything to their inventors.

If you do have a revolutionary idea for a new product, you are likely to need all the help you can get to bring it to market. Inventors often have difficulty in communicating their ideas to others. These ideas are often a long way from being a recognizable product at the time when most help (financial or otherwise) is needed.

case study

When Mark Sanders, a young graduate, put his proposal for Strida, a revolutionary folding bicycle, up to venture capitalists for financial support, the only projections he could include with any degree of certainty were costs.

The business proposal for which he sought backing was to take his brain-child from the drawing board to a properly costed production prototype. For this he needed about two years' living expenses, the use of a workshop and a modest amount of materials.

Sanders's business plan detailed how he would develop the product over this period and, as a result, the concept was backed by James Marshall, one-time manager of golfer Greg Norman. Marshall put together the manufacturing and marketing elements of the business plan, and by Christmas of the second year the Strida was in full-scale production and on sale through many stores such as Harrods, Next Essentials, John Lewis, House of Fraser and Kelvin Hughes.

Help for inventors

Before deciding to go ahead with a business idea based on an invention, you should seek as much help and advice as possible. See Sections 4 and 7 for help and advice for Innovation and Technology.

Using other people's ideas

You may not have a business idea of your own, but nevertheless feel strongly that you would like to work for yourself. There is nothing unusual about this phenomenon. Sometimes an event such as redundancy (as with Tim Waterstone), early retirement or a financial windfall may prompt you into searching for a business idea. Business ideas themselves very often come from the knowledge and experience gained in previous jobs, but then take time to come into focus. Often you will need a good flow of ideas before one arrives that appeals to you and that appears viable.

You can trawl for ideas and opportunities by reading magazines such as *Business Opportunity Digest*, which, as the name suggests, presents the bones of a number of ideas each month. Or you can read papers and periodicals which advertise other people's opportunities. The *Sunday Times*, *The Times* on Fridays, the *Financial Times* on Tuesdays, the *Daily Telegraph* on Mondays and the *Guardian* all have sections on opportunities and ideas for small business.

When answering advertisements for other people's business ideas, do take precautions to ensure you are not simply about to become a victim of someone else's fraudulent venture.

The Advertising Standards Authority warns that not all 'Get rich quick' offers are genuine. These advertisements have multiplied in the recession and are luring otherwise sophisticated people into bogus mail order schemes.

The ASA believes that 'fooling all of the people all of the time' is entirely possible when the product or service is interesting or persuasive enough.

Recent complaints include a mailshot saying: 'No more telephone bills for you – ever'. For £7.50, GP Services of Huntingdon, Cambs, offered to disclose details of a technique which had been 'tried, tested and proven', which required no equipment or capital and which was 'currently being used throughout the UK'. The method was just to contact British Telecom's customer services department and ask to be disconnected.

Upholding complaints against the firm, the authority ruled that it 'exploited consumers' credulity'.

The authority also says that advertisements offering easy ways to earn cash are 'gaining in audacity' as the recession deepens. One offered guaranteed annual earnings of £35,000 to people able to sell 45 titles a week from home, but a complainant who sent £149 for more information was unable to make any money.

Another scheme included testimonials to demonstrate its claim of part-time earnings of £5,000 a month from home. The testimonials were challenged and the mailshot was amended to read that monthly earnings could amount to '£1,000s'.

This chapter has four sections: Finding a Business Idea, Joining a Co-operative, Franchising and finally Is the Business Right for You?

■ FINDING A BUSINESS IDEA

If you know what kind of business you want and you plan either to start from scratch or, if you are already in business, to grow from your existing base, then these ideas and opportunities may not be for you. There are, however, a very large number of people who simply know that they would like to work for themselves – quite what at they are not sure.

There is nothing unusual about this phenomenon – sometimes an event such as redundancy, early retirement or a financial windfall may prompt you into searching for a business opportunity, or perhaps into extending the scope of an existing business idea. Business ideas themselves very often come from the knowledge and experience gained in previous jobs, but they take time to germinate. More usually people only really start to think seriously (and usefully) about an idea when it becomes an opportunity.

Although you may not know exactly what you want to do, you will have certain resources and skills. Contacting people with complementary 'features' is one way of getting into business, or expanding an existing business.

There are a number of organizations and publications that put people in touch with business opportunities and new products.

Sources of further information

European Business Centre Network, Rue d'Arlon 80, 1040 Brussels, Belgium (Tel: 00 322 2959421; Fax: 00 322 2962572). This centre was set up in 1972 to assist small and medium-sized firms to contact and co-operate with companies with similar interests in the EEC. The centre was established on an experimental basis for a period of three years, but proved sufficiently popular to become a permanent service providing information to companies on economic, legal, tax and financial aspects of cross-frontier co-operation and integration. In addition, the centre acts as a 'marriage bureau' for small and medium-sized firms, putting potential partners in touch with one another and assisting in preliminary discussions.

Any firm seeking the centre's help is asked to provide certain information about itself, and to define exactly what type of partner or what type of co-operation it wants. All the information supplied, and any queries received, are treated as strictly confidential, and no names are revealed without the agreement of all parties. The centre will search its files for a suitable partner and, if the application cannot be matched, will, if the firm agrees, circulate a summary of its requirements, with no names mentioned, to its 'correspondents' in all EC countries.

The Business Exchange, 21 John Adam Street, London WC2N 6JG (Tel: 0171 930 8965; Fax: 0171 930 8437). Set up by Grant Thornton and several other leading accountants, this is a market for buying and selling quality family-owned businesses in the price range £800,000 to £15 million. Data is fed in by chartered accountants, solicitors, actuaries and banks throughout the country.

Business Opportunity Profiles (BOPs) are two-sided factsheets covering almost 300 popular business ideas, ranging from abattoirs and breweries to worm-farming, taking in furniture-making, greetings cards and sandwich shops on the way.

Each factsheet gives a market overview, some data on customers, competitors, promotional methods, start-up costs, qualifications and training, legal issues, further reading and some useful addresses. The whole 300 come for £190; however, your local library or Enterprise Agency may hold them, and, as a subscriber, they can give permission for a copy to be made. Contact Project North East (Tel: 0191 261 7856).

Christie & Co, 2/6 York Street, London W1A 1BP (Tel: 0171 486 4231; Fax: 0171 935 4032). Through its 20 regional offices, Christie's claims to be the country's leading agent for buying and selling pubs, hotels, nursing homes and newsagents. The company also provides commercial mortgages, insurance, business valuations and a stock-taking service through a subsidiary company.

LINC (Local Investment Networking Company) is a nationwide business introduction service, run by seven enterprise agencies which help small businesses find capital and management help, and for people who want to invest and sometimes work in those firms. The service has been run on a local basis around the country for as long as six years but has now been launched nationwide. LINC offers investors a much wider choice of business opportunities and provides entrepreneurs with more potential sources of finance.

A bulletin is published monthly with details of investment opportunities and companies for sale from all the participating LINC agencies. In some cases it is also possible to match companies and individuals where it is appropriate.

The Investors' Club is for people who wish to invest and sometimes work in small firms. Membership of the club costs £50 per annum; this includes annual subscription to the bulletin and inclusion on the investor database, and allows attendance at investors' meetings for a small charge (subject to availability of seats). Investors' meetings enable those seeking finance to present their plans and ideas to investors giving a much clearer indication of the business and how it operates. Details of future investors' meetings and locations can be found at the back of the bulletin. To register, simply complete the form at the end of the bulletin and return it to the address indicated together with a cheque for the appropriate amount.

Those seeking finance using LINC need to produce a business plan (sample plans available) indicating clearly the amount of finance required. Firms should be prepared to offer an equity share in return for the investment received though in some cases a mixture of equity and loan finance may be possible.

Entrepreneurs who need assistance in completing a business plan should consult their nearest LINC office or local enterprise agency. A modest one-off registration fee is payable. To contact your nearest LINC see Section 6.

The Manufacturers' Agents Association (MAA), Somers House, 1 Somers

Road, Reigate RH2 9DU (Tel: 01737 241025; Fax: 01737 224537) can advise you on becoming an agent in almost any trade. Membership costs £63.25 (£34.50 subscription, £28.75 entrance fee). If you are choosing this route to self-employment take on more than one agency. And make sure you have a written agreement, preferably using the standard MAA Agreement Form which costs £3.45.

Singer & Friedlander Ltd, 21 New Street, Bishopsgate, London EC2M 4HR (Tel: 0171 623 3000; Fax: 0171 623 2122) operates a company register for those who want to buy a company, sell one or merge with suitable partners. The register is confidential. Its fees, on a graduated scale, are payable only on completion of a satisfactory transaction.

Tourism: the National Tourist Board provides a service advising potential investors and operators of new business opportunities. The English Tourist Board's annual reports usually list several hundred possible projects (see Section 2 for addresses).

Publications
101 Great Money Making Ideas by Mark Hempshell, published by Northcote House in 1989; price £5.99. Divided into sections like creative and artistic, practical, and desk businesses. Each idea has project facts, pros, cons, how to operate, how much you can earn.

101 Ways to start a Business by Christine Ingham, published by Kogan Page in 1992; price £8.99. Describes a range of full-time and part-time business ideas, many of which can be run from home. Each idea describes whom it would appeal to, pros, cons and possibilities for expansion.

A New Career After Forty: a practical guide to mid-life opportunities by John Bird, published by Northcote House in 1993; price £9.99. Takes the fear out of redundancy and gives encouragement to all those who should have left conventional work to start their own thing years ago. It draws on actual experiences and covers a wide range of career options for the over-forties.

Acquisitions Monthly. This magazine (Tel: 01892 515454) publishes a new three-monthly index prepared by accountancy firm Stoy Hayward, which monitors prices paid for private companies. This will enable owners of private companies to follow trends in unquoted company acquisitions and help them to assess a fair price for their own businesses. Based on completed acquisitions, it will track the ratio between the purchase price of private companies sold during a three-month period and their historical earnings.

Business Opportunities Digest, 28 Charles Square, London N1 6HT. A monthly subscription magazine, price about £39.50 for 12 issues. Introduces and explains business ideas and how to make them work for you.

The Business Search and Insolvency Supplement published by Venture Capital Report Ltd, Boston Road, Henley-on-Thames RG9 1DY. Subscription £40 p.a. (banker's order) or £45 p.a. (cheque). A fortnightly supplement which contains details of businesses in receivership, liquidation and administration and a list of auctions. All entries in these categories are placed free of charge. Businesses may advertise in For Sale/Wanted section but are charged.

Business Start-ups for Professional Managers by Pat Richardson and Laurence Clarke, published by Kogan Page in 1993; price £9.99.

Daily Telegraph Business Network published on Mondays: hundreds of business opportunities and companies for sale, required, strategic alliances sought, funds available or required. Summaries are in the paper; full details on up to three opportunities cost £15 + VAT.

Entrepreneur published by American Entrepreneurs Association, 2392 Morse Avenue, Irvin, CA 92714, USA. Subscription $37.97 p.a. (to be paid in US funds and drawn on US banks). This monthly publication gives a very invigorating view of American business opportunities, by the hundred.

The Entrepreneur's Guide to Buying and Selling a Business by Luke Johnson, published by Butterworth-Heinemann in 1994; price £12.95. This hands-on guide to acquiring or selling a business cuts through the mystique associated with mergers and acquisitions, focusing on the deal-making process, examining such areas as how to instruct lawyers preparing contracts and finding private venture capitalists. Contents: Why do deals?; Who does deals?; Finding the deal; Investigating the deal; Negotiating the deal; Financing the deal; Making the deal legal; Making the deal work; Correcting bad deals; Making money from the deal.

£500 a Week from Car Boot Sales by Roger Morgan, published by Imperia Books in 1993; price £9.99 (available direct: Tel: 0171 372 3800). Describes how to succeed with very little capital. Plenty of case studies, how to get stock for next to nothing, win the best pitches, and how to turn browsers into buyers. Plus it discloses the secrets of how to tell real antiques from junk!

Going Freelance: a guide to self-employment with minimum capital by Godfrey Golzen, published by Kogan Page in 1993; price £8.99. The first part looks at essentials from cutting tax liability, legal obligations and how to get a clear brief and so on. Second part describes 40 opportunities for freelance professionals and lists basic skills, aptitudes and equipment required, the market, how to find work, fees and more.

Great Ideas for Making Money by Niki Chesworth, published by Kogan Page/Daily Express in 1994; price £6.99.

Home Run, 79 Black Lion Lane, London W6 9BG (Tel: 0181 741 2440; Fax: 0181

846 9244). This is a magazine aimed at helping people who have been made redundant, want to get out of the rat race or who have recently retired but want to stay active by starting up in business for themselves. The newsletter comes out ten times a year; price £54 per annum.

Homing In, from Chris Oliver, 56 London Road, Milborne Port, Sherborne, Dorset DT9 5DW. A newsletter for people working from home containing business ideas, examples and explanations.

How to Buy a Business by Peter Farrell, published by Kogan Page in 1988; price £12.95 hb, £5.95 pb. This guide for the small businessman examines the advantages and risks of buying a business. Contents: 1 Why buy? 2 Why is it for sale? 3 What are you buying? 4 Judging the track record. 5 Evaluating the assets. 6 What is the right price? Can you afford it? 7 Paying for it.

How to Run a Part-time Business by Barry Hawkins, published by Piatkus in 1993; price £8.99. Deals with most of the important issues and gives newcomers a good feel for what to expect as they become established. The author packs a lot in, from choosing a business and generating ideas, to contract and consumer law.

How to Start a Business from Home by Graham Jones, published by How To Books in 1991; price £7.99. Choose the right business for you with this guide to home-based opportunities. Also covers business plans, pricing, attracting and keeping customers etc.

How to Work from Home by Ian Phillipson, published by How To Books in 1992; price £7.99. Enjoyable and informative: the basics of working from home – create and design your space, employ staff and set the ground rules, maintain motivation and handle stress, and more.

Making a Living from a Craft by Fiona McCleary, published by Cumbria College of Art and Design in 1990; price £14.95.

Making Money from Your Garden by Barty Phillips, published by Piatkus in 1992; price £7.99. Covers every angle of making money from gardening, from selling crops as food or decoration, to selling your skills as a gardener, designer or flower arranger; plus mail order services and plants for offices.

Multi-level Marketing by Peter Clothier, published by Kogan Page in 1993; price £9.99. Multi-level marketing offers great potential wealth, but it has a mixed reputation and is not suitable for everybody. Learn how it works, where to get advice, the law and good practice.

Profit Through the Post by Alison Cork, published by Piatkus in 1994; price £15.00. A must for anyone wanting to set up and run a successful mail order business. Based on the author's own considerable success, it covers all the issues in a practical and realistic way.

Running Your Own Mail Order Business by Malcolm Breckman, published by Kogan Page in 1992; price £9.99. An invaluable and practical guide for those with limited budgets wanting to start and run a mail order business.

The Small Business Resource Bank: Volume 1 – 'Ideas to start-up', Volume 2 – 'Start up to growth', by Paul Moran et al, published by National Extension College in 1990; price £90 per volume or £170 for both.

Starting Up Your Own Business, 101 ways to do it on £500 or less by Ross McBennet, published by Mercury Business Paperbacks in 1990; price £5.99.

Think Up a Business by Barrie Hawkins and Grant Badge, published by Rosters in 1990; price £7.95. This shows how to come up with ideas for a new business suited to your personal talents and requirements.

Working for Yourself Without Capital by B H Elvy, published by Macmillan in 1994; price £6.99.

Venture Capital Report, Boston Road, Henley-on-Thames RG9 1DY (Tel: 01491 579999). This publication gives details of entrepreneurs and their business ventures, inviting people with money to invest, often on a partnership basis. Price £200 p.a.

Working for Yourself by Godfrey Golzen, published by Kogan Page; price £10.00. This is the very successful *Daily Telegraph* book, with its 16th edition published July 1994. Apart from useful sections on the general mechanics of starting a business, tax, raising money, etc, there is a Directory of Opportunities. In this section you are given an insight into the pros and cons of some 60 different types of business, together with addresses and contact points to follow up those of interest to you. (This is a good starting point in the opportunity search.)

Newspapers

One of the best ways to keep abreast of current business opportunities is to read a selection of national and local papers. Start off with as wide a range as you can afford (or visit your library) to get the flavour of each. Then once you have made a selection, keep searching. Many articles give details of useful follow-up addresses.

The major papers with Business Opportunities sections include:
Sunday Times – Small Business Focus.
London *Evening Standard* (Mondays) – Business Options.
Daily Telegraph (Mondays) – Business Monitor and Business Network.
The Times (Tuesdays) – Your Own Business and Business Opportunities.
Financial Times (Tuesdays) – Growing Business Opportunities;
(Saturdays) – Business Start-ups.

■ JOINING A CO-OPERATIVE

Although the most commonly known co-operatives are the high street shops and supermarkets, there is another, lesser-known variety, the workers' co-operatives – where workers share control and decision-making equally, and not in relation to their financial stake. They split off from the more successful retail movement, reached a peak of 1,000 or so outlets at the turn of the century, then declined (almost to the point of extinction).

In 1978, the Industrial Common Ownership Act, 1976, gave workers' co-operatives a much needed shot in the arm. Various estimates put the number of workers' co-operatives operating in the UK in 1988 at around 1,400, employing about 30,000 people. About a fifth of all co-operatives are in the Greater London area. Certainly, if the growth of supporting organizations and agencies is anything to go by, this seems a conservative estimate.

In order to meet the legal requirements a co-operative must conform to the following rules:

- **Conduct of business** The members must benefit primarily from their participation in the business, i.e. as workers, not merely as investors.
- **Control** Each member has equal control through the principle of 'one person one vote'. Control is not related to the size of financial stake in the business.
- **Interest repayments** A co-operative cannot pay an unlimited return on loan or share capital. Even in good years, interest payments will be limited in some specified way.
- **Surplus** This may be wholly retained in the business or distributed in part to the members in proportion to their involvement, e.g. according to hours worked.
- **Membership** This must be open to anybody satisfying the qualifications of membership.

The main attraction of workers' co-operatives is the greater level of involvement in control and decision-making in the workplace. Since workers' co-operatives tend to remain small scale it is this, rather than financial benefits, that attract people though there are a growing number of larger and expanding co-operative enterprises. The sector itself is increasingly moving towards a wider definition of common ownership that encompasses any form of democratic employee-controlled enterprise, and there is some evidence that the growth of interest in ethical investment is resulting in improved access to finance for such structures.

The Industrial Common Ownership Movement (ICOM), Vassalli House, 20 Central Road, Leeds LS1 6DE (Tel: 0113 2461738/7 Fax: 0113 2440002). ICOM was formed in 1971 to promote the principles and practice of co-operative working within enterprises, particularly in the form of common ownership. Today it serves as a national federation and lobby group for workers' co-operatives and their support agencies.

In 1992 ICOM widened its remit to embrace all democratic employee-controlled enterprises. This move was a recognition of the growing interest in workplace democracy and an acknowledgement that democratic structures other than co-operatives may be more relevant. ICOM's purpose is to promote and support democratic employee control of enterprises of every kind and to represent those who practise it. It espouses and advocates the principles of co-operation, common ownership, workplace democracy, equal opportunity and social justice.

ICOM provides a range of services to workers' co-operatives, the voluntary sector, charities, housing co-operatives and community business projects. Services provided by ICOM as part of the basic membership subscription include:

- an advice service which offers specialist information on legal issues affecting workers' co-operatives; sources of finance and related matters
- information news-sheets and a quarterly journal providing both news and a forum to debate issues of interest to the co-operative movement.

ICOM members also have access to a further range of services, on a fee-paying basis, including extensive legal and registration services. As a Programme Manager for the European Social Fund's training money, ICOM oversees and co-ordinates applications from a variety of co-operatives and co-operative support agencies.

ICOM is financially independent and receives its income from members' subscriptions and the sale of services. It is active within a number of national networks, and was a founder member of CECOP, the European federation of workers' co-operatives. ICOM is democratically controlled by its members and is managed by a General Council elected each year at the Annual General Meeting. This Council represents the interests of members to government departments, the EC, local authorities, trade unions and the rest of the co-operative movement.

ICOM also provides a comprehensive range of books on subjects relating to democracy in the workplace and its practical implementation;. details of publications are available on request (a selection of titles is listed on page 120).

Co-operative support organizations

England
Barnsley: Barnsley Enterprise Centre, 1 Pontefract Road, Barnsley, South Yorkshire S71 1AJ (Tel: 01226 733291).
Basildon: Basildon CDA, c/o Basildon Unemployed Workers Centre, 1 The Gore, Basildon SS14 2EA (Tel: 01268 289420; Fax: 01268 289473).
Birmingham: Birmingham CDA, Co-operative Enterprise Centre,

111–119 Bishop Street, Birmingham B5 6JL (Tel: 0121 622 6973; Fax: 0121 622 1554).
– Birmingham Employment Initiatives Unit, 138 Digbeth, Birmingham B5 6DR (Tel: 0121 643 4343).
– Capital Strategies Ltd, 23 Hamstead Road, Handsworth, Birmingham B19 1BX (Tel: 0121 515 1956).
– Co-Enterprise Birmingham, 138 Digbeth, Birmingham B5 6DR

(Tel: 0121 643 4343).
– Radical Routes Ltd, 24 South Road, Hockley, Birmingham B18 5NB (Tel: 0121 551 1679).
Black Country: Black Country CDA (Central Office), West Midlands House, Gypsy Lane, Willenhall WV13 2HA (Tel: 0121 609 7100; Fax: 0121 609 7103).
– Black Country CDA (Dudley Office), 89 High Street, Dudley DY1 1QP (Tel: 01384 239664; Fax: 01384 458825).
– Black Country CDA (Sandwell Office), Sandwell Business Advice Centre, Victoria Street, West Bromwich B70 8ET (Tel: 0121 525 2204; Fax: 0121 525 2206).
Blackburn: Bootstrap (Blackburn) Ltd, 35 Railway Road, Blackburn BB1 1EZ (Tel: 01254 680367; Fax: 01254 680672).
Bolton: Bolton Neighbourhood Economic Development Agency, Bolton Enterprise Centre, Washington Street, Bolton, Lancashire BL3 5EY (Tel: 01204 22213).
Bradford: Bradford CDA, Unit 3–4, Theatre Royal Workshops, Snowden Street, Bradford BD1 3DT (Tel: 0113 2461738).
Bristol: Avon CDA, 49 Colston Street, Bristol BS1 5AX (Tel: 0117 9254711; Fax: 0117 9258881).
Cambridge: Cambridge CDA, The Business Advice Centre, 71a Lensfield Road, Cambridge CB2 1EN (Tel: 01223 60977).
– Social Economy Consortium Ltd, 16 Ditton Walk, Cambridge CB8 5QE (Tel: 01223 566116).
Cheshire: Cheshire Community Business Ltd, The Bluecoat Centre, Upper Northgate Street, Chester CH1 4EH

(Tel: 01244 603059).
Cleveland: Cleveland Cooperative Development Agency, 10a Albert Road, Middlesbrough, Cleveland TS1 1QA (Tel: 01642 210224; Fax: 01642 251842).
Coventry: Coventry CDA, Unit 15, The Arches Industrial Estate, Spon End, Coventry CV1 3JQ (Tel: 01203 714078; Fax: 01203 712483).
Derbyshire: Derbyshire Enterprise Board (Economic Development) Ltd, Derbyshire Business Development Centre, Beaufort Street, Derby DE2 6AX (Tel: 01332 384404; Fax: 01332 292852).
Devon: Devon CDA (Exeter Office), 2nd Floor, Eastgate House, High Street, Exeter EX4 3JT (Tel: 01392 410222; Fax: 01392 410222).
– Devon CDA (Plymouth Main Office), 138 North Road East, Plymouth, Devon PL4 6AQ (Tel: 01752 223481).
Dorset: Dorset Co-operative Development Agency, c/o Lytchett Minster Village Stores, 56 Dorchester Road, Lytchett Minster, Poole BH16 6JE (Tel: 01202 622200).
Durham: Durham Co-operative Development Assosiation, New College, Framwellgate Moor, Durham DH1 5ES (Tel: 0191 386 4404; Fax: 0191 386 4404).
East Anglia: East Anglian Co-operative Development Association, Denmar House, River Way, Harlow CM20 2PD (Tel: 01279 451440; Fax: 01279 454108).
East Sussex: Robert Tressell Workshops, Station Yard, Devonshire Road, Hastings, East Sussex TN34 1NF (Tel: 01424 722213).

Essex: Essex CDA, Office 3, Colchester Enterprise Centre, 154 Magdalen Street, Colchester CO1 2JX (Tel: 01206 765608).
Gloucester: Gloucester CDA, c/o Pat Stokes, ComTAW Ltd, 1st Floor, 15 High Street, Lydney, Glos GL15 5DP (Tel: 01594 841964).
Harlow: Harlow CDA, Latton Bush Centre, Southern Way, Harlow, Essex CM18 7BL (Tel: 01279 446446; Fax: 01279 434681).
Hull: Humberside CDA (Hull Office) 1st Floor, Ferensway Chambers, 79 Ferensway, Hull HU2 8LD (Tel: 01482 28160; Fax: 01482 589656).
Kent: Kent Co-operative Support Organization, The Enterprise Agency of East Kent, The Old Town Hall, Market Street, Margate CT9 1EU (Tel: 01843 290205; Fax: 01843 230802).
Kingston: Kingston and Richmond CDA, 58b London Road, Kingston-upon-Thames, Surrey KT2 6QA (Tel: 0181 549 9159).
Kirklees: Kirklees Metropolitan Council Economic Development Unit, Co-operative Development Officer, 5th Floor, Kirklees House, Market Street, Huddersfield HD1 2EY (Tel: 01484 422133 ext 2266).
Lancashire: Lancashire CDA (Central Office), Enterprise House, 17 Ribblesdale Place, Preston, Lancashire PR1 3NA (Tel: 01772 203692/203020; Fax: 01772 204129).
– Lancashire CDA (Lancaster Office), Whitecross Mill, Whitecross, Lancaster LA1 4XH (Tel: 01524 388517).
Leeds: Belle Isle Community Enterprises Ltd, Unit 1, Open Access Workshops, Middleton, Leeds LS10 3NZ (Tel: 0113 2762466).

– Industrial Common Ownership Movement Ltd, Vassalli House, 20 Central Road, Leeds LS1 6DE (Tel: 0113 2461738; Fax: 0113 2440006).
Leicester: Braunstone Employment Project Ltd, 9 Cantrell Road, North Braunstone, Leicester LE3 1SD (Tel: 0116 2892186).
– Leicester and County CDA, 94 New Walk, Leicester LE1 7EA (Tel: 0116 2547837; Fax: 0116 2546608).
Liverpool: CDS Training for Enterprise Ltd, 36 Slater Street, Liverpool L1 4BX (Tel: 0151 708 6213).
London: CAG Consultants, Antonia House, 262 Holloway Road, London N7 6NE (Tel: 0171 607 7017/8; Fax: 0171 704 7840).
– Chisel Ltd, 188a Brockley Road, London SE4 3RN (Tel: 0181 694 1840; Fax: 0181 694 1921).
– CRS London Region Political Committee, 78–102 The Broadway, London E15 1NL (Tel: 0181 534 4201).
– Doddington and Rollo Community Association, The Community Centre, Charlotte Despard Ave, London SW11 5TE (Tel: 0171 720 0335).
– Greenwich Co-operative Development Agency, 22 Bardsley Lane, London SE10 9RF (Tel: 0181 293 9804; Fax: 0181 293 9448).
– Hackney Co-operative Developments Ltd, 16 Dalston Lane, Hackney, London E8 3AZ (Tel: 0171 254 4829).
– Hounslow CDA, c/o Red Lemon, 333 Chiswick High Road, London W4 4HS (Tel: 0181 995 4295; Fax: 0181 995 4295).
– Industrial Common Ownership

Finance, Antonia House, 262 Holloway Road, London N7 6NE (Tel: 0171 700 3711/3757; Fax: 0171 700 0086).
– Islington Business Development Agency, Islington Enterprise Centre, 135 Upper Street, London N1 1QP (Tel: 0171 226 2783; Fax: 0171 354 1518).
– Lambeth CDA, The Co-op Centre, Unit 5, 11 Mowll Street, London SW9 6BG (Tel: 0171 582 0003; Fax: 0171 793 0426).
– London Co-op Training, The Print House, 18 Ashwin Street, London E8 3DL (Tel: 0171 254 7051; Fax: 0171 923 4280).
– London ICOM, 1st Floor, 18 Ashwin Street, Hackney, London E8 3DL (Tel: 0171 249 2837).
– Marketing Resource Centre, Antonia House, 262 Holloway Road, London N7 5NE (Tel: 0171 700 4171).
– Tower Hamlets CDA, 84 White Horse Road, London E1 0ND (Tel: 0171 791 0450).
– Turkish Speaking Co-op Development Project, Unit 1, Holles House, Overton Road, London SW9 7JN (Tel: 0171 733 7148).
– Waltham Forest EDU, 195–197 Wood Street, Walthamstow, London E17 3NU (Tel: 0181 527 5544 ext 4912).
Luton: Bedfordshire CDA, The Business Centre, Kimpton Road, Luton LU2 0LB (Tel: 01582 23456; Fax: 01582 419422).
Manchester: Co-operative Union Ltd, Holyoake House, Hanover Street, Manchester M60 0AS (Tel: 0161 832 4300).
– Manchester Local Action Team, 9th Floor, Town Hall Extension, Manchester M60 2LA (Tel: 0161 234 1513).
Middlesbrough: East Middlesborough

Community Venture, 2nd Floor, Beresford Buildings, The Greenway, Thorntree, Middlesborough TS3 9MB (Tel: 01642 230314).
Milton Keynes: Co-operative Research Unit, Systems Group, Open University, PO Box 136, Walton Hall, Milton Keynes MK7 6BD (Tel: 01908 652102).
Northampton: Industrial Common Ownership Finance, 12–14 Gold Street, Northampton NN1 1RS (Tel: 01604 37563; Fax: 01604 36165).
– Northamptonshire CDA, 36A Milton Street, Northampton NN2 7JF (Tel: 01604 791990; Fax: 01604 791959).
Northumberland: Northumberland County Council, County Hall, Morpeth, Northumberland NE61 2EF (Tel: 01670 533000; Fax: 01670 510476).
Norwich: Norwich City Council, City Planning Department, City Hall, Norwich NR2 1NH (Tel: 01603 622233 ext 2524; Fax: 01603 760006).
Nottinghamshire: Nottinghamshire CDA, Dunkirk Road, Dunkirk, Nottingham NG7 2PH (Tel: 0115 9705700).
Oldham: Co-operative Enterprise North West, c/o Rhodes Bank Chambers, 2 Prince Street, Oldham OL1 1EL (Tel: 0161 832 4300; Fax: 0161 833 9374).
Oxfordshire: Oxfordshire CDA, The Northway Centre, Maltfield Road, Headington, Oxford OX3 9RF (Tel: 01865 741384).
Redditch: Redditch CDA, Town Hall, Alcester Street, Redditch, Worcestershire B98 8AH (Tel: 01527 64252 ext 3375).
Salford: Salford CEDA (Start Up), 9

Broadway, Salford, Manchester M5 2TS (Tel: 0161 872 3838).
Sandwell: Sandwell Metropolitan Borough Council, Economic Development Unit, Sandwell Council House, Oldbury, Warley, West Midlands B69 3DE (Tel: 0121 569 2090)
Sheffield: Sheffield Co-op Development Group Ltd, Aizlewood's Mill, Nursery Street, Sheffield S3 8GG (Tel: 0114 2823100; Fax: 0114 2823150); also Women's Training Network (Tel: 0114 2823172).
Smethwick: Community Enterprise Development and Information Centre (Sandwell) Ltd, Smethwick Enterprise Centre, 128b Oldbury Road, Smethwick, Warley, West Midlands B66 1JE (Tel: 0121 565 0026).
Southampton: Southampton Area CDA, Exmoor House, Methuen Street, Southampton, Hants SO2 0SQ (Tel: 01703 230529; Fax: 01703 235175).
Stockton-on-Tees: Stockton-on-Tees Borough Council, PO Box 34, Municipal Buildings, Church Road, Stockton-on-Tees TS18 1LE (Tel: 01642 670067; Fax: 01642 616315).
Sunderland: Sunderland Common Ownership Enterprise Resource Centre, 44 Mowbray Road, Hendon, Sunderland, Tyne and Wear SR2 8EL (Tel: 0191 565 0476; Fax: 0191 514 3450).
Wakefield: Wakefield Economic Development Dept, Wakefield MDC, PO Box 92, 22 Cheapside, Wakefield WF1 1XS (Tel: 01924 295825).
Wansbeck: Wansbeck District Council ERU, Wansbeck Business Centre, Wansbeck Business Park, Rotary Parkway, Ashington, Northumberland NE63 8QZ (Tel: 01670 856666).

West Midlands: West Midlands Co-operative Finance, Wellington House, 31–34 Waterloo Street, Birmingham B2 5TJ (Tel: 0121 236 8855/3942).

Wales

Cardiff: Wales Co-op Development and Training CT, Llandaff Court, Fairwater Road, Cardiff CF5 2XP (Tel: 01222 554955; Fax: 01222 578586).
– Cardiff and Vale CDA, 127 Bute Street, Cardiff CF1 5LE (Tel: 01222 494411).
Gwynedd: Wales Co-op Development and Training CT, Council Offices, Bron Castell Stryd Fawr, Bangor, Gwynedd LL57 1YU (Tel: 01248 364729).
– Antur Waunfawr Ltd, Bryn Pistyll, Waunfawr, Caernarfon, Gwynedd LL55 4BJ (Tel: 01286 650721).
Merthyr Tydfil: Wales Co-op Development and Training CT, c/o Made Ltd, Merthyr Tydfil Industrial Park, Pentre Bach, Merthyr Tydfil CF48 4DR (Tel: 01433 692233).
Port Talbot: Port Talbot CDA, 2nd Floor Royal Buildings, Talbot Road, Port Talbot, West Glamorgan SA13 1DN (Tel: 01639 895173).
West Glamorgan: West Glamorgan Common Ownership Development Agency, 10 St Helens Road, Swansea, West Glamorgan SA1 4AN (Tel: 01792 653498).

Scotland

Glasgow: Drumchapel Opportunities, 51/53 Dunkenny Square, Glasgow G15 8NB (Tel: 0141 944 4923; Fax: 0141 944 1429).
– Scottish Co-operative Development Company Ltd, Templeton Business Centre, Templeton Street, Bridgeton,

Glasgow G40 1DA
(Tel: 0141 554 3797;
Fax: 0141 554 5163).
Lothian: The National Network of Community Businesses, Society Place, West Calder, West Lothian EH55 8EA (Tel: 01506 871370)
Ross and Cromarty: Ross and Cromarty District Council (Business Information Service), Ferintosh Business Centre, Station Road, Dingwall, Ross-shire IV15 9JE

(Tel: 01349 863737;
Fax: 01349 865126).
Stirling: Community Enterprise Support Unit, Unit 35, Stirling Enterprise Park, Kerse Road, Stirling FK7 7RP (Tel: 01786 50969; Fax: 01786 79611).

Northern Ireland
Northern Ireland CDA, 23/25 Shipquay Street, Derry BT48 6DL (Tel: 01504 371733).

Other useful organizations
Industrial Common Ownership Finance, 4 St Giles Street, Northampton NN1 1AA (Tel: 01604 37563). Formed by ICOM in 1973, ICOF Ltd now operates independently. It provides half the money required by co-operatives in short- to medium-term loans from six months to six years, with a monthly repayment after an initial capital holiday. The minimum sum it will consider is £1,000 and the maximum is £50,000, though usually loans start from £2,500.

Registry of Friendly Societies, 15 Great Marlborough Street, London W1V 2AX (Tel: 0171 437 9992). The register can give information about the legal requirements of forming a co-operative.

Assistant Registrar of Friendly Societies, 58 Frederick Street, Edinburgh EH2 1NB (Tel: 0131 226 3224).

Publications
Co-operative Businesses in the UK: 1993 Directory published by ICOM/OU; price £12.90. Annual activity and contact details of 1,100+ UK worker co-ops from the results of the 1992–93 survey by the Open University's Co-operative Research Unit.

Employee Ownership – Legal and Tax Aspects by John Nelson-Jones and Graeme Nuttall, published by Fourmat Publishing; price £19.90. Examines the law relating to workers' co-ops, employee-controlled companies, employee trusts and employee buy-outs.

Going for Growth by Jim Brown, John Bound and Lydia Baker, published by ICOM; price £5.55. A marketing handbook for co-operatives and other ethical small businesses. The result of a year-long DTI-funded action research project.

How to Start a Worker Co-op published by ICOM Co-Publications; price £1.00. A short A4 illustrated booklet for people thinking of starting their own business as a co-operative.

The Workers' Co-operative Handbook by Peter Cockerton and Anna Whyatt, published by ICOM Co-Publications; price £4.25. The most widely read and comprehensive guide to all aspects of setting up a worker co-operative.

■ FRANCHISING

Franchised sales in the UK exceeded £4.5 billion in 1993. According to the Survey of UK Franchising, sponsored by the National Westminster Bank and the BFA, about 373 business format franchise systems are now on offer in the UK, down from 432 in 1991. However, only a small percentage of those franchisors have got their operations together properly, and so could be viewed as a sound investment proposition for prospective franchisees.

The Survey further revealed that the average number of franchised units per chain is 36, with some 18,100 outlets in all. Over 184,000 people are employed in franchising in the UK.

The factors that fuelled the growth of franchising in the 1980s were equally divided between changes in the economic and in the political climates. The recession of the early 1980s generated more people with large redundancy payments, who elected after losing their jobs to go into business for themselves instead. Franchising seemed to offer a way of combining the independence of self-employment with the security of a proven business formula. In the 1990s many of these features are still at play in the UK economy.

Market factors have helped too. The growth in popularity of fast food as a result of changing lifestyles, for example, has helped to stimulate demand for franchised food outlets. The growing number of women entering work has encouraged demand for dry-cleaning services, home-help agencies and the emergence of US-style convenience stores which meet a need for early and late shopping in neighbourhood areas.

The government has also increasingly recognized the importance of new businesses in job creation and economic growth. This has led to a range of stimulatory measures aimed at the small-business sector in general, but with an inevitable overspill that has benefited the franchise sector.

The banks, accountancy firms and legal practices have also worked in their various way to legitimize franchising and to encourage and advise would-be franchisees.

Business format franchising in the UK is forecast to top £10 billion by 1997, with most sectors experiencing some growth. Ahead in the growth league will be service-type operations and those franchises with a relatively low entry cost.

Franchising is a marketing technique used to improve and expand the distribution of a product or service. The franchisor supplies the product or teaches the service to the franchisee, who in his turn sells it to the public. In return for this, the franchisee pays a fee and a continuing royalty, based usually on turnover. The advantage to the franchisee is a relatively safe and quick way of getting into business for himself, but with the support and advice of an experienced organization close at hand.

The franchisor can expand his distribution with the minimum strain on his own capital and have the services of a highly motivated team of owner–managers. Franchising is not a path to great riches, nor is it for the truly independent spirit, as policy and profits will still come from 'on high'.

Before taking out a franchise it is essential that you consult your legal and financial advisers. You must also ask the franchisor some very searching questions to prove his competence. You will need to know if he has operated a pilot unit in the UK – an essential first step before selling franchises to third parties. Otherwise, how can he really know all the problems, and so put you on the right track? You will need to know what training and support is included in the franchise package, the name given to the start-up kit provided by franchisors to see you successfully launched. This package should extend to support staff over the launch period and give you access to back-up advice. You will need to know how substantial the franchise company is. Ask to see their balance sheet (take it to your accountant if you cannot understand it). Ask for the track record of the directors (including their other directorships).

Organizations

Franchise associations

The British Franchise Association, Thames View, Newtown Road, Henley-on-Thames, Oxfordshire RG9 1HG (Tel: 01491 578049). The British Franchise Association was formed in 1977 by a number of leading British companies engaged in the distribution of goods and services under franchise and licensee agreements. The aims of the BFA include establishing a clear definition of ethical franchising standards to help the public, press, potential investors and government bodies to identify sound business opportunities. All BFA members have to abide by a stringent code of business practice and have to undergo a detailed accreditation procedure before being accepted as members. The BFA acts as the spokesman for the official view on responsible franchising.

The International Franchise Association, 1350 New York Avenue, NW 900 Washington, DC 20005, USA. Founded in 1960, this is a non-profit organization representing 350 franchising companies in the USA and around the world. It is recognized as the spokesman for responsible franchising. It could be particularly useful in providing information on the growing number of 'new' franchises arriving in the UK with claims of US parentage. It serves as a resource centre for both current and prospective franchisors and franchisees, as well as for the government and media.

The IFA has been instrumental in developing legislation that regulates and safeguards franchising from abuse by fraudulent operators. The Association has also testified on behalf of programmes that assist women and minorities to become more involved in business through franchising.

IFA members share a common purpose, which has not changed since the founding of the organization – to promote franchising as a responsible method of doing business. As a condition of membership, all IFA members must subscribe to and uphold IFA's Code of Ethics.

To keep pace with the rapid changes taking place in franchising, IFA provides its members with lobbying and government relations, seeking to safeguard the very practice of franchising at the state, national and international level. Also offered by the IFA are hundreds of educational programmes and seminars throughout the year, extensive marketing and public relations campaigns, franchise shows and educational publications, international trade missions, and special programmes to encourage minority participation in franchising.

The IFA sponsors the International Franchise Expo, the largest gathering of franchise companies in the world, which features over 300 of the best franchise companies as well as a wide variety of educational seminars.

National Franchise Association Coalition, PO Box 366, Fox Lake, Illinois 60020, USA. The coalition was formed in 1975 by franchisees in order to provide a centre for the expression of the franchisees' viewpoints, as distinct from those of the franchisors. No such organization exists in the UK, but the American experiences provide some interesting lessons. There are areas of problems and dispute even between ethical and established franchise organizations and their franchisees.

European national associations

European Franchise Federation, Boulevard des Italiens 9, 75002 Paris, France

Austrian Franchise Association, Parkring 2, A-1010 Wien, Austria

Belgian Franchise Association, Rue St Bernard 60, B-1060 Brussels, Belgium

Danish Franchise Association, Amaliegade 31a, DK-1256 Copenhagen K, Denmark

Dutch Franchise Association, Arubalaan 4, 1213 VG Hilversum, The Netherlands

French Franchise Association, Boulevard des Italiens 9, 75002 Paris, France

German Franchise Association, St Paul-Strasse 9, D-8000 Munich 2, Germany

Irish Franchise Association, 13 Frankfield Terrace, Summerhill South, Cork, Republic of Ireland

Italian Franchise Association, Corso di Porta Nuova 3, 20121 Milan, Italy

Norwegian Franchise Association, Astveitkogen 41, 5084 Tertnes Bergen, Norway

Portuguese Franchise Association, Avenida Duque de Lovle 90, R/C DTO, 1000 Lisbon, Portugal

Spanish Franchise Association, Jose Lazaro Galdiano 4, 28036 Madrid, Spain

Swedish Franchise Association, PB 5512, S-11485 Stockholm, Sweden

Swiss Franchise Association, Haldenstrasse 33-35, CH 6006 Lucerne, Switzerland

Non-European associations

Franchisors Association of Australia, PO Box 94, Wilberforce NSW 2756, Australia

Canadian Franchise Association, 88 University Avenue, Toronto, Ontario, Canada M5J IT6

Israeli Franchise Association, Corex Building, Maskit Street, Herzlia Pituach 46733, Israel

Japanese Franchise Association, Elsa Building 602, 3-13-12 Roppongi, Minato-Ku, Tokyo, Japan

Mexican Franchise Association, Michelet 30, Col Nueva Anzures, 11590 Mexico DF, Mexico

South African Franchise Association, PO Box 18398, Hillbrow 2038, Republic of South Africa

The Franchise Centre. Advice on choosing the right franchise is now available in Manchester, seven days a week (Greenwood Business Centre, Goodiers Drive, Manchester M5 4QH; Tel: 0161 877 7788). The Franchise Centre is a free, independent organization, funded by the Department of Trade and Industry, where businessmen can obtain display materials, brochures and information without being hassled by salesmen.

Education

The following organizations regularly run courses on franchising:

Chartered Institute of Marketing and The British Franchise Association, Moor Hall, Cookham, Maidenhead, Berkshire SL6 9QH (Tel: 016285 24922).
Franchise Development Services Ltd, Castle House, Castle Meadow, Norwich NR2 1PJ (Tel: 01603 620301).
Franchise World, James House, 37 Nottingham Road, London SW17 7EA (Tel: 0181 767 1371).
Patent and trade mark agents
Ladas & Parry, 52–4 High Holborn, London WC1V 6RR (Tel: 0171 242 5566).
Contact: I C Baille.

Franchise consultants
David Acheson Partnership, 101 Gloucester Terrace, Lancaster Gate, London W2 3HB (Tel: 0171 402 4514).
Contact: D Acheson.
Ernst and Young, Rolls House, 7 Rolls Buildings, Fetter Lane, London EC4A 1NH (Tel: 0171 928 2000). Contact: Dr B A Smith.
FMM Consultants International Ltd, 46–8 Thornhill Road, Streetly, Sutton Coldfield, West Midlands, B74 3EH

(Tel: 0121 353 0031). Contact: M Matthews.
FMM Consultants International Ltd, 48 Corstorphine High Street, Edinburgh EH12 7SY (Tel: 0131 334 8040).
Contact: Andrew James.
FMM Consultants International Ltd, 27 Brighton Road, Crawley, West Sussex RH10 3NW (Tel: 01293 535453).
Contact: J Gooderham.
Franchise Development Services Ltd, Castle House, Castle Meadow, Norwich NR2 1PJ (Tel: 01603 620301).
Contact: Roy Seaman.
Hallmark International, 4th Floor, Vandale House, Post Office Road, Bournemouth, Hampshire BH1 1BT (Tel: 01202 751175).
Contact: A Newton.
The Hambleden Group, 28 Mount Sion, Tunbridge Wells, Kent TN1 1TW (Tel: 01892 515533).
Contact: B Duckett.
Stoy Hayward Franchising Services, 8 Baker Street, London W1M 1DA (Tel: 0171 486 5888).
Contact: A Griggs.

Two important questions you should ask anyone offering their services in this field are:

- Has the consultant been involved in successful franchising at a high level?
- Has he demonstrated his ability to advise?

Ask to speak to some of his past clients. If the consultant is taking commission on the sale of the franchises his client is launching, there could well be an undesirable conflict of interest.

Exhibitions

Blenheim Queensdale, Blenheim House, 630 Chiswick High Road, London W4 5BG (Tel: 0181 742 2828). Contact: S Sweeney. Organizers of the National Franchise Exhibitions in Birmingham and London.

Solicitors

Addeshaw Sons & Latham, Dennis House, Marsden Street, Manchester M2 1JD (Tel: 0161 832 5994). Contact: G Lindrup.

Adlers, 22–26 Paul Street, London EC2A 4JH (Tel: 0171 481 9100). Contact: R King.

Bird Semple Fyfe Ireland, 249 West George Street, Glasgow G2 4RB (Tel: 0141 221 7090). Contact: F Nicolson.

Bristows Cooke & Carpmael, 10 Lincolns Inn Fields, London, WC2A 3BP (Tel: 0171 242 0462). Contact: M Anderson.

Brodies, 15 Atholl Crescent, Edinburgh EH3 8HA (Tel: 0131 228 3777). Contact: J C A Voge.

Church Adams Tatham & Co, Chatham Court, Lesbourne Road, Reigate, Surrey RH2 7FN (Tel: 01737 240111). Contact: B J Haynes.

David Bigmore & Co, Glade House, 52–54 Carter Lane, London EC4V 5EA (Tel: 0171 379 6656). Contact: D Bigmore.

Donne Mileham & Haddock, 42–46 Frederick Place, Brighton, East Sussex BN1 1AT

(Tel: 01273 329833). Contact: A J Trotter.

Field Fisher Waterhouse, 41 Vine Street, London EC3N 2AA (Tel: 0171 481 4841). Contact: Mark Abell.

Hopkins & Wood, 2–3 Cursitor Street, London EC4A 1NE (Tel: 0171 404 0475). Contact: K O'Connor.

Howard Jones & Company, 32 Market Street, Hoylake, Wirral, Merseyside L47 2EB (Tel: 0151 632 3411). Contact: G E Howard Jones.

Jaques & Lewis, Senator House, 85 Queen Victoria Street, London EC4V 4JL (Tel: 0171 919 4500). Contact: Martin Mendelsohn.

Lawrence Tucketts, Shannon Court, Corn Street, Bristol BS99 7JZ (Tel: 0117 9294861). Contact: R M Staunton.

Leathes Prior, 74 The Close, Norwich, Norfolk NR1 4DR (Tel: 01603 610911). Contact: G C Wilcock.

Levy & Macrae, 266 St Vincent Street, Glasgow G2 5RL (Tel: 0141 307 2311). Contact: T Caplan.

Mundays, Crown House, 40 Church Road, Claygate, Esher, Surrey KT10 0LP (Tel: 01372 467272). Contact: M Ishani.

Needham & James, Windsor House, Temple Row, Birmingham B2 5LF (Tel: 0121 200 1188). Contact: John H Pratt.

Owen White, Senate House, 62–70 Bath Road, Slough, SL1 3SR (Tel: 01753 536846). Contact: Anton Bates.

Paisner & Co, Bouverie House, 154 Fleet Street, London, EC4A 2DQ (Tel: 0171 353 0299). Contact: J S Schwarz.

Payne Marsh Stillwell, 6 Carlton Crescent, Southampton, Hampshire SO1 2EY (Tel: 01703 223957). Contact: G H Sturgess.

Peters & Peters, 2 Harewood Place, Hanover Square, London W1R 9HB (Tel: 0171 629 7991). Contact: Raymond Cannon.

Ross & Craig, Swift House, 12A Upper Berkeley Street, London W1H 7PE (Tel: 0171 262 3077). Contact: J Horne.

Wragge & Company, Bank House, 8 Cherry Street, Birmingham B2 5JY (Tel: 0121 233 1000). Contact: G D Harris.

Chartered accountants

BDO Binder Hamlyn, Ballantine House, 168 West George Street, Glasgow G2 2PT (Tel: 0141 248 3761). Contact: C R J Foley.

Kidsons Impey, Carlton House, 31–34 Railway Street, Chelmsford, Essex CM1 1NJ (Tel: 01245 269595). Contact: D V Collins.

Menzies, Ashby House, 64 High Street, Walton-on-Thames, Surrey KT12 1BW (Tel: 01932 247611). Contact: T M Gale.

Rees Pollock, 7 Pilgrim Street, London EC4V 4DR (Tel: 0171 329 6404). Contact: W A J Pollock.

Touche Ross, Hill House, 1 Little New Street, London EC4A 3TR (Tel: 0171 936 3000). Contact: P Small.

Banks

Barclays Bank plc, Business Sector Marketing Department, PO Box 120, Longwood Close, Westwood Business Park, Coventry CV4 8JN (Tel: 01203 694242). Contact: J S Perkins.

Lloyds Bank plc, Retail Banking UKRB, PO Box 112, Canon's Way, Bristol BS99 7LB (Tel: 0117 9433138). Contact: R W Hinds.

Midland Bank plc, Franchise Unit, Midland Enterprise, Ground Floor, Courtwood House, Silver Street Head, Sheffield S1 1RG (Tel: 0114 2529037). Contact: Dai Rees.

National Westminster Bank plc, Commercial Banking Services, Franchise Section, National Westminster Tower, Level 21, 25 Old Broad Street, London EC2N 1HQ (Tel: 0171 920 5966). Contact: P Stern.

The Royal Bank of Scotland plc, 42 St Andrew Square, Edinburgh EH2 2YE (Tel: 0131 556 8555). Contact: G Rose.

Publications

Business Franchise Magazine, Newspaper House, Tannery Lane, Penketh, Cheshire WA5 2UD (Tel: 01925 724326). A bi-monthly magazine aimed at the potential franchisee, containing information about existing franchises, interviews with franchisors, and updated reports on new franchise opportunities. It is also packed with advertising from various franchisors, and solicitors offering help with all the legal aspects of franchising.

The Dow Jones-Irwin Guide to Franchises, Peter G Norback and Crain Norback, May 1983. A thorough investigation of franchising, organized by franchise categories. Once again it covers only the American scene, but it does provide some useful pointers.

Financial Management for the Small Business: The Daily Telegraph Guide by Colin Barrow, published by Kogan Page, 2nd edition 1988; price £9.99 pb.

The Franchise Magazine, Franchise Development Services, Castle House, Castle Meadow, Norwich NR2 1PJ. A monthly publication.

Franchise Opportunity Handbook, US Government Printing Office, Administrative Division (SAA) Washington, DC 20402, USA. The handbook provides an interesting insight into the official American views on franchising and also gives an idea of the scope of the franchising phenomenon.

Franchise Reporter, Franchise Publications, James House, 37 Nottingham Road, London SW17 7EA, has eight issues a year. It is intended to keep you up to date with UK franchise news between the quarterly issues of *Franchise World* (see below).

Franchise Rights, a Self-Defense Manual for the Franchisee by Alex Hammond (Hammond and Marton, 1185 Avenue of the Americas, New York, NY 10036, USA). The manual contains perceptive insight into franchisee/franchisor relationships – forewarned is forearmed.

Franchise World, Franchise Publications, James House, 37 Nottingham Road, London SW17 7EA, has all the latest news on new franchise opportunities, new consultancies and sources of finance. Each issue has a franchise directory, which describes the franchise organizations and gives some idea of the cost of entry.

A Guide to Franchising by Martin Mendelsohn, published by Cassell, 5th edition revised 1993. A very sound introduction to the advantages and disadvantages of franchising, it covers the basic principles including the 'franchise contract' which formalizes the relationship between the franchisor and the franchisee.

Law for the Small Business: The Daily Telegraph Guide by Patricia Clayton, published by Kogan Page, 7th edition 1991; price £10.95 pb. Explains all the relevant Acts and their likely effect on traders.

The franchise directory

Key 1   Minimum start-up capital
2   1st UK franchise
3   No. of UK franchised outlets
4   No. of UK companies operated (including 'pilots')
5   BFA member
–   Information not available

	1	2	3	4	5
Advanced Windscreen Repairs Ltd, Windscreen House, 19 Buttermere Road, Orpington, Kent BR5 3WD (Tel: 01276 473876) Contact: Dave Williams A windscreen-repair franchise based on a simple-to-learn but technically sophisticated repair system.	£3,500	1992	1	2	No
AlphaGraphics Printshops of the Future (UK) Ltd, Pavilion House, Valley Bridge Road, Scarborough, North Yorkshire YO11 1UY (Tel: 01723 500450) Contact: Paul Anderson Advanced design, copy and print solutions.	£165,500	1988	14	2	No
Amtrak Express Parcels Ltd, Company House, Tower Hill, Bristol BS2 0EQ (Tel: 0117 9272002) Contact: David Hadley National and international express parcel carrier.	£18,250	1987	203	1	Yes
Apollo Despatch, Apollo House, 28–30 Hoxton Square, London N1 6NN (Tel: 0171 739 8444) Contact: Norman Grossman, Franchise Director Urgent motorcycle and van despatch service incorporating overnight, international and Red Star deliveries.	£35,000	1991	5	4	Ass.

	1	2	3	4	5
Apollo Window Blinds, Fountain Crescent, Inchinnan Business Park, Inchinnan, Renfrewshire PA4 9RE (Tel: 0141 812 3322) Contact: Kate Wilson Retail of custom-made blinds and curtains to the domestic and commercial markets, via retail outlets or mobile/home-based operations. Manufacturing option available in some cases.	£5000 – £40,000	1975	90	1	Yes
ASC Network plc, 24 Red Lion Street, London WC1R 4SA (Tel: 0171 831 6191) Contact: J Sucharewicz The ASC Group was established 22 years ago and specializes in providing business consultancy services. Their specially designed financial options programme is the backbone of their concept. The company aims to ensure job security, income and a satisfactory career development. Applicants must be well established to meet selection requirements.	£15,000	1990	26	1	No
Athena, Franchise Department, PO Box 918, Edinburgh Way, Harlow, Essex CM20 2DU (Tel: 01279 641125) Contact: Richard Aquilina, Franchise Director Athena is a leading retailer of prints, posters, frames and greeting cards.	£100,000	1987	67	122	No
Autela, Regal House, Birmingham Road, Stratford-upon-Avon, Warwickshire CV37 0BN (Tel: 01789 4145452) Contact: R B Taylor Automotive parts distribution. Wholesale motor component distribution to the market trade and allied industries from commercial property sites.	£45,000 – £50,000	1982	25	38	Yes

	1	2	3	4	5
Autosmart Ltd, Lynn Lane, Shenstone, Lichfield, Staffordshire WS14 0DH (Tel: 01543 481616) Contact: Caroline Fidler Cleaning chemicals and systems for the automotive and transport markets.	£15,000	1978	100	–	No
Bass Lease Company, 60–61 Lionel Street, Birmingham B3 1JE (Tel: 0121 233 9889) Contact: Richard Gardner Runs an expanding estate of public houses to suit a variety of styles and operation.	–	–	–	–	No
Budget Rent a Car International Inc, 41 Marlowes, Hemel Hempstead, Hertfordshire HP1 1LD (Tel: 01442 232555) Contact: Bernard Glover Car, van and truck rental.	£75,000	1966	132	40	Yes
Burger King , UK, Europe, Middle East and Africa, Cambridge House, Highbridge Industrial Estate, Oxford Road, Uxbridge, Middlesex UB8 1UN (Tel: 01895 206200) Contact: Bruce Hodgson Quick-service fast-food restaurant.	–	1980	120	80	Yes
Burger Star, 206 Bath Road, Cheltenham, Gloucestershire GL53 7NE (Tel: 01242 528884) Contact: Simon Daws Hamburger and pizza takeaway.	£75,000	1987	3	1	No
Card Connection, Park House, South Street, Farnham, Surrey GU9 7QQ (Tel: 01252 733177) Contact: Simon Hulme Publishes exclusive range of greeting cards.	£16,000	1992	31	–	Pro.

	1	2	3	4	5
Catermat Fresh Drinks, 13 Redhills Road, South Woodham Ferrers, Chelmsford, Essex CM3 5UJ (Tel: 01245 322465) Contact: Steven Pritchard Supply fresh coffee, vending and cold drink systems with complete range of ingredients.	£3,000	1989	6	5	No
Chem-Dry, Suite D, Annie Reed Court, Annie Reed Road, Beverley, North Humberside HU17 0LF (Tel: 01482 872770) Contact: Mark Hutchinson Franchise in carpet upholstery and curtain cleaning and maintenance.	£9,000 – £13,000	1987	323	2	Yes
Choices Home Sales Ltd, 6 High Street, Crawley, West Sussex RH10 1BJ (Tel: 01293 565644) Contact: Simon Shinerock Estate agency, mortgage brokers, financial planning, conveyancing, lettings and management, general insurance.	£3,500	1990	4	1	No
Cico Chimney Linings Ltd, Westleton, Saxmundham, Suffolk IP17 3BS (Tel: 01728 648608) Contact: R J Hadfield Relining of domestic and non-domestic chimneys and flues by the Cico cast-in-situ method to prevent leakage and down-draught.	£21,000	1982	18	–	Ass.
Circle 'C' Convenience Stores Ltd, 24 Fitzalan Road, Roffey, Horsham, West Sussex RH13 6AA (Tel: 01403 268888) Contact: Richard Perkins, Property and Franchise Director Convenience Stores open seven days a week selling wide range of goods.	£50,000	1982	45	19	Yes

	1	2	3	4	5
Clifford's Dairies, 4 Northcourt Road, Abingdon, Oxfordshire OX14 1PL (Tel: 01235 553519) Contact: Helen Butler Franchise milk and goods delivery service.	£6,500 – £8,000	1987	230	133	No
Colour Counsellors Ltd, 3 Dovedale Studios, 465 Battersea Park Road, London SW11 4LR (Tel: 0171 978 5023) Contact: Marlene Robinson Home-based interior design service which uses a unique colour-coded design system.	£5,000	1982	51	1	Yes
Complete Weed Control Ltd, 7 Astley House, Cromwell Business Park, Banbury Road, Chipping Norton, Oxfordshire OX7 5SR (Tel: 01608 644044) Contact: R W Turner Weed control service to local authorities, government departments, industry, amenity and commercial areas – wherever weed growth presents a problem in non-agricultural areas.	£25,000	1982	20	0	No
Computa Tune, 9 Petre Road, Clayton Park, Clayton-le-Moors, Accrington, Lancashire BB5 5JB (Tel: 01254 391792) Contact: Teresa Chaplow Mobile engine tuning and servicing. Guaranteed for 5,000 miles/six months.	£9,950	1986	110	–	Yes
The Cookie Coach Company, Horsfield Way, Bredbury Park Industrial Estate, Bredbury, Stockport, Cheshire SK6 2TE (Tel: 0181 470 7719) Contact: Adrian K Lewis Van sales distribution of cookies, cakes and confectionery into a wide range of independent retail trade sectors.	£5,000	1983	49	7	No

■

	1	2	3	4	5
Countrywide BTC, 6–8 Cornmarket, Louth, Lincolnshire LN11 9PV (Tel: 01507 601633) Contact: P A Stevens Business transfer consultants.	25,000	1986	4	1	No
Countrywide Garden Maintenance Services Ltd, 164–200 Stockport Road, Cheadle, Cheshire SK8 2DP (Tel: 0161 428 4444) Contact: Martin Stott Garden maintenance service to the private, industrial and commercial sectors on a yearly contract basis.	£25,000	1986	27	1	Yes
Coversure Insurance Services Ltd, 13 High Street, Huntingdon, Cambridgeshire PE18 6TE (Tel: 01480 457527) Contact: Mark Coverdale Personal lines insurance franchise.	£20,000	1989	18	1	No
Create-a-Book, 29 Roydon Road, Diss, Norfolk IP22 3LN (Tel: 01379 652396) Contact: Jane Hutton-Williams Personalized books for children and grown-ups.	£2,000 – £3,500	1989	40	1	No
Crimecure Ltd, Shield House, Station Approach, Yaxley, Peterborough, Cambridgeshire PE7 3EG (Tel: 01733 240448) Contact: Shirley Howlett Domestic, commercial and industrial security installers: intruder alarm systems, fire-systems, closed-circuit television systems.	£18,000	1986	24	1	No
Decorating Den UK, South West Region, Bowditch, Longbridge, Membury, Axminster, Devon EX13 7TY (Tel: 0140488 789) Contact: Sarah Bell Interior decorating franchise, developed in the USA.	£5,500	1989	26	4	Pro.

	1	2	3	4	5
Domino Financial Services, Agriculture House, 31 Trull Road, Taunton, Somerset TA1 4QQ (Tel: 01823 286460) Contact: J F Smith VAT consultancy dealing primarily with the retail market, retail scheme calculations and assessment work.	£18,000	1992	5	–	No
Dominos Pizza, 5–7 Clarence Street, Staines TW18 4SU (Tel: 01784 462444) Contact: William Ewbank Home delivery pizza.	£85,000	1987	77	1	No
Donut King, 1 Station Parade, Eastbourne, Sussex BN21 1BE (Tel: 01323 649687) Contact: Mr and Mrs Geard Canadian-style doughnut/coffee shop.	£60,000	1993	1	3	No
Driver Hire, West End House, Legrams Lane, Bradford BD7 1NH (Tel: 01274 726002) Contact: J P Bussey Blue-collar employment agencies.	£16,500	1985	27	2	Ass.
Dyno-Locks, Zockoll House, 143 Maple Road, Surbiton, Surrey KT6 4BJ (Tel: 0181 481 2200) Contact: Nicolette O'Leary Mobile emergency locksmith service for door and lock opening.	£17,000	1987	60	–	Yes
Dyno-Rod plc, Zockoll House, 143 Maple Road, Surbiton, Surrey KT6 4BJ (Tel: 0181 481 2200) Contact: Nicolette O'Leary Drain, sewer and pipe cleaning and maintenance specialists.	£30,000	1965	130	-	Yes
Dyno-Services, Zockoll House, 143 Maple Road, Surbiton, Surrey KT6 4BJ (Tel: 0181 481 2200) Contact: Nicolette O'Leary Dyno-Services is a 24-hour emergency property care and repair service covering roofing, plumbing and glazing.	£16,500	–	–	–	Yes

	1	2	3	4	5
Eismann Homeservice, Margarethe House, Eismann Way, Phoenix Park Industrial Estate, Corby, Northampton- shire NN17 1ZB (Tel: 01536 407010) Contact: Carole Dawson Homeservice quality frozen foods.	–	–	–	–	Pro.
The Eurotrade Exchange Company Ltd, 29 Brenkley Way, Blezard Business Park, Newcastle NE13 6DS (Tel: 0191 217 0340) Contact: Anthony Craggs Eurotrade is a business-to-business barter network in the UK, offering a range of services to the business community, including cash-free credit loans and cashless purchasing options.	£3,500 – £7,500	1992	23	4	No
Fatty Arbuckle's American Diner, Arbuckle House, High Street, Poole, Dorset BH15 1BP (Tel: 01202 668909) Contact: Adrian Lee An American-style diner/restaurant serving generous portions of food in a relaxed atmosphere for all the family.	£100,000	1991	4	3	No
Favorite Fried Chicken, 7 Davy Road, Gorse Lane Industrial Estate, Clacton on Sea, Essex, CO15 4XD (Tel: 01255 222568) Contact: M Kirk Franchisor of fast-food takeaway chain.	£100,000	1986	47	8	No
Freewheel – The Bicycle Specialists, Buckingham House East, The Broadway, Stanmore, Middlesex, HA7 4EA (Tel: 0181 954 7798) Contact: Simon Matthews Network of quality cycle retailers.	£25,000	1989	7	3	No

	1	2	3	4	5
Gild Associates Ltd, Gild House, 64–8 Norwich Avenue West, Bournemouth BH2 6AW (Tel: 01202 762531) Contact: Geoffrey Whittle Consultants specializing in identifying and reducing commercial business rates.	£3,000	1992	3	–	No
Giltsharp Technology (UK) Ltd, Suite 44, Concourse House, Dewsbury Road, Leeds LS11 7DF (Tel: 0113 2706004) Contact: S M Hardcastle Giltsharp technicians provide a service of product sales and servicing facilities to the hairdressing and catering trades, utilizing a mobile unit that functions as both workshop and showroom.	£15,000	1991	28	2	No
Greenalls Inns, PO Box 2, Greenalls Ave, Wilderspool, Warrington WA4 6RH (Tel: 01925 51234) Contact: Brian King Public-house retailing drink, food and accommodation.	£20,000	1990	227	1,400	Yes
Gun-Point Ltd, Thavies Inn House, 3–4 Holborn Circus, London EC1N 2PL (Tel: 0171 353 1759) Contact: Hugh Chamberlain Repointing brick and stone buildings.	£8,000	1983	17	–	Yes
Highway Windscreens (UK) Ltd, 64–68 Rose Lane, Norwich NR1 1PT (Tel: 01603 617921) Contact: P Milburn Windscreen replacement; 24-hour emergency glazing in houses, offices and shops; car sunroofs; car alarms.	£38,000	1980	40	4	No
Hometune, 1st Floor, 1 Broad Street, Crewe, Cheshire CW1 3DE (Tel: 01270 250046) Contact: Bryan Fretton Mobile vehicle engine tuning, servicing and security.	£18,000	1968	141	2	Yes

	1	2	3	4	5
House of Colour Ltd, 4 Dudrich House, Princes Lane, London N10 3LU (Tel: 0181 444 3621) Contact: Lynn Elvy Colour analysis and image consultants.	£6,500	1986	68	–	Ass.
Humana International, 231 Tottenham Court Road, London W1P 9AE (Tel: 0171 872 9044) Contact: Douglas G Bugie National network of independent recruitment businesses. Specializes in executive and middle management recruitment for assignments in the £20,000–£70,000 income range.	£10,000	1992	11	1	No
In-toto Ltd, Wakefield Road, Gildersome, Leeds LS27 0QW (Tel: 0113 2524131) Contact: M C Eccleston Retailers of quality fitted kitchens, offering a complete service of design, planning and installation to householders and the building industry.	£45,000	1980	45	–	Yes
Kall-Kwik Printing (UK) Ltd, Kall-Kwik House, 106 Pembroke Road, Ruislip, Middlesex HA4 8NW (Tel: 01895 632700) Contact: Clive Sawkins A national printing franchise comprising 203 Kall-Kwik centres, each offering a full range of print, copying and design services to the local business community.	£35,000	1979	203	–	Yes
Kentucky Fried Chicken, Colonel Sanders House, 88–97 High Street, Brentford, Middlesex TW8 8BG (Tel: 0181 569 7070) Contact: Simon Bartholomew Fast-food restaurants.	£200,000	1965	212	82	Yes

	1	2	3	4	5
Kloster International Franchise, The Old Market House, 36 High Street, Buckingham MK18 1NU (Tel: 01280 822077) Contact: Simon Hartley Selling a wine personalization concept to business and leisure sectors.	£15,990	1992	10	–	Pro.
Krogab, Mere Court, Chelford, Macclesfield, Cheshire SK11 9BD (Tel: 01625 860086) Contact: Mark Edwards Supply of beverage systems and products to hotels, restaurants and the catering market.	£35,000	1990	10	1	No
Lakeside Security Shutters, Unit 8, Beaufort Court, Beaufort Road, Plasmarl, Swansea SA6 8JG (Tel: 01792 771117) Contact: Phil Lake Manufacture and installation of continental-style security shutters in a variety of colours for both the domestic and commercial markets.	£10,000	1989	11	2	No
M & B Marquees, Premier House, Tennyson Drive, Pitsea, Basildon, Essex SS13 3BT (Tel: 01268 558002) Contact: John Mansfield M & B Marquees operates a network of marquee-hire outlets providing a service to both domestic and commercial markets.	£50,000	1985	30	1	Ass.
Mastersharp, 28 Glen Road, Boscombe, Bournemouth, Dorset BH5 1HS (Tel: 01202 396002) Contact: P Addison Mobile hi-tech tool valeting and renovation.	£10,500	1988	18	–	No
McDonald's, 11–59 High Road, East Finchley, London N2 8AW (Tel: 0181 883 6400) Contact: Roberta Gower Fast-service restaurant.	£25,000	1986	52	420	Yes

	1	2	3	4	5
Minster Cleaning Services, 8 Astor House, 282 Lichfield Road, Four Oaks, Sutton Coldfield, West Midlands B74 2UG (Tel: 0121 308 3610) Contact: Alan Haigh, Senior Partner Marketing and management of an office cleaning service to banks, commerce and industry.	£15,000 – £30,000	1990	3	2	Ass.
Mixamate Concrete, 11 Westdown, Great Bookham, Surrey KT23 4LJ (Tel: 01372 456714) Contact: Peter Slinn A specialized service to builders and home improvers for the provision of mixed concrete.	£19,000	1982	27	–	Yes
Mr Cod, 6–7 High Street, Woking, Surrey GU21 1BG (Tel: 01483 755407) Contact: J Brewer Fast-food fish and chip/chicken takeaway/restaurant business.	£50,000	–	–	–	No
Nationwide Investigations (Franchises) Ltd, Nationwide House, 86 Southwark Bridge Road, London SE1 0EX (Tel: 0171 928 1799) Contact: S R Withers Private investigators providing a professional investigation service for the legal profession, commerce, industry and the general public.	£7,500	1978	15	20	Yes
Novus Windscreen Repair, 2nd Floor, Bridge House, Gibbons Industrial Park, Dudley Road, Kingswinford, West Midlands DY6 8XF (Tel: 01384 401860) Contact: Colin Edgar Windscreen repair (not replacement).	£5,000	1985	74	2	No

	1	2	3	4	5
Oaise UK Ltd, Unit 4, Forest Close, Ebblake Industrial Estate, Verwood, Dorset BH31 6DQ (Tel: 01202 829700) Contact: Vince Coda Production and delivery of bottled water and fruit juice on a door-to-door basis.	£3,995	1992	13	1	No
One Stop Community Stores Ltd, Raeburn House, Hulbert Road, Waterlooville, Hampshire PO7 7JT (Tel: 01705 267321) Contact: Christopher Curtis Convenience stores.	£120,000	–	–	70	Ass.
PDC Copyprint, 1 Church Lane, East Grinstead, West Sussex RH19 3AZ (Tel: 01342 315321) Contact: Stephen Ricketts High street business printing and design services.	£37,000	1982	33	1	Yes
Perfect Pizza Ltd, Perfect Pizza House, The Forum, Hanworth Lane, Chertsey, Surrey KT16 9JX (Tel: 01932 568000) Contact: David Brodala Pizza delivery and takeaway franchise.	£25,000	1982	150	15	Yes
Poppins Restaurants, 28 Sudley Road, Bognor Regis, West Sussex PO21 1ER (Tel: 01243 864647) Contact: A L Robinson Table service family restaurants, normally situated in town centres.	£60,000	–	40	–	No
Practical Car and Van Rental Ltd, 137–145 High Street, Bordesley, Birmingham B12 0JU (Tel: 0121 772 8599) Contact: Bolton Agnew Practical is an add-on franchise. The company only franchises to existing garage owners. Car and van rental.	£25,000	1984	192	1	Yes

	1	2	3	4	5
Prontaprint Ltd, Executive Offices, Coniscliffe House, Darlington, DL3 7EX (Tel: 01325 483333) Contact: Chris Gillam Business service centre chain offering printing, high volume copying and other business-related products and services to the local business community.	£110,000	1971	279	1	Yes
Property Sales Partnership, 149 High Street, Tonbridge, Kent TN9 1DH (Tel: 01732 771351) Contact: Paul Sadler Estate agency franchise.	£80,000	1992	11	3	Ass.
Rainbow International Carpet Dyeing and Cleaning Company, Willow Court, Cordy Lane, Underwood, Nottinghamshire NG16 5FD (Tel: 01773 715352) Contact: Melvin Lusty Carpet dyeing, cleaning, tinting, repair, upholstery cleaning, deodorization, flood and fire restoration, curtain cleaning, fibre protection, fire retardant treatment, general soft furnishings maintenance.	£15,600	1991	30	1	No
The RSBS Group, 103 Bute Street, Cardiff CF2 6AF (Tel: 01222 455410) Contact: Jeff Powell Business transfer agents acting for clients in the sale of going concern businesses in the retail, catering, industrial and care home market.	£45,000	1992	4	8	No
Ryman the Stationer, Franchise Department, PO Box 918, Edinburgh Way, Harlow, Essex CM20 2DU (Tel: 01279 641125) Contact: Richard Aquilina Ryman is a leading specialist commercial stationer, catering primarily for the small business and office stationery user.	£100,000	1986	16	86	No

	1	2	3	4	5
Screen Savers (UK) Ltd, The Thatched House, Hollybank Road, West Byfleet, Surrey KT14 6JD (Tel: 01932 355177) Contact: Carl Bechgaard Nationwide repair service (not replacement) of stone-damaged windscreens on all types of vehicles.	£7,800	1990	9	1	Pro.
ServiceMaster Ltd, 308 Melton Road, Leicester LE4 7SL (Tel: 0116 2610761) Contact: Don Rudge Daily cleaning services for commerce and industry; carpet and upholstery services for the insurance and domestic market; high quality home cleaning service for the domestic market; furnishing repairs, french polishing, leather restoration for commercial and private customers.	£12,000 – £25,000	1959	333	–	Yes
SGO Decorative Glass, PO Box 65, Norwich, Norfolk NR6 6EJ (Tel: 01603 4885454) Contact: T Tarr The design and manufacture of decorative glass products sold to the trade.	£45,000	1986	14	1	Ass.
Signs Express, 25 Kingsway, Norwich, Norfolk NR2 4UE (Tel: 01603 762680) Contact: David Corbett Sign makers.	£25,000	1992	4	1	Ass.
Signsprint UK, The Lodge Cottage, Harbour Walk, Seaham, Durham SR7 7DS (Tel: 0191 510 0740) Contact: Steve Halliman Computerized signmaking and design.	£8,500	–	–	–	No
Sketchley Recognition Express Ltd, PO Box 7, Rugby Road, Hinckley, Leicestershire LE10 2NE (Tel: 01455 238133) Contact: Simon Hobson Manufacturer of personalized name badges, signage, vehicle livery, suppliers of corporate jewellery, button and embroidered badges, trophies and awards.	£32,000	1979	21	1	Yes

	1	2	3	4	5
Snappy Snaps Franchises Ltd, 12 Glenthorne Mews, 115 Glenthorne Road, London W6 0LJ (Tel: 0181 741 7474) Contact: Don Kennedy Photographic mini-labs – high street shops, offering a one-hour colour film developing and printing service.	£25,000	1987	58	1	Yes
Spudulike, 34–38 Standard Road, London NW10 6EU (Tel: 0181 965 0182) Contact: Ron Snipp Baked potato restaurants.	£40,000	1981	30	19	Yes
Square 1 Cleaning Services, 2 Cranleigh Avenue, Rottingdean, Brighton, East Sussex BN2 7GT (Tel: 01273 305016) Contact: Anthony Delow Domestic and commercial cleaning; carpet, fabric and upholstery cleaning and proofing.	£15,000	1987	14	–	No
Swinton Insurance, Swinton House, 6 Great Marlborough Street, Manchester M1 5SW (Tel: 0161 236 1222) Contact: Peter Lowe High street insurance specialists.	£12,000	1984	290	450	Yes
Techclean Services, VDU House, Old Kiln Lane, Churt, Farnham, Surrey GU10 2JH (Tel: 01428 713713) Contact: D L Cooper Cleaning all types of hi-tech equipment, computers, faxes, printers, photo-copiers, power stations, control centres, computer rooms.	£5,000	1986	42	–	Yes

	1	2	3	4	5
Thrifty Car Rental, The Old Court House, Hughenden Road, High Wycombe, Buckinghamshire HP13 5DT (Tel: 01494 474767) Contact: Andrew Burton Car rental franchise system, providing licensees with a full starter pack together with fleet and insurance programmes.	£25,000	1988	30	1	No
Trafalgar Cleaning Chemicals, Unit 4, Gillmans Industrial Estate, Natts Lane, Billingshurst, West Sussex RH14 9EZ (Tel: 01403 785111) Contact: John Thompson The supply of cleaning and maintenance chemicals to the motor and transport industries.	£5,000	1987	30	5	No
Training Skills Ltd, 103 Bute Street, Cardiff CF2 6AD (Tel: 01222 465743) Contact: Chris Juan-Hofer Training services for personal computer and Mac users in local centres. Training courses available on a wide range of topics and proprietary software.	£10,000	1992	2	1	No
Travail Employment Group, 24 Southgate Street, Gloucester GL1 2DP (Tel: 01452 307645) Contact: Colin Rogers Temporary and permanent recruitment services in almost all skill disciplines including commercial, industrial, driving, technical, catering, executive.	£50,000	1985	26	6	Yes
Trust Parts Ltd, Unit 7, Groundwell Industrial Estate, Crompton Road, Swindon, Wiltshire SN2 5AY (Tel: 01793 723749) Contact: Robin Bourne From a fleet of 80 sales vans, Trust Parts supply a wide range of brand leader and own brand engineering and maintenance consumables and tools to all types of engineering workshops and industrial maintenance departments.	£21,000	1986	8	72	Yes

	1	2	3	4	5
Tune-Up Ltd, 23 High Street, Bagshot, Surrey GU19 5AF (Tel: 01276 451199) Contact: A Stevens Mobile engine tuning and servicing for all cars and light vans (including diesels).	£13,500 – £15,000	1988	77	–	Ass.
Tyrefix Ltd, Taylors Piece, 9–11 Stortford Road, Great Dunmow, Essex CM6 1DA (Tel: 01371 876640) Contact: Sue Kearns On-site plant tyre repair and replacement service.	£45,000	1989	10	2	No
Val-U-Pak, Valuefuture plc, Clare Lodge, 41 Holly Bush Lane, Harpenden, Hertfordshire AL5 1PT (Tel: 01582 460977) Contact: Jeff Frankling Co-operative direct mail.	£3,750	1989	45	–	No
Waiters on Wheels, 28 Glen Road, Boscombe, Bournemouth, Dorset BH5 1HS (Tel: 01202 396002) Contact: P Addison Fast-food own menu delivery service – no cooking required.	£6,950	1993	–	1	No
The Wedding Guide, Suite 5, Churchill House, Horndon Industrial Park, West Hornden, Essex CM13 3XD (Tel: 01277 811002) Contact: Terry Steel Complete marketing package for suppliers of wedding services plus planning directory for brides.	£6,800	1991	8	2	No
Wetherby Training Services, Flockton House, Audby Lane, Wetherby, West Yorkshire LS22 4FD (Tel: 01937 583940) Contact: David Button Secretarial and computer training centre franchise.	£15,000	1977	165	4	Yes

■ IS THE BUSINESS RIGHT FOR YOU?

Here is an exercise which might help your decision process.

Take a sheet of paper and draw up two columns. In the left-hand column, list all your hobbies, interests and skills. In the right-hand column, translate them into possible business ideas. For example:

Interest/skills	Business ideas
Motor cars	Motor car dealer/repair garage/home tuning service
Cooking	Restaurant/home catering service/bakery shop providing produce for freezer outlets
Gardening	Supplier of produce to flower or vegetable shop/running a nursery/running a garden centre/landscape design
Typing	Typing authors' manuscripts from home/typing back-up service for busy local companies/running a secretarial agency

... and so on.

Having done this exercise, you need to balance the possibilities against the criteria; which are most important to you? These might be: small amount of capital required; good anticipated profit; secure income; work satisfaction; no need to learn new skills; variety of work; the possibility of working hours that suit your lifestyle; opportunity to meet new people; minimal paperwork; opportunity to travel.

Select your criteria

You may have other criteria not on this list. Decide the most important criteria and place them in order of importance. Allocate each chosen criterion a weighting factor of between 1 and 5. Now list the possible business opportunities you have identified from the first exercise and measure them against the graded criteria.

A simple example: Jane Clark, an ex-secretary with school-age children, needed work because her husband had been made redundant and was busy looking for another job. She wasn't in a position to raise much capital, and she wanted her hours to coincide with those of her children. She wanted to run her own show and she wanted to enjoy what she did. The criteria she selected were:

Criteria	Weighting factor (out of 5)
Minimal capital required	5
Possibility to work hours that suit lifestyle	5
No need to learn new skills	4
Minimal paperwork	3
Work satisfaction	2
Opportunity to meet interesting people	1

Since minimal capital was a very important criteria for Jane she gave it a weighting factor of 5, whereas the opportunity to meet interesting people, being far less important to her, was only weighted 1.

Jane then gave each of her three business ideas a rating, in points (out of 5), against these criteria. A secretarial agency needed capital to start so was given only 1 point. Back-up typing needed hardly any money and was allocated 5 points. Her worked-out chart looked like this:

		Secretarial agency		Back-up typing		Authors' manuscripts	
	Weighting factor	points	score	points	score	points	score
Criteria							
Minimal capital	5x	1 =	5	5 =	25	4 =	20
Flexible hours	5x	1 =	5	3 =	15	5 =	25
No new skills	4x	2 =	8	5 =	20	5 =	20
Work satisfaction	3x	4 =	12	1 =	3	3 =	9
Minimal paperwork	2x	0 =	0	4 =	8	5 =	10
Meeting people	1x	4 =	4	3 =	3	4 =	4
Total score			34		74		88

The weighting factor and the rating point multiplied together give a score for each business idea. The highest score indicates the business that best meets Jane's criteria. In this case, typing authors' manuscripts scored over back-up typing since Jane could do it exactly when it suited her.

Teleworking

Teleworking – or, as it is sometimes called, telecommuting – has long been billed as the working pattern of the future. Los Angeles is its irrefutable headquarters; before the recent earthquake damaged thousands of offices and businesses, the metropolis had an estimated 600,000 telecommuters.

In the first two weeks after the quake, 2,750 people called a hotline set up by the regional telephone company, Pacific Bell, to field questions on telecommuting. Southern California's telecommuting centres were inundated with enquiries and found themselves drawing up waiting-lists and even expansion plans.

Telecommuting was first mooted more than 20 years ago, and research shows 7.6 million Americans telecommute, 6.1% of the 129 million workforce. Almost all are white-collar workers who do so part-time, for an average of two days a week.

A survey several years ago by US West (one of a number of telephone companies beating the telecommuting drum) showed that productivity among a pilot group who became telecommuters, in 14 states, shot up 20%. Electronic commuting in the USA can produce net savings of $8,000–9,000 (£5,400–6,100) per employee per year, through higher output and lower costs.

It is estimated that there are some 500,000 self-employed teleworkers in the UK. That is about one is seven of the self-employed population and one in sixty of the total workforce (still below that of Los Angeles).

Architects, accountants, solicitors, programmers, designers, tour operators, writers, secretaries, translaters, copywriters, indexers are just a handful of the sorts of people who can work, at least for part of the time, remote from their customers.

Teleworking is certainly a major area of business opportunity for small firms, which looks set to grow rapidly over the next decade.

Teleworking offers

The advantage for individuals, whether employees or self-employed, is the removal of daily commuting. Not only are there evident savings on public transport fares, or on petrol and car maintenance (and nervous energy), but the hours previously expended on commuting can now be spent more productively.

Hand in hand with this goes the flexibility that teleworking brings. Since it's based on the premise that the physical location of work is becoming less and less relevant, as a teleworker you have the freedom to live where you want.

Most teleworkers do have to visit an office sometimes, of course, and in many businesses there will still be a need to meet clients and attend industry events.

Nearly all parts of the UK lend themselves to teleworking provided they are within reasonable reach of computer maintenance, express courier services and the like – so teleworking allows you to place personal and family considerations, rather than the job, at the top of your priorities.

Flexibility is not only in location, but also in time. However, it's important if you're teleworking to establish some core hours when you will always be available for telephone meetings or video conferences. But especially for those with young families or community involvements, teleworking makes scheduling a lot easier.

These flexibilities also make teleworking especially attractive to people who are returning to work after a long absence, such as former full-time parents. While office culture may have changed radically and, to the returner, uncomfortably so in two decades, teleworking can be a temporary measure allowing them to ease back into working life, or a long-term solution which makes the most of older people's skills without forcing them into an unfamiliar life.

The teleworker's equipment

Though many people would characterize teleworking as a product of the information age, PCs are not essential to its operation – fax and other forms of telecommunications are much more important.

However, on a practical level the PC does help the teleworker simply because it gives an individual command over a range of functions as varied as financial analysis (spreadsheets) and graphic design (desktop publishing). And, of course, digital data held on a PC is more easily portable than that held in an analogue form. For example one CD-Rom disc can replace several bookshelves' worth of information.

In this way the PC not only makes it easier for teleworkers to exchange information between themselves, but also makes working at home in quite cramped conditions practical.

For teleworkers in Britain, perhaps the most important telecommunications technology is ISDN, the Integrated Services Digital Network. ISDN connection gives access to digital telephone lines – not to be confused with the now almost universal digital telephone exchanges – which can carry far more data (have a great bandwidth) than ordinary copper wire telephone connections.

The basic ISDN configuration available from BT is called ISDN2, which provides the user with two ISDN channels, each capable of carrying 64 kilobits of information per second. Each channel is almost seven times faster than the 9.6 kilobit per second modems most people use.

ISDN2 actually includes a third channel as well, but this is used only to transmit control information and does not add to the bandwidth available for your data transmissions.

At the moment the next step upwards is to ISDN30 which provides 30 64 kilobit per second channels, but BT are soon to introduce an intermediate level called ISDN6. Because the ISDN signal is digital from start to finish, ISDN users do not need modems to translate data from digital into analogue and back again, although you will still need an ISDN adapter to make the physical connection to your computer.

You can use ISDN to transmit voice or fax, but there's little point – the copper wire system already handles these adequately. Where it really comes into its own is in high-speed data transmission – theoretically you could send a megabyte in a little over two minutes – and in video conferencing.

Each participant in a video conference usually has a camera mounted on the top of his or her monitor, and can see other participants in a window on the monitor. Video conferencing systems are the first practical mass-market application of ISDN, and they require its high bandwidth because they are an attempt to send moving images over telecommunications links in real time.

So in future teleworkers may be able to hold meetings and face-to-face discussions with clients, suppliers and others without leaving their home.

Home office setup

What equipment you require will, as ever, depend on the business you're in.

A sensible basic configuration would have at its heart a 486-based PC with ample hard-disk space – because it may be more cost-effective to store frequently used information on your own machine rather than incur telephone charges dialling up a central source.

Self-employed teleworkers will almost certainly need a laser printer, or at least a decent inkjet, regardless of profession, because marketing yourself and creating a good image are important parts of the job.

A 9600-baud modem should be seen as a bare minimum for communications. Although electronic mail is perfectly possible at the old 2400 or even 1200-baud speeds, downloading files takes so much longer that the minimal cost advantage of buying one of these is soon eliminated by phone bills.

Software, too, depends largely on the job, although a wordprocessor and communications package are essential to everyone – as is a decent set of disk and file management utilities, such as Norton Utilities, because there is no computer department down the corridor to come to your aid when things go wrong. For the same reason, a virus-checker is important.

Scheduling and project-management software can be useful when your time is flexible to make sure you are allocating enough to each task – remember, as a teleworker you are more likely to be paid by results than by hours at the desk – as is an electronic address book, to store the many different phone, fax and electronic mail contacts you will use.

New forms of software, such as groupware and remoteware, also make teleworking easier. Groupware products are those such as Lotus Notes which, unlike traditional single-user software packages, are designed for collaborative working in groups. Remoteware, as the name suggests, is software intended for remote workers who can log in to a company's central mainframe or PC servers and use the computer just as if they were at head office.

All these products help take the technical strain out of teleworking and make communications transparent – the home office becomes just another office.

Another technology which helps teleworkers is the fax card. These slot into the back of the PC and allow you to send faxes direct from the screen to another PC, if it has an appropriate card too, or an ordinary fax machine.

Beyond the computer, a fax machine is almost indispensable, even if you prefer a fax card or fax modem for outgoing material – receiving faxes straight into the PC can eat up disk space at a frightening rate.

Install a separate line for the fax, or, if that's beyond your means, invest in one of the answering machines which can automatically detect faxes and route them to the machine.

The telephone itself is the teleworker's primary tool. Make sure the handset is one you can comfortably hold on your shoulder while typing or leafing through documents, and look for a machine which can store frequently used numbers.

Services such as Call Waiting – which alerts you while you're engaged on the phone that someone else is trying to call you – are worth investing in too, though these add to the phone bill.

If you do expect to be away from your 'tele office' – or would like freedom from interruption when you are there – you could consider investing in a Virtual Personal Assistant (VPA). The VPA, invented by Andest Communications of Milton Keynes, looks like a cross between a telephone answering machine and a mouse. It works as a digital answering machine, a voice mailbox and a V32bis data modem and it can store and forward faxes (it doesn't have a built-in printer to print them out). The VPA can be used as a standalone machine, or linked to PC or Apple Macintosh. In being 'easy for anyone to use' the VPA is claimed to 'remove many of the barriers to teleworking'. It costs £499 plus VAT. (Tel: 0162 875577.)

Video conference system

PictureTel Live PCS100 video conferencing system runs on a desk-top computer using Windows-based software to connect users at up to 16 sites via an ISDN2 digital telephone line which BT can install.

An impressive system. Although there is a slight delay in receiving speech this is no more than a satellite-connected international telephone call. Also, the picture is not as clear as video film and movements are jerky.

It is easy to operate via Windows-based icons which form an on-screen menu. To make a call you flash up the phone book on your screen by pointing and clicking at the relevant icon on the menu and it is dialled automatically. The phone book stores up to 1,000 numbers and can be stored on disk.

When the phone rings, you point and click at the answer box which flashes on to the screen, or pick up the handset for a private call. When used in loud audio mode, a mute on the handset can be pressed to stop your conversation being heard at the other end. There is also a headset option.

Other impressive features include the chalkboard on which users at different sites can write and draw simultaneously. The Talk Box allows conference minutes to be written on-screen then saved, while the clipboard can transfer parts of files between different computers or send whole documents to another computer for viewing and commenting.

The psychological benefits of seeing the person you are talking to are huge. It is expensive to buy but after the initial outlay there is only the cost of calls to consider. These are slightly higher than normal since the system uses dual telephone lines. The price of £4,995 plus VAT (excluding the computer) includes two software cards, camera, camera stand, handset and connecting cables.

For details and demonstrations, telephone PictureTel (01753 673000). A rental service is available from ATS Technirent (Tel: 01344 411011).

Telecottages

If all this equipment is a bit beyond your means, or if you rightly feel that technology is changing very rapidly, you could either join or set up your own telecottage.

A telecottage is a small business designed to give local people – the self-employed and other small businesses – access to wider business networks via IT equipment and services. Just as you would rent time on a washing machine in a launderette, so in a telecottage you can rent time on a keyboard (rates vary between £2 and £6 an hour for use of a computer). In addition to computers, faxes, scanners, laser printers, modems, desk-top publishing equipment and, in some cases, video conferencing facilities can also be used at the telecottage for an hourly fee. Some of them also train and recruit freelances – often women returning to work – to take on contract work for larger companies. Telecottages within the Welsh network, for example, have undertaken projects for such clients as the Welsh Office, for whom they provide English/Welsh translation services, and a government department in London, for whom a large data-inputting project was sub-contracted to them by ICL. Buoyed by this success, Welsh eyes are now turning towards the wider European market.

Even as major employers like BT are seeing the sense of this and beginning to contemplate telecottages of their own, the cutting edge is moving on. In December 1993 planning permission was granted for the world's first televillage, at Crickhowell in the Brecon Beacons National Park.

There are other, more community-based developments. Set up in 1990 by Highlands and Islands Enterprise, Orkney Islands Council and British Telecom, the 'telecottage' in the old schoolhouse on the Island of Hoy offers computer, fax and copying facilities to the 450 islanders. The business is now self-financing under a local management committee, and its biggest users are local professional people.

The Telecottage Association, sponsored by BT, was formed in April 1993 as a non-profit-distributing company to encourage teleworking principally, although not exclusively, in rural areas. Already it has 80 local telecottages, and 1,300 members. A £24.50 annual membership includes an information kit, a magazine, *Teleworker*, an annual conference and reduced rates at association seminars and conferences. Though it is not necessary to be a member to use a telecottage, the association can tell you where there is an electronically hooked-up 'cottage' near you.

Since February 1994, the association has offered a 20-week course in business administration and information-technology operation. BT sponsorship is bringing down the cost of course fees. The course, approved by City and Guilds, is aimed at practical tuition covering business efficiency, financing, self-management and the practicalities of data transmission. The eventual aim is to use about 60 telecentres as a focus for the course work. Enquiries: Lynn Chadwick, The Telecottage Association Training (Tel: 01538 386674).

The National Association of Teleworkers was founded in 1992. The Association aims to:

- bring together teleworkers and the purchasers of services provided by teleworking;
- provide information and advice to telecommuters and their employers;
- promote high standards of teleworking through its Code of Conduct;
- record the teleworking services provided by its members and their professional qualifications and experiences on a Members' Register;
- promote awareness of teleworking;
- represent its members at national level to policy makers and influencers;
- promote the training of teleworkers.

Membership of the National Association of Teleworkers is relevant to a wide range of individuals and companies who use teleworking in their business or profession. These include:

- technical authors
- software support

- accountants
- public relations specialists
- software programmers
- office services providers
- systems analysts
- management consultants
- graphic designers
- journalists
- salespeople
- training providers
- marketing and telesales
- data entry services
- academics
- printers and typesetters

Annual membership costs £39.95 plus VAT.

Sources of help and further information

The Telecottage Association. Membership: Wren Telecottage, Freepost CV2312, Kenilworth, Warwickshire CV8 2RR (no stamp required inside UK). Or ring toll-free telephone number 0800 616008 and ask for Telecottage Association membership form, or contact: Alan Denbigh, ACRE, executive director Telecottage Association, BT Teleworking Adviser (Tel: 0145 383 4874).

The National Association of Teleworkers, Deer Park Telecentre, Weston, Honiton, Devon EX14 0PG (Tel: 01404 47467; International +44 404 41266; Fax: 01404 46598), welcomes individual members.

BT and Mercury both provide information on teleworking, the latter having recently set up a partnership with computer manufacturer DEC to advise companies.

BT have produced an excellent document on the economics of teleworking, which includes an analysis of the costs and savings for employers. Tel: 01800 800 854.

The Rural Development Commission (which has local offices – see Section 2), Scottish Enterprise (041 248 2700), and the Department of Trade and Industry (071 215 5000) can also provide advice; the DTI has a teleworking Special Interest Group (SIG).

Other useful publications include: *Teleworking Acceptance, Benefits and Management*: published by Organisation and Technology Research Ltd, 256 Edgware Road, London W2 1DS (Tel: 0171 402 3574); *Teleworking in the 1990s – a view from the home*: a research report by Sussex University (Tel: 01273 678 165).

4 | *Exploiting high, and not so high, technology*

Technology presents considerable opportunities to inventors and users alike. It also presents a number of problems. Inventors have difficulty in communicating their ideas to commercial organizations. These ideas are often a long way from being a recognizable product at the time when most help (financial or otherwise) is needed. A growing number of institutions, organizations and services now aim to provide just this understanding and assistance.

On the other hand, there are many small businesses which could make considerable use of new technology, if only they knew how. Computers, faxes and modems are just the most obvious development, where dull, repetitive tasks can be done quickly, leaving the entrepreneur free to perform more important tasks, and to provide greater mobility.

The following material should give you an appreciation of what is happening to solve these technological communication problems.

■ SCIENCE PARKS, INNOVATION & TECHNOLOGY CENTRES

In 1973 an experiment was begun to encourage the growth of technical innovation in the USA. The basic idea was to bring inventors, entrepreneurs and academics together physically on or near the college campus. By adding some government funds to provide buildings, materials and equipment, it was hoped that the right environment to identify and stimulate new products and services would then be created. Although at the start these 'Innovation Centres' would be heavily subsidized, they were expected to become substantially self-supporting. This, no doubt, was the motivation in ensuring that a good business school was on the campus too (a lesson that UK emulators have not universally followed).

The American experiment seems to show that the college–industry centres can and do flourish. By 1978 these centres had played a major part in forming some 30 new and largely technology-based businesses. They employed on average 40 people each, and some had sales returns of well over $1 million per annum. By the 1990s, some 80 centres were operating around the USA based on such colleges as Carnegie-Mellon and the Massachusetts Institute of Technology. In the UK (and elsewhere) similar deliberations were taking place. For example, in 1969 a decision was taken to encourage the expansion of science-based industry close to Cambridge. This would take advantage of the considerable concentration there of scientific expertise, equipment and libraries. The resultant Science Park was officially opened in 1975.

A growing number of organizations are now concerned with improving the lot of the inventor–entrepreneur. Some of these seem to offer little more than premises and a sympathetic ear. Others are rather less than high-technology based. However, most of them are extremely young, and at least half have expressed a desire to provide practical as well as technological help to small, new, innovation-based businesses. This situation represents a considerable improvement when compared to the UK inventor's lot in the 1980s.

There are now over 40 science parks in the UK, clustered under the loose umbrella of the UK Science Parks Association, 44 Oaks Road, Sutton Coldfield, West Midlands B74 2TL (Tel: 0121 308 8815). The rents for units will vary considerably, from around £10 per square metre to around £25.

Key 1 Opening date
2 Number of companies
3 Range of unit size (sq. metres)
4 Venture capital fund
5 Grants available

England	1	2	3	4	5
Aston Science Park, Birmingham Technology Limited, Business and Innovation Centre, Love Lane, Aston Triangle B7 4BJ (Tel: 0121 359 0981; Fax: 0121 359 0433) Contact: Barbara Richards Managed by Birmingham Technology Limited (BTL), a joint venture by the City of Birmingham, Lloyds Bank plc and Aston University.	1983	60	14–465+	Yes	No
Beaconside Technology Park, 3 Martin Street, Stafford ST16 2LH (Tel: 01785 223121; Fax: 01785 215286) Contact: Stephen Read The park will be situated on a site of approximately 30 acres on the eastern outskirts of Stafford. It is envisaged that strong links with Staffordshire University, which is adjacent to the site, will provide excellent facilities in the fields of technology, computing research and the commercial exploitation of innovative ideas.	–	–	–	–	–

	1	2	3	4	5
Belasis Hall Technology Park, Billingham, Cleveland TS23 4AZ (Tel: 01642 370301; Fax: 01642 370288) Contact: George Hunter Owned jointly by Imperial Chemical Industries and English Estates. Expertise of ICI available to tenants.	1988	61	4,645–9,290	No	Yes
Birmingham Research Park, Vincent Drive, Edgbaston, Birmingham B15 2SQ (Tel: 0121 471 4988; Fax: 0121 472 5738) Contact: Dr Derek Burr Managed by Birmingham Research Park Ltd, which is jointly owned by the University of Birmingham and Birmingham City Council.	1986	17	350+	Yes	No
Brunel Science Park, Cleveland Road, Uxbridge, Middlesex UB8 3PH (Tel: 01895 272192; Fax: 01895 256581) Contact: Peter Russell Funded solely by the University.	1983	21	372–1,200+	Yes	No
Cambridge Science Park, Trumpington Road, Cambridge CB2 2LD (Tel: 01223 841841) Contact: Henry Bennett Has been developed by Trinity College.	1970	79	37–279+	Yes	Yes
Chilworth Research Centre, The Cottage, Southampton SO1 7JF (Tel: 01703 767420; Fax: 01703 766190) Contact: Shirley Smith Shareholders are University of Southampton Holdings Limited and Southampton Economic Development Corporation Limited (the City of Southampton).	1986	25	46–465	No	No

	1	2	3	4	5
Cranfield Technology Park, Cranfield Institute of Technology, Cranfield, Bedford MK43 OAL (Tel: 01234 752731; Fax: 01234 751637) Contact: David Newens Being developed by Cranfield Institute of Technology (CIT).	1991	–	9,700	No	No
Durham Mountjoy Research Centre, Unit 1A, Durham DH1 3SW (Tel: 0191 374 2599; Fax: 0191 374 2591) Contact: John Turner Now owned and managed by a company wholly owned by the University of Durham. It was orginally developed by English Estates in co-operation with the University, Durham City Council and Durham County Council.	1986	22	37	No	Yes
Harefield Mediparc, Trafalgar House Business Parks, Devonshire House, Mayfair Place, London W1A 3AG (Tel: 0171 499 9020; Fax: 0171 495 2078) Contact: Mark Wyatt A joint initiative between Harefield Hospital, one of the world's most renowned cardiothoracic hospitals, and Trafalgar House Business Parks.	1991	–	–	No	No
Highfields Science Park, Nottingham City Council, Lawrence House, Clarendon Street, Nottingham NG1 5NT (Tel: 0115 9483500; Fax: 0115 9475944) Contact: Sarah Waring Owned by Nottingham City Council, with the co-operation of the University of Nottingham.	1984	38	96–557	No	No

	1	2	3	4	5
Listerhills Science Park at University of Bradford, Bradford BD7 1DP (Tel: 01274 383170; Fax: 01274 720910) Contact: Dr G Humphreys English Estates, the University of Bradford and the City of Bradford Metropolitan Council are partners in this development.	1982	27	97–468	No	Yes
Loughborough Technology Centre, Leicestershire County Council, Glenfield, Leicester LE3 8RE (Tel: 01533 656963) Contact: David Berry Funded by Leicestershire County Council and managed by the Director of Property. A close liaison has been developed with Loughborough University of Technology, Loughborough College and Loughborough College of Art and Design, whose facilities and expertise are made available to the tenants through Loughborough Consultants Limited, an independent company operating from the university campus.	1984	12	25–91	No	No
Manchester Science Park, Lloyd Street North, Manchester M15 4EN (Tel: 0161 226 1000; Fax: 0161 226 1001) Contact: Tom Broadhurst Shareholders: Manchester City Council, UMIST, University of Manchester, Ciba-Geigy plc, Courtaulds Advanced Materials, Ferranti International plc, Granada Television Ltd. Also supported by Manchester Business School and Manchester Polytechnic.	1983	18	21–680	Yes	Yes

	1	2	3	4	5
Merseyside Innovation Centre Ltd, 131 Mount Pleasant, Liverpool L3 5TF (Tel: 0151 708 0123; Fax: 0151 707 0230) Contact: Brian Job A company limited by guarantee, associated with the University of Liverpool and the Liverpool Polytechnic.	1981	12	929	No	Yes
Newcastle Technopole Central Business and Technology Park, Trafalgar Street, Newcastle upon Tyne NE1 2LA (Tel: 0191 230 2288; Fax: 0191 230 3222) A joint development between A F Budge Limited and Tyne and Wear Development Corporation, with Science Cities Limited as managing agents.	–	–	–	–	–
Newlands Science Park, University of Hull, Cottingham Road, Hull HU6 7RX (Tel: 01482 465139; Fax: 01482 466477) Contact: Nigel Halford Financed by English Estates, the University of Hull and Kingston upon Hull City Council. The university leased land on the campus for a development funded and planned by English Estates.	1984	15	20–100	No	Yes
Oxford Science Park, Robert Robinson Avenue, Oxford OX4 4GA (Tel: 01865 784000; Fax: 01865 784004) Contact: George Deacon First phase being developed as a joint venture between Magdalen College, Oxford, and the Prudential Assurance Company.	1991	24	–	Yes	Yes

	1	2	3	4	5
Reading University Innovation Centre, University of Reading, Philip Lyle Building, Whiteknights, Reading RG6 2BX (Tel: 01734 318978; Fax: 01734 861894) Contact: Alison Ansell Organization set up to facilitate contributions by the university to companies.	1989	11	1,580	No	No
St John's Innovation Park Cambridge, Cowley Road, Cambridge CB4 4WS (Tel: 01223 420252; Fax: 01223 420844) Contact: Walter Herriot Accommodation for technological companies, and provides close links with the university.	1987	69	12–483	No	No
Sheffield Science Park, Cooper Building, Arundel Street, Sheffield S1 2NS (Tel: 0114 2724140; Fax: 0114 2720379) Contact: Marion Adkins Phase 1, The Cooper Building, developed by Sheffield City Council in conjunction with Sheffield University and Sheffield City Polytechnic. The Cooper Building is run by Sheffield Science Park Company which has representation from the university, polytechnic, Midland Bank, Chamber of Commerce, MSF (the Manufacturing Scientific and Financial trade union), English Estates and British Steel Industries Limited. English Estates have developed Phase 2 of the site and are responsible for its letting and management.	1988	25	70–372	No	No

	1	2	3	4	5
South Bank Technopark, 90 London Road, London SE1 6LN (Tel: 0171 928 2900; Fax: 0171 928 3908) Contact: Mike Saunders Funded by the Prudential Corporation and managed by a company whose board includes representatives from the Prudential, the Polytechnic of the South Bank and various other interested local organizations.	1987	43	19+	No	No
Surrey Research Park, 30 Frederick Sanger Road, Guildford, Surrey GU2 5YD (Tel: 01483 579693; Fax: 01483 68946) Contact: Dr Malcolm Parry Wholly owned by the university's Foundation Fund.	1986	58	25–10,000	No	No
TWI Technology Park, Abington Hall, Abington, Cambridge CB1 6AL (Tel: 01223 891162; Fax: 01223 892588) Contact: George Salter The park will be managed by TWI Technology Ltd, a wholly owned subsidiary of the Welding Institute.	To be established in 1995/6				
University College London Ventures Ltd, Gower Street, London WC1E 6BT (Tel: 0171 380 7701; Fax: 0171 380 7220) Contact: Dr Jeff Skinner UCL Ventures Ltd (UCLv) is a partnership between University College London (UCL) and County NatWest Ventures. Representatives from KPMG Peat Marwick and Speechly Bircham Solicitors act as advisers to the board.	1989	5	–	Yes	No

	1	2	3	4	5
University of East Anglia Science Park, Norwich, Norfolk NR4 7TJ (Tel: 01603 56161; Fax: 01603 58553) Contact: John Brind Not yet established.					
University of Warwick Science Park Ltd, Barclays Venture Centre, Sir William Lyons Road, Coventry CV4 7EZ (Tel: 01203 418535; Fax: 01203 410156) Contact: David Rowe A limited liability company with the following shareholders: University of Warwick, Coventry City Council, Warwickshire County Council, West Midlands Enterprise Board.	1983	64	40–2,500	Yes	Yes
Westlakes Science and Technology Park, Ingwell Hall, Moor Row, Cumbria CA24 3JZ (Tel: 01946 590818; Fax: 01946 590929) Contact: Pam States Partners: West Cumbria Development Fund Ltd and Rural Development Commission.	To be established in 1995/6]				
Winfrith Technology Centre, Dorchester, Dorset DT2 8DH (Tel: 01305 251888; Fax: 01305 202811) Contact: Jonathan Harrison Already provides a location for advanced scientific services. AEA Technology, who own WTC, are assessing the feasibility of forming a science park enclave within the existing development. This work is being carried out in collaboration with Bournemouth Polytechnic.					

	1	2	3	4	5
York Science Park, University of York, Heslington, York YO1 5DD (Tel: 01904 432915; Fax: 01904 432917) Contact: Professor A Robards Partners: University of York and P & O Developments Limited.	1991	1	500–3,000	No	No

Wales

	1	2	3	4	5
Aberystwyth Science Park, Development Board for Rural Wales, 25 Maengwyn Street, Machynlleth, Powys SY20 8EB (Tel: 01654 702053; Fax: 01654 702613) Contact: Nia Williams A joint venture between the University College of Wales (UCW), Aberystwyth and the Development Board for Rural Wales.	1983	12	500+	Yes	Yes
Cardiff Business Technology Centre, Senghenydd Road, Cardiff CF2 4AY (Tel: 01222 372311; Fax: 01222 373436) Contact: Eileen Turner Instigated by South Glamorgan County Council and University of Wales College of Cardiff. These have now been joined by representatives from other higher education establishments and the private sector.	1988	16	12–72	No	No
Menai Technology Enterprise Centre (MENTEC), c/o Economic Development Department, Gwynedd County Council, Caernarfon, Gwynedd LL55 1SH (Tel: 01286 679397; Fax: 01286 673324) Contact: Dafydd Jones Has received financial backing from the Welsh Office through the Urban Programme; a joint venture between Gwynedd County Council, Arfon Borough Council, and University College of North Wales, Bangor.	1987	6	61.5	Yes	Yes

	1	2	3	4	5
Newtech Science Park, Deeside Industrial Park, Clwyd CH5 2NT (Tel: 01244 289881; Fax: 01244 280002) Contact: John Allen Principal partners in its development are Clwyd County Council and the North East Wales Institute. The Welsh Development Agency is responsible for the construction of the present industrial units on site. Newtech also provides its services through a second base in the Wrexham Technology Park (see below).	1983	15	58–485	No	No
University College of Swansea Innovation Centre, Singleton Park, Swansea SA2 8PP (Tel: 01792 295556; Fax: 01792 295613) Contact: Eifion Griffiths A joint initiative between the Welsh Development Agency and the University College of Swansea.	1986	19	30–150	No	No
Wrexham Technology Park, Croesnewydd Hall, Wrexham, Clwyd LL13 7YP (Tel: 01978 290694; Fax: 01978 290705) Contact: John Roberts Partners: Clwyd County Council, the North East Wales Institute of Higher Education, Clwyd Health Authority.	1984	25	30–150	Yes	No

Scotland

	1	2	3	4	5
Heriot-Watt University Research Park, Riccarton, Edinburgh EH14 4AP (Tel: 0131 449 7070; Fax: 0131 449 7076) Contact: Ian Dalton Entirely developed by Heriot-Watt University from its own resources.	1971	36	139–2,230	Yes	No

	1	2	3	4	5
Stirling University Innovation Park, Scottish Metropolitan Alpha Centre, Innovation Park, Stirling FK9 4NF (Tel: 01786 70080; Fax: 01786 51030) Contact: Stewart Cameron Shareholders are the University of Stirling, Central Regional Council and Scottish Enterprise.	1986	22	40–630	Yes	No
West of Scotland Science Park, Glasgow G20 0SP (Tel: 0141 946 7161; Fax: 0141 945 1591) Contact: Sandie McGee A joint initiative between Scottish Enterprise and the Universities of Glasgow and Strathclyde.	1983	20	77–340	Yes	Yes

Northern Ireland

	1	2	3	4	5
Antrim Technology Park, IDB Regional Office, Unit 2A, Belfast Road, Antrim BT41 1QS (Tel: 018494 61538; Fax: 018494 28075) Contact: George Dillan Wholly owned by the Industrial Development Board for Northern Ireland (IDB). It is being developed with the support and co-operation of the Queen's University of Belfast and the University of Ulster.	1985	8	700–1,100	No	Yes

■ RESEARCH ASSOCIATIONS AND ORGANIZATIONS

There are some 100 research organizations in the UK, which are the centres of knowledge in their respective fields. If the product or idea that you are developing (or want to use) comes within their sphere of interest, they may well be of use. They have extensive information systems, and can usually guide enquirers to appropriate sources of data or other help.

BHRA Fluid Engineering,
Cranfield, Beds MK43 0AJ
(Tel: 01234 750422;
Fax: 01234 750074).

BIBRA Toxicology International,
Woodmansterne Road, Carshalton,
Surrey SM5 4DS (Tel: 0181 643 4411;
Fax: 0181 661 7029).

Brewing Research Foundation,
Lyttel Hall, Nutfield, Redhill RH1 4HY
(Tel: 01737 82272.)
Brick Development Association,
Woodside, Winkfield, Windsor, Berks
SL4 2DX
(Tel: 01344 885651;
Fax: 01334 890129)
British Glass Confederation,
Northumberland Road, Sheffield
S10 2UA (Tel: 0114 2686201;
Fax: 0114 2681073).
Contact: H C D Brown.
**The British Internal Combustion
Engine Research Institute Ltd,**
111–112 Buckingham Avenue, Slough
SL1 4PH (Tel: 01753 27371). Contact:
I Brown, Director.
British Leather Confederation, King's
Park Road, Moulton Park, Northamp-
tonshire NN3 1JD
(Tel: 01604 494131;
Fax: 01604 648220).
Contact: C B Wood.
Building Research Establishment,
Garston, Watford WD2 7JR
(Tel: 01923 894040;
Fax: 01923 664010).
**Building Services Research and
Information Association,**
Old Bracknell Lane West, Bracknell,
Berks RG12 4AH
(Tel: 01344 426511;
Fax: 01344 487575).
Contact: Anne King.
**CERAM (Ceramic Research
Association),** Queens Road, Penkhull,
Stoke-on-Trent ST4 7LQ
(Tel: 01782 45431;
Fax: 01782 412331).
Contact: R C Edgar.
**Construction Industry Research and
Information Association,** 6 Storey's
Gate, London SW1P 3AU
(Tel: 0171 222 8891;
Fax: 0171 228 1708).

Contact: Louise Harrison.
**Cranfield Unit for Precision
Engineering,** Cranfield Institute of
Technology, Cranfield, Beds MK43
0AL (Tel: 01234 750111).
Contact: Professor P A McKeown,
Director.
Fabric Care Research Association,
Forest House Laboratories, Knaresbor-
ough Road, Harrogate, North Yorks
H62 7LZ (Tel: 01423 885977; Fax:
01423 880045).
Contact: C J Tebbs.
**Furniture Industry Research
Association,** Maxwell Road, Stevenage
SG1 2EW (Tel: 01438 313168;
Fax: 01438 72767).
Contact: P R Hinton.
**The Horticultural Research
Association,** Wellesbourne, Warwick
CV35 9EF (Tel: 01789 470382;
Fax: 01789 470552).
Institute of Biology, 20–22
Queensbury Place, London SW7 2DZ
(Tel: 0171 581 8333;
Fax: 0171 823 9409).
Institute of Materials, 1 Carlton
House Terrace, London SW1Y 5DB
(Tel: 0171 839 4071;
Fax: 0171 839 2289).
Contact: Helen Turkdogan. Covers all
materials – plastics, rubber, ceramics,
powders.
Institute of Sheet Metal Engineering,
Exeter House, 48 Holloway Road,
Birmingham B1 1NQ
(Tel: 0121 622 2860;
Fax: 0121 666 6316).
Contact: M A Ruston.
Institute of Wood Science, Stocking
Lane, Hughenden Valley, High
Wycombe, Bucks HP14 4NU
(Tel: 01494 565374).
Contact: M W Holloway.
**Machine Tool Technologies
Association,** 62 Bayswater Road,

London W2 3PS
(Tel: 0171 402 6671;
Fax: 0171 724 7250).
Contact: Paul Harbinson.
The Paint Research Association,
Waldegrave Road, Teddington, Middx
TW11 8LD
(Tel: 0181 977 4427;
Fax: 0181 943 4705).
Contact: J A Bernie.
PERA (Production Engineering
Research Association) International,
Melton Mowbray, Leicestershire LE13
0PB (Tel: 01664 501501;
Fax: 01664 501264).
Contact: A Housdan.
PIRA International (Paper and Board,
Printing and Packaging Industries
Research Association), Randalls Road,
Leatherhead, Surrey KT22 7RU
(Tel: 01372 376161;
Fax: 01372 377526).
Contact: Donna West.
Royal Aeronautical Society,
4 Hamilton Place, London W1V 0BQ
(Tel: 0171 499 3515;

Fax: 0171 499 6230).
Contact: Noelle Meredith.
Society of Glass Technology,
20 Hallam Gate, Sheffield S10 5BT
(Tel: 0114 2663168;
Fax: 0114 2665252).
Contact: J. Costello.
Timber Research and Development
Association, Stocking Lane,
Hughenden Valley, High Wycombe,
Bucks HP14 4ND
(Tel: 01494 563091;
Fax: 01494 565487).

Other institutes include:
British Association for the
Advancement of Science, Fortress
House, 23 Savile Row, London
W1X 1AB (Tel: 0171 494 3326;
Fax: 0171 734 1658).
Contact: Peter Briggs.
The Research and Development
Society, 47 Belgrave Square, London
SW1X 8QX (Tel: 0171 235 6111; Fax:
0171 259 6002).
Contact: Clive Jones.

■ COMPUTERS

If you have not already bought a computer then there are a number of organizations, periodicals and books that may help you to make the best decisions. You will need to know something of what a computer can and cannot do, and exactly what work you want done. If your business involves or is likely to involve repetitious, routinized, time-consuming and usually boring tasks, the chances are that a computer could do them better. Typically, small businesses put their book-keeping, management accounts, payroll, mailing and price lists and wordprocessing functions on to a computer. Sales management systems are available to analyse customers: how long they take to pay up; how much on average they order; and when their next order is due.

Finding your solution

Once you have decided what you want done, then you have to find the software and hardware to meet your needs. The software is the program or instructions that have to be given to the computer in order to process your data and produce the information you want.

Finding out about software means reading the computer magazines, talking to manufacturers and users, going to exhibitions and getting demonstrations from software houses.

If you are considering computerizing your accounts you should talk first to your accountant, and the Inland Revenue and Customs and Excise to ensure your system will meet their needs.

An increasing number of 'standard' software packages are available for specific trades and professions. Packages include those for small shops, such as pharmacies, and for medical practices and estate agents. Your trade association will be watching these developments, and they should be able to help you find out more. Keeping a watch in your trade magazine will also show you what enterprising people are getting up to in this area.

It is highly likely that your needs and the available software will not quite match. In this case you will need to customize the software to your own requirements by writing, or having written, additional programs.

Finally, you will have to decide on the hardware – the computer itself. Your choice of software will pre-select the computer best suited to your needs, but you can still choose whether to buy (or lease) your own, or to use a computer bureau on a time-sharing basis. It is very likely that the complexities and unfamiliarity of the field, combined with the overwhelming apparent choice of systems, will leave you confused.

Sources of further information and advice

The Association of Independent Computer Specialists, Leicester House, 8 Leicester Street, London WC2H 7BN (Tel: 0171 437 0678). Founded in 1972. The association's members are consultants, programmers, software designers and specialists in various aspects of computer applications, including communications. They set and maintain standards of competence and integrity in the independent provision of computer-related services.

The Association of Professional Computer Consultants, Penn House, 16 Peterborough Road, Harrow HA1 2YN (Tel: 0181 422 6460). Founded in 1982. The association's Code of Professional Conduct ensures that members' clients receive objective, impartial advice and services. Members are not allowed to supply (directly or indirectly) hardware or software, nor are they allowed to write software themselves for sale to their clients. They must not benefit from sales and agency commissions, introductory commissions, or trading links with computer industry suppliers. Contact the association with details of your problem(s) and the sort of expertise you need and they will send you details of experienced independent and professional consultants, usually in your area.

British Computer Society, 13 Mansfield Street, London W1M 0BP (Tel: 0171 637 0471; Fax: 0171 631 1049). The professional body for information technology.

Business Equipment and Information Technology Association, Leicester House, 8 Leicester Street, London WC2H 7BN (Tel: 0171 437 0678; Fax: 0171 437

4901). Field of expertise covers communications, data processing, dictation, filing and storage equipment, mailing systems etc.

Computing Services Association, Hanover House, 73–74 High Holborn, London WC1V 6LE (Tel: 0171 405 2171; Fax: 0171 404 4119). The industry association for the computing software and services industry in the UK. It is able to assist those starting their own business or running a business through three services:

- A paper, titled 'Choosing an IT System', is available free of charge.
- Businesses with an IT system requirement may briefly detail this to CSA who will circulate this as a Business Enquiry to all 380 members. This offers the enquirer two advantages: it is possible by this route to seek out the experts in their field who may already have 'packaged solutions', and they will be dealing with reputable and experienced companies. The service is available under a box number maintained by CSA to ensure confidentiality, or companies may contact the enquirer directly. Contact Tracey Battams at CSA for more information.
- Briefing notes on 'Choosing a Consultant' and 'Choosing a System Supplier' are available free of charge.

Data Protection Registrar, Springfield House, Water Lane, Wilmslow, Cheshire SK9 5AX (Tel: 01625 535711). See Section 7, on legal issues.

Independent National Computing Association, Austen Suite, 2nd Floor, Austen House, 1 Upper Street, Fleet, Hampshire GU13 9PE (Tel: 01252 811173; Fax: 01252 811175). Association of independent freelance computer consultants. Monthly newsletter and helpline, free to members and potential members.

Information Technology Centres (ITeCs as they are generally called) were first launched in 1982 with the objective of encouraging young people and the business community to understand and make use of new technology. They still have a major training role with young people and are an important source of employees to local companies.

Many ITeCs now also offer IT consultancy, hardware and software sales and support particularly relevant to the small to medium-sized enterprise in addition to the business applications training provided to large organizations.

For the address of your nearest ITeC contact NAITEC, Suffolk Enterprise Centre, Russell Road, Ipswich IP1 2DE (Tel: 01473 288000; Fax: 01473 2524889).

Internet

The world's biggest computer network with more than 25 million users, growing at 20% per month, Internet connects you to anyone, anywhere with a computer and a modem. It is used by universities, research establishments, libraries, government departments and business users as a cheap and reliable means of electronic communication.

It is the most comprehensive international electronic data highway in the world, and firms are lining up to offer services to Internet subscribers. In many cases using Internet is cheaper than an international phone call or fax.

To join the Internet you need a reasonably powerful desktop or laptop computer that you connect to the telephone line with a modem, which costs between £150 and £400.

You must then join one of the providers that have negotiated a top-level Internet connection. Some have established local access in several cities (important in cutting long-distance phone bills).

The following are some of the groups that provide commercial and private users a connection to the Internet. Their services vary widely, but all offer e-mail and the ability to read what is on the Internet.

In general, the higher the fee the more the service is aimed towards business and the more after-sales service is provided. One such provider is Compuserve.

For the 1.9 million customers of the on-line network Compuserve, the subscription gives these personal computer users in 138 different countries access to a global network of electronic mail, virtual shopping, on-line news and information services, and a collection of chat areas where you can discuss almost everything.

Compuserve is the friendly face of on-line computing. The software for Windows and Macintosh PCs, which the company gives away with the initial subscription fee, hides the impenetrable command codes of big-world computing behind the scenes and translates them into easy point-and-click routines.

To send an e-mail message just click on the names of the people you want to talk to. To book an airline seat, fill in an on-screen form with your dates, cities and meal requirements, and the computer will hunt for the best price.

The British subscriber base to Compuserve is only 45,000 at the moment but it is expected to double over the next year as the variety of local services grows. Subscribers have access to live British traffic information, British news from the Press Association, European railway timetables, newspaper libraries (including that of *The Times*), on-line information from the AA's travel books, and live share prices from the Stock Exchange.

Compuserve also exchanges electronic mail with Internet, and will, increasingly, bring on-line direct access to Internet services too.

Spending hours accessing this vast wealth of information could prove expensive. After the initial entry fee of £26.45, Compuserve charges around £6 a month for the subscription, £5 an hour for using the service between peak hours (8 a.m. to 7 p.m. Monday to Friday) and between £2.50 and £6 an hour extra for using 'extended services', such as forums about products or professional topics.

There will also be an extra hourly surcharge (up to £2) if you access the service indirectly, say through a phone link operated by another company, such as Mercury.

The monthly subscription includes an allowance of 60 free e-mail messages, with a small charge per message if you exceed that amount. Pulling information out of private databases will generate extra charges which vary from up to £20 for a company search to less than £1 for a newspaper library cutting.

Used wisely, Compuserve can be extremely cost-effective, charged weekly to your credit card. You should find the cheapest phone route into the system, which may not be the shortest. For example, it is cheaper in Cornwall to make a long-distance phone call on Mercury into a direct Compuserve node in London than to phone a local node which attracts a surcharge because it is not run directly by the network itself.

You can keep costs down if you stay on-line for the shortest time possible. Unless you are joining off-peak, make sure you read and write electronic mail off-line.

BBC Networking Club
Local access: London, Edinburgh, Bristol, Birmingham, Manchester, Cambridge.
Fees: £12 a month plus VAT.
The BBC is planning a combined bulletin board and Internet feed. It might take over the home-user market.
Tel: 0181 576 7799.

CityScape
Local access: London, Cambridge, Edinburgh.
Fees: IP Gold, £50 registration + £180 a year, or CityScape e-mail, £400 a year.
Most user-friendly of all the providers, specializing in customers with no prior knowledge of the Internet.
Tel: 01223 566950.

CIX
Local access: London.
Fees: £25 registration and £6.50 a month plus 6p per minute usage charge.
The most popular UK bulletin board, good for e-mail but does not provide full Internet fee.
Tel: 01492 641961.

Demon Internet
Local access: London, Manchester, Liverpool, Warrington, Edinburgh.
Fees: £12.50 registration and £10 a month. No time charges. The biggest low-cost provider of a raw Internet feed.
Tel: 0181 349 0063.

The Direct Connection
Local access: London.
Fees: from £10 a month, unlimited use, with no time charges.
A sophisticated package with fees rising according to the number of services used.
Tel: 0181 317 0100.

Eunet GB

Local access: London, Bracknell, Cambridge, Canterbury, Birmingham.
Fees: from £95 a quarter.
Aiming at international business. Good for connections to east Europe.
Tel: 01227 475497.

Exnet Systems

Local access: London and Edinburgh.
Fees: £300 per annum; Internet supplement is £9 a month with special prices for resellers.
Aimed at users who want to offer their own services.
Tel: 0181 244 0077.

Greennet

Local access: London.
Fees (non-commercial standard): £5 a month + £3.60 an hour (peak) or £2.40 (off-peak). The alternative Internet link-up, specializing in pressure groups etc.
Tel: 0171 608 3040.

On-Line

Local access: London.
Fees: £9.99 a month or £2.00 an hour.
Specializing in international connections.
Tel: 0181 558 6114.

Pipex

Local access: London, Cambridge, Edinburgh.
Fees: dial-up services start at £400 per annum.
The most comprehensive of the UK providers, offering every available service.
Tel: 01223 250120.

Win-Net Mail and News

Local access: London.
Fees: from £6.75 per month (based on £3.25 per hour).
Several premium services are offered.
Tel: 0181 863 1191.

Faxing on Internet

Low-cost faxing, via Internet: by connecting a computer to the telephone line with a modem and accessing the Internet by a local phone call, a fax can be sent across the world to a distant computer which, for the price of another local call, will fax the document to its destination. The cost is almost always much lower than for the one long-distance call.

A sender types a destination fax number in the message header of the document being prepared and the computer does the rest. It looks at the number and decides which participating computer is nearest to it. If it finds none near the destination, it sends a message saying the fax could not be delivered.

Ever more computers attached to the Internet are being configured to allow this intelligent and cheap faxing facility. London is served by several college computers, as is much of America and east Canada. Connections are growing all the time.

Senders can also fax to several fax machines by this method, or even a combination of fax machines and traditional e-mail recipients.

For more details contact InterFax on 001 215 584 0300; FAXINET on 001 617 522 8102 or Unigate (for faxing to Russia) on 001 206 649 5619.

Using a telephone on Internet

The M.Phone looks like a conventional telephone, but slide out the keyboard and it becomes a computer which, according to the developer, M.Power of New York, makes access to the Internet and other on-line information services as easy as writing a note.

With a menu-driven interface, users can make an ordinary telephone call or dial through to on-line services such as home banking, Compuserve, and e-mail through the Internet. At the heart of the M.Phone lies a signal-processing chip with inbuilt software that can be updated over the phone line. It also includes facilities for adding peripherals such as disk drives and printers.

The M.Phone is now in American shops costing $300 (£200), and is beginning to appear in Britain. If you can't wait for local availability, Tel: 001 212 593 0906.

Open University Customer Services Box 76, Milton Keynes MK7 6AN (0908 274066). The Open University has a number of home study courses covering computing in business.

Trade Association Your trade association will be able to keep you abreast of computing developments in your trade or industry. *The Directory of British Associations*, published by CBD Research Limited, Beckenham, Kent, lists all Trade Associations. The directory is in most reference libraries.

Publications

There are numerous publications that serve all sectors of this growing market-place. Most popular computers have a magazine associated with them. Directories of the latest software and hardware are regularly published in monthly magazines and new products are tested and reviewed.

When reading reviews, watch out for words like 'easy to use', 'usable', and 'user-friendly'. Most reviewers have many years' experience using computers, and what is easy to them is not necessarily easy for a beginner. The best they can tell you is that a product is easier to use than other ones they have seen. But very often the easiest product to use is the one most like the one you already know. The advent of Windows, the graphical user interface for the PC, has modified that rule, but not that much.

Individual reviewers also have their own prejudices, which may not be obvious. Most reviews of word processors, for example, mention the word counter because this is the first thing a journalist, writing to length, needs. It is not a feature most business people need to worry about. If you're planning a purchase, therefore, the best advice is to read more than one review, and use the reviews to eliminate obviously wrong choices. Then try to get more information about or see live demonstrations of the remaining products.

Useful publications include:
Better Buys for Business, a sort of *Which?* for the office, is available from Managing your Business Ltd, 7 Cromwell Road, London SW7 2HR.

How to Computerize Your Small Business by Patrick D O'Hara, published by Wiley in 1993; price £12.95.

Business Computing Primer by John Edwards and Colin Lewis, published by Pitman in 1994; price £15.99.

How to Get IT Right in Business – a video series produced in association with the Department of Trade and Industry. The videos set out to help you make informed judgements and know what questions to ask of suppliers. Priced at £95 each, there are six videos in the series.
    Details from: IFS International, Wolsley Business Park, Kempston, Bedford MK42 7BT (Tel: 01234 853605; Fax: 01234 854499).

Newspapers
The *Sunday Times*, *Daily Telegraph* and *The Times* all have regular weekly sections that review current computing issues, in an informed and jargon-free manner.

PC Today – *Solutions for Small Business*, price £3.95, monthly from most newsagents. This is a very good source of ideas and information on all computing issues, pitched at a level appropriate to the small and medium-sized firm.

Computer – video-based training
Whether you are a complete beginner or already know your way around a PC and now wish to expand your skills, the *Sunday Times* range of videos offers effective training at good value. For beginners: two videos, using plain English, explain all you need to know to get started. *Your First PC* covers basic techniques and the jargon; *Microsoft Windows* introduces the popular Windows software; £16.99 each (inc. VAT) plus P&P.

How to Get the Best from Your PC: a series of 17 videos offering a range of clear, detailed explanations of basic computer concepts and essential topics:

Word Processing 1	Communications
Word Processing 2	Networks
Spreadsheets 1	Choosing a Micro
Spreadsheets 2	Teleworking
Databases 1	Computer Security
Databases 2	Computer Aided Design
Desktop Publishing 1	How to Computerize your Accounts
Desktop Publishing 2	Developing a Business-led Computer
Accounts	Strategy

Price £14.99 each (exc. VAT) plus P&P. All 17 videos are on offer for £199 (exc. VAT) plus P&P and saving over £80. To order or request a free brochure, contact Taylor Made Films, PO Box 2000, Andover SP10 3XY (Tel: 01264 335577; Fax: 01264 334999).

The National Computing Centre is the UK centre for information technology. Backed by, and in co-operation with, government, the IT industry and IT users, NCC directs technical programmes, administers national schemes and develops products and services to promote the effective use of information technology.

The following services are of particular interest to new computer users:

■ *'Guidelines' for IT management*
The monthly 'Guidelines' keeps managers up to date and points them towards sources of further information.
■ *Briefing*
By providing a strategic overview of IT issues in a concise monthly report, 'Briefing' saves valuable executive time, giving background information on wider strategy and policy arguments, distilled by experts. It covers subjects such as software cost estimation, benchmarking, client server computing and much more.
■ *'Interface'*
Their monthly magazine keeps members abreast of what is happening in the IT world, with listings, events, articles on current technology, and all the NCC news.
■ *IT Alert*
Rushed to you whenever a 'hot' issue requires immediate action or comment, this bulletin draws the attention of NCC members to urgent issues and deadlines which directly affect their day-to-day activities in IT.
■ *Survey of IT Users*
A comprehensive annual survey of IT usage in the UK, aimed at NCC members. A reliable and factual review of trends and attitudes, invaluable when needing to justify IT expenditure.
■ *HelpDesk*
'One call can save the cost of joining the NCC'. The HelpDesk's ever growing database of answers to previous enquiries means it can respond immediately, or put you in touch with further sources of information.

Specially trained staff deal with your enquiries, record the details and check that you are satisfied with the response.

■ *LinkLine*
The 'marriage bureau' for members. Specific help and guidance from someone who has faced the same problem, researched the same idea and made the right decision. They put you in direct contact with sympathetic organizations, then they monitor the outcome for the benefit of others.

■ *Regional associations*
NCC members automatically belong to a regional asociation. Responding to local needs, each of the 60 regional associations runs its own programme of workshops and seminars, conducts its own surveys and sets up its own working parties. Whether you are looking for new business contacts or a forum for discussion, you will have every opportunity to participate. Every member can stand for election to the Regional Committee, each has a vote in the selection process.

■ *Special interests*
Interest groups debate such issues as IT security, the law and communications, quality and training. They bring together the leading authorities in the industry, facilitate interaction and provide a source of support, influence and intelligence for their members and to the wider IT community. Membership costs £395 per annum (excluding VAT), which may sound a lot – but it's a lot less costly than making a wrong investment in either software or hardware.

National Computing Centre, Oxford House, Oxford Road, Manchester M1 7ED (Tel: 0161 228 6333; Fax: Sales 0161 237 1558; Membership 0161 236 8049).
National Computing Centre, Cowcross Court, 77 Cowcross Street, London EC1M 6BP (Tel: 0171 490 5828; Fax: 0171 490 8628).
National Computing Centre, Anderston House, 389 Argyle Street, Glasgow G2 8LR (Tel: 0141 204 1101; Fax: 0141 204 3725).
National Computing Centre, The Crescent Centre, Temple Back, Bristol BS1 6EZ (Tel: 0117 9277077; Fax: 0117 9298496).

■ OTHER SOURCES OF INFORMATION AND ADVICE ON TECHNOLOGY AND RELATED MATTERS

Apart from science parks, there are a number of other organizations and services useful to the innovator. In this section you can find out how to meet other inventors; how to get someone else to do all the work of developing, patenting and marketing your product, and then pay you a fee; how to find financial institutions that understand technology and can give more than just financial help. (See also Section 6.)

British Technology Group (BTG), 101 Newington Causeway, London SE1 6BU (Tel: 0171 403 6666). Funded by national government. In 1981 the British Technology Group was formed out of the late National Enterprise Board and the National Research Development Corporation. It is now privatized. The organization has a portfolio of 400 investments in industrial companies. In addition, about 200 research and development projects are being funded at British universities.

BTG can provide finance for technical innovation in any field of technology. This finance is available to any company or individual entrepreneur, either as equity or loan capital. BTG is the main channel for exploiting technology from universities, polytechnics, research councils and government research establishments. It has a portfolio of 1,800 UK patents, 600 licences and over 400 revenue-earning innovations.

For small companies they have two schemes:

- *The Small Company Innovation Fund (SCIF).* This was established in September 1980 to provide finance where the business as a whole is innovative. Despite having advanced only £1 million spread over two dozen projects since its inception, BTG are keen to hear from innovative entrepreneurs needing the services of SCIF.
- *Oakland Finance Ltd,* established in March 1981, provides loans of up to £50,000 for technological or more traditionally based companies.

BTG produces a booklet 'Help for the Inventor'.

Greater London Enterprise Technology, 63–67 Newington Causeway, London SE1 6BD (Tel: 0171 403 1742). Contact: Michael Cooley. As well as having funds to invest in technology-based ventures in London, in April 1987 they set up a £500,000 fund for product development. This is to enable innovatory products from companies and universities to realize their commercial potential. Marketing and financial advice is also provided to support the ventures they back.

3i Ventures, is the high-technology arm of Investors in Industry plc, 91 Waterloo Road, London SE1 8XP (Tel: 0171 928 7822). Generally its approach is effective for situations calling for investments of £200,000 or more. In whatever form its funds are provided it expects them to be at substantial risk. Other than in exceptional circumstances they ask for a significant but minority shareholding in the business.

Innovation Centres. Their founding purpose is to offer a valuable resource to people with ideas for original or improved products.

Supported variously by local authorities, central government, higher education and the private sector, innovation centres offer – often free or at merely nominal cost – commercial services unavailable at affordable prices. These include technical and commercial appraisal; advice on legal protection; design or redesign; prototype manufacture and assessment; sourcing of materials, information or further help; negotiation with potential manufacturers or sponsors; marketing assistance.

Two such centres are described below. To locate others see your local phone book.

Cornwall Innovation Centre Ltd, Rosewarne, Camborne, Cornwall TR14 0AB (Tel: 01209 612670; Fax: 01209 612671). Founded in 1984 by the Cornwall County Council and the Council for Small Industries in Rural Areas (CoSIRA). The aim was, and still is, to improve opportunities for employment and wealth creation in the county by encouraging and assisting people and firms with new ideas to bring them successfully to the market-place.

People from existing industries were involved from the beginning, as it was intended that it should be run primarily by those with direct experience of the problems involved. It is now operated and managed by senior men and women from industry, the Cornwall College and various public services, on an entirely voluntary basis.

The work of the Centre is divided into two parts. On the one hand it helps individuals who have made particular inventions to protect them and have them produced and marketed. On the other, it organizes general educational and promotional events to improve awareness of all aspects of the exploitation of innovation.

Help to individuals includes:
■ technical and commercial appraisal of projects;
■ advice and assistance in making patent applications;
■ re-design to meet market or production requirements;
■ introductions to organizations that might undertake advanced development, production or marketing.

The Centre works under a strict undertaking of confidentiality. People who wish to use its services are first invited to complete a simple form giving some general information about their idea and of the help they feel they need. This then becomes a guarantee that the idea will not be used or divulged to an outside party without the consent of the applicant. Discussing an idea with the Centre is a private matter and does not prevent a patent from being obtained. The Centre will advise on avoiding those actions which might well invalidate a patent application.

The Cornwall Innovation Centre does not duplicate the work of other organizations. It will put applicants in touch with any agency that can offer specialized help in particular areas such as legislation, grants and finance.

An initial interview and appraisal of the applicant's innovation is given entirely free of charge. If this shows that the idea has a good chance of commercial success, and detailed help from the Centre is required, a nominal charge, currently £25, is made purely to contribute towards the administrative costs involved. This charge may be waived in certain exceptional cases.

South London Innovation Centre and Skill Exchange Ltd, 1–4 Brixton Hill Place, London SW2 1HJ (Tel: 0181 671 4055). The Centre assists any person who has an innovative design or novel redesign of an existing product. Their services are free of charge. The Centre has a well-equipped metal workshop and wood workshop, with trained supervisors who will help clients in the development of their product. Computer-aided design facilities are also available.

The Centre can purchase materials on behalf of the client and will assist the client through from basic design concept to manufacture. It is open Monday to Friday, 9 a.m. to 5 p.m. Interested parties should contact Ian Swanson (Tel: 0181 678 0628 or 0181 671 4055: Fax: 0181 678 0612).

The Chartered Institute of Patent Agents, Staple Inn Buildings, High Holborn, London WC1V 7PZ (Tel: 0171 405 9450); Fax: 0171 430 0471. The institute itself does not run an advisory service, although it will give advice on patents, trade marks and designs where possible. It publishes *The Register of Patent Agents*, which lists the names and business addresses of all the patent agents qualified to practise before the Patent Office. More details on individual agents are available; price £10.00.

The Institute runs a free advisory clinic staffed by patent agents, which is held on Tuesdays from 5 p.m. to 7 p.m. (by appointment only, in half-hour sessions).

The patent agent will be able to give advice on all aspects relating to making application for patents, trade marks and designs, as well as on infringement of these or of protection and on passing off matters. He may also be able to give advice on the exploitation of any invention protected by patent, although this is not specifically within his field of operation. The patent agents will work to a fixed scale of charges relating to the work done, in the same way as a solicitor charges, rather than taking a share in the commercial success of an invention.

Innovations and Inventions Fair, Co-sponsored by Institute of Patentees and Inventors, held annually. Hundreds of ideas and inventions, concepts, proto-types, designs and models on show plus seminars on intellectual property, technology transfer, financing inventions, selling your invention.

Institute of International Licensing Practitioners Ltd, 105 Onslow Square, London SW7 3LU (Tel: 0171 584 5749; Fax: 0171 244 8741). Licensing practitioners can help you find customers to license your invention to, if you cannot exploit it yourself. They keep a register of members and their specialist areas of expertise. Copies are available from the secretary.

The Institute of Inventors, 19 Fosse Way, Ealing, London W13 0BZ (Tel: 0181 998 3540; Fax: 0181 991 1309). This is a self-supporting institute run by inventors for inventors. It can help with patent application, prototypes and commercialization of suitable inventions.

The Institute of Patentees and Inventors, Suite 505a, Triumph House, 189 Regent Street, London W1RV 7WF (Tel/Fax: 0171 242 7812). The institute was founded in 1919 to further the interests of patentees and inventors. It gives advice and guidance to members on all aspects of inventing, from idea conception to innovation and development. Its journal, *Future*, comes out quarterly and helps to keep members up to date. Its *New Patents Bulletin* acts as a liaison with industry, bringing members' inventions to the notice of specialized manufacturing firms. Exhibitions of new inventions are organized frequently by IPI.

Institute for Social Inventions, 20 Heber Road, London NW2 6AA (Tel: 0181 208 2853; Fax: 0181 452 6434). Promotes social innovations for improving the quality of life.

The Inventors' Information Guide, Published by the Centre for Commercial Law Studies, Queen Mary and Westfield College, University of London (0171 975 5555 ext 5322).

PA Technology, Cambridge Laboratory, Melbourn, Royston, Herts SG8 6DP (Tel: 01763 261222; Fax: 01763 260023). Their major role is the development of commercially successful products for companies. The service begins with a clear definition of the commercial and market constraints and extends through initial concept development, technical and commercial feasibility studies, ergonomic design and styling, prototype design and construction, production and manufacturing engineering, market research and market launch, packaging and supporting graphics. Each project is managed by an experienced team of senior consultants who are recognized authorities in their field and have in-depth experience in international project and business development.

SCEPTRE, Sheffield Centre for Product Development and Technological Resources, Sheffield Hallam University, City Campus, Pond Street, Sheffield S1 1WB (Tel: 0114 2533450; Fax: 0114 2533352. Practical help to improve your product. Workshop facilities include:

lathes for metal and wood	shot-blast cleaner
Bridgeport and Parkson milling machines	electronics equipment
	surface and cylindrical grinders
band saw, jig saw, circular saw	planer-thicknesser
plastics moulding vacuum former	guillotine and folder
TIG, gas and spot welder	pillar drill and radial arm drill

You can use their machines to test out your ideas. Cost: £6 plus VAT per hour of use (or they can do it for you, to a fixed price quotation).

Use their qualified staff and extensive backup resources to help you sort out your technical problems:

patents, copyright	sources of finance
British standards	directories and indexes
European regulations	practical problem-solving
manufacturers and suppliers of parts	troubleshooting
	test rig and prototype building
grants and information on	

In addition they can provide a short course tailored to your needs to last for several weeks or just half a day.

Technology Evaluation and Marketing Ltd (TEaM), 2 Whitton Road, Martin's Heron, Bracknell, Berks RG12 6QZ (Tel: 01344 411000; Fax: 01344 411000). Main activities are helping researchers and businesses with technology transfer. They offer the following types of service:

- *Technology assessment.* Evaluation of the commercial prospects for innovations and estimation of the potential market size and returns.
- *Technology marketing.* Contacts with appropriate market sectors to ensure perceptions of market needs are matched by reality.
- *Technology audit.* Review of a technology area within a laboratory or business to identify opportunities and exploitation routes.
- *Technology searching.* Assessment of company technology needs and finding sources of solutions.
- *Business planning.* Assistance with preparation of business plans with emphasis on financial implications of proposed technologies.
- *Patents consultancy.* Appraisal of patent prospects and advice on cost-effective protection of IPR for commercial exploitation.
- *Exploitation and licensing.* Negotiation of contracts or licence deals as an alternative route to realizing value from innovations.

Technology Exchange Centre Ltd, South Bank Technopark, 90 London Road, London SE1 6LH (Tel: 0171 465 8880). A non-profit company limited by guarantee, formed to assist the smaller manufacturing enterprise to find new products and processes by licence and also to help them find manufacturers elsewhere for their own development. Under the EEC SPRINT programme the Exchange has a collaboration with regional development authorities in Belgium, Spain, Greece, France, Denmark and Ireland.

They maintain close links with the major databanks in the USA, Europe and Japan and the development authorities, universities and research establishments around the world. A catalogue of offers and requests for technology is published quarterly and circulated to licensing agents, journals and managing directors seeking new products in many countries.

The Exchange links with organizations seeking technology for developing countries and obtains early notification of development needs involving the supply of capital plant and technology that can be licensed.

5 | *Finding out about your market*

■ SIZING UP THE MARKET

You need to ensure that there are enough customers out there, with sufficient money to spend, to create a viable market-place for your products or services. You must also see who else will be competing against you for their business.

In other words you need to research your market. This is something that potential financial backers – be they banks or other institutions – will insist on. And in this they are doing you a favour. Many businesses started with private money (such as redundancy payments) fail, because the market was not thoroughly researched at the outset. Whatever your business idea, you must undertake some well-thought-out market research before you invest any money or approach anyone else to invest in your venture.

You do not have to pay professional companies to do your research. You can gather information more effectively (and cheaply) yourself. This 'DIY' market research will have two purposes:

■ To build credibility for the business idea, the entrepreneur must prove, first to his or her satisfaction and later to outside financiers, that he or she thoroughly understands the market-place for the new product or service. This will be vital if resources are to be attracted to build the new venture.

■ To develop a realistic market entry strategy for the new business, based on a clear understanding of genuine customer needs and ensuring that product quality, price, promotional methods and distribution chain are mutually supportive and clearly focused on target customers.

The Army motto: 'Time spent in reconnaissance is rarely time wasted' holds true for business as well. You will need to research in particular:

■ your customers: who will buy your goods and services? What particular customer needs will your business meet? How many of them are there?

■ your competitors: which established companies are already meeting the needs of your potential customers? What are their strengths and weaknesses?

■ your product or service: how should it be tailored to meet customer needs?

■ the price you should charge: what would be perceived as giving 'value for money'?

- the promotional material needed to reach customers: what newspapers and journals do they read?
- your location: from where could you reach your customers most easily, at minimum cost?

Research, above all else, is not just essential in starting a business but, once launched, must become an integral part in the on-going life of the company. Customers and competitors change; products don't last for ever. Once started, however, on-going market research becomes easier, as you will have existing customers (and staff) to question. It is important that you regularly monitor their views on your business (as the sign in the barber shop stated: 'We need your head to run our business') and develop simple techniques for this purpose (e.g. questionnaires for customers beside the till, suggestion boxes with rewards for employees).

First steps

Before embarking on your market research you should first set clear and precise objectives, rather than just setting out to find interesting general information about the market. For example, if you are planning to open a shop selling to young fashion-conscious women, your research objective could be: to find out how many women aged 18–28, in the income range £18,000+ p.a., live or work within two miles of your chosen shop position. The next step is to see if someone else has the answers already.

Market research conjures up images of people with clipboards accosting you in the street – and you might well have to do that. But much of the information you need will already be published, so some of your market research activity, at least, can be done in a comfortable chair in a good library. For instance, the official Census of Population will supply you with demographic data on size, age and sex of the local populace, and there is a wealth of government and other published statistics to enable you to work out the size and shape of the market nationwide and the expenditure per head of population.

This type of research is called desk research and it is well worth doing first.

Desk research

There is increasingly a great deal of secondary data available in published form. It is accessible via business sections of public libraries and it can help you quantify the size of the market sectors you are entering and determine trends in those markets. In addition to populations of cities and towns (helpful for quantification of markets), libraries frequently purchase reports which analyse growth in different business sectors. Government statistics, showing trends in the economy and in individual sectors, are also held. It is important that business founders can demonstrate that their sector is growing (is the wind behind you, like Anita Roddick with the green movement behind her 'natural' beauty products?), or if the sector is declining, it must be demonstrated why a product/service will be different and will not be affected by the trend (e.g. although in the UK car manufacturing has declined, the makers of 'Kit Cars' have focused on a growing profitable niche of enthusiasts).

If no one has answered your questions then you are into field research, involving field-work in collecting specific information for the market.

Field research

This allows you to gather information directly related to your venture. For instance, entrepreneurs interested in opening a classical music shop in Exeter, aimed at young people, were encouraged when desk research showed that of a total population of 250,000, 25% were under 30. However, it did not tell them what percentage of this 25% was interested in classical music nor how much money each potential customer might spend.

Field research (questionnaire in street) provided the answer of 1% and £2 a week spent, suggesting a potential market of only £65,000 a year (250,000 x 25% x 1% x £2 x 52)! The entrepreneurs sensibly decided to investigate Birmingham and London instead.

But at least the cost had been only two damp afternoons spent in Exeter, rather than the horror of having to dispose of a lease of an unsuccessful shop.

Field-work is now becoming quite big business. In the UK alone expert market research companies now turn over more than £200 million a year. Most field-work carried out consists of interviews, with the interviewer putting the questions to a respondent. We are all becoming accustomed to it, whether being interviewed while travelling or resisting the attempts of enthusiastic salesmen posing as market researchers on doorsteps ('sugging' as this is known has been illegal since 1986). The more popular forms of interviews are:

■ personal (face to face) interview 55% (especially for consumer markets)
■ telephone 32% (especially for surveying companies)
■ post 6% (especially for industrial markets)
■ test and discussion group 7%

Personal interviews and postal surveys are clearly less expensive than getting together panels of interested parties or using expensive telephone time. Telephone interviewing requires a very positive attitude, courtesy, an ability not to talk too quickly and listening while sticking to a rigid questionnaire. Low response rates on postal surveys (normally less than 10%) can be improved by accompanying letters, explaining the purpose of the survey and why respondents should reply; by offering rewards for completed questionnaires (small gift); by sending reminder letters and, of course, by providing pre-paid reply envelopes.

All methods of approach require considered questions. In drawing up the questionnaire attention must be paid to:

■ defining your research objectives: what exactly is it that you vitally need to know? (e.g. how often do people buy, how much?).
■ identifying the customers to sample for this information (e.g. for DIY prod-

ucts, an Ideal Home Exhibition crowd might be best).
- how you are going to undertake the research (e.g. face to face in street).
- how you will analyse the data. If it involves complex multi-choice questions you may need to plan in advance to use a computer to help you process the data. This will involve coding the questions. An even better idea is to keep it so simple you don't need a computer!

When you are sure of the above, and only then, you are ready to design the questionnaire. There are six simple rules to guide this process:
1.   Keep the number of questions to a minimum.
2.   Keep the questions simple. Answers should be either Yes/No/Don't Know or offer at least four alternatives.
3.   Avoid ambiguity – make sure the respondent really understands the question (avoid vague words such as 'generally', 'usually', 'regularly').
4.   Seek factual answers; avoid opinions.
5.   Make sure at the beginning you have a cut-out question, to eliminate unsuitable respondents (e.g. those who never use product/service).
6.   At the end, make sure you have an identifying question to show a cross-section of respondents.

The introduction to a face-to-face interview is important; make sure you are prepared, either carrying an identifying card (e.g. student card, watchdog card) or with rehearsed introduction (e.g. 'Good morning, I'm from Greenwich University [show card] and we are conducting a survey and would be grateful for your help'). You may also need visuals of the product you are investigating (samples, photographs), to ensure the respondent understands. Make sure these are neat and accessible. Finally try out the questionnaire and your technique on your friends, prior to using them in the street. You will be surprised at how questions which seem simple to you are incomprehensible at first to respondents!

The size of the survey undertaken is also important. You frequently hear of political opinion polls taken on samples of 1,500–2,000 voters. This is because the accuracy of your survey increases with the size of sample as the following table shows:

Random sample of:	Points within which 95% of surveys are right:
250	6.2
500	4.4
750	3.6
1,000	3.1
2,000	2.2
6,000	1.2

So, if on a sample size of 600, your survey showed that 40% of women in the town drove cars, the true proportion probably lies between 36% and 44%. For small businesses, a minimum sample of 250 is recommended.

An example of how information can be gleaned from relatively cheap and easy research is shown below. Remember, above all, however, that questioning is by no means the only or most important form of field-work. Sir Terence Conran, when questioned on a radio programme, said that he undertook few formal interviews and implied that he did no market research field-work at all. Later in the programme, however, he confessed to spending nearly half of his time visiting competitors, inspecting new and rival products etc. Visiting exhibitions, buying and examining competitors' products (as the Japanese have so painfully done, in disassembling piece by piece competitive cars, deciding in the process where cost-effective improvements could be made) are clearly important field-work processes.

Just as importantly, test marketing by selling off stalls on a Saturday, or taking part in an exhibition, gives an opportunity to question interested customers and can be the most valuable field-work of all. All methods are equally valid, and results of each should be carefully recorded for subsequent use in presentations and business plans.

Once the primary market research (desk and field research) and market testing (stalls and exhibitions) are complete, pilot testing of the business should take place in one location or customer segment before launching fully into business. Only then can you make a reasonably accurate prediction of sales and the cash-flow implications for your business.

■ MARKETING INFORMATION

The information listed here is just a small proportion of the data available. This section is divided into four areas: Company and product data, UK; Company and product data, overseas; Market and industry data, UK; and Market and industry data, overseas.

Company and product data provides information on home and overseas companies, their products or services, profiles and profitability. Market and industry data provides information on the markets serviced by those companies, their size, growth and other characteristics. There are a number of reference sources that do not rest easily in one section, and they will have been placed in the most suitable location and cross-referenced in order to help you find your way round.

Company and product data, UK

The Analyst's Service provides cards on UK quoted and unquoted companies. The cards contain the following information: name and business of the company together with details of subsidiaries and associates; the date on which the company was registered (formed), along with any change of name or status (e.g. private to public); directors – their positions (chairman, managing director, etc) and their shareholdings as well as the names of the company secretary, bankers, auditors and solicitors. Ten years' profit and loss accounts and at least three years' balance sheets are given, together with sources and applications of funds statements. The highest and lowest share price over the ten-year period is also given, as well as the chairman's latest statement on the company position. A news card is published three or four times a year, giving details of dividends declared, board changes, acquisitions, liquidations, loans raised and other elements of operating information. A selection of these cards is held in many reference libraries. Six months' subscription is £370. Extel Financial Ltd, Fitzroy House, 13–17 Epworth Street, London EC2A 4DL (Tel: 0171 251 3333; Fax: 0171 251 2725).

Extel's Handbook of Market Leaders brings together details on 750 major quoted companies. Though not a substitute for the cards it does provide a quick reference guide to the financial performance of major companies. Published twice a year, in January and July, at £110 per annum.

Companies Registration Office.

This keeps records of all limited companies. For England and Wales these records are kept at Companies House, Crown Way, Maindy, Cardiff, South Glamorgan CF4 3UZ (Tel: 01222 380801) and for Scotland at the Registrar of Companies for Scotland, 102 George Street, Edinburgh EH2 3JD (Tel: 0131 225 5774). For Northern Ireland the Companies Registration Office is at 64 Chichester Street, Belfast BT1 4JX (Tel: 01232 234488).

The records kept include financial statements, accounts, directors' names and addresses, shareholders, and changes of name and structure. The information is available on microfiche at £1 per company, and can be photocopied at 10p per sheet. This service is available to visitors only. There are a number of commercial organizations that will obtain this information for you.

Credit Rating Company Appraisal, ICC Information Group Ltd, Crwys House, 33 Crwys Road, Cardiff CF2 4YF (Tel: 01222 383454; Fax: 01222 668954). Each credit report assesses the financial stability of a company, suggests a credit ceiling and gives an indication of the company's overall creditworthiness.

ICC Financial Surveys produce 200 business sector reports analysing the performance of some 12,000 leading UK companies over a three-year period. For each sector (for example, window manufacturers, retail chemists, the toy industry or computer equipment) key performance ratios are shown for each company in the sector and an average for the sector as a whole. You can therefore use this information to compare your performance, actual or projected, against an industry standard. There are 19 key ratios, and they cover profitability, liquidity, asset utilization, gearing, productivity and exports. Growth rates are monitored, including sales, total assets, capital employed, average wages and exports.It is thus possible to see quickly which company is growing the fastest in your sector and to compare your growth against the best, the worst or the average. Reports are priced between £165 and £195 each, and further details are available from ICC Information Group Ltd, Field House, 72 Oldfield Road, Hampton, Middlesex TW12 2HQ (Tel: 0181 783 1122; Fax: 0181 783 0049).

ICC Information Group Ltd, Field House, 72 Oldfield Road, Hampton, Middlesex TW12 2HQ (Tel: 0181 783 0977; Fax: 0181 783 1940).

Industrial Performance Analysis: a financial analysis of UK industry and commerce. A ratio analysis of 27 industries subdivided into 200 sectors. Also gives average performances for sectors. It is based on over 25,000 companies which go into the ICC Business Ratio series. This information could provide some pointers as to how profitable certain business sectors really are and give ideas on the cost of entry.

Jordan's Business Information Service, Jordan House, 21 St Thomas Street, Bristol BS1 6JS (Tel: 0117 9230600; Fax: 0117 9230063; e-mail: Telecom Gold 74: JOR007. Their Company Search Department can get you information on any UK company in 'Companies House', and their Rapid Reply Service can guarantee despatch within a few hours. Alternatively, if you really are in a hurry, they have a telex, a telephone service, and e-mail. They also produce a range of annual business surveys covering most industries.

Key British Enterprises published by Dun & Bradstreet Ltd, Holmers Farm Way, High Wycombe, Buckinghamshire HP12 4UL (Tel: 01494 424295; Fax: 01494 422260). Information on 50,000 UK companies that between them are responsible for 90% of industrial expenditure. *KBE* is very useful for identifying sales prospects or confirming addresses, monitoring competitors and customers or finding new suppliers. As well as giving the names, addresses, telephone, fax and telex numbers of the main office of each company, it gives branch addresses, products indexed by SIC (Standard International Code), sales turnovers (UK and overseas), directors' names and responsibilities, shareholders, capital structure, trade names and number of employees.

KBE splits information on an alphabetical and geographical basis. By using the directory you can quickly establish the size of business you are dealing with and what other products or services it offers. It is very often important to know the size of a firm – if, for example, your products are confined to certain types of business. A book-keeping service is unlikely to interest a large company with several hundred employees; they would have their own accounts department. Conversely, a very small company may not need a public relations consultant. The directory is available with updates and is on-line through Data-Star Dialog Europe (see on-line sources, page 00).

Kompass is published in four volumes: Volumes I and II are indexed by product or service to help find suppliers, indicating whether they are manufacturers, wholesalers or distributors. It can be very useful indeed on certain occasions to be able to bypass a wholesaler and get to the manufacturer direct.
Volume III gives basic company information on the 30,000 suppliers identified from Volume I. These include the addresses, telephone and telex numbers, bankers, directors, office hours and the number of employees. Volume IV gives financial data on these companies over a three-year period giving: turnover,

profit before tax, fixed assets, current assets, shareholders' funds and the ulti-mate holding company, if any. This directory is also available on CD-ROM. Kompass Publishers, Windsor Court, East Grinstead House, East Grimstead, West Sussex RH19 1XA (Tel: 01342 326972; Fax: 01342 315130).

The London Gazette, published by HMSO daily, provides the official notices on companies, including bankruptcies and receiverships. It may be too late for you to do much by the time it reaches the *Gazette.* Her Majesty's Stationery Office, London Gazette Office, Room 413 Publications Centre, 51 Nine Elms Lane, London SW8 5DR (Tel: 0171 873 0011; Fax: 0171 873 8463).

McCarthy Information Services, McCarthy Information Ltd, Manor House, Ash Walk, Warminster, Wilts BA12 8PY (Tel: 01985 215151; Fax: 01985 217479). Provides a comprehensive press comment service monitoring the daily and financial press. From some 50 papers and journals they extract information on quoted companies each day and unquoted companies each week. The service is provided on subscription, and a modestly priced Back Copy Service seems the most likely one to appeal to small business. The subscription is £42 per annum, and 82p per page copied. Alternatively, an on-line service through FT-Profiles and a microfiche service are also offered.

MacMillan's Unquoted Companies provides financial profiles for 20,000 of Britain's top unquoted companies. It gives details on business sector, sales, profits, number of employees and directors. It is published by ICC Business Pub-lications, Freepost, Hampton, Middlesex TW12 1BR.

Research Index is an index to news, views and comments from the UK national daily papers plus around 150 periodicals in every field. The material is chosen carefully to include most items that would interest the business user, both on individual companies and on industries. Over a period of a year it includes around 130,000 items, and since the first edition over a million refer-ences have been made. By using it, even the smallest business can have at its fingertips the knowledge for information retrieval equivalent to the most sophisticated libraries. Published by Business Surveys Ltd, Broadmayne House Farm, Osmington Drive, Broadmayne, Dorset DT2 8EP (Tel: 01305 853704; Fax: 01305 854162).

The Retail Directory published by Newman Books Ltd, 32 Vauxhall Bridge Road, London SW1V 2SS (Tel: 0171 973 6402; Fax: 0171 233 5056). Gives details of all UK department stores and private shops: the names of executives, and mer-chandise buyers as well as addresses and telephone numbers, early closing days, etc. It also covers multiple shops, co-operative societies, supermarkets and many other retail outlets. If you plan to sell to shops, this is a useful starting point, with around 1,305 department stores and large shops and 4,821 multiple-shop firms and variety stores listed in 1,346 pages. If you are already selling retail, this directory could help you expand your prospects list quickly. The directory also identifies high turn-over outlets for main product ranges. There is a useful survey, showing retail activities on each major shopping street in the country. It gives the name and nature of the retail businesses in each street. A separate volume contains shop surveys for the Greater London area, with 27,830 shops listed by name, street number and trade. The head offices of 1,130 multiples are given, as are 233 surveys showing what sort of shops are in any area. This can be used for giving sales people useful contacts within their territory.

Sales Growth 1000. A directory listing the fastest-growing 1,000 companies in the UK, with financial data. A sister directory, called *Profit Growth 1000*, is also published by ICC Information Group, Field House, 72 Oldfield Road, Hampton, Middlesex TW12 2HQ (Tel: 0181 783 1122; Fax: 0181 783 0049).

Sell's Product and Service Directory published by Benn's Business Information Services Ltd, Riverbank House, Angel Lane, Tonbridge, Kent TN9 1SE (Tel: 01732 362666; Fax: 01732 770483). It lists over 65,000 firms alphabetically, with name, trade, address, telephone number and telex numbers. Using a classified cross-reference system, it covers more than 25,000 products and services. There is a guide to several thousand trade names cross-referenced back to each company. The two remaining sections include a contractors' section, advertising firms seeking contract work, and a business information section. If you only know the trade name and want to find out who makes the product, then this directory will help you. You can then use it to find competitive sources of supply of similar products or services.

Who Owns Whom (UK) published by Dun & Bradstreet. Volume I lists parent companies, showing the structure of a group as a whole and the relationship with member companies. Volume II lists subsidiaries and associates showing their parent companies. It covers 100,000 companies, is updated four times a year, and is available on-line through Data-Star Dialog Europe. Dun & Bradstreet Ltd, Holmers Farm Way, High Wycombe, Buckinghamshire HP12 4UL (Tel: 01494 424295; Fax: 01494 422260).

Company and product data, overseas

Export/Import United Kingdom Monthly Statistics. Contains current and cumulative monthly statistics for 10,000-plus products giving value and various measures of quantity. Classified by tariff code and country, it covers all EC countries, USA, Japan, Canada and others, as well as UK. Business and Trade Statistics Ltd, Lancaster House, 45 More Lane, Esher, Surrey KT10 8AP (Tel: 01372 463121; Fax: 01372 469847).

Extel European Companies Service supplies cards on individual companies throughout Europe. Each card contains financial history, directors and other information. Available from: Extel Financial Ltd, Fitzroy House, 13–17 Epworth Street, London EC2A 4DL (Tel: 0171 251 3333; Fax: 0171 251 2725).

Funk and Scott International and European Indexes provide a worldwide index to company news appearing in several hundred English-language papers and journals. They have an index for the USA too. You can use this service to find out what has been happening to a company that has not shown up in its figures, for example, new products cancelled, strikes, acquisitions, divestments, and board changes.

ICC American Company Information Service, ICC Information Group Ltd, 16–26 Banner Street, London EC1Y 8QE (Tel: 0171 250 4149). They can provide reports on 12,000 US public companies. The report includes the Annual Report and Accounts and the IOK Corporate Structure report on subsidiaries, directors, prominent shareholders and company properties. These cost approximately £50 for each company.

ICC European Company Information Services. Through company registries and information services throughout Europe, ICC can provide various reports, including financial accounts, status reports and annual returns on companies registered in Belgium, Denmark, France, Germany, Holland, Norway, Sweden, Channel Islands, Italy, Portugal and Spain. A thousand European company accounts are kept on file in the UK ready for immediate despatch. The cost of the information is from £40 per company.

International Dun's Market Identifiers covers over 500,000 companies in 143 countries. It lists details on sales, directors and products/services provided by Standard International Code. It is available on the Dialog on-line database. Dun & Bradstreet Ltd, Holmers Farm Way, High Wycombe, Buckinghamshire HP12 4UL (Tel: 01494 424295; Fax: 01494 422260).

Jordan's Overseas Company Information, Jordan House, 21 St Thomas Street, Bristol BS1 6JS (Tel: 0117 9230600; Fax: 0117 9230063; e-mail: Telecom Gold 74: JOR007). Covers the whole world with an international network of agents and information sources. Information on companies varies from country to country, as does the speed with which that information can be retrieved. Still, this is certainly one of the best ways of finding out about a company that is not included in a general directory either because it is too small or too new. Of course, you may need much more detailed information on a particular company than is normally provided in a directory, and this information service may be able to provide it.

Kompass Directories, similar to UK directories, are available for Belgium and Luxemburg, Denmark, West Germany, France, Holland, Italy, Australia, Brazil, Indonesia, Morocco, Norway, Singapore, Spain, Sweden and Switzerland (Kompass address given in UK listing).

McCarthy's Australian Service
McCarthy's European Information Service

McCarthy's North American Service
See earlier listing in UK section for more details of above three services.

Principal International Business, published by Dun & Bradstreet, gives the basic facts about 50,000 businesses in 135 countries. As well as the business name, address and telex and its main activities, it tells you if the company is a subsidiary of a larger corporation; whether they import or export; how many employees they have; their latest sales volume; and the name of the chief executive. Its cover of companies in each country is not great: nearly 8,000 in the USA; 6,000 in Germany; 5,500 in France; 4,000 in Japan; and 2,000 businesses in the UK. This represents only a small percentage of the businesses in any one country, but they are the principal ones.

Standard and Poor's Register of Corporations, Directors and Executives. The Corporation Record, Volume I, has a wealth of information on the financial structure and performance of 45,000 of the most significant American corporations. There is also a list of the subsidiary companies cross-referenced to parents. Volume II contains the individual listings of 700,000 people serving as officers of these corporations, together with some personal details on their education and fraternal membership. Volume III contains a series of indexes that complement the first two volumes.

Store Buyer International lists 9,000 buyers in major stores throughout Europe. Published by Manor House Press Ltd, 3rd Floor, Hill House, McDonald Road, off Highgate Hill, London N19 5NA (Tel: 0171 281 6767; Fax: 0171 281 8087).

Thomas's Register of American Manufacturers consists of 16 volumes, making it probably the most comprehensive directory on the market. Volumes 1–8 list products alphabetically, giving the manufacturer's name. Volumes 9 and 10 list company names alphabetically, giving addresses with zip codes and telephone numbers, together with branch offices, capital ratings and company officials. An American trademark index is given in Volume 10. Volumes 11–16, called Thomcat, contain catalogues of companies, bound alphabetically and cross-referenced in the first ten volumes. In all a formidable work, this is useful either to find an American source of supply or a potential customer for your product. The catalogues provide an insight into the way in which American companies market their wares.

Wall Street Journal Index provides a monthly and annual review of published material on the USA. It is in two sections. The first gives company news, and the second gives general business news. Both are alphabetical and provide brief abstracts of the activities in question. It is somewhat similar to what the FT has to say about a company, product or personality.

Who Owns Whom (Australasia and Far East). Details are as below.

Who Owns Whom (Continental Europe) is published in two volumes. The first is similar to the UK volume, and the second volume has a section on foreign investment. (See listing in UK section for more details.)

Who Owns Whom (North American edition) is perhaps the definitive directory of US multinational subsidiaries. Canadian companies are also covered.

Market and industry data

Businesses have to take part in censuses in much the same way as do individuals. This information, showing purchasers, stocks, capital expenditure and so on, is available for all the main UK industries, in the *Annual Report on the Census of Production.* The Business Monitor Series covers this and other areas in considerable detail each month and quarter. *Mintel Retail Business* is a monthly publication that examines consumer goods markets. By taking an area at a time it can produce quite comprehensive studies on spending patterns and the underlying reasons for them.

If you want a piggyback on someone else's research, then *Reports Index* is a quick reference guide to several thousand market studies, carried out on UK products and markets, available for purchase at quite modest prices. If you do not find a reference book in this section covering the field you are interested in, then the *Guide to Official Statistics* from HMSO will probably show you where to find it. Overseas markets are particularly well covered with the Euromonitor publications, which provide comprehensive comparative information on European and international markets. *Market Data Reports on European Industries* shows growth and size trends of 24 industries in eight countries over the past seven years. The *International Directory of Published Market Research* provides a useful insight into who has done what in the market research field, and a number of useful indexes on other international data sources are also identified.

Market and industry data, UK

The A–Z of Business Information Sources. A loose-leaf directory published annually with four updates. It is arranged alphabetically, from Abrasives to Zoos. Just turn to the subject of interest and choose the source most suitable to your needs. The directory costs £140.25 and is available in good reference libraries. Published by Croner Publications Ltd, Croner House, London Road, Kingston-upon-Thames, Surrey KT2 6SR (Tel: 0181 547 3333; Fax: 0181 547 2637).

Annual Abstract of Statistics, available from HMSO, is the basic source of all UK statistics. Figures are given for each of the preceding ten years, so trends can be recognized.

Benn's Media Directory published by Benn Information Services, Sovereign Way, Tonbridge, Kent TN9 1RW (Tel: 01732 362666; Fax: 01732 770483). Published in three volumes.

British Rate and Data **(BRAD).** Published by Maclean Hunter Ltd, Maclean Hunter House, Chalk Lane, Cockfosters Road, Barnet, Hertfordshire EN4 0BU (Tel: 0181 242 3000; Fax: 0181 242 3134). Whatever market you are interested in, it is almost certain to have a specialized paper or journal, which will be an important source of market data. *BRAD* lists all newspapers and periodicals in the UK and Eire, and gives their frequency and circulation volume, price, their executives, advertising rates and readership classification.

British Rate and Data Advertisers and Agency List is produced four times a year, and lists all advertising agencies, their executives and their customers' brand names. It also covers market research and direct mail companies.

Business Monitors are the medium through which the Government publishes the business statistics it collects from over 400,000 enquiry forms. They are the primary – and very often the only – source of detailed information on the sectors they cover. The Monitors can help businessmen to monitor trends and trace the progress of 4,000 individual products, manufactured by firms in 160 industries. Monitors can also be used to rate your business performance against that of your industry and measure the efficiency of different parts of your business.

The Monitors are published in three main series. The Production Monitors are published monthly, quarterly and annually. The quarterly is probably the most useful, with comprehensive yet timely information. The Service and Distributor Monitors cover the retail market, the instalment credit business, the motor trade, catering and allied trades and the computer service industry, among others. Finally, there are Miscellaneous Monitors covering such topics as shipping, insurance, import/export ratios for industry, acquisitions and mergers of industrial and commercial companies, cinemas and tourism. The Annual Census of Production Monitors covers virtually every sector of industry, and includes data on total purchases, total sales, stocks, work in progress, capital expenditure, employment, wages and salaries. It includes analyses of costs and output, of establishments by size, of full- and part-time employees by sex, and of employment, net capital expenditure and net output by region.

You can use the information – particularly that from the size analysis table – to establish such ratios as gross output per head, net output per head, net to gross output, and wages and salaries to net output. With these as a base, you can compare the performance of your own business with the average for firms of similar size and for that with your particular industry as a whole. For example, you can discover your share of the market, and compare employment figures, increases in sales and so on.

Most of the reference libraries will have a selection of the Business Monitor Series. Individual monitors can be bought from Her Majesty's Stationery Office, 51 Nine Elms Lane, London SW8 5DR (Tel: 0171 873 0011). They are all individually priced.

Euromonitor UK Market Reports produce over 90 separate reports covering over 90 consumer and industrial markets. Contact: Euromonitor Publications

Ltd, 87–88 Turnmill Street, London EC1M 5QU (Tel: 0171 251 8024; Fax: 0171 608 3149).

Family Expenditure Survey, published by HMSO, shows in great detail income and expenditure by type of household for the UK and includes some regional analyses – produced annually.

Guide to Official Statistics is the main guide to all government-produced statistics, including ad hoc reports. It is published by HMSO. Available from Her Majesty's Stationery Office, 51 Nine Elms Lane, London SW8 5DR (Tel: 0171 873 0011). However, a brief free guide is available each year from the Press and Information Service, Central Statistical Office, Cabinet Office, Information Department, Horse Guards Road, London SW1P 3AL (Tel: 0171 270 6363/4).

Key Note Reports produce concise briefs on various sectors of the UK economy. Each Key Note contains a detailed examination of the structure of an industry, its distribution network and its major companies; an in-depth analysis of the market, covering products by volume and value, market shares, foreign trade and an appraisal of trends within the market; a review of recent developments in the industry, highlighting new product development, corporate development and legislation; a financial analysis of named major companies, providing data and ratios over a three-year period together with a corporate appraisal and economic overview; forecasts on the future prospects for the industry, including estimates from Key Notes, own database and authoritative trade sources. There is a very useful appendix detailing further sources of information – recent press articles, other reports and journals.

Over 100 market sectors are covered, including such areas as adhesives, after-dinner drinks, bicycles, butchers, commercial leasing, health foods, road haulage, public houses, travel agents and women's magazines. Key Note Publications Ltd, Field House, 72 Oldfield Road, Hampton, Middlesex TW12 2HQ (Tel: 0181 783 0977; Fax: 0181 783 1940).

Market Forecasts give five-year forecasts for some 200 consumer markets at an annual cost of £250. Available from: Market Assessment Publications, The BLA Group, 2 Duncan Terrace, London N1 8BZ (Tel: 0171 278 9517; Fax: 0171 278 6246).

Market Information Manual covers over 450 product markets, with regional breakdown and retail outlets. Sections of the manual are sold seperately from around £250. Available from Neilsen, Neilsen House, London Road, Headington, Oxford, Oxfordshire OX3 9RX (Tel: 01865 742742; Fax: 01865 742222).

Market Intelligence is a monthly publication providing reports on the performance of new products and a wide range of specific areas of consumer expenditure. It covers several specific consumer goods markets each month, combining published data and original research to make the studies as exhaustive as possible. Comprehensive data on leisure and retail markets is also given. They provide research services and have an on-line service. Further details from Mintel International Group, 18–19 Long Lane, London EC1A 9HE (Tel: 0171 606 6000; Fax: 0171 606 5159).

Marketing and Distribution Abstracts, published eight times a year by MCB University Press Ltd, 62 Toller Lane, Bradford, West Yorkshire BD8 9BY (Tel: 01274 480916; Fax: 01274 543576). This surveys 200 journals worldwide and provides an index to abstracts of appropriate articles and reports in the field.

Marketing Surveys Index published by Marketing Strategies for Industry (UK) Ltd, 32 Mill Green Road, Mitcham, Surrey CR4 4HY (Tel: 0181 640 6621). A digest of current market research surveys that are available for sale, worldwide, updated each month. It covers almost every sector of the economy.

McCarthy's Industrial Services provides a similar service on products and markets as their service on quoted and unquoted companies. The industry service is classified into 13 industry groups: agricultural and animal and vegetable raw materials; building and civil engineering; finance; general engineering; electrical and electronic engineering; chemicals and chemical engineering; miscellaneous industrial manufacturers; consumer goods manufacture; transport and transport equipment; marketing; distribution and consumer services; communications and communications equipment; mining and minerals and energy. Within the main industry group lie about 350 subsections. Marketing for example ranges from auto vending, franchising to street markets, as well as the more predictable department stores and supermarket groups.

Information is provided at £2.50 per page. A phone call to McCarthy will tell you how many pages are involved, as naturally the size varies with the volume of news in a given area. The Back Numbers Service seems good value for small businesses.

Office of Population Censuses and Surveys produce demographic statistics for each county in England and Wales from the latest census. These provide data not only on total populations in each area, but also on occupations, economic groups, etc. Similar reports for Scottish and Northern Ireland regions are also available. There is a reference library at OPCS, St Catherine's House, 10 Kingsway, London WC2B 6JP (Tel: 0171 396 2235).

Reports Index is a bi-monthly index to reports in every field published and available for sale. Its sources include Government publications, HMSO as well as non-HMSO, market research organizations, trade and professional associations, public bodies, stockbrokers, educational establishments, EC, industrial and financial companies. Again the cost is modest at £230 per annum. Business Surveys Ltd, Broadmayne House Farm, Osmington Drive, Broadmayne, Dorset DT2 8EP (Tel: 01305 853704; Fax: 01305 854162).

Retail Business, published monthly by the Economist Intelligence Unit, covers the economic aspects of the UK retail trade, with emphasis on consumer goods market research, distribution patterns and sales trends.

Retail Intelligence is a bi-monthly publication also from Mintel, covering in considerable depth the consumer goods marketed.

Social Trends, published by HMSO, brings together key social and demographic data on many aspects of the UK economy – useful charts and graphs.

Sources of Unofficial UK Statistics covers some 1,000 regular statistical publications. Data comes from trade associations, professional bodies, stockbrokers, private companies, academic institutions and banks. Gower Publishing Company Ltd, Gower House, Craft Road, Aldershot, Hampshire GU11 3HR (Tel: 01252 331551; Fax: 01252 344405).

Market and industry data, overseas

British Business magazine's European Community Information Unit offers a free service to businesses in Britain by answering general enquiries about EEC matters and referring business enquiries to experts in official circles (details in UK section).

European Directory of Non-official Statistical Sources, contains 2,000 sources in Western Europe. These include banks, trade associations, professional bodies, market research agencies and academic institutions. Available from Euromonitor Publications Ltd, 87–88 Turnmill Street, London EC1M 5QU (Tel: 0171 251 8024; Fax: 0171 608 3149).

Economist Intelligence Unit, 40 Duke Street, London W1A 1DW (Tel: 0171 493 6711; Fax: 0171 499 9767) produces each quarter some 83 separate reviews covering 160 countries, evaluating growth prospects, assessing opportunities and examining local and international problems. It provides a business-oriented analysis of the economic state of the countries examined.

European Marketing Data and Statistics, published by Euromonitor Publications Ltd, is an annual handbook containing comparative information about European markets. *International Marketing Data and Statistics* is a companion volume that covers North and South America, Asia, Africa and Australasia. Contact: Euromonitor Publications Ltd, 87–88 Turnmill Street, London EC1M 5QU (Tel: 0171 251 8024; Fax: 0171 608 3149).

Industrial Market Research Reports provide international market research covering over 20 major sectors, worldwide. Also available on-line via Data-Star. Contact: Frost & Sullivan Ltd, Sullivan House, 4 Grosvenor Gardens, London SW1W 0DH (Tel: 0171 730 3438; Fax: 0171 730 3343).

Statistics – Europe, Africa, America, Asia and Australasia are four guides to sources of statistics for social, economic and market research. They are published by CBD Research Ltd, Chancery House, 15 Wickham Road, Beckenham, Kent BR3 2JS (Tel: 0181 650 7745; Fax: 0181 650 0768).

UN Demographic Yearbook gives population statistics on 165 countries, based on each country's census data. Available from: Her Majesty's Stationery Office, 51 Nine Elms Lane, London SW8 5DR (Tel: 0171 873 0011).

■ FINDING THE INFORMATION

Now that you have an idea of the considerable mass of data that is available about companies, their products and markets, the next problem that remains is to track it down. Fortunately many of the directories and publications are kept in reference sections of major libraries up and down the country.

If you know exactly what information you want, then your problem is confined to finding a library or information service that has that information.

Specialist libraries

Apart from your local library there are hundreds of specialist libraries concentrated in government departments, major industrial companies, trade organizations, research centres and academic institutes. Two useful publications that will help find out about these are listed below.

ASLIB Directory of Information Sources in the UK. In two volumes. Volume 1 covers science, technology and commerce. Volume 2 covers social sciences, medicine and humanities. The directories list 6,500 libraries giving name, address, type of organization, contact name and subject coverage. ASLIB, the Association for Information Management, Information House, 20–24 Old Street, London EC1V 9AP (Tel: 0171 253 4488; Fax: 0171 430 0514).

Guide to Government Departments and Other Libraries is available from the Science Reference Library, 25 Southampton Buildings, Chancery Lane, London WC2A 1AW (Tel: 0171 323 7472; Fax: 0171 323 7930). As the title indicates, this book concentrates on libraries in government departments and agencies, and particularly avoids duplicating the ground covered by the ASLIB Directory. The entries are arranged by subject covered, supplemented by an alphabetical index of the libraries, their locations, phone numbers and opening hours.

Not all the libraries covered in these directories are open to the public for casual visits. However, many will let you use their reference facilities, by appointment.

Guide to Libraries and Information Units, published annually by the British Library, Science Reference and Information Service, 25 Southampton Buildings, London WC2A 1AW.

British Institute of Management Library and Management Information Centre, Management House, Cottingham Road, Corby, Northants NN17 1TT (Tel: 01536 204222; Fax: 01536 201651). Open Monday to Friday, 9.30 a.m. to 5 p.m. The library houses one of the largest specialist collections of management literature in Europe. This includes much valuable information not generally available. The services are for BIM members who can use the library in person or make enquiries by letter or telephone.

The library also produces extremely valuable reading lists covering a wide range of topics. These provide a selective guide to books, directories and periodicals in any of 170 specific areas. They also publish *A Basic Library of Management* which lists 300 or so of the more useful books in the management field.

British Library, Science Reference and Information Service (SRIS). This is the national library for modern science, technology and commerce, and for patents, trade marks and designs. It has the most comprehensive reference collection in Western Europe of such literature from the whole world. It serves the information needs of research and development scientists, technologists and engineers, industry and commerce, and is used by information officers, researchers, abstractors, technical journalists, industrial managers, librarians, patent and trade mark agents. It is open to any adult member of the public and no reader's pass is required. Enquiries are welcome by telephone, fax, telex, courier or mail as well as from personal callers. There are special services providing business, patent, scientific, technical, environmental and Japanese information, and on-line searching of computerized databases; photocopying and linguistic help are also available. A charge is made for some services; further details on request: 25 Southampton Buildings, Chancery Lane, London WC2A 1AW (Tel: general enquiries 0171 323 7494/7496).

Stock Serials: over 67,000 (c25,000 current titles); abstracting serials: c1,400; monographs: c251,000; patent specifications: c34,683,000; dictionaries and glossaries; trade directories: 2,000; market surveys: 2,500; trade literature and company information.

Reading rooms
25 Southampton Buildings, Chancery Lane, London WC2A 1AW (Tel: general enquiries 0171 323 7494/7496; British and EPO patent enquiries 0171 323 7919; foreign patents 0171 323 7902; business information 0171 323 7454 (quick enquiry service) and 0171 323 7457 (priced research service); Japanese information (0171 323 7924; science and technology information (including on-line searching) 0171 323 7477; environmental information 0171 323 7955; IRS-Dialtech – the UK National Centre for the European Space Agency's ESA–IRS scientific and technical bibliographic information service – 0171 323 7951/7946/7481; Fax: reading room 0171 323 7495; business information 0171 323 7453; industrial property 0171 323 7912; patent photocopies 0171 323 7930; BT Gold: 81:BLI 404.

Stock and subject coverage Physical sciences and technologies; engineering; business information on companies, markets and products (2,000 trade and business directories, 2,000 market research reports, 1,500 trade and business journals, McCarthy Cards, Extel Cards and a collection of company annual reports); British, European and Patent Co-operation Treaty patents; trade marks.

Hours Main reading room 9.30 a.m. to 9 p.m.; 10 a.m. to 1 p.m. Saturday; foreign patents reading room (in Chancery House) 9.30 a.m. to 5.30 p.m.

Kean Street, London WC2B 4AT (Tel: 0171 323 7288; Fax: 0171 323 7290).

Subject coverage Life sciences and technologies, including biotechnology, medicine and agriculture; earth sciences, mathematics; astronomy.

Hours: 9.30 a.m. to 5.30 p.m.

Publications Free: *SRIS Newsletter;* priced: list available from Marketing and Public Relations (Tel: 0171 323 7472).

BSI (British Standards Institution), Linford Wood, Milton Keynes MK14 6LE (Tel: 01908 220022; Customer Services (Information): 01908 226888; Fax: 01908 320856).

Stock The BSI Library holds around 600,000 international and foreign standards, codes of practice, regulations and technical requirements.

Services Foreign and international standards and regulations are available for loan to BSI subscribing members (British Standards may not be borrowed). Library tokens are used to borrow documents: these can be purchased through Customer Services. An enquiry service is available in all aspects of standards information (longer enquiries may be chargeable). Bibliographical details of British Standards are available on-line via Standardline or on the PERINORM CD-ROM which also includes details of international, European and some foreign national standards. Various current awareness services are provided including *Worldwide Standard Information* which is a monthly subject listing of all documents received in the Library. An archival set of withdrawn and superseded British Standards is maintained, photocopies of which may be purchased. Current standards and other publications may be ordered from BSI Publications Department.

Availability The Library is open to the public, 9.30 a.m. to 5 p.m.

Publications *British Standards; BSI Standards Catalogue* (annually); *Catalogue Supplement* (monthly update to Catalogue); *BSI News* (monthly); *Instep* (quarterly publication on information services); translations of foreign standards; Information Services publications (mostly export related).

Central Statistical Office Library, Government Buildings, Cardiff Road, Newport, Gwent NP9 1XG (Tel: 01633 812973; Fax: 01633 812599). Enquiries: Ext 2973

Stock and subject coverage Official statistical series; trade directories; periodicals and monographs on statistical theory; computer technology; general and Civil Service management.

Availability Open to the public for reference, 9 a.m. to 5 p.m. (last admission 4.30 p.m.).

Services Telephone enquiry service in the field of UK statistics; written enquiry service; public reading room.

Publications Library periodicals holdings list; *CSO Bulletins* series; *Business Monitor Catalogue; Government Statistics – a Brief Guide to Sources; UK in Figures.*

City Business Library, 1 Brewers Hill Garden, London EC2V 5BX (Tel: 0171 638 8215)

Stock and subject coverage Current financial and business data, including newspapers and periodicals – maximum file length is 5 years; UK quoted annual reports for 5 years, and a selection of overseas reports; Extel and McCarthy card series; extensive range of current UK and overseas trade directories; selection of market research reports; limited statistical information for UK and overseas.

Availability Freely available for reference use – this is a very busy library, so priority is given to personal visitors.

Hours: 9.30 a.m. to 5 p.m.

Services Business Information Focus (fee-based service offering on-line, research and photocopying services) (Tel: 0171 600 1461; Fax: 0171 600 1185).

Publications List of newspaper and periodical holdings.

Business Information Network

The Business Information Network is an association of libraries and information units committed to providing quality business information services to their user community. Their joint resources and expertise are publicized to business users as one network in order to raise public awareness of what already exists in libraries, and to encourage more people to make use of the information. The Network also enables members to provide a service which is more effective by improving the quality of referrals and providing access to a wider range of resources.

Many of the member libraries of the Network have access to European Information Centres, European Documentation Centres, BC-NET, etc. Any individual or organization can use the resources within the Network by contacting their nearest Network library. Charges vary depending on the Library and the nature of the request. Main contact points are listed below. For further information on the Business Information Network contact: Network Manager, Business Information Network, 25 Southampton Buildings (Room 255), London WC2A 1AW (Tel: 0171 323 7499; Fax: 0171 323 7453).

England

Aston University, Library and Information Services, Aston University, Aston Triangle, Birmingham B4 7ET (Tel: 0121 359 3611; Fax: 0121 359 7358).

Avon County Council, Central Library, College Green, Bristol BS1 5TL (Tel: 0117 9276121, ext 253; Fax: 0117 9226775).

Bedfordshire County Council,
Luton Central Reference Library,
St George's Square, Luton LU1 2NG
(Tel: 01582 454580;
Fax: 01582 24638).
**Berkshire County Library and
Information Service,** County
Reference Library, Abbey Square,
Reading, Berkshire RG1 3BQ
(Tel: 01734 509245;
Fax: 01734 589039).
**Bexley London Borough Library
Service,** Central Reference Library,
Townley Road, Bexleyheath
DA6 7HT (Tel: 0181 301 5151;
Fax: 0181 313 7872).
Birmingham University,
Main Library, Birmingham, West
Midlands B15 2TT
(Tel: 0121 414 5823;
Fax: 0121 471 4691).
**Bolton Metropolitan Borough
Council,** Central Library, Le Mans
Crescent, Bolton BL1 1SE
(Tel: 01204 397013;
Fax: 01204 363224).
**Bradford Libraries and Information
Service,** Central Library, Prince's Way,
Bradford, West Yorkshire BD1 1NN
(Tel: 01274 753656;
Fax: 01274 395108).
British Library, Document Supply
Centre (BLDSC), Boston Spa,
Wetherby, West Yorkshire LS23 7BQ
(Tel: 01937 546023;
Fax: 01937 546333).
Bromley Libraries, Business Informa-
tion Service, Central Library, High
Street, Bromley, Kent BR1 1EX
(Tel: 0181 290 0145;
Fax: 0181 313 0475).
Buckinghamshire County Library,
Reference and Information Service,
County Reference Library, Walton
Street, Aylesbury, Buckinghamshire
HP20 1UU (Tel: 01296 382245;

Fax: 01296 382405).
**Cambridgeshire Libraries and Infor-
mation Service,** Cambridge Central
Library, 7 Lion Yard, Cambridge CB2
3QD (Tel: 01223 65252;
Fax: 01223 62786).
Cheshire Libraries Arts and Archives,
Cheshire Information Service,
Ellesmere Port Library, Civic Way,
Ellesmere Port, South Wirral
L65 0BG (Tel: 0151 355 2286;
Fax: 0151 355 6849).
Essex County Library, Essex County
Library, Goldlay Gardens,
Chelmsford, Essex CM2 0EW
(Tel: 01245 284981;
Fax: 01245 492780).
**Gloucestershire County Council, The
Reference Library,** Clarence Street,
Cheltenham, Gloucestershire
GL50 3JT (Tel: 01242 582269;
Fax: 01242 510373).
Hampshire County Library,
Winchester Reference Library, 81
North Walls, Winchester, Hampshire
SO23 8BY (Tel: 01962 846059; Fax:
01962 856615).
**Hereford and Worcester County
Libraries,** County Library HQ, County
Hall, Spetchley Road, Worcester WR5
2NP (Tel: 01905 766240;
Fax: 01905 763000).
**Humberside County Council, Central
Library,** Albion Street, Hull, Humber-
side HU1 3TF (Tel: 01482 224040;
Fax: 01482 24786).
Kent Arts and Libraries, Chatham
Library, Riverside, Chatham, Kent
ME4 4SN (Tel: 01634 843589;
Fax: 01634 827976).
Kirklees Cultural Services, Business
Information Service, Huddersfield
Reference Library, Princess Alexandra
Walk, Huddersfield HD1 2SU.
(Tel: 01484 446804/5;
Fax: 01484 531983).

Lancashire County Library, Harris Library, Market Square, Preston, Lancashire PR1 2PP (Tel: 01772 204583; Fax: 01772 555527).
Liverpool City Libraries, Central Library, William Brown Street, Liverpool L3 8EW (Tel: 0151 225 5434; Fax: 0151 207 1342).

London
British Library Business Information Service, BL Business Information Service, 25 Southampton Buildings, London WC2A 1AW.
Free quick enquiry service (Tel: 0171 323 7454; Fax: 0171 323 7453).
Priced business information service (Tel: 0171 323 7457; Fax: 0171 323 7453).
DTI Library and Information Services, Enquiry Unit, Victoria Street Library and Information Centre, Room 136, 123 Victoria Street, London SW1E 6RB (Tel: 0171 215 6452; Fax: 0171 215 5665).
Royal Borough of Kensington and Chelsea, Central Library, Phillimore Walk, London W8 7RX (Tel: 0171 937 2542; Fax: 0171 937 0515).

Newcastle upon Tyne City Libraries and Arts, Central Library, Princess Square, Newcastle upon Tyne NE99 1DX (Tel: 0191 261 0691; Fax: 0191 261 1435).
Newcastle upon Tyne, University of Northumbria, The Library, University of Northumbria, Ellison Place, Newcastle upon Tyne NE1 8ST (Tel: 0191 232 6002, ext 4135).
Northumberland County Library, Central Library, The Willows,

Morpeth, Northumberland NE61 1TA (Tel: 01670 512385; Fax: 01670 518012).
Oxfordshire County Council, Dept of Leisure and Arts, Library Services HQ, Holton, Oxford OX9 1QQ (Tel: 01865 815549/815337; Fax: 01865 810207).
Rotherham Metropolitan Borough Council, Central Library, Walker Place, Rotherham, South Yorkshire S65 1IH (Tel: 01709 382121, ext 3613; Fax: 01709 823650).
Suffolk County Council Information Centre, Central Library, Northgate Street, Ipswich, Suffolk IP1 3DE (Tel: 01473 252477; Fax: 01473 230758).
Wakefield Business and Technical Information Centre, Five Towns Research Centre, Welbeck Street, Castleford, West Yorkshire WF10 1DR (Tel: 01977 519625, ext 204).
Warwickshire County Council, Rugby Library, St Matthew's Street, Rugby, Warwickshire CV21 3B2 (Tel: 01788 542687; Fax: 01788 542687).
Wiltshire Library and Museum Service, Information Unit, Bythesea Road, Trowbridge, Wiltshire BA14 8BS (Tel: 01225 713727; Fax: 01225 713993).
Wolverhampton University, The Library, Compton Park, Compton Road West, Wolverhampton WV3 9DX (Tel: 01902 323644).

Wales
Clwyd Library and Information Service, County Civic Centre, Mold, Clwyd CH7 6NW (Tel: 01352 753605; Fax: 01352 753662).
Gwynedd County Library Service, Mentec Centre, Deiniol Road, Bangor, Gwynedd LL57 2UP

(Tel: 01248 354103;
Fax: 01248 352497).
**Llanelli Borough Council, Central
Library**, Vaughan Street, Llanelli,
Dyfed SA15 3AS (Tel: 01554 773538;
Fax: 01554 750125).
South Glamorgan County Library,
Central Library, St David's Link,
Frederick Street, Cardiff CF1 4DT
(Tel: 01222 382116;
Fax: 01222 238642).

Scotland
Glasgow City Libraries, Business Users
Service, The Mitchell Library, North
Street, Glasgow G3 7DN
(Tel: 0141 248 3997;
Fax: 0141 248 5027).
Scottish Science Library, 33 Salisbury
Place, Edinburgh EH9 1SL
(Tel: 0131 667 9554;
Fax: 0131 662 0644).

Northern Ireland
Belfast Public Libraries, Central
Library, Royal Avenue, Belfast BT1

1EA (Tel: 01232 243233;
Fax: 01232 332819).

Also these private companies have
extensive business libraries.
Dun & Bradstreet Europe Ltd,
Holmers Farm Way, High Wycombe,
Buckinghamshire HP12 4UL
(Tel: 01494 422000;
Fax: 01494 422260).
Extel Financial Ltd, Fitzroy House,
13–17 Epworth Street, London EC2A
4DL
(Tel: 0171 251 3333, ext 8628/9;
Fax: 0171 490 1340).
Global Scan, 28 Scrutton Street,
London EC2A 4RQ
(Tel: 0171 377 8872;
Fax: 0171 247 4194).
Jordans and Sons Ltd, 47 Brunswick
Place, London N1 6EE
(Tel: 0171 253 3030;
Fax: 0171 251 0825).
Keystroke Knowledge, Upper Butts,
Orcop, Hereford HR2 8SF (Tel: 01981
540263; Fax: 01981 540734).

Before making a special journey it would be as well to telephone and make sure
the library has the reference work you want.

Do not neglect your local library. A visit to Kensington and Woolwich
libraries was a very pleasant surprise. Gloucestershire is also among a growing
band of progressive County Libraries aiming to serve local business needs in the
information field. Their librarian has produced a very useful guide to their free
commercial service for the county's business communities.

■ HELP WITH MARKET RESEARCH

The most cost-effective way for a new or small business to get help with market
research is to secure the services of a student, who is being supervised by professionals and with some appreciation of the problems a small business has. A
national network provides just such a service.

The Shell Technology Enterprise Programme (STEP) is designed to help small
and medium-sized businesses take advantage of the skills and abilities of the
local undergraduate population at a low cost and to help solve business problems. Participating companies benefit from the skills and enthusiasm of a bright

and intelligent undergraduate targeted at a particular project – a problem or opportunity.

Typical benefits include:
- increased sales potential
- new product design
- increased customer base
- reduced costs
- identification of new business opportunities
- increased efficiency
- new business plan
- environmental improvements
- increased export potential
- improved health and safety.

The students are paid a training allowance of £100 per week. Up to 50% of the allowance will be subsidized by a STEP sponsor. In addition to this you will be asked to make a contribution towards the student's travel expenses. Projects take place in July and August and last for eight weeks. STEP is run by local agencies at over 70 locations around the UK.

The students will be second- or penultimate-year undergraduates with suitable academic and/or work experience. You will be provided with details of several suitable students, from which you can make a final choice.

Prior to starting their placements, the students will be provided with induction training by the local agency. The training will include: an introduction to SMEs, project management, time management, report writing and presentation techniques. At the end of the placement all the students produce a written report and give a short presentation of the results.

The placements will be closely monitored by your local managing agent and will include at least one visit during the course of the placement.

You are eligible to take part if you:
- have a project of a commercial or technical nature which can be completed by a penultimate-year undergraduate in eight weeks;
- operate as an independent business with under 200 employees;
- can commit the necessary resources to supervise the project and provide the student with an insight into business.

If you are interested in participating in the programme, contact: Andrew Driver, Administrator, Shell Technology Enterprise Programme (STEP), 11 St Bride Street, London EC4A 4AS (Tel: 0171 936 3556; Fax: 0171 936 3531).

Area offices for STEP are listed below.

England
London/South East
Kent Kent Technology Transfer Centre. Contact: Lorraine Wildman (Tel: 01227 763414).

London (East) Urban Learning Foundation. Contact: Gill Holmes (Tel: 0171 476 8801).

London (North) Barfield Enterprise Training. Contact: Sheila Boad

(Tel: 0181 447 1000).
London (South East) Sira Test and
Certification. Contact: Steve Lower
(Tel: 0181 467 2636).
Sussex Sussex Technology Transfer
Centre. Contact: Patsie Sutcliffe
(Tel: 01278 678388).
Thames Valley Thames Valley
Technology. Contact: Peter Russell
(Tel: 01865 784888).

East
Bedfordshire University of Luton.
Contact: Gordon Weller
(Tel: 01582 489246).
Cambridge St John's Innovation
Centre. Contact: Howard Waller
(Tel: 01223 421116).
Essex Essex Business Centre. Contact:
Vanessa Vollans (Tel: 01245 283030).
Norfolk Business Development
Centre. Contact: Martin Lott
(Tel: 01603 633577).

South West
Avon Bristol and Avon Enterprise
Agency. Contact: Ashley E Dyer
(Tel: 0117 9272222).
Devon and Cornwall Action
Consultants Training.
Contact: Roy Robinson
(Tel: 01803 862271).
Gloucestershire Gloucestershire
Chamber of Commerce.
Contact: John Cripps
(Tel: 01452 385151).
Isle of Wight Isle of Wight Enterprise
Agency.
Contact: Hammie Tappenden
(Tel: 01983 529120).
Somerset Sedgemoor District Enter-
prise Centre. Contact: Mary Hall
(Tel: 01278 452978).
Wiltshire Great Western Enterprise.
Contact: Louis Vanderpump
(Tel: 01793 488088).

West Midlands
Birmingham Black Business in
Birmingham. Contact: Sena Kwame
(Tel: 0121 631 2860).
Coventry University of Warwick
Science Park. Contact: Stephen Brown
(Tel: 01203 418535).
Dudley Dudley Business Venture.
Contact: Ian Milroy
(Tel: 01384 231283).
Hereford and Worcester Hereford and
Worcester TEC.
Contact: Lisa King
(Tel: 01905 723200).
Sandwell Sandwell Enterprise.
Contact: Tim Moore
(Tel: 0121 500 5412).
Shropshire Shropshire TEC.
Contact: Roy Ellis
(Tel: 01952 291471).
Staffordshire Staffordshire
Development Agency.
Contact: Mary Bloomer
(Tel: 01785 277371).
Walsall Quest Business Technology
Centre. Contact: Geoff Henderson
(Tel: 01922 22122).

East Midlands
Derbyshire North Derbyshire Enter-
prise Agency. Contact: Jim Callendar
(Tel: 01246 207379).
Lincolnshire Lincolnshire Business
School. Contact: Mike Neale
(Tel: 01522 568866).
Northamptonshire Kettering Business
Venture.
Contact: Ted George
(Tel: 01536 513840).
Nottinghamshire Nottingham Trent
University. Contact: Philip Donnelly
(Tel: 0115 9486412).

Yorkshire and Humberside
Doncaster DONBAC.
Contact: Katherine Moffat

(Tel: 01302 340320).

Humberside Humberside EBP.
Contact: Malcolm Thompson
(Tel: 01482 856622).

Leeds Leeds Development Agency.
Contact: Helen King
(Tel: 0113 2474643).

Sheffield Sheffield Enterprise Agency.
Contact: Andrew Martin
(Tel: 0114 2755721).

North West

Barrow in Furness Barrow Borough
Council. Contact: Duncan Spilsbury
(Tel: 01229 825500).

Bolton Bolton Business Ventures.
Contact: Gillian Hunt
(Tel: 01204 391400).

Carlisle and Eden Cumbria and
Ellesmere Port Enterprise Agency.
Contact: Sally Gosmore
(Tel: 0151 348 1163).

East Lancashire Pendle Enterprise
Trust. Contact: Ron Morrish
(Tel: 01282 698001).

Kendal and South Lakeland Cumbria
TEC.
Contact: Celia Hunter-Wetenhall
(Tel: 01539 735407).

Liverpool Parliament Street
Industrialists Association.
Contact: Tony Haines
(Tel: 0151 709 8932).

Manchester Trafford Business
Venture. Contact: Rebecca Perrin
(Tel: 0161 848 4317).

Preston Preston Business Venture.
Contact: Pauline Greene
(Tel: 01772 563941).

South and East Cheshire South and
East Cheshire TEC.
Contact: Sarah Hillyerd
(Tel: 01606 737009).

West Cumbria Cumbria TEC.
Contact: Barbara Cannon
(Tel: 01900 669911).

Wigan Wigan and District Chamber
of Commerce.
Contact: Dave Sculthorpe
(Tel: 01942 496591).

Wirral Cleveland Street Business
Association. Contact: Mark Basnett
(Tel: 0151 670 1616).

North East

Cleveland Teesside Training Enterprise. Contact: Peter Bianchi
(Tel: 01642 433295).

Co. Durham Derwentside Industrial
Development Agency.
Contact: Joyce Robson
(Tel: 01207 509124).

South Tyneside TEDCO.
Contact: Joanne Dobson
(Tel: 0191 455 4300).

Tyne and Wear Tyne and Wear
Enterprise Trust.
Contact: Roger Turner
(Tel: 0191 261 4838).

Scotland

Aberdeen Aberdeen Enterprise Trust.
Contact: Jim Swanson
(Tel: 01224 582599).

Ayrshire Ayrshire EBP.
Contact: Sue Jones
(Tel: 01563 72929).

Bathgate and Livingston West
Lothian Business Development.
Contact: Alistair Shaw
(Tel: 01506 633906).

Coatbridge Monklands Enterprise.
Contact: Stewart Robinson
(Tel: 01236 423281).

Dunbarton Dunbartonshire
Enterprise. Contact: John Gillies
(Tel: 0141 951 2121).

Dumfries and Galloway Dumfries and
Galloway Enterprise.
Contact: Helen Scoular
(Tel: 01387 54444).

Fife Glenrothes Enterprise Trust.
Contact: Arthur Stutt
(Tel: 01592 630599).

Glasgow Glasgow Opportunities.
Contact: Hugh Stevenson
(Tel: 0141 221 0955).
Hamilton Hamilton Enterprise Development Co.
Contact: Helen Jamieson
(Tel: 01698 429425).
Inverurie Gordon Enterprise Trust.
Contact: Jackie Hall
(Tel: 01467 621166).
Motherwell Motherwell Enterprise Development Co.
Contact: Sharon Reynolds
(Tel: 01698 269333).
Perth Perthshire Enterprise Co.
Contact: Robert Main
(Tel: 01738 29114).

Wales
Bangor University College North

Wales. Contact: Keith Marshall
(Tel: 01248 351151).
Cardiff Cardiff and Vale Enterprise.
Contact: Kay Williams
(Tel: 01222 494411).
Powys Powys County Council.
Contact: Gareth Jones
(Tel: 01597 826376).
Swansea West Glamorgan Enterprise.
Contact: Eunydd Thomas
(Tel: 01792 885197).

Northern Ireland
Belfast and Newry Innovation Centre
Belfast.
Contact: Bill McKendry
(Tel: 01232 894534).
Londonderry Noribic Ltd.
Contact: Jim McColgan
(Tel: 01504 264242).

Other sources of help with market research

In addition to the STEP programme you should contact the university of college nearest to you, listed in Section 8. They will have students or staff who can help with research.

On-line databases

There are now thousands of database services, worldwide. The business databases worldwide which are accessible from the UK are listed in the Directory, *Business-Line Company Information*, available from Euromonitor Publications Ltd, 87–88 Turnmill Street, London EC1M 5QU (Tel: 0171 251 8024; Fax: 0171 608 3149).
Data-Star Dialog Europe, Haymarket House, 1 Oxendon Street, London SW1Y 4EE (Tel: 0171 930 7646; Fax: 0171 930 2581). A major publisher of technical, business and financial information, worldwide, operating two on-line services, Dialog and Data-Star. Publishes *Key British Enterprises, Who Owns Whom*.
Echo, PO Box 2373, L1023 Luxembourg. Technical and commercial information on the EEC.
EUSIDIC, European Association of Informaiton Services, 37 Val St André, PO Box 1416, L1014 Luxembourg (Tel: 00 352 250 750 220; Fax: 00 352 250 750 222). Represent on-line database users and run conferences and seminars.
FT Profile, PO Box 12, Sunbury-on-Thames, Middlesex TW16 7UD (Written enquiries only.) Provides international news and comment, company reports and marketing data.
Infocheck provides detailed information on over 420,000 companies and basic

information on approximately one million. Hosts: Infocheck, Data-Star, Gateways, FT Profile, British Telecom. The Infocheck Group Ltd, Godmersham Park, Godmersham, Canterbury, Kent CT4 7DT (Tel: 01227 813000; Fax: 01227 813100).

Mead Data, 1 St Katherine's Way, London E1 9UN (Tel: 0171 488 9187). Publishes, among others, an international legal information service, LEXIS.

■ MARKETING ORGANIZATIONS AND THEIR SERVICES

The organizations that look after the interests of professional marketeers can also give considerable help to newcomers and small businesses. At least two of these organizations, the Institute of Marketing and the British Overseas Trade Board, have unrivalled libraries and information banks in their respective fields. The Institute of Marketing, with its unique low-cost advisory service, is one particularly useful organization. Many others, including the Market Research Society and the Institute of Management Consultants, provide specialist members' directories. These can put you in touch with someone with recent experience in the areas of your concern. Although you will have to pay for their services, you will improve the chances of solving your problem first time round.

Education is also a strong point of many organizations. The Institute of Sales and Marketing and the British Direct Marketing Association hold frequent short courses on most aspects of sales and marketing, as does the Institute of Marketing itself.

The Advertising Association, Abford House, 15 Wilton Road, London SW1V 1NJ (Tel: 0171 828 2771; Fax: 0171 931 0376). The association was formed in 1926, and is primarily a federation of organizations with a major interest in advertising. As such it sets out to promote greater awareness of the effectiveness and purpose of all types of 'paid-for space' in the media. Two services of possible interest are its publications of advertising expenditure statistics and forecasts in all media, and its education programme, run through CAM, listed below.

Association of Exhibition Organizers Ltd, Market Towers, Nine Elms Lane, London SW8 5NQ (Tel: 0171 627 3946; Fax: 0171 498 0574).

British Consultants Bureau, 1 Westminster Palace Gardens, 1–7 Artillery Row, London SW1P 1RJ (Tel: 0171 222 3651; Fax: 0171 222 3664). This is an independent, non-profit-making association of British consulting firms of all disciplines. BCB's main purpose is to promote the interest of British consultants overseas. However, the bureau publishes a comprehensive directory, giving detailed information about all their members, their experience and their expertise. This is available to commercial firms.

The British Direct Marketing Association, Grosvenor Gardens House, 35 Grosvenor Gardens, London SW1W 0BS (Tel: 0171 630 7322; Fax: 0171 828 7125). The association brings together the three main groups of people who influence the way in which products and services are marketed direct to customers. These groups are: direct mail houses, who prepare and market lists of prospective customers; financial, insurance, commercial and manufacturing firms; publishers and professional organizations that market direct (i.e. not via retailers), and advertising agencies and consultancies that specialize in direct marketing methods.

The BDMA is growing rapidly both in size and stature. It has played an important role in helping the customer to choose whether or not he wants to receive more advertising mail through the post. Its education programme of short courses and workshops, covering the use of direct mail, is extensive. The BDMA also produces a number of useful books that introduce the subject to the novice, or sharpen up older hands.

British Exhibition Venues Association, Mallards, Five Ashes, Mayfield, East Sussex TN20 6NN (Tel: 01435 872244; Fax: 01435 872696).

British Institute of Management, Management House, Cottingham Road, Corby, Northants NN17 1TT (Tel: 01536 204222; Fax: 01536 201651). Their services to members include information and advisory functions, and a research and education programme. They also have a Centre for Physical Distribution Management, which covers transport, warehousing, inventory control, materials handling and packaging matters. This is more an institute for professional managers than just for marketeers, but its wider vision is particularly useful for small businesses.

British List Brokers Association Ltd, 16 The Pines, Broad Street, Guildford, Surrey GU3 3BH (Tel: 01483 301311; Fax: 01483 303533).

British Promotional Merchandise Association, Suite 12, 4th Floor, Parkway House, Sheen Lane, East Sheen, London SW14 8LS (Tel: 0181 878 0738; Fax: 0181 878 1053). Promotional product and services information for member companies and non members. Associated company: Promotions News Ltd. Advisory desk, members' publication *Promotions News*, BPMA Yearbook.

Chartered Institute of Marketing, Moor Hall, Cookham, Maidenhead, Berks SL6 9QH (Tel: 016285 24922; Fax: 01628 531381). The institute has nearly 25,000 members and is the largest and most comprehensive body in the field. It has a substantial library and a wide range of publications. There are few subjects in the field to which the institute cannot provide a useful pointer.

Communication Advertising and Marketing Education (CAM) Foundation, Abford House, 3rd Floor, 15 Wilton Road, London SW1V 1NJ (Tel: 0171 828 7506; Fax: 0171 976 5140). This is the authoritative body on what and where to study in the marketing field.

Design Business Association, 29 Bedford Square, London WC1B 3EG (Tel: 0171 631 1510; Fax: 0171 580 2338). Represents, promotes and supports the UK design consultancy sector, with over 200 members providing design services in product, graphic and environmental design. The DBA runs professional practical training for designers and design managers, also the bi-annual Design Effectiveness Awards. Publishes design management guides and 'Professional Practice in Design Consultancy'.

Direct Mail Information Service, 5 Carlisle Street, London W1V 5RG (Tel: 0171 494 0483; Fax: 0171 494 0455). Research into direct mail and marketing, research publishing, information service.

Direct Mail Services Standards Board Ltd, 26 Eccleston Street, London SW1W 9PY (Tel: 0171 824 8651; Fax: 0171 824 8574). Self-regulatory organization for direct mail industry. It is sponsored by the Advertising Standards Authority and the Royal Mail. The DMSSB works closely with the direct mail industry to ensure compliance with the advertising codes. Does not deal directly with complaints from the public.

The Direct Marketing Association (UK) Ltd, Haymarket House, 1 Oxendon Street, London SW1Y 4EE (Tel: 0171 321 2525; Fax: 0171 321 0191).

Direct Selling Association, 29 Floral Street, London WC2E 9DP (Tel: 0171 497 1234; Fax: 0171 497 1344). For those involved in selling to people at home, including party selling. Provides information and statistics; organizes conferences, training and exhibitions. Has a free leaflet: *Shopping at Home.*

Exhibition Bulletin, The London Bureau, 266–272 Kirkdale, Sydenham, London SE26 4RZ (Tel: 0181 778 2288; Fax: 0181 659 8495). International directory of exhibitions; updates and issues monthly.

Exhibition Fact Finder, Batiste Publications Ltd, Pembroke House, Campsbourne Road, London N8 7PE (Tel: 0181 340 3291; Fax: 0181 341 4840). Conference and exhibitions in UK. Circulation 6,000+ to organizers of conferences and exhibitions.

Industrial Market Research Association, 11 Bird Street, Lichfield, Staffs WS13 6PW (Tel: 01543 263448). The association represents over 1,000 members of the profession of Industrial Market Research in the UK. Although it does produce a directory of members, this is not generally available.

Institute of Customer Care, St John's House, Chapel Lane, Westcott, Surrey RH4 3PJ (Tel: 01306 876210; Fax: 01306 888910). Institute of Public Relations, Gate House, St John Square, London EC1M 4DH (Tel: 0171 253 5151). The institute is mainly concerned with keeping professional standards high and promoting general awareness of the role of public relations.

Institute of Management Consultants, 32–33 Hatton Garden, London EC1N 8DL (Tel: 0171 242 2140; Fax: 0171 830 4597). The institute has 3,300 individual members, and publishes the journal *Consult.* As a free service to industry it operates a client enquiry service, putting enquirers in contact with members with appropriate skills.

The Institute of Sales and Marketing Management, 31 Upper George Street, Luton, Beds LU1 2RD (Tel: 01582 411130; Fax: 01582 453640). Professional body for sales and marketing personnel. Provides professional training courses, and a wide range of benefits – personal, financial and professional.

Institute of Sales Promotion, Arena House, 66–68 Pentonville Road, Islington, London N1 9HS (Tel: 0171 837 5340; Fax: 0171 837 5326). Professional association for everyone in the promotions marketing industry. Their Consultants Register is available to non-member prospective clients, as is their information service, which holds a comprehensive reading list on the subject.

London Exhibition Venues Association, 137 Sheen Road, Richmond, Surrey TW9 1YJ (Tel: 0181 940 3431; Fax: 0181 332 1920). Director G V Smith.

Mail Order Protection Scheme, National Newspapers, 16 Took's Court, London EC4A 1LB (Tel: 0171 405 6806; Fax: 0171 404 0106).

Mail Order Traders Association, 100 Old Hall Street, Liverpool L3 9TD (Tel: 0151 227 4181; Fax: 0151 227 2584).

Mail Order Traders Association of Great Britain, 25 Castle Street, Liverpool L2 4TD (Tel: 0151 236 7581).

The Management Consultancy Information Service, 32 Blenheim Avenue, Gants Hill, Ilford, Essex IG2 6SQ (Tel: 0181 554 4695). Keeps records on management consultancy firms and individual consultants. Offers a free confidential service to potential clients to help find the right person for your task.

The Market Research Society, 15 Northburgh Street, London EC1V 0AH (Tel: 0171 490 4911; Fax: 0171 490 0608). This is the professional body for those concerned with market, social and economic research. It has 3,500 members and is the largest body of its kind in the world. Apart from a programme of education, research and publications of primary interest to members, the society produces a directory of organizations providing market research services. The directory provides background information on the 210 research agencies, their executives, experience and the size in sales turnover. Some of the organizations are quite small, with turnovers below £50,000 per annum, whereas others have a turnover of several million pounds. They also publish the *International Research Directory.*

The Marketing Society, Derwent House, Stanton House, 206 Worple Road, London SW20 8PN (Tel: 0171 879 3464; Fax: 0171 879 0362). The society was formed 30 years ago. One of its main objectives is to raise the reputation and understanding of marketing among general management, government, the Civil Service, trade unions and educationalists.

The Newspaper Society (Marketing Dept), Bloomsbury House, Bloomsbury Square, 74–7 Great Russell Street, London WC1 BDA (Tel: 0171 636 7014; Fax: 0171 631 5119). Single point of entry to book advertising in any of 1,000 local newspapers. They offer a computerized database service that can provide all relevant facts and figures about these local papers and the areas in which they operate.

Public Relations Consultants Association, Willow House, Willow Place, Victoria, London SW1P 1JH (Tel: 0171 233 6026; Fax: 0171 828 4797). The association produces a wide range of guidance papers and other publications.

Sales Promotion Consultants Association, PO Box 1578, London E1 9FR (Tel: 0171 702 8567; Fax: 0171 702 8570).

Women in Direct Marketing, Royal Mail House, 148–166 Old Street, London EC1V 9HQ (Tel: 0171 250 2365; Fax: 0171 250 2021).

Women in Marketing and Design, 9 Greenside Road, London W12 9JQ (Tel: 0181 749 3847; Fax: 0181 743 1715). A network group for all women working or studying in the design and marketing industries. Aims: to pursue professional recognition, address industry issues and encourage the development of professional and personal skills.

■ SPECIALIST SERVICES FOR EXPORTING

The British Overseas Board, with its wide range of expertise and services, is of considerable use to first-time exporters. Apart from a wealth of information and statistics, its Market Entry Guarantee Scheme can provide an important part of the funding which a small firm needs to enter a new market.

The Institute of Export is the professional body in the field, and two other services are particularly interesting. Scanmark, run from Buckinghamshire College of Higher Education, undertakes research into overseas markets at a fraction of the cost of the commercial research organizations. The Export and Overseas Trade Advisory Panel Ltd performs a rather different role. Using their panel of expert advisers, they not only help you to evaluate an overseas market opportunity but will guide you through the red tape, too.

SITPRO (the Simplification of International Trade Procedures Board) will also be able to help with export documentation systems that will save exporters time and money, and the BBC Service to Exporters is always keen to hear interesting exporting stories.

Organizations

Export Market Information Centre (EMIC) is provided by the Department of Trade and Industry (DTI) to enable British exporters to carry out desk research into overseas markets. The centre has statistics on overseas trade, production, price, employment, population; foreign trade and telephone directories; development plans and overseas mail order catalogues. Department of Trade and Industry, 123 Victoria Street, London SW1E 6RB (Tel: 0171 215 5444; Fax: 0171 215 4231). Contact your local DTI office initially.

The following services for exporters are also available from the DTI, but will eventually be provided by Business Link outlets (see Section 2 for description of business links).

- There is an automated service matching companies to new export intelligence received daily by DTI. This is available through Prelink (Tel: 0181 900 1313). The government offers on-line access from your office computer to all its export intelligence through FT Profile (Tel: 01932 76144), the electronic database owned by the *Financial Times.*
- **Market Information Enquiries** will assemble a tailor-made package of information on export opportunities for products, processes or services. It charges £35 for basic information and then in four-hour units for more complicated enquiries ranging from an initial £70 up to £355 for between 16 and 24 hours' work.
- **The Export Marketing Research Scheme** is more specific and detailed, providing professional advice and financial support, whether the work is done in-house or by a professional consultant.
- **The Export Representative Service** will help find a representative overseas through the government's own experts in the market concerned. The charge is £355 for up to 24 hours' work, £710 for up to 48 hours and £1,065 for longer.
- **Overseas Status Reports** provide assessments of the suitability of potential

representatives or companies you want to do business with, but not credit-worthiness. Charges are similar to those for Market Information Enquiries.

- **Trade Fair Support** pays for half the space and gives a fixed construction grant for up to three exhibitions in each market, but up to five in Japan and some parts of Germany and the US.
- **New Products from Britain** is a media relations service; £60 buys a professionally written news story aimed at securing editorial coverage in appropriate media in target markets.
- **Trade missions,** organized by chambers of commerce or trade associations, are subsidized. Many companies find them a cheap way of sampling a market at first hand and for making contacts for subsequent visits. Reciprocal social obligations will usually involve attending a couple of receptions.
- **The Programme Arranging Service** usually builds on market information obtained through Market Information Enquiries, the Export Marketing Research Scheme or the Export Representative Service. It helps arrange appointments and gives advice on local business and culture in your target market.
- **In-Market Help** goes one step further, offering accompanied visits by local commercial experts and a de-briefing afterwards to help you consider your next steps.

British Food Export Council, 301–344 Market Towers, 1 Nine Elms Lane, London SW8 5NQ (Tel: 0171 622 0188; Fax: 0171 627 0616). Helps with promoting the export of UK fresh and processed foods, drinks and associated products.

British International Freight Association, Redfern House, Browells Lane, Feltham, Middx TW13 7EP (Tel: 0181 844 2266; Fax: 0181 890 5546). Advice on movement of goods, worldwide.

British Knitting and Clothing Export Council, 7 Swallow Place, London W1R 7AA (Tel: 0171 493 6622; Fax: 0171 493 6276). Advises members on export sales and marketing matters in the knitting and clothing fields.

The DTI Business in Europe, Kingsgate House, 66 Victoria Street, London SW1E 6SW (Tel: 0171 215 4703; 0171 215 6140). Enquiries about doing business in Europe.

Export Group for the Constructional Industries, Kingsbury House, 15–17 King Street, London SW1Y 6QU (Tel: 0171 930 5377).

Institute of European Trade and Technology, 29 Throgmorton Street, London EC2N 2AT (Tel: 0171 628 9770; Fax: 0171 628 7692). Aims to promote awareness of the benefit of trade and technological collaboration between European organizations.

The Institute of Export, 64 Clifton Street, London EC2A 4HB (Tel: 0171 247 9812; Fax: 0171 377 5343). The institute aims to contribute to profitable exporting by providing a forum for the exchange of experience and information between exporters. It also promotes education and training throughout the whole field of exporting. Its regular journal, *Export,* is a good way of getting into the export picture.

Institute of Linguists, 24a Highbury Grove, London N5 2EA (Tel: 0171 359 7445). Will advise on industrial and technical translations – ask for the Translators' Guild.

International Chamber of Commerce, 14–15 Belgrave Square, London SW1X 8PS (Tel: 0171 823 2811; Fax: 0171 235 5447). Promotes international trade through various services and publications.

The London Chamber of Commerce runs residential beginners' courses in French, Arabic, German, Spanish and Portuguese, Italian, Japanese and Mandarin Chinese, which guarantee to teach you to speak and write 450 words of the new language in six days. It does not sound a lot, perhaps, but when used in multiple combinations 450 words provide an extremely useful basic preliminary vocabulary of expressions and phrases. Also available are intermediate and advanced courses in French and intermediate courses in German and Spanish. The courses have been designed by Professor Robert Boland specifically for the mature student, and make a complete departure from the school language lab routine. For more information contact LCCI, 69 Cannon Street, London EC4A 5AB (Tel: 0171 248 4444 ext 337).

Simplification of International Trade Procedures Board (SITPRO), 29 Glasshouse Street, London W1R 5RG (Tel: 0171 287 3525; Fax: 0171 287 5751). This is an independent body set up by the Department of Trade. Its objective is to simplify trade documents and procedures and so make international trade easier for British companies. The board would like to know of any persistent problems in international trade documents and procedures, to help it decide on future priorities for action. SITPRO News is available on request. SITPRO also produces a range of publications, one of which, *Top Form,* is a useful guide through a complex process.

The board has an advisory consultancy service which will visit sites and will provide technical help for exporters. Marketing any product overseas means that you will have to comply with the laws of the land (safety and environmental); national standards; certification practices; and customer needs. This service can supply detailed information on foreign regulations; identify, supply and assist in the interpretation of foreign standards and other technical requirements; provide translations; and help with obtaining foreign approval.

A technical enquiry service is operated specifically to deal with the day-to-day problems of exporters, many of which are answerable over the telephone. The charge depends on the amount of research and the time involved. A range of fees is charged for more detailed and difficult enquiries.

Publications

The major accounting firms and banks produce guides to doing business in most major overseas markets.

Croner's Reference Book for Exporters, from Croner Publications Ltd, Croner House, London Road, Kingston-upon-Thames, Surrey KT2 6SR (Tel: 0181 547 3333; Fax: 0181 547 2637). This is a loose-leaf and regularly updated service that keeps exporters up to date on all exporting procedures. It is available on a ten-day free approval offer. Price £60.50.

Directory of Export Buyers in the United Kingdom, 1987, by Tookey and published by Trade Research Publications, 6 Beech Hill Court, Berkhamsted, Herts HP4 2PR (Tel: 014427 3951). The conventional wisdom of successful exporting recommends that you should travel abroad to contact buyers. However, firms abroad are increasingly establishing buying offices in this country in order, among other reasons, to look for new sources of supply. It is estimated that orders for about 20% of British exports are negotiated and signed in the UK, and mainly by people listed in this directory. The entries are indexed by countries bought from, products bought and foreign firms bought for.

■ SPECIALIST SERVICES FOR IMPORTING

British Importers Confederation, 3rd Floor, 152–160 City Road, London EC1V 2NP (Tel: 0171 490 7262). The confederation was founded in 1972, and represents some 3,500 importers. It is the only organization protecting the interests of importers whatever the goods concerned. Membership fees are modest and members include a significant number of one-man importers or smaller firms, as well as such companies as Shell and Unilever. Because of its close relationship with the UK Government and the EEC Commissions, the confederation is usually aware of likely changes in import procedures long before they occur. This knowledge and other information form an important part of the service that the confederation can provide for small businesses.

Croner's Reference Book for Importers accurately spells out the regulations and procedures to import goods of any nature into the UK. It covers import controls, exchange controls, VAT, marketing of goods, customs and excise, and transit and transhipment insurance. The book is in loose-leaf form and the service includes a regular supply of amendments. From Croner Publications Ltd, Croner House, London Road, Kingston-upon-Thames, Surrey KT2 6SR (Tel: 0181 547 3333; Fax: 0181 547 2637).

Directory of British Importers covers 4,000 companies indexed by countries/market imported from and product type. It includes brand and trade names. Contact: Trade Research Publications, 6 Beech Hill Court, Berkhamsted, Hertfordshire HP4 2PR (Tel: 01442 863951; Fax: 01442 230772).

■ BOOKS AND PERIODICALS ON MARKETING

Be Your Own PR Expert by Bill Penn, published by Piatkus Books in 1993; price £8.99. The complete guide to publicity and public relations.

Campaign, Haymarket Publications Ltd, 22 Lancaster Gate, London W2 3LY (Tel: 0181 943 5000). A weekly mainly concentrating on advertising and agency matters. Price £1.30.

The Creative Handbook, published by British Media Publications, Windsor Court, East Grinstead, West Sussex RH19 1XA (Tel: 01342 326972). Annual, listing all creative services, e.g. illustrators, model makers, photographers, cartoonists. Price £92.50.

Desk Research by Peter Jackson, published by Kogan Page in 1994; price £12.95.

Do-It-Yourself Advertising by Fred Hahn, published by John Wiley & Son in 1993; price £9.95. How to produce your own ads, brochures, catalogues, direct mail etc.

Do Your Own Advertising by Alistair Crompton, published by Business Books in 1991; price £7.99. The guide for everyone who runs a small business.

Exhibition Bulletin, 266/272 Kirkdale, Sydenham, London SE26 4RZ (Tel: 0181 778 2288). Provides a monthly list of all exhibitions in the UK.

Manual of Market Research by Hibbert, published by Blackwells in 1994; price £19.99.

Marketing – a weekly subscription-only publication from Haymarket Publications (address above).

Marketing, an Introductory Text by Martin Christopher and Malcolm McDonald, published by Macmillan in 1995; price £12.99. Refreshing, practical and set firmly in the UK environment.

Marketing Breakthroughs – a monthly worldwide review of new marketing techniques. World Business Publications, 4th Floor, Britannia House, London N12 9RY (Tel: 0181 446 5141).

Marketing Ideas for the Small Business by P W and P F Stewart, published by Mercury Business Books in 1990; price £6.99. Forty promotional campaigns that small firms can use.

Marketing, Management, Analysis, Planning and Control by Philip Kotler, published by Prentice Hall in 1991 (7th edition); price £22.95. The most lucid and comprehensive book on the subject. Generally accepted as the standard text, and though illustrated liberally with American examples, the theory is both readable and understandable.

Selling by Mail Order Made Easy by John Kremer, published by McGraw-Hill in 1992; price £19.95. A step-by-step guide to organizing and carrying out a successful direct marketing programme.

Selling by Phone by Linda Richardson, published by McGraw Hill in 1992; price £14.95.

Selling Services and Products by McDonald Morris, published by Butterworth-Heinemann in 1994; price £10.95.

Successful Market Research in a Week by Matthew Housden, published by Headway in 1993; price £5.99.

6 | *Raising the money*

■ PREPARING YOUR CASE

There is rarely a true shortage of money to finance the launching of new businesses and the growth of existing ones. What are scarce are good, small-company propositions. At least, that is the argument put forward by the financial institutions themselves. There is certainly an element of truth in this view, but the quality of the propositions owes much to the poor groundwork and planning of some budding entrepreneurs. The starting point for any search for funds is to determine how much is needed, and then to demonstrate the security that the likely investor will then enjoy.

The accepted way in which proposals for funds are put forward is through a business plan. The business plan brings together the marketing and operational aspects of the business or proposed business, and expresses these actions in terms that a financial institution will understand. Not surprisingly, these institutions will expect the plan to contain financial statements both actual and projected. Section 11 shows how to prepare your first business plan, and suggests organizations and publications that can help.

■ THE DIFFERENT TYPES OF MONEY

Your cash-flow projections will provide a good idea of how much money your business will need, when it is required and for how long.

The next step is where to go and find this finance. Before considering possible sources of finance, you should categorize your needs into fixed or working capital. Fixed capital is money tied up in things the business intends to keep over longer periods of time, such as property, equipment, vehicles etc. Working capital is the money used to finance the day-to-day operations. The stock, for example, and any money required to finance your customers until they pay up, are elements of working capital, as are all other running costs and overheads.

Your own capital

Obviously the first place to start is to find out exactly how much you have to invest in the business. You may not have much in ready cash, but you may have valuable assets that can be converted into cash, or other borrowing. The difference between your assets and your liabilities is your 'net worth'. This is the maximum security that you can offer for any money borrowed, and it is hoped that the calculations below will yield a pleasant surprise.

Table 6.1 Matching finance to business needs

Type of capital	Business needs	Financing method
Fixed capital	Acquiring or altering a property; buying equipment, such as cookers, ovens, photocopiers, or vehicles; the franchise fee and other 'start-up' package costs such as training	Your own capital; term loans; hire purchase; leasing; sale and leaseback; venture capital; government loan guarantee scheme; mortgage loan
Working capital	Raw materials or finished goods; money to finance debtors; dealing with seasonal peaks and troughs, loan guarantee scheme expansion or unexpected short-term problems; paying royalties	Your own capital; bank overdraft; factoring; trade credit; government

Table 6.2: Your net worth

Assets		Liabilities	
Cash in hand and in the bank, building society, national savings or other deposits	£	Overdraft	£
		Mortgage	£
		Other loans	£
Stocks and shares	£	Hire purchase	£
Current redemption value of insurances	£	Tax due, including capital gains	£
Value of home	£	Credit cards due	£
Any other property	£	Garage, local shop accounts due	£
Motor car(s) etc	£	Any other financial obligations	£
Jewellery, paintings and other marketable values	£		
	£		
Any money due to you	£		
Value of existing businesses	£		
Total assets	£	Total liabilities	£
Net worth = Total assets – Total liabilities:	£		

External funds

There are a number of different types of external money which a growing company can tap into.

Debt is money borrowed most usually from a bank and which one day you will have to repay. While you are making use of borrowed money you will also have to pay interest on the loan.

Equity is the money put in by shareholders, including the proprietor, and money left in the business by way of retained profit. You don't have to give the shareholders their money back, but they do expect the directors to increase the value of their shares, and if you go public they will probably expect a stream of dividends too.

If you don't meet the shareholders' expectations then they won't be there when you need more money – or if they are powerful enough they will take steps to change the board.

Cash-flow financing is a general title that covers overdrafts which are repayable on demand and receivables financing in its many forms. Receivables financing – factoring and invoice discounting – is a facility whereby funding is provided against sales invoices. As sales grow, so does funding.

Hire purchase and leasing are other ways to finance fixed assets.

Franchising is another way to finance a growing business. People are invited to 'invest' in your business by paying you a fee to set up a branch in their own area. In this way you can expand the business across the country largely using their money.

Grants are also available in some circumstances to help the government of the day, or increasingly the European Community, achieve its own objectives. If their aims are in line with your own, their grants can be a useful help. But the strategy calling for the cash must be capable of standing on its own.

To most of us, raising money is synonymous with a visit to our local bank manager. Though not the only source of finance, the banks are a good starting point.

There are over a dozen clearing banks, as the high street bankers are usually called, and they are in serious competition with each other for new business. It is as well to remember that bank managers are judged on the quantity and quality of their lending and not on the deposits they take. If they cannot successfully lend, they can't make a profit for the bank.

For most satisfactory new business propositions the clearing bankers would normally be happy to match pound for pound the money put up by the owner, i.e. 1:1 gearing. They will also recommend a 'package' of funds – part term loan, part overdraft and perhaps part government loan guarantee – that best suits the type of business you are interested in starting up. For example, if the business you are considering is a service, requiring few physical assets, serving cash customers and expecting to break even in the first year, then you may be advised to take a small term loan and a larger overdraft facility. This will give you the money you need to start, without upsetting the long-term security of the business. The converse relationship between loan capital and overdraft may be prudent if you are considering a 'capital-intensive' business such as a restaurant.

The banks offer a wide range of services in their own right. Through wholly or partially owned subsidiaries, they cover virtually every aspect of the financial market. For franchisees their services include overdrafts, term loans, factoring, leasing and the government loan guarantee scheme. As well as providing funds, the clearing banks have considerable expertise in the areas of tax, insurance and financial advice generally.

Overdrafts

Bank overdrafts are the most common type of short-term finance. They are simple to arrange: you just talk to your local bank manager. They are flexible, with no minimum level. Sums of money can be drawn or repaid within the total amount agreed. They are relatively cheap, with interest paid only on the outstanding daily balance. Of course, interest rates can fluctuate, so what seemed a small sum of money one year can prove crippling if interest rates jump suddenly. Normally you do not repay the 'capital': you simply renew or alter the overdraft facility from time to time. However, overdrafts are theoretically repayable on demand, so you should not use short-term overdraft money to finance long-term needs, such as buying a lease, or plant and equipment.

There is evidence that many small firms are too dependent on overdraft financing and as a consequence are unnecessarily exposed to the mercy of their bankers. Midland Bank, however, claim the position is changing with only £4bn of their £12.5bn lent to small firms provided as overdrafts.

Term loans

These are rather more formal than a simple overdraft and cover periods of up to three, three to ten and ten to twenty years respectively. They are usually secured against an existing fixed asset or one to be acquired, or are guaranteed personally by the directors (proprietors). This may involve you in some costs for legal fees and arrangement or consultants' fees, so it may be a little more expensive than an overdraft, but unless you default on the interest charges you can be reasonably confident of having the use of the money throughout the whole term of the borrowing.

The interest rates on the loan can either be fixed for the term or variable with the prevailing interest rate. A fixed rate is to some extent a gamble, which may work in your favour, depending on how interest rates move over the term of the loan. So if general interest rates rise, you win, and if they fall, you lose. A variable rate means that you do not take that risk. There is another benefit to a fixed rate of interest. It should make planning ahead a little easier with a fixed financial commitment; with a variable overdraft, a sudden rise can have disastrous consequences. The banks have been quite venturesome in their competition for new and small business accounts. One major clearer had a scheme which offered free banking to new businesses for one year – even if they were overdrawn – provided the limit had been agreed.

The key innovation in such schemes is that the loan will be subordinated to other creditors, with the bank repaid before the shareholders but after all the other creditors if the company fails. In return for this risk they are likely to want an option on up to 25% of the company's capital.

Government loan guarantee for small businesses

Government loan guarantees for small businesses were introduced in March 1981 for an initial period of three years and were extended in the 1984 and later

Budgets. To be eligible for this loan, your proposition must have been looked at by an approved bank and considered viable, but should not be a proposition that the bank itself would normally approve. You can be a sole trader, partnership or limited company wanting funds to start up or expand. The bank simply passes your application on to the Department of Trade and Industry, using an approved format.

This is an elementary business plan, which asks for some details of the directors, the business, its cash needs and profit performance, or projection of the business. There are no formal rules on size, number of employees or assets, but large businesses and their subsidiaries are definitely excluded from the scheme. The other main exclusions are in the fields of agriculture, horticulture, banking, commission agents, education, forestry (except tree-harvesting and saw-milling), house and estate agents, insurance, medical and veterinary, night clubs and licensed clubs, pubs and property, and travel agencies.

The loans can be for up to £250,000 (small loans up to £15,000 can be approved without reference) and repayable over two to seven years. It may be possible to delay paying the capital element for up to two years from the start of the loan, but monthly or quarterly repayments of interest will have to be made from the outset. The loan itself, however, is likely to be expensive.

Once approved by the Department of Trade, the bank lends you the money at bank rate plus 4 or 5% and the government guarantees the bank 85% of its money if you fail to pay. In return for this the government charges you a 0.5 to 1.5% 'insurance' premium on the 85% of the loan it has taken on risk. Borrowers would be expected to pledge all available business assets as a security for the loan, but they would not necessarily be excluded from the scheme if there were no available assets. Their personal assets should already be fully committed to the venture.

The rule certainly seems to be to ask for as much as you need, plus a good margin of safety – going back for a second bite too soon is definitely frowned upon. You do not have to take all the money at once. At the discretion of your bank manager, you can take the money in up to four slices, but each slice must be 25% or more.

There are now 30 banks operating the scheme, and 18,000 loans worth over £600 million have been made. The average loan has been fairly constant at £33,000. A number of franchisees have received funds under this scheme including franchise-holders with household names such as Prontaprint.

■ WHERE YOU CAN GET THE MONEY

Clearing banks

This is the general name given to the high street bankers. We immediately think of the big four banks – Barclays, Lloyds, Midland and the National Westminster – when we think of 'clearers'. However, there are another dozen or so that fit within the general meaning of 'clearing and domestic deposit bank'.

In addition to providing a source of funds, the clearing banks have considerable expertise in the areas of tax, insurance and financial advice generally. Very little of this expertise will rest in your local branch office. The bank's regional and main head offices are where these centralized services are provided.

As you probably already have a bank account, this may be your starting point in looking for money for business. Do not forget, however, that the banks are in competition with one another and with other lenders. So shop around if you do not get what you want first time. Incidentally their charges to commercial customers vary too, so ask for figures before signing up.

The banks are becoming quite adventurous in their competition for new and small business accounts, and now all the clearers offer some special inducement to attract new small business accounts. For example, the Co-operative Bank offers free banking, even to companies with an overdraft, provided it is kept within agreed limits.

Some of the banks have a small-firms specialist, one of whose tasks is to help new, small-business clients get the best out of their banking services. To get an opinion from one of these specialists would be a good way of finding the possibilities of getting finance and how best to go about it.

Clearing and other domestic deposit banks

Allied Irish Banks Ltd, 64/66 Coleman Street, London EC2R 5AL (Tel: 0171 588 0691). Contact: Declan Flynn.

Bank of Ireland, 36 Queen Street, London EC4R 1BN (Tel: 0171 329 4500). Contact: Area Manager.

Bank of Scotland, Business Banking, PO Box 12, Uberior House, 61 Grassmarket, Edinburgh EH1 2JF (Tel: 0131 442 7777; Fax: 0131 243 5948). Contact: A D Paton.

Barclays Bank plc, Small Business Services, Business Sector Marketing Department, PO Box 120, Longwood Close, Westwood Business Park, Coventry CV4 8JN (Tel: 01203 694242; Fax: 01203 532699). Contact: David Swallow.

Clydesdale Bank plc (a member of the Midland Banking Group), 30 St Vincent Place, Glasgow G1 2HL (Tel: 0141 248 7070). Contact: A K Denholm.

Co-operative Bank plc, 1 Balloon Street, Manchester M60 4EP (Tel: 0161 832 6262). Contact: J Cowburn.

Coutts & Co (a member of the National Westminster Bank Group), 440 Strand, London WC2R 1QS (Tel: 0171 379 6262). Contact: A Beale and J Lucas.

Girobank plc, 10 Milk Street, London EC2V 8JH (Tel: 0171 600 6020). Contact: David Barber.

Lloyds Bank plc, Retail Banking UKRB, PO Box 112, Canons House, Canons Way, Bristol BS99 7LB (Tel: 01272 433433; Fax: 01272 433079). Contact: Michael Shaw.

Midland Bank plc, 2nd Floor, Griffin House, 41 Silver Street Head, Sheffield S1 3GG (Tel: 0114 2529477; Fax: 0114 2529770). Contact: Stuart White.

National Westminster Bank plc, Level 10, Drapers Gardens, 12 Throgmorton Avenue, London EC2N 2DL (Tel: 0171 374 3355;

Fax: 0171 454 2111).
Contact: Jane Bradford.
Northern Bank Ltd (a member of the
Midland Bank Group), Corporate
Finance Department, PO Box 183,
Donegal Square West, Belfast BT1 6JS
(Tel: 01232 245277).
Contact: A O'Hanlon.
The Royal Bank of Scotland,
PO Box 183, 42 St Andrews Square,
Edinburgh EH2 2YE

(Tel: 0131 556 8555).
Contact: J Byers.
Ulster Bank Ltd (a member of
National Westminster Bank Group),
35–39 Waring Street, Belfast BT1 2ER
(Tel: 01232 235232).
Contact: T McCurly.
Yorkshire Bank plc, 20 Merrion Way,
Leeds LS2 8NZ (Tel: 0113 2441244).
Contact: D Mortimer.

Factors

Factoring is generally only available to a business that invoices other business customers for its services. Factoring can be made available to new businesses, although its services are usually of most value during the early stages of growth.

Factoring is an arrangement which allows you to receive up to 80% of the cash due from your customers more quickly than they would normally pay. The factoring company buys your trade debts and provides a debtor accounting and administration service. In other words, it takes over the day-to-day work of invoicing and sending out reminders and statements. This can be a particularly helpful service to a small expanding business. It allows the management to concentrate on expanding the business, with the factoring company providing expert guidance on credit control, 100% protection against bad debts, and improved cash flow.

You will, of course, have to pay for factoring services. Having the cash before your customers pay will cost you a little more than normal overdraft rates. The factoring service will cost between 0.5 and 3.5% of the turnover, depending on volume of work, the number of debtors, average invoice amount and other related factors. You can get up to 80% of the value of your invoice in advance, with the remainder paid when your customer settles up, less the various charges just mentioned.

If you sell direct to the public, if you sell complex and expensive capital equipment or expect progress payments on long-term projects, then factoring is not for you. If you are expanding more rapidly than other sources of finance will allow, this may be a useful service. All other things being equal, it should be possible to find a factor if your turnover exceeds £25,000 per annum, though the larger firms will look for around £100,000 as the economic cut-off point.

The Association of British Factors and Discounters is at 1 Northumberland Avenue, Trafalgar Square, London WC2N 5BW (Tel: 0171 930 9112). Contact: Michael Burke. Only 11 of the UK's 39 factoring companies are members of the Trade Association. Factors provide around £20bn of trade finance to some 8,000 companies, who are for the most part small firms with an annual turnover below £5m.

Members of the Association of British Factors and Discounters

Alex Lawrie Factors Ltd, Beaumont House, Beaumont Road, Banbury, Oxfordshire OX16 7RN (Tel: 01295 272272; Fax: 01295 271634).

Barclays Commercial Services Ltd, Aquila House, Breeds Place, Hastings, East Sussex TN34 3DG (Tel: 01424 430824; Fax: 01424 461692).

Century Ltd, Southbrook House, 25 Bartholomew Street, Newbury, Berkshire RG14 5LL (Tel: 01635 31517; Fax: 01635 31703).

Griffin Factors Ltd, 21 Farncombe Road, Worthing, West Sussex BN11 2BW (Tel: 01903 205181; Fax: 01903 214101).

Hill Samuel Commercial Finance Ltd, Boston House, The Little Green, Richmond, Surrey TW9 1QE (Tel: 0181 940 4646; Fax: 0181 940 6051).

International Factors Ltd, PO Box 240, Sovereign House, Church Street, Brighton, Sussex BN1 3WX (Tel: 01273 321211; Fax: 01273 207651).

Kellock Ltd, Abbey Gardens, 4 Abbey Street, Reading, Berks RG1 3BA (Tel: 01734 585511; Fax: 01734 502480).

Lombard NatWest Commercial Services Ltd, Smith House, PO Box 50, Elmwood Ave, Feltham, Middlesex TW13 7QD (Tel: 0181 890 1390; Fax: 0181 751 3367).

Royscot Factors Ltd, Exchange Court, 3 Bedford Park, Croydon, Surrey CR0 2AQ (Tel: 0181 686 9988; Fax: 0181 680 1799).

Trade Indemnity-Heller Commercial Finance Ltd, Park House, 22 Park Street, Croydon, Surrey CR9 1RD (Tel: 0181 681 2641; Fax: 0181 681 8072).

UCB Invoice Discounting Ltd, Wren House, Sutton Court Road, Sutton, Surrey SM1 4TE (Tel: 0181 307 7744; Fax: 0181 307 7740).

Leasing companies

This is a way of getting the use of vehicles, plant and equipment without paying the full cost at once. Operating leases are taken out where you will use the equipment for less than its full economic life – for example, a car, photocopier, vending machine or kitchen equipment. The lessor takes the risk of the equipment becoming obsolete, and assumes responsibility for repairs, maintenance and insurance. As you, the lessee, are paying for this service, it is more expensive than a finance lease, where you lease the equipment for most of its economic life and maintain and insure it yourself. Leases can normally be extended, often for fairly nominal sums, in the latter years.

The obvious attraction of leasing is that no deposit is needed, leaving your working capital free for more profitable use elsewhere. Also, the cost is known from the start, making forward planning more simple. There may even be some tax advantages over other forms of finance. However, there are some possible pitfalls, which only a close examination of the small print will reveal. So do take professional advice before taking out a lease.

Hire purchase companies

This differs from leasing in that you have the option at the start to become the owner of the equipment after a series of payments have been made. The interest is usually fixed and often more expensive than a bank loan. However, manufacturers (notably car makers) often subsidize this interest, so it pays to shop around both for sources of hire purchase finance and manufacturers. Leasing and hire purchase is a £22.5bn business.

Information on leasing and hire purchase is obtainable from:

The Finance and Leasing Association, 18 Upper Grosvenor Street, London W1X 9PD (Tel: 0171 491 2783; Fax: 0171 629 0396).

Abbey National Treasury Services plc, Abbey House, Baker Street, London NW1 6XL (Tel: 0171 612 4000; Fax: 0171 486 6872).
Contact: R Garratt.

Alliance & Leicester Personal Finance Ltd, Heritage House, 61 Southgates, Leicester LE1 5RR (Tel: 0116 2515333; Fax: 0116 2621 993).
Contact: T M Hilliard.

Anglo Leasing plc, Anglo House, 2 Clerkenwell Green, London EC1R 0DH (Tel: 0171 253 4300; Fax: 0171 251 4300).
Contact: A E Leesmith.

Barclays Direct Lending Services, Barclays Bank plc, Central Retail Services Division, Northampton NN1 1SG (Tel: 01604 256700; Fax: 01604 256799).
Contact: P Georgeu.

BNP Leasing Ltd (BNP UK Holdings Ltd), 8–13 King William Street, London EC4P 4HS (Tel: 0171 895 7025; Fax: 0171 283 2848).
Contact: J I Dean.

Canadian Imperial Bank of Commerce, Cotton's Centre, Cotton's Lane, London SE1 2QL (Tel: 0171 234 6536; Fax: 0171 407 4132).
Contact: P M D Jones.

Capital Leasing Ltd (Bank of Scotland Group), PO Box 49, 4 Melville Street, Edinburgh EH3 7NZ

(Tel: 0131 453 1919; Fax: 0131 243 8423).
Contact: J McCabe.

Carolina Leasing Ltd (NationsBank Europe Ltd), New Broad Street House, 35 New Broad Street, London, EC2N 2EH (Tel: 0171 638 8888; Fax: 0171 588 9150).
Contact: J R Clargo.

Chartered Trust plc (Standard Chartered plc), 24–26 Newport Road, Cardiff CF2 1SR (Tel: 01222 473000; Fax: 01222 495180).
Contact: A C Webb.

Citibank Trust Ltd (Citicorp, USA), St Martin's House, 1 Hammersmith Grove, London W6 0NY (Tel: 0181 846 8100; Fax: 0181 846 8488).
Contact: P A Cohen.

City Leasing Ltd (Morgan Grenfell Group plc), 23 Great Winchester Street, London EC2P 2AX (Tel: 0171 588 4545; Fax: 0171 826 7130).
Contact: G Michie.

Clyde General Finance Ltd (National Australia Group UK Ltd), Mirren Court South, 119 Renfrew Road, Paisley PA3 4EA (Tel: 0141 887 3070; Fax: 0141 840 1807).
Contact: A Webster.

Co-operative Bank plc (Co-operative Wholesale Society Ltd), PO Box 101, 1 Balloon Street, Manchester M60 4EP (Tel: 0161 832 3456; Fax: 0161 839 2387).
Contact: M Cluett.

Daiwa Europe Bank plc (Daiwa Securities Co Ltd, Tokyo), City Tower,

40 Basinghall Street, London EC2V
5DE (Tel: 0171 315 3900;
Fax: 0171 315 3970).
Contact: I Paterson.

DeLage Landen Leasing Ltd
(Rabobank Nederland, Utrecht),
Belvedere House, Vale Avenue,
Tunbridge Wells, Kent TN1 1DJ
(Tel: 01892 518111;
Fax: 01892 517888).
Contact: S J Robinson.

Enskilda Corporate Leasing Ltd (Skandinavska Enskilda Banken),
2–6 Cannon Street, London EC4M
6XX (Tel: 0171 588 3494;
Fax: 0171 329 6944).
Contact: D M Cree.

First National Bank plc (First National Finance Corp. plc), First National
House, College Road, Harrow, Middlesex HA1 1FB (Tel: 0181 861 1313;
Fax: 0181 863 4322).
Contact: K W Horlock.

Forthright Finance Ltd (Bank of Wales plc), Lambourne Crescent, Llanishen,
Cardiff CF4 5UP (Tel: 01222 396131;
Fax: 01222 231128).
Contact: J Skeldon.

Forward Trust Group Ltd (HSBC Holdings plc), 145 City Road, London
EC1V 1JY (Tel: 0171 833 5146;
Fax: 0171 490 0993).
Contact: G W Evans.

Frizzell Banking Services Ltd
(Marsh McLennan Group), County
Gates House, 300 Poole Road,
Bournemouth, Dorset BH1 3NQ
(Tel: 01202 295544;
Fax: 01202 858712).
Contact: T W Trinder.

Guinness Yokohama Leasing Ltd
(Guinness Mahon Holdings plc), 32 St
Mary at Hill, London EC3P 3AJ
(Tel: 0171 982 9234;
Fax: 0171 982 9248).
Contact: I Blower.

Hambros Bank Ltd (Hambros plc),
41 Tower Hill, London EC3N 4HA
(Tel: 0171 480 5000;
Fax: 0171 702 9825).
Contact: A G Mallin.

HFC Bank plc (Household
International (UK) Ltd), North Street,
Winkfield, Windsor, Berkshire SL4
4TD (Tel: 01344 890000;
Fax: 01344 890014).
Contact: T Arndt.

Hill Samuel Asset Finance Ltd
(TSB Group plc), 100 Wood Street,
London EC2P 2AJ
(Tel: 0171 600 6000;
Fax: 0171 920 3880).
Contact: A W Jukes.

Hitachi Credit (UK) plc, Hitachi
Credit House, Stables Courtyard,
Church Road, Hayes, Middlesex UB3
2UH (Tel: 0181 561 8486;
Fax: 0181 561 1206.
Contact: D G Anthony.

IAF Group plc, 107 Cannon Street,
London EC4N 5AD
(Tel: 0171 929 5306;
Fax: 0171 929 7974).
Contact: R W Price.

IBJ Leasing (UK) Ltd (IBJ Leasing Co
Ltd), Bracken House, One Friday
Street, London EC4M 9JA
(Tel: 0171 236 2222;
Fax: 0171 236 5555).
Contact: M Kono.

**International Brokerage & Leasing
Ltd** (Den norske Bank AS), 20 St
Dunstan's Hill, London EC3R 8HY
(Tel: 0171 621 1111;
Fax: 0171 626 7400).
Contact: S G Smith.

Japan Leasing (UK) Ltd (Japan Leasing
Corp, Japan), 8th Floor, Berkshire
House, 168–173 High Holborn,
London WC1V 7AA
(Tel: 0171 240 4080;
Fax: 0171 836 4903).

Contact: B G Bailey.

Julian Hodge Bank Ltd (The Carlyle Trust Ltd), 30 Windsor Place, Cardiff, South Glamorgan CF1 3UR (Tel: 01222 371726; Fax: 01222 222597). Contact: R E Cave.

Kleinwort Benson Ltd (Kleinwort Benson Group plc), 20 Fenchurch Street, London EC3P 3DB (Tel: 0171 623 8000; Fax: 0171 929 2672). Contact: A J White.

Kredietfinance Corporation Ltd (Kredietbank NV, Belgium), 14/15 Quarry Street, Guildford, Surrey GU1 3UY (Tel: 01483 504290; Fax: 01483 303387). Contact: A M Standing.

Lazard Equipment Leasing Ltd (Lazard Brothers & Co Ltd), 21 Moorfields, London EC2P 2HT (Tel: 0171 588 2721; Fax: 0171 628 2485). Contact: Mrs H Britton.

Lease Plan UK Ltd (ABN AMRO NV, Netherlands), Thames Side, Windsor, Berkshire SL4 1TY (Tel: 01753 868268; Fax: 01753 841060). Contact: A Foley.

Lloyds Bowmaker Finance Group (Lloyds Bank plc), Finance House, 51 Holdenhurst Road, Bournemouth, Dorset BH8 8EP (Tel: 01202 299777; Fax: 559177). Contact: D A Baggaley.

Lombard North Central plc (National Westminster Bank Group), Lombard House, 3 Princess Way, Redhill, Surrey RH1 1NP (Tel: 01737 774111; Fax: 01737 760031). Contact: M Maberly.

Nationwide Trust Ltd (Nationwide Building Society), Nationwide House, 20 Lower Dagnall Street, St Albans, Herts AL3 4RR (Tel: 01727 832241; Fax: 01727 834508).

Contact: E Borton.

Royal Bank Leasing Ltd (Royal Bank of Scotland plc), The Quadrangle, The Promenade, Cheltenham, Glos GL50 1PX (Tel: 01242 226200; Fax: 01242 222743). Contact: C R Freeborough.

Schroder Leasing Ltd (Schroder Group), Townsend House, 160 Northolt Road, Harrow, Middlesex HA2 0PG (Tel: 0181 422 7101; Fax: 0181 422 4402). Contact: J P Addison.

SocGen Lease Ltd (Société Générale Banking Group), 60 Gracechurch Street, London EC3V 0HD (Tel: 0171 626 5400; Fax: 0171 929 1332). Contact: J D Walker.

Southern Finance Company Ltd, Southern House, Shirley Road, Southampton, Hants SO1 3EY (Tel: 01703 226745; Fax: 01703 224745). Contact: W B Tracy.

TSB Asset Finance Ltd (TSB Group plc), 99 Glassford Street, Glasgow G1 1DL (Tel: 0141 307 2079; Fax: 0141 307 2071). Contact: G C Smith.

Union Discount Finance & Leasing Ltd (The Union Discount Company of London plc), 39 Cornhill, London EC3V 3NU (Tel: 0171 623 1020; Fax: 0171 929 2110). Contact: J H Bradley.

United Dominions Trust Ltd (TSB Group plc), 116 Cockfosters Road, Cockfosters, Barnet, Herts EN4 0DY (Tel: 0181 447 2447; Fax: 0181 447 2601/2). Contact: G R Bird.

S G Warburg & Co (Leasing) Ltd (S G Warburg & Co Ltd), 1 Finsbury Avenue, London EC2M 2PA (Tel: 0171 860 0311;

Fax: 0171 860 0860).
Contact: D M M Beever.
West Merchant Bank Ltd (WestLB
(Europa) AG), 33–36 Gracechurch
Street, London EC3V 0AX
(Tel: 0171 623 8711;
Fax: 0171 626 1610).
Contact: J Swaine.
**Woodchester Investments (UK Hold-
ings) Ltd** (Woodchester Investments
plc), Woodchester House, Docklands,
London E14 9GL (Tel: 0171 538 4191;
Fax: 0171 537 2210).
Contact: A Iversen.

Wrenwood Group Finance Ltd,
Lancaster House, Blackburn Street,
Radcliffe, Manchester M26 9TS
(Tel: 0161 723 1628;
Fax: 0161 725 9160).
Contact: P F Whiting.
**Yorkshire Bank Asset Finance
(National Australia Group UK Ltd),**
Brunswick Point, Wade Lane, Leeds,
West Yorkshire LS2 8NQ
(Tel: 0113 2315000;
Fax: 0113 2465875).
Contact: I H Gill.

Trade credit

Once you have established credit-worthiness, it may be possible to take advantage of trade credit extended by suppliers. This usually takes the form of allowing you anything from seven days to three months from receiving the goods, before you have to pay for them. However, if your franchisor is the main source of supply, you may have very little flexibility in this area. Even if you have a choice, you will have to weigh carefully the benefit of taking this credit against the cost of losing any cash discounts offered. For example, if you are offered a 2.5% discount for cash settlement, then this is a saving of £25 for every £1,000 of purchase. If the alternative is to take six weeks' credit, then the saving is the cost of borrowing that sum from, say, your bank on overdraft. So if your bank interest rate is 16% per annum, that is equivalent to 0.31% per week. Six weeks would save you 1.85%. On £1,000 of purchase you would save only £18.50 of bank interest. This means that the cash discount is more attractive.

Rural Development Commission

The Rural Development Commission is a government agency whose objective is to revitalize country areas in England by helping to establish small rural firms and to encourage existing ones to become more prosperous. 'Rural' is defined as an area with fewer than 10,000 inhabitants.

The Commission normally expect the major part of your funding to be arranged with a commercial lending source. However, they have a limited loan fund which can be used to finance part of the costs of a project, up to a maximum of £75,000 over a two- to twenty-year period.

They can also provide grants towards the cost of converting buildings of all descriptions into workshops, including the cost of installing or upgrading mains services). Contact: Rural Development Commission, 141 Castle Street, Salisbury, Wiltshire SP1 3TP (Tel: 01722 336255), and county offices throughout England. See Section 2 for fuller details.

Credit unions

Credit unions have always been an attractive option for people on low incomes, providing a cheap and convenient alternative to banks and building societies, but recommendations in February 1994 by the Department of Trade and Industry (DTI) could catapult them into the big league.

The DTI has proposed to raise the ceiling on loans and savings from £5,000 to 1.5% of the total liabilities of the union, meaning a large union with funds of £1m could provide a £15,000 loan, bringing them more into line with banks and building societies.

Some self-employed people such as taxi drivers have formed a credit union. They can then apply for loans to meet unexpected capital expenditure either for repairs, refurbishments or technical upgrading.

At the moment, however, just finding a credit union may be a problem. There are more than 400 unions around the country, but less than one in 300 people belong to one, compared with more than one in three in Canada, Ireland and Australia. Clearly, the movement has a long way to go, but the DTI proposals and recommendations tabled by the National Consumer Council (NCC) could pave the way for a very prosperous future.

Among the NCC proposals is a plan to broaden the definition of the 'common bond' which must exist between members of any credit union – the workplace, local community or ethnic origin, for example. Its proposals could enable company employees without a scheme available at work to join a credit union in the area around the workplace, currently forbidden under the terms of the Credit Union Act.

Certainly, few could argue about the attractiveness of an annual interest rate of 30% less than the high-street lenders.

Members have to save regularly to qualify for a loan, though there is no minimum deposit and, after ten weeks, members with a good track record can borrow up to five times their savings, though they must continue to save while repaying the loan. There is no set interest rate, but dividends are distributed to members from any surplus, usually about 5% a year. This too compares favourably with bank interest on deposit accounts.

Another aspect restricting expansion is finding volunteers who can be trained to run the unions. The NCC has recommended that official training systems are established, and also intends to lobby local authorities to provide funding to help get unions started. Banks are also targeted to provide free banking for credit unions, so far only provided by the Co-operative Bank.

For those considering setting up a credit union, the National Federation of Credit Unions (NFCU) says you need at least seven fully trained volunteers and a minimum of 21 members. All unions must register with the Registry of Friendly Societies. Training leading to enrolment lasts five months and costs about £200. New unions must also take out an insurance policy, which costs about £100 a year, to protect members' funds. The Open University's Community Education department has a useful starter pack on credit unions. Further information can be obtained from the NFCU (Tel: 0191 257 2219) or the Association of British Credit Unions (Tel: 0171 582 2626).

Local Exchange Trading Systems (LETS)

Almost 200 LETS schemes have been set up, more than three-quarters of them in 1993. Some have only a dozen members while the largest, in Manchester, has over 380. All in all, over 10,000 people are involved in this method of trading. Anyone who joins a scheme offers skills or services, such as plumbing, gardening or the use of a photocopier, to other members. A price is agreed in whatever notional currency has been adopted, but no money changes hands. The system is more ambitious than straight barter. The provider receives a credit on his or her account kept by a local organizer and a debit is marked up against the user. The person in credit can then set this against other services.

The trades that have used LETS successfully include restaurateurs, plumbers, carpenters, lawyers, retailers of all descriptions, cycle shops, freelance writers, piano teachers, translation agencies, cleaners, typists, gardeners, tree surgeons, security guards, book-keepers and child-minders.

No interest is paid on LETS, and all the usual tax and Value Added Tax rules apply to businesses trading in this way.

The benefits of using LETS are that you can start trading and grow with virtually no start-up capital. All you need are time and saleable skills – once you have 'sold' your wares, payment is immediate by way of a LETS credit. Also by using LETS the wealth is kept in the local community, which means customers in your area may be able to spend more with you. For example, one shop that used to accept 25% of the value of its goods in LETS was surprised at how sharply its turnover increased when it increased the proportion to 50%.

One of the keys to success in using LETS is to have an enterprising organizer who can produce, maintain and circulate a wide-ranging directory of LETS services and outlets.

The trend to go local is escalating. In 1993 the central body Letslink UK had 30,000 enquiries. A year later the 3,000 people who paid £6.50 for a start pack are putting their researches into action and there are dozens of launches in the pipeline.

Contact: Letslink UK, 61 Woodcock Road, Warminster, Wilts BA12 9DH (Tel: 01985 217871).

Venture capital providers

Over 50 providers of venture capital are members of the British Venture Capital Association, formed in 1983 to help to further the provision of such financing in the UK.

In the decade to 1990, the UK venture capital industry has grown from a score of firms investing £66 million a year to over 200 who back new and growing firms to the tune of £1.65 billion. The UK venture capital industry is the largest in Europe and second only to the USA in world importance.

The largest player in this market is 3i's (Investors in Industry), formed in 1945, who account for around half of all this type of funding, with stakes in over 5,000 businesses. They are the only venture capital firm with a comprehensive UK regional office structure.

The British Venture Association, 3 St Catherine's Place, London SW1E 6DX (Tel: 0171 233 5212), publishes an annual directory of providers, free each year.

Table 6.3 shows where venture capitalists put their money, in terms of the stage of the venture.

Table 6.3: Venture financing by stage of business

Stage	%
Pre-start-up	10
Start-up	25
Early stage development	28
Late stage development	26
Management buy-out	11
	100

Accountants KPMG Peat Marwick, in conjunction with the journal *Venture Economics*, also maintain a comprehensive database of venture capitalists. This allows them to extract on a selective basis details of various capital sources as potential investment candidates.

For further details contact: KPMG Peat Marwick, 1 Puddle Dock, Blackfriars, London EC4V 3PD (Tel: 0171 236 8000).

UK venture capital providers

Key 1   Minimum investment   MBI: Management Buy-In
      2   Stage of investment   MBO: Management Buy-Out
      3   Industry preferences
      4   Geographic preferences

	1	2	3	4
3i plc, 91 Waterloo Road, London SE1 8XP Tel: 0171 928 3131 Fax: 0171 928 0058 Contact: Malcolm Gloak	£100K	All	All	UK, Europe
Abacus Development Capital Ltd, 52 Welbeck Street, London W1M 5RL Tel: 0171 935 4160 Fax: 0171 935 4171 Contact: Wendy Pollecoff	£100K	Early stage onwards	Food industry	UK, Israel
Abingworth Management Ltd, 26 St James's Street, London SW1A 1HA Tel: 0171 839 6745 Fax: 0171 930 1891 Contact: Anthony Montagu	£500K	All	All	UK, W Europe, N America

■

	1	2	3	4
Abtrust Fund Managers Ltd, 10 Queens Terrace, Aberdeen AB9 1QJ Tel: 01224 631999 Fax: 01224 647010 Contact: Hugh Little	£100K	Venture purchase of quoted shares	All	UK, W Europe
Advent International plc, 39 Victoria Street, London SW1H 0EE Tel: 0171 333 0800 Fax: 0171 333 0801 Contact: Douglas Brown	£1m	Venture purchase of quoted shares	Computer, chemical & material, consumer, media	UK, W Europe, E Europe, N America, Asia
Advent Ltd, 25 Buckingham Gate, London SW1E 6LD Tel: 0171 630 9811 Fax: 0171 828 1474/4919 Contact: David Cooksey	£250K	Expansion & services	Communications, computer medical/health	UK, W Europe, N America
AIB Venture, 12 Old Jewry, London EC2R 8DP Tel: 0171 606 5800 Fax: 0171 606 5818 Contact: Kim Martin, Philip Wilson	£500K	All except start-up	Most industries would be considered, except new technology and property related	UK, Ireland
Alta Berkeley Associates, 9–10 Savile Row, London W1X 1AF Tel: 0171 734 4884 Fax: 0171 734 6711 Contact: Bryan Wood	£250K	Start-up, other early stage onwards	Communications, computer related, biotechnology, medical/health, chemical & materials, media, environmental	UK, W Europe

	1	2	3	4
Apax Partners & Co Ltd, 15 Portland Place, London W1N 3AA Tel: 0171 872 6300 Fax: 0171 636 6475 Contact: Ronald Cohen	£500K	All except seed	All	UK
BancBoston Capital, 39 Victoria Street, London SW1H 0ED Tel: 0171 932 9053 Fax: 0171 932 9117 Contact: Andrew Kellett	£500K	Expansion, secondary purchase/replacement capital, MBO, MBI, acquisition	All	UK, N America
Barclays Development Capital Ltd, 4th Floor, Pickfords Wharf, Clink Street, London SE1 9DG Tel: 0171 407 2389 Fax: 0171 407 3362 Contact: Michael Cumming	£500K	Expansion, secondary purchase/replacement capital, rescue/turnaround, MBI, MBO, refinancing, bank debt	All	UK, USA, France, Australia
Barclays Venture Capital Unit, Clerkenwell House, 67 Clerkenwell Road, London EC1R 5BH Tel: 0171 242 4900 Fax: 0171 242 2048 Contact: Chris Gammon	£100K	Expansion, secondary purchase/replacement capital, MBO, MBI	All	UK
Baring Capital Investors Ltd, 140 Park Lane, London W1Y 3AA Tel: 0171 408 1282 Fax: 0171 493 1368 Contact: Otto van der Wyck	£3M	Expansion, MBO, MBI	All sectors considered	W Europe
Baring Venture Partners Ltd, 140 Park Lane, London W1Y 3AA Tel: 0171 408 0555 Fax: 0171 493 5153 Contact: Paul Bailey	£35K	Seed, start-up, other early stage	All	W Europe, N America

	1	2	3	4
Barnes Thomson Management Services, 120 Wigmore Street, London W1H 9FD Tel: 0171 487 3870 Fax: 0171 487 3860 Contact: Kenneth Barnes	£250K	Early stage onwards	Computer related	UK
Baronsmead plc, Clerken-well House, 67 Clerkenwell Road, London EC1R 5BH Tel: 0171 242 4900 Fax: 0171 242 2048 Contact: Robert Wilson	£200K	Expansion, secondary purchase/replacement capital, MBO, MBI, refinancing bank debt	All	UK
Birmingham Technology (Venture Capital) Ltd, Aston Science Park, Love Lane, Aston Triangle, Birmingham B7 4BJ Tel: 0121 359 0981 Fax: 0121 359 0433 Contact: Derek Harris	£20K	Start-up, expansion	Computer related, other electronics related, medical/health related	No preference
The British Linen Bank Ltd, 4 Melville Street, Edinburgh EH3 7NZ Tel: 0131 243 8322 Fax: 0131 243 8324 Contact: Charles Young	£250K	Venture purchase of quoted shares, expansion, MBO, MBI	Medical/health related, industrial products & services, other manufacturing	UK
British Steel (Industry) Ltd, Scotland, Bridge House, Bridge Street, Sheffield, S3 8NS Tel: 0114 2731612 Fax: 0114 2701390 Contact: Vernon Smith	£10K	Seed, start-up, other early stage onwards	All sectors considered except construction, property, retail, agriculture, financial services	England, Scotland, Wales

	1	2	3	4
Brown Shipley Venture Managers Ltd, Founders Court, Lothbury, London EC2R 7HE Tel: 0171 606 9833/6555 Fax: 0171 600 2279 Contact: David Wills bank debt	£1M	Expansion, secondary purchase/replacement capital, MBO, MBI, refinancing bank debt	All	UK, W Europe
Cairnsford Associates Ltd, Upper Kingswell, Top Floor, 58-62 Heath Street, London NW3 1EN Tel: 0171 431 0881 Fax: 0171 794 7052 Contact: Tania Slowe	£200K	Early stage onwards	Communications, computer & other electronics related, medical/health, energy, transportation, chemical & materials, industrial automation, industrial products & services, consumer related, other manufacturing, other services	UK
Cambridge Capital Management Ltd, 13 Station Road, Cambridge CB1 2JB Tel: 01223 312856 Fax: 01223 65704 Contact: Chris Smart	£200K	Expansion, secondary purchase/replacement capital	All	East Anglia, East Midlands
Candover Investments plc, 20 Old Bailey, London EC4M 7LN Tel: 0171 489 9848 Fax: 0171 248 5483 Contact: Stephen Curran	£1M	MBO, MBI	All	UK, W Europe

	1	2	3	4
Capital for Companies Ltd, 3 Park Court, Park Cross Street, Leeds LS1 2QH Tel: 0113 2438043 Fax: 0113 2422259 Contact: Barry Anysz	£100K	All except seed, start-up & venture purchase of quoted shares	Medical/ health, transport, chemical, industrial automation, product & services, consumer, other manufacturing, leisure	N England, i.e. M62 corridor and North East
Capital Partners International Ltd, Disney Place House, 14 Marshalsea Road, London SE1 1HL Tel: 0171 378 7992 Fax: 0171 378 6328 Contact: Christoph von Luttitz	£10K	All	Computer, medical/ health, industrial products/ services, consumer, other manufacturing & services	UK, W Europe, E Europe, N America
Causeway Capital Ltd, 7 Hanover Square, London W1R Tel: 0171 495 2525 Fax: 0171 491 2050 Contact: Lionel Anthony	£2M	Expansion, secondary purchase/replacement capital, MBO, MBI	All	UK
Charterhouse Development Capital Ltd, Watling Street, London EC4M 9BJ Tel: 0171 248 4000 Fax: 0171 329 4252 Contact: Gordon Bonnyman	£500K	Expansion, bridge finance, secondary purchase/replacement capital, rescue/turnaround, MBO, MBI	All	UK, W Europe
CINVen Ltd, Hobart House,Grosvenor Place, London SW1X 7AD Tel: 0171 245 6911 Fax: 0171 389 7173 Contact: Robin Hall	£500K	Start-up onwards	All	UK, W Europe

	1	2	3	4
Close Investment Management Ltd, 36 Great St Helen's, London EC3A 6AP Tel: 0171 283 2241 Fax: 0171 638 5624 Contact: John Snook	£1M	Venture purchase of quoted shares	All	UK
Clydesdale Bank Equity Ltd, 30 St Vincent Place, Glasgow G1 2HL Tel: 0141 248 7070 Fax: 0141 223 3724 Contact: Neil Kennedy	£250K	Expansion onwards	All except property, financial ser- vices, film & TV and very high tech	UK, mainly Scotland
Compass Investment Management Ltd, Osprey House, 78 Wigmore Street, London W1H 9DQ Contact: Peter Dale	£300K	Funds fully invested	All	N America
Cornwall Enterprise Board Investment Ltd, Trevint House, Strangways Villas,Truro, Cornwall TR1 2PA Tel: 01872 223883 Fax: 01872 42470 Contact: John Berry	£25K	All	All	Cornwall
CVC Capital Partners Ltd, Hudson House, 8–10 Tavistock St, London WC2E 7PP Tel: 0171 438 1488 Fax: 0171 438 1419/1420 Contact: Michael Smith	£1M	Expansion onwards	All	UK, W Europe, E Europe
Derbyshire Enterprise Board Ltd, 95 Sheffield Road, Chesterfield, Derbyshire S41 7JH Tel: 01246 207390 Fax: 01246 221080 Contact: Alan Moore	£50K	All	All	Derbyshire

	1	2	3	4
The Doncaster Enterprise Agency (Finance), 19–21 Hallgate, Doncaster DN1 3NA Tel: 01302 340320 Fax: 01302 344740 Contact: Brian Crangle	£20K	Seed, start-up onwards	All	Yorkshire & Humberside
Dunedin Ventures Ltd, Dunedin House, 25 Ravelston Terrace, Edinburgh EH4 3EX Tel: 0131 315 2500 Fax: 0131 332 1234 Contact: Brian Finlayson	£250K	All	All	UK
EM Warburg, Pincus & Co Int Ltd, 20 St James's Street, London SW1A 1ES Tel: 0171 321 0129 Fax: 0171 321 0881 Contact: Michael Hoffman	£5M	Expansion, 'special situations', i.e. buy-outs, recapitalizations, etc	All	W Europe
Eagle Star Investment Managers Ltd, 60 St Mary Axe, London EC3A 8JQ Tel: 0171 929 1111 Fax: 0171 283 2187 Contact: Carol Ames	£1M	Expansion, MBO, MBI, refinancing bank debt	All	UK, W Europe
ECI Ventures, Brettenham House, Lancaster Place, London WC2E 7EN Tel: 0171 606 1000 Fax: 0171 240 5050 Contact: David Wansbrough	£1M	Venture purchase of quoted shares onwards	All	UK, W Europe
Electra Innvotec Ltd, 65 Kingsway, London WC2B 6QT Tel: 0171 831 9901 Fax: 0171 240 8565 Contact: Peter Dohrn	£250K	Start-up onwards	All except retailing, construction, property, financial services & leisure	UK, W Europe, N America

■

	1	2	3	4
Electra Kingsway Ltd, 65 Kingsway, London WC2B 6QT Tel: 0171 831 6464 Fax: 0171 430 1632 Contact: Hugh Mumford	£5M	Expansion onwards	All	UK, W Europe, USA
Enterprise Equity (NI) Ltd, Bulloch House, 2 Linehall St, Belfast BT2 8PP Tel: 01232 242500 Fax: 01232 242487 Contact: Declan Glynn	£50K	Start-up onwards	All	N Ireland only
Eurocontinental (Advisers) Ltd, 5th Floor, 30 Coleman St, London EC2R 5AE Tel: 0171 600 1689 Fax: 0171 600 1967 Contact: Albert Gabizon	£350K	Early stage onwards	Prefer traditional industries, service sector and advanced technologies	W Europe
Euroventures (UK), Suite 355, The Quorum, Barnwell Road, Cambridge CB5 8RE Tel: 01223 415689 Fax: 01223 413817 Contact: Ian Barton	£100K	Expansion	Communications, computer & other electronics related	UK, W Europe
Finlay Ventures, Finlay House, 10–14 West Nile Street, Glasgow G1 2PP Tel: 0141 204 1321 Fax: 0141 204 4254 Contact: Peter Homer	£100K	Expansion, MBO	Electronics related, medical/ health, chemical & materials, industrial automation, products & services, other manufacturing & services	UK

	1	2	3	4
Fleming Ventures Ltd, 7 Tower Walk, St Katharine's Way, London E1 9UR Tel: 0171 480 6211 Fax: 0171 481 1156 Contact: Bernard Fairman	£500K	Early stage, expansion	Communications, computer & electronics related	UK, W Europe, N America
Foreign & Colonial Ventures Ltd, 8th Floor, Exchange House, Primrose Street, London EC2A 2NY Tel: 0171 782 9829 Fax: 0171 782 9834 Contact: James Nelson	£1M	All, but prefer later stage	All	UK, W Europe
Gartmore Venture Capital, Gartmore House, 16–18 Monument Street, London EC3R 8AJ Tel: 0171 782 2000 Fax: 0171 782 2658 Contact: Michael Walton	£300K	Venture purchase of quoted shares onwards	All	UK, W Europe, N America
GLE Development Capital, 63–67 Newington Causeway, London SE1 6BD Tel: 0171 403 0300 Fax: 0171 403 1742 Contact: David Walburn	£100K	Expansion onwards	All	Greater London
Goldman Sachs International Ltd, Peterborough Court, 133 Fleet Street, London EC4A 2BB Tel: 0171 774 1000 Fax: 0171 774 4123 Contact: Charles Bott	£10M	All except seed, start-up, early stage & rescue/ turnaround	All	UK, W Europe, N America, Asia, Latin America
Granville Development Capital Ltd, Mint House, 77 Mansell Street, London E1 8AF Tel: 0171 488 1212 Fax: 0171 481 3911 Contact: Michael Proudlock	£500K	Expansion onwards	All	UK, W Europe

	1	2	3	4
Great Winchester Capital Fund Managers, 21 Great Winchester Street, London EC2N 2HH Tel: 0171 588 7575 Fax: 0171 638 4239 Contact: Anthony Campling	£250K	All except seed	All	UK
Gresham Trust plc, Barrington House, Gresham Street, London EC2V 7HE Tel: 0171 606 6474 Fax: 0171 606 3370 Contact: Trevor Jones	£300K	Expansion onwards	All	UK
Grosvenor Venture Managers Ltd, Commerce House, 2–6 Bath Road, Slough SL1 3RZ Tel: 01753 811812 Fax: 01753 811813 Contact: Robert Drummond	£300K	Early stage onwards	All	UK
Guinness Mahon Development Capital Ltd, 32 St Mary at Hill, London EC3P 3AJ Tel: 0171 623 6222 Fax: 0171 623 4313 Contact: Gordon Power	£250K	Expansion onwards	Interested in businesses able to exploit intellectual property rights through licensing. Access to Asia/Pacific region	UK
Hambro European Ventures Ltd, 41 Tower Hill, London EC3N 4HA Tel: 0171 480 5000 Fax: 0171 702 9827 Contact: Gilbert Chalk	£250K	Venture purchase of quoted shares onwards	All	UK, W Europe

	1	2	3	4
Hambros Advanced Technology Trust, 20–21 Tooks Court, Cursitor Street, London EC4A 1LB Tel: 0171 242 9900 Fax: 0171 405 2863 Contact: Harry Fitzgibbons	£200K	Early stage, expansion	Communications, computer & other electronics related, biotechnology, medical/ health, environmental	UK
Henderson Venture Managers Ltd, 3 Finsbury Avenue, London EC2M 2PA Tel: 0171 410 4415 Fax: 0171 410 4407 Contact: Andrew Evans	£1M	Expansion onwards	All except property, early stage hi-tech, biotech & exploration of natural resources	UK, W Europe
HIT Investments plc, Hillsdown House, 32 Hampstead High St, London NW3 1QD Tel: 0171 794 0677 Fax: 0171 433 1405 Contact: Guy Hallifax	£500K	All except seed & start-up	All except food & property	UK
Hodgson Martin Ltd, 36 George Street, Edinburgh EH2 2LE Tel: 0131 226 7644 Fax: 0131 226 7647 Contact: Allan Hodgson	£100K	Expansion onwards	Construction, consumer related, other manufacturing, financial services, other services, leisure, environmental	UK, W Europe, N America
Industrial Development Board for Northern Ireland, IDB House, 64 Chichester Street, Belfast BT1 4JX Tel: 01232 233233 Fax: 01232 231328 Contact: Charles Harding	Open	Start-up, expansion	Manufacturing & tradeable services only	Northern Ireland

	1	2	3	4
Industrial Technology Securities Ltd, 1a The Broadway, Market Place, Chalfont St Peter, Bucks SL9 9DZ Tel: 01753 885524 Fax: 01753 882359 Contact: Jan Berglund	£150K	Seed, start-up, expansion, MBO	Communications, computer & other electronics related, biotechnology, medical/ health, energy, industrial automation, other manufacturing, environmental	UK
Ivory & SIME Development Capital, 1 Charlotte Square, Edinburgh EH2 4DZ Tel: 0131 225 1357 Fax: 0131 225 2375 Contact: Mark Tyndall	£500K	All stages other than early	All, except agriculture	UK, W Europe, N America
Kleinwort Benson Development Capital Ltd, 10 Fenchurch Street, London EC3M 3LB Tel: 0171 956 6600 Fax: 0171 626 8616 Contact: Barry Dean	£250K	Expansion onwards	All	UK, W Europe
Korda & Co Ltd, 18–20 Farringdon Lane, London EC1R 3AU Tel: 0171 253 5882 Fax: 0171 251 4837 Contact: Rick Armitage	£50K	Seed, start-up, other early stage	Communications, computer & other electronics related, industrial automation, environmental	UK, W Europe
Lancashire Enterprises plc, Enterprise House, 17 Ribblesdale Place, Preston, Lancs PR1 3NA Tel: 01772 203020 Fax: 01772 880697 Contact: David Hall	£500K	Seed, start-up onwards	All	NW England

■

	1	2	3	4
Larpent Newton Ltd, 4th Floor, 24–26 Baltic Street, London EC1Y 0TB Tel: 0171 251 9111 Fax: 0171 251 2609 Contact: Charles Breese	£250K	Start-up, other early stage	Communications, computer & other electronics, medical/health, industrial products & services, media	England
Lazard Ventures, 21 Moorfields, London EC2P 2HT Tel: 0171 588 2721 Fax: 0171 638 2141 Contact: Tom Glucklich	£300K	Early stage, expansion onwards	All	UK, W Europe
Legal & General Ventures Ltd, Bucklersbury House, 3 Queen Victoria St, London EC4N 8EL Tel: 0171 489 1888 Fax: 0171 528 6655 Contact: Charles Peal	£1M	Expansion onwards	All	UK, W Europe
Lica Development Capital Ltd, 102 Jermyn Street, London SW1Y 6EE Tel: 0171 839 7707 Fax: 0171 839 4363 Contact: Stephen Hill	£100K	Expansion onwards	Communications, computer & other electronics, medical/health, transportation, industrial automation, industrial products & services, other manufacturing, media, environmental	EC, W Europe, E Europe
Lloyds Development Capital Ltd, 48 Chiswell Street, London EC1Y 4XX Tel: 0171 600 3226 Fax: 0171 522 5889 Contact: Ron Hollidge	£400K	All except seed, start-up & early stage	All except property development	UK

	1	2	3	4
London Oxford & Kobe Development Co Ltd, Alton House, 174-177 High Holborn, London WC1V 7AA Tel: 0171 836 1225 Fax: 0171 240 7460 Contact: Reg Clark	£500K	All except MBO, MBI. Prefer early stage	All	UK, W Europe, E Europe
London Wall Investments, 25 Copthall Avenue, London EC2R 7DR Tel: 0171 638 5858 Fax: 0171 382 8155 Contact: Martin Pritchard	£2M	Expansion, MBO, MBI	All	UK
Lothian Enterprise Ltd, 21 Ainslie Place, Edinburgh EH3 6AJ Tel: 0131 220 2100 Fax: 0131 225 2658 Contact: Kathy Greenwood	£10K	Seed, start-up, other early stage, expansion, MBO, MBI	All except property & retail	Scotland, Lothian region
March Investment Funds, Telegraphic House, Waterfront 2000, Salford Quays, Manchester M5 2XW Tel: 0161 872 3676 Fax: 0161 848 0181 Contact: William Hopkins	£100K	Expansion onwards	All	NW England
Mercury Development Capital, 33 King William Street, London EC4R 9AS Tel: 0171 280 2508 Fax: 0171 280 2820 Contact: Ian Armitage	£2.5M	Expansion onwards	All	UK, W Europe, N America
Midland Growth Capital, Midland Bank plc, Watling Court, 47–53 Cannon Street, London EC4M 5SQ Tel: 0171 260 7935 Fax: 0171 260 6767 Contact: Robert Henry	£100K	Expansion onwards	All	UK

	1	2	3	4
Montagu Private Equity Ltd, 10 Lower Thames Street, London EC3R 6AE Tel: 0171 260 9911 Fax: 0171 220 7265 Contact: Ian Forrest	£750K	Expansion onwards	All	UK, W Europe
Morgan Grenfell Development Capital Ltd, 23 Great Winchester St, London EC2P 2AX Tel: 0171 588 4545 Fax: 0171 826 6482 Contact: Robert Smith	£2M	Expansion onwards	Transportation, industrial automation, products & services, consumer, other manufacturing & services, media, agriculture	UK, W Europe
MTI Managers Ltd, Langley Place, 99 Langley Road, Watford, Herts WD1 3PE Tel: 01923 250244 Fax: 01923 247783 Contact: Paul Castle	£250K	Start-up, other early stage, expansion onwards	All	England, Wales
Murray Johnstone Developments Ltd, 7 West Nile Street, Glasgow G1 2PX Tel: 0141 226 3131 Fax: 0141 248 5636 Contact: David MacLellan	£500K	Expansion onwards	All	UK, W Europe
Nash, Sells & Partners Ltd, 25 Buckingham Gate, London SW1E 6LD Tel: 0171 828 6944 Fax: 0171 828 9958 Contact: John Nash	£500K	All, emphasis on later stage	Healthcare facilities & services, leisure, environmental, food, chemicals & infrastructure	UK
NatWest Ventures Ltd, 135 Bishopsgate, London EC2M 3UR Tel: 0171 628 2444 Fax: 0171 375 6262 Contact: David Shaw	£500K	Venture purchase of quoted shares, expansion onwards	All	UK, W Europe, E Europe

	1	2	3	4
Newmarket Venture Capital plc, 40 Clifton Street, London EC2A 4DX Tel: 0171 377 1507 Fax: 0171 377 1327 Contact: Caroline Vaughan	£250K		Current fund fully invested	UK, N America
North of England Ventures, Cheshire House, 18–20 Booth St, Manchester M2 4AN Tel: 0161 236 6600 Fax: 0161 236 6650 Contact: Peter Folkman	£250K	Expansion onwards	All	England, Wales
Northern Ireland Innovation Programme Investments Ltd, Howard House, 1 Brunswick Street, Belfast BT2 7GE Tel: 01232 241619 Fax: 01232 439899 Contact: John Stringer	£20K	Seed, start-up, other early stage	All	N Ireland
Northern Venture Managers Ltd, Northumberland House, Princess Square, Newcastle upon Tyne, NE1 8ER Tel: 0191 232 7068 Fax: 0191 232 4070 Contact: Tim Levett	Open	All except seed	All	Scotland, N England
Phildrew Ventures, Triton Court, 14 Finsbury Square, London EC2A 1PD Tel: 0171 628 6366 Fax: 0171 638 2817 Contact: Charles Gonszor	£1M	Start-up onwards	Construction, transportation, chemical & materials, industrial products & services, consumer, other manufacturing & services, leisure, environmental	UK

	1	2	3	4
Phoenix Fund Managers Ltd, 1 Laurence Pountney Hill, London EC4R 0EU Tel: 0171 638 3818 Fax: 0171 638 3487 Contact: Martin Smith	£1M	Secondary purchase/replacement capital, rescue/turnaround, MBO, MBI, refinancing bank debt	All	UK, W Europe
Piper Investment Management Ltd, Eardley House, 182–184 Campden Hill Road, London W8 7AS Tel: 0171 727 3866 Fax: 0171 727 8969 Contact: Christopher Curry	£250K	Start-up onwards	Consumer related, leisure	UK
Postel Development Capital, Standon House, 21 Mansell Street, London E1 8AA Tel: 0171 702 0888 Fax: 0171 481 8001 Contact: John Brakell	£1M	Expansion onwards	All	UK, W Europe
Prelude Technology Investments Ltd, 280 Science Park, Milton Road, Cambridge CB4 4WE Tel: 01223 423132 Fax: 01223 420869 Contact: Robert Hook	£10K	Seed, start-up, other early stage	All	UK
Prudential Venture Managers Ltd, Audrey House, Ely Place, London EC1N 6SN Tel: 0171 831 7747 Fax: 0171 831 9528 Contact: Paul Brooks	£1M	Expansion onwards	All	UK, W Europe
Quayle Munro Ltd, 42 Charlotte Square, Edinburgh EH2 4HQ Tel: 0131 226 4421 Fax: 0131 225 3391 Contact: Rod Petrie	£150K	Start-up onwards	All	UK

	1	2	3	4
Quester Capital Management Ltd, 2 Queen Anne's Gate Buildings, Dartmouth Street, London SW1H 9BP Tel: 0171 222 5472 Fax: 0171 222 5250 Contact: John Spooner	£100K	Start-up onwards	All	UK, W Europe, N America, Asia
Rothschild Asset Management Ltd, Five Arrows House, St Swithin's Lane, London EC4N 8NR Tel: 0171 280 5000 Fax: 0171 623 6261 Contact: Jeremy Curnock Cook	£100K	Seed, start-up onwards	Biotechnology, medical/health related	Worldwide
Rothschild Ventures Ltd, New Court, St Swithin's Lane, London EC4P 4DU Tel: 0171 280 5000 Fax: 0171 283 0242 Contact: Jeremy Dawson	£300K	Expansion onwards	All except biotechnology, medical/ health, finan- cial services, agriculture	UK, W Europe
Schroder Ventures, 20 Southampton St, London WC2E 7QG Tel: 0171 632 1000 Fax: 0171 240 5072 Contact: Jon Moulton	£500K	Start-up, onwards	All	UK
Scottish Enterprise, 120 Both- well Street, Glasgow G2 7JP Tel: 0141 248 2700 Fax: 0141 204 3648 Contact: Pamela Stewart	£50K	Start-up, expansion, rescue/ turnaround, MBO, MBI	All	Scotland
Seed Capital Ltd, Boston Road, Henley-on-Thames RG9 1DY Tel: 01491 579999 Fax: 01491 579825 Contact: Lucius Cary	£5K	Seed	Innovative engineering	England (within one hour's drive of Henley-on- Thames)

	1	2	3	4
The South West Scotland Investment Fund Ltd, 118 English St, Dumfries DG1 2DE Tel: 01387 61769 Fax: 01387 60029 Contact: Donald MacKinnon	£50K	Start-up/ expansion	All	Dumfries & Galloway only
Sumit Equity Ventures Ltd, Edmund House, 12 Newhall Street, Birmingham B3 3EJ Tel: 0121 236 1222 Fax: 0121 233 4628 Contact: Lindsay Bury	£200K	All except seed & start-up	All	UK
Sun Life Investment Management Services Ltd, 107 Cheapside, London EC2V 6DU Tel: 0171 606 7788 Fax: 0171 378 1865 Contact: David Bays	£500K	All except seed & start-up	All	UK, W Europe
Tayside Enterprise Board Ltd, 1st Floor, Royal Exchange Building, Panmure Street, Dundee DD1 1DZ Tel: 01382 26339 Fax: 01382 26339 Contact: David Evans	£25K	Follow-on investment in existing investments only	Follow-on investments	Tayside only
Thompson Clive & Partners Ltd, 24 Old Bond Street, London W1X 3DA Tel: 0171 491 4809 Fax: 0171 493 9172 Contact: Nat Hone	£500K	Early stage expansion, rescue/turn-around, MBO, MBI, small quoted	Communica-tions, computer & other elec-tronics, medical/ health, indus-trial automa-tion, products & services, envi-ronmental	UK, W Europe, N America
Transatlantic Capital Ltd, 33 Harley House, Marylebone Road, London NW1 5HF Tel: 0171 224 1193 Fax: 0171 224 1563 Contact: Gordon Dean	£25K	Early stage, development, expansion	Biotechnology, medical/health, environmental	UK, W Europe, N America

	1	2	3	4
Trinity Capital Partners, 123 Buckingham Palace Road, London SW1W 9SL Tel: 0171 828 8001 Fax: 0171 828 8017 Contact: John Walker	£250K	Start-up onwards	All	UK, W Europe, N America
Tufton Associates Ltd, Little Tufton House, 3 Dean Trench St, London SW1P 3HB Tel: 0171 222 8151 Fax: 0171 222 0312 Contact: Lars Ahrell	£250K	Expansion onwards	Energy, transportation, industrial products & services, consumer, other manufacturing	UK, W Europe, Scandinavia
Ulster Development Capital Ltd, 1 Arthur Street, Belfast BT1 4GA Tel: 01232 246765 Fax: 01232 232982 Contact: Edmund Johnston	£50K	Other early stage onwards	All	N Ireland
Venture Founders Ltd, West Court, Salamander Quay, Harefield, Uxbridge, Middlesex UB9 6NZ Tel: 01895 824015 Fax: 01895 823099 Contact: Joe Frye	£100K	Expansion, development & later stage	Computer & other electronics related, biotechnology, medical/health related	England
Venture Link Investors Ltd, Tectonic Place, Holyport Road, Maidenhead, Berks SL6 2YG Tel: 01628 771050 Fax: 01628 770392 Contact: Jonathan Welfare	£200K	Start-up, other early stage. Product development financing	All except property & films	UK, dedicated Welsh fund
Welsh Development Agency, Pearl House, Greyfriars Road, Cardiff CF1 3XX Tel: 01222 222666 Fax: 01222 223243 Contact: Martin Briggs	£5K	All	All except agriculture, media, retail, leisure	Wales

	1	2	3	4
West Midlands Enterprise Board Ltd, Wellington House, 31–34 Waterloo Street, Birmingham B2 5TJ Tel: 0121 236 8855 Fax: 0121 233 3942 Contact: Peter Collings	£100K	Expansion onwards	All	West & East Midlands
Yorkshire Bank Development Capital Ltd, 4 Park Cross St, Leeds LS1 2QL Tel: 0113 2442848 Fax: 0113 2340959 Contact: George Shiels	£500K	Expansion, MBO, MBI	All	UK, W Europe
Yorkshire Enterprise Ltd, St Martin's House, 210–212 Chapeltown Road, Leeds LS7 4HZ Tel: 0113 2374774 Fax: 0113 2374922 Contact: Donald Law	£100K	Start-up onwards	Computer & other electronics, chemical & materials, industrial automation, products & services, consumer, other manufacturing	Yorkshire & Humberside
Yorkshire Fund Managers Ltd, St Paul's House, Park Square, Leeds LS1 2PJ Tel: 0113 2442585 Fax: 0113 2441425 Contact: Philip Cammerman	£250K	Start-up, other early stage onwards	All except biotechnology, construction, agriculture & environmental	Yorkshire & Humberside
Yorkshire Venture Capital Ltd, Don Valley House, Savile Street, Sheffield S4 7UQ Tel: 0114 2722272 Fax: 0114 2725718 Contact: Paul Gilmartin	£200K	Expansion onwards	All except property	UK

Business angels

For small sums of money, from a few thousand pounds upwards, you could contact a business angel. An angel is a private individual who is willing to put their money and perhaps their efforts into your business. Various industry estimates suggest that upwards of £6.5 million of angel's money is looking for investment homes. Not only will angels put in smaller sums of money than conventional venture capital providers, they will be more prepared to back start-ups and riskier projects – if the chemistry is right.

So how do you get in contact with an angel? You will need to use an introductory agency or 'marriage bureau' such as LINC, who circulate to subscribing investors a regular bulletin of abbreviated information on business projects. If you are seeking finance through LINC you should submit a business plan indicating the amount of finance required (sample plans and counselling services are available). Having once been accepted as a bona fide proposal you will be charged a small fee for as many bulletin entries (around 50 words) as are felt necessary. Also a longer, two-page summary business plan will be prepared to help any enquirers requesting further details. There are now 20 local enterprise agencies in the LINC Network, covering much of the country. You can obtain more details from: LINC, 4 Snow Hill, London EC1A 2BS (Tel: 0171 236 3000).

The whole angels sector was given a boost in the 1993 Budget with the introduction of the Enterprise Investment Scheme (EIS). The key features of the scheme, which is intended to raise £60 million a year for small firms, are:

- up-front tax relief at 20% in investments of qualifying unquoted equity;
- no tax on capital gains;
- income and capital gains tax relief on losses;
- a maximum annual investment of £100,000;
- companies may raise up to £1 million a year;
- investors may become paid directors.

Angel Networks include:

The Bedfordshire Investment Exchange, Bedfordshire TEC, 2 Railton Road, Woburn Road Industrial Estate, Kempston, Bedfordshire MK42 7PN (Tel: 01234 843100; Fax: 01234 843211). Contact: Jennifer Carley.

Blackstone Franks Chartered Accountants, Barbican House, 26–34 Old Street, London EC1V 9HL (Tel: 0171 250 3300; Fax: 0171 250 1402). Contact: Vivienne Askew.

Capital Connections, East Lancashire TEC, Red Rose Court, Clayton Business Park, Clayton-le-Moors, Accrington, Lancashire BB5 5JR (Tel: 01254 301333; Fax: 01254 399090). Contact: Business Development Manager.

Daily Telegraph Business Network, 112 High Holborn, London WC1V 6JS (Tel: 0171 538 7172; Fax: 0171 831 2179). Contact: Gavin Wetton.

Devon and Cornwall Business Angels Programme, Trevint Ltd, Trevint House, Strangways Villas, Truro, Cornwall TR1 2PA (Tel: 01872 223883; Fax: 01872 42470). Contact: Anyone within the organization.

Enterprise Adventure Ltd, The Enterprise Pavilion, London Square, Cross Lanes, Guildford, Surrey GU1 1UG (Tel: 01483 458111; Fax: 01483 504675). Set up in June

1994 by Peter Benton, former deputy chairman of British Telecom. Through its venture list service they aim to build up a computer-based national data base that will act as a clearing house for 'angels' (investees) to be matched to small firms looking for money. Companies seeking funds pay £300 for a quality assessment by a consultant. Individual investors pay £500 and intermediaries such as accountants pay £1,000.

Gloucestershire Enterprise Agency, Enterprise House, Brunswick Road, Gloucester GL1 1HG (Tel: 01452 501411; Fax: 01452 305664). Contact: Mike Blackie.

Hilling Wall Corporate Finance, 43 South Street, Mayfair, London W1Y 5PD (Tel: 0171 495 1302; Fax: 0171 495 1303). Contact: Andrew Wall.

Informal Register of Investment Services (IRIS), Parkview House, Woodvale Office Park, Woodvale Road, Brighouse, West Yorkshire HD6 4AB (Tel: 01484 406297; Fax: 01484 400672). Contact: Geoffrey Sentance.

Interim Management (UK) Ltd, 8 Bloomsbury Square, London WC1A 2LP (Tel: 0171 404 6772; Fax: 0171 405 1541). Contact: Alan Horn.

Investors Forum, Portman House, Portland Road, Newcastle NE2 1AQ (Tel: 0191 261 4108; Fax: 0191 261 4108). An equity matching service for companies seeking funds between £10,000 and £250,000.

Investors in Hertfordshire, Hertfordshire TEC, New Barnes Mill, Cottonmill Lane, St Albans, Hertfordshire AL1 2HA (Tel: 01727 852313; Fax: 01727 841449). Contact: Graeme Falconer.

Local Investment Networking Company (LINC), 4 Snow Hill, London EC1A 2BS (Tel: 0171 236 3000; Fax: 0171 329 0226). Contact: Fiona Conoley.

Milton Keynes Business Venture (MKBV), Medina House, 314 Silbury Boulevard, Milton Keynes MK9 2AE (Tel: 01908 660044; Fax: 01908 233087). Contact: Colin Offer.

Principality Financial Management, 3rd Floor, Alexandra House, Swansea SA1 5ED (Tel: 01792 474111; Fax: 01792 474112). Contact: Peter Phillips.

Techinvest, South and East Cheshire TEC, PO Box 37, Dalton Way, Middlewich, Cheshire CW10 0HU (Tel: 01606 737009; Fax: 01606 734201). Contact: Vivienne Upcottgill. Based in Cheshire and one of the DTI's five demonstration programmes, Techinvest is one of the more successful regional introduction services. Started in February 1993, it has 79 angels on its books and says it has raised more than £1m for 20 deals in 12 businesses (£500,000 was provided in one deal by a venture capital group). The service offers companies seeking money a subsidized advisory service during which consultants put the proposal into shape. It also runs investor meetings and plans to open them to the public for a fee next month.

Techinvest sends some of its proposals to VCR and some to LINC for inclusion in its national bulletin. Investors and companies pay £200 to join – £400 if their cases are published through VCR if cash is successfully raised. The source of future funding is uncertain.

Venture Capital Report (VCR), Boston Road, Henley-on-Thames, Oxon RG9 1DY (Tel: 01491 579999; Fax: 01491 579825). Contact: Lucius Cary.

WINSEC Corporate Exchange, WINSEC Financial Services Ltd, 1 The Centre, Church Road, Tiptree, Colchester, Essex CO5 0HF (Tel: 01621 815047; Fax: 01621 817965). Contact: Claude Brownlow.

Other sources of capital

British Technology Group (BTG)

Funded by the government, the BTG provides finance for companies and individuals who want to develop their own technology or to start up a business using products they have developed themselves. The primary criterion is that the project should be based on a new invention, contain a significant technical innovation, or be an important evolutionary improvement on an existing product. Over the past five years they have invested £40 million in some 300 projects all over the UK. Contact: British Technology Group, 101 Newington Causeway, London SE1 6BU (Tel: 0171 403 6666).

The Capital Exchange, Wyvern Centre, Barrs Court Road, Hereford HR1 1EG (Tel: 01432 342484; Fax: 01432 263550). Produces a monthly magazine, *The Gazette*, listing and describing business proposals seeking money. Membership costs £75 per annum and an insert in the magazine costs £120.00. They also have a local adviser network to help you put together your proposal.

The GLE Business Incentive Scheme

This is the second largest fund for start-ups. Details from: Greater London Enterprise (Tel: 0171 403 0300).

Venture Capital Report (VCR)

A monthly publication of investment opportunities circulated to about 900 subscribers. Each issue contains details of ten or so business projects. VCR charges a flat fee of £350 (see listing earlier for contact) for preparing articles and, in addition, a percentage fee on any risk capital raised. VCR have their own small seed-corn fund, and back a number of ventures themselves.

Grants and soft loans

One further possible source of money is a grant. The EC, the government and many local authorities give grants for one purpose or another. Various estimates put the total figure of grant aid available at between £1 billion and £2 billion a year. *Government Funding for UK Business* and *European Community Funding for Business Development* are both published annually by Kogan Page Ltd, priced around £13.00 each.

Before you rush off and search for this 'free money' do remember that being eligible for a grant does not necessarily mean that your business idea is viable. You may be able to get a grant in a rural area, but if you are miles away from your customers, the grant will not compensate for the loss of your market. Establish that your business idea is truly viable before you apply for grants and soft loans. Some sources of funds include:

Crafts Council

The Council is a registered charity working for the Minister of Arts, offers business advice to artists, craftsmen and women, as well as providing a subsidy for craft project. They have a 'setting up scheme' to help with the cost of setting up a first workshop. Contact: Crafts Council, 44a Pentonville Road, Islington, London N1 9BY (Tel: 0171 278 7700; Fax: 0171 837 6891).

Local authorities
Many local authorities provide access to both finance and advice for business start-ups. Certain areas such as the Highlands and Islands of Scotland, and Wales, have substantial grant aid available. Contact: Your Local Authority Industrial Development Department.

The Prince's Youth Business Trust
This Trust helps unemployed or disadvantaged 18–26-year-olds with a viable business idea to get started. They provide grants and soft loans, but to get considered you need a business plan (see Section 11). Their advisers can help you put the plan together and provide support and encouragement to all recipients for at least a year after the money is put in.

One new business that has succeeded with the Trust's help is Julie Titterton and Joanne Hartshorne's hairdressing salon Altering Images, based in Little Eaton, Derbyshire. The salon was started with a loan of £5,000 from the Prince's Youth Business Trust. To secure the money, Julie Titterton and Joanne Hartshorne interviewed door-to-door to find out which salons were most patronized and how willing clients were to change; their loan covered the advance payment of the shop's lease and had to be paid back within three years. The pair planned to repay it within a year, and to support themselves have also taken part in the Government-run Enterprise Allowance Scheme.

Contact: The Prince's Youth Business Trust, 5th Floor, Cleveland Place, London SW1Y 6JJ (Tel: 0171 321 6500).

Livewire
This is another scheme to help young people (16–25) to get their own business started up. It is run all over the UK as a competition, with the winners getting good four-figure prizes, and everyone getting help and advice. The initiative came from Shell UK, but now has many other supporters. Contact: Livewire, Freepost, Newcastle upon Tyne NE1 1BR.

Contact your local TEC or LEC. Support for new businesses is provided through Training and Enterprise Councils (TECs) and Local Enterprise Councils (LECs in Scotland). The previously named Enterprise Allowance Scheme is run by these organizations under a variety of names and with differing features. (See Section 2.)

■ KEEPING THE BOOKS

Before you get started all your financial data are projections. Once you get going the information flow needs to 'go live' and capture all the relevant trading transactions.

If you are starting out as a sole trader or in a partnership, even if your turnover is likely to be below £15,000 p.a., you should keep records to generally meet Company Act requirements, as these will help your dealings with the tax authorities. The Inland Revenue can investigate business accounts and records for all sizes of business where there is reason to believe the profits may have been understated. The onus is therefore on you and your records to either agree or dispute the amount demanded by the tax authorities.

Company Act 1985: requirements for keeping books and records

If you are trading as a Limited Company it is a requirement of Company Law to keep adequate books and records 'sufficient to show and explain the company's transactions'. Section 221 of the Companies Act 1985 states:

(1) Every Company shall cause accounting records to be kept. The accounting records shall be sufficient to show and explain the Company's transactions, and should:
   (a) disclose with reasonable accuracy, at any time, the financial position of the Company at that time, and
   (b) enable the Directors to ensure that any Balance Sheet and Profit and Loss Account prepared under this part comply with the requirements of this Act as to the form and content of Company accounts and otherwise.

(2) The accounting records shall in particular contain:
   (a) entries from day to day of all sums of money received and expended by the Company, and the matters in respect of which the receipt and expenditure takes place, and
   (b) a record of the assets and liabilities of the Company.

(3) If the Company's business involves dealing in goods the accounting records shall contain:
   (a) statement of stock held by the Company at the end of each financial year of the Company.
   (b) all statements of stock-takings from which any such statements of stock as is mentioned in paragraph (a) has been or is to be prepared and
   (c) except in the case of goods sold by way of ordinary retail trade, statements of all goods sold and purchased showing the goods and the buyers and sellers in sufficient detail to enable all these to be identified.

There are also statutory requirements to keep VAT and PAYE records. Both the Inland Revenue and HM Customs and Excise carry out visits to ensure the requirements are met.

Finally, and more important than any of the above statutory reasons for maintaining the books and records, is the fact that they provide the information necessary for decision-making. Record-keeping is not therefore just an exercise to be carried out to keep your accountants happy, it is a necessary part of business survival. However, to be of any use the books must be written up on a daily basis.

Choosing a book-keeping and accounting system

In order to get financial control you need to install a book-keeping system before you start trading. This should tell you how much you have in the bank; how much you owe; and how much you are owed (a bare minimum). All the systems reviewed can do this.

The following is a brief survey of book-keeping systems. They are divided into four categories: 'shoe boxes'; do-it-yourself books; accountants only; and computer based systems.

'Shoe box' systems

This is for the simplest businesses, which need relatively little financial control beyond cash, bank accounts, accounts payable and accounts receivable.

At its simplest you need four shoe boxes, a bank paying-in-book and a cheque book (the last two can tell you how much you have in the bank). You keep two boxes for unpaid invoices (one for sales, one for purchases, services and so on). You transfer the invoices into the other two boxes (one for sales, one for purchases, etc) when each invoice is paid. By adding all the invoices in one box (sales, unpaid invoices) you can find out how much you are owed and by adding another (purchase unpaid) you find out how much you owe.

You keep every record relating to the business, too. This is a perfectly adequate system unless you need some form of cash control or some profit information and you need it fast. It is, however, not too good on credit control. Essentially this system is only for the smallest firms.

DIY systems

These are normally hardback, bound books with several sections to them, each part ruled and already laid out for the entries. Each one has a set of instructions and examples for each section.

All the DIY systems have some advantages and disadvantages in common:

Advantages – Each one tries to assist the small-business person by allowing some measures of financial control, especially over cash and bank balances. They almost always include VAT sections and Profit and Loss sections. They aim, in the large part, to make an accountant unnecessary, or at least to minimize your expense in that area.

Disadvantages – None of these systems will work unless it is kept up regularly – which means weekly at a minimum, and preferably daily. As a drawback this cannot be over-emphasized. Unless you currently regularly keep a diary, these books are probably not for you. If not kept properly they can cost you more in accountancy fees rather than less. Other disadvantages are that they often assume some prior knowledge from the user even though they give instructions. Their instructions sometimes leave much to be desired, relying largely on worked examples that are difficult to follow. They compartmentalize people and business, and they tend to ignore such expenses as 'use of home as office' (for example, home telephone bills), many of which may be tax allowable. Finally, many people also find that they would rather not use these books as the basis for dealing with their Inspector of Taxes and would rather have their accountants do this. In these circumstances you are going to need an accountant anyway, and your inspector is much more likely to pay attention to him in any case.

Accountant-only systems
The accountant-only systems are those for the more complex (possibly larger) small businesses, and will be designed by your accountant. They often need trained book-keepers to run them. However, the training period can be relatively short (anything from one day upwards). The book-keeper handles the routine matters, and your accountant the non-routine.

Computer-based accounting systems
There are many small computer systems that will carry out the book-keeping and accountancy functions needed by a small business. But, like all systems, they are only as good as the quality of the information put in. The other major problems with computer systems are these: selecting the equipment in a market with many models with claimed advantages; making sure that you have the necessary extra equipment; making sure that you have the software (programs) capable of handling your information and record needs; and, finally, ensuring that you can use the machine efficiently.

However, once your financial information is on a computer the range of useful data you can get is significantly better than from any manual system. Comparing one period with another and preparing graphs and trends is simple and quick. If you already have a computer then you should consider this option first.

To take one example: in June 1994 Intuit, a US software house, released QuickBooks 2.0 for Windows with which they hope to achieve a major market share of the small-business market. QuickBooks costs £149.95 (or £157.62 inc VAT) from Intuit, including postage and packing, and free telephone support.

QuickBooks will print sales invoices and cheques, and handle bills from suppliers, cheque payments and cheque receipts. Traditional accounts packages work on a 'summarize and carry forward' base: once a transaction has been entered on to the computer its original details are lost. By contrast, these new packages retain all transactions in full detail, and from anywhere in the program a couple of keystrokes or mouse clicks can display any invoice or payment exactly as it was entered: you have instant access to all your files and management information.

Figure 6.1 Accounting software – features compared

Facility	Account II	Anagram	Global 3000	MAP Premiere	Money Manager	Pastel 3	Pegasus Senior	QuickBooks	Sage Sovereign	Sage Sterling	Simply Accounting	Sure Accounts Plus	Tetra 2000
Sales orders	●	●	●	●			●		●	●		●	
Job costing/estimating	●	●	●			●	●			●	●		
Stock control	●	●	●	●	●	●	●		●	●	●	●	●
Bill of materials		●		●			●		●	●			●
Purchase orders	●	●	●	●			●		●	●			●
Invoicing	●	●	●			●	●	●	●	●		●	●
Ledgers													
Sales	●	●	●	●	●	●	●	●	●	●	●	●	●
Purchase	●	●	●	●	●	●	●	●	●	●	●	●	●
Nominal	●	●	●	●	●	●	●	●	●	●	●	●	●
Retail/POS							●						
Fixed assets	●		●		●		●						●
Payroll	●		●	●			●	●					●
BACS	●		●	●			●						●
Intrastats		●	●				●						●
Report generator	●		●			●	●	●	●		●	●	●
Spreadsheet	●						●						
Operating system													
Dos	●	●	●	●	●	●	●	●	●			●	●
Unix	●		●				●		●				●
Windows								●	●		●		
Price (under £200)				●	●	●	●	●	●		●	●	

Contact numbers for software:
Accounts II, Accounting Software, Tel: 0181 742 3737
Anagram, Anagram Systems, Tel: 01403 259551
Global 3000, Sutton Computing, Tel: 0121 354 4492
MAP Premiere, MAP Computer Products, Tel: 0161 624 5662
Money Manager, Connect Software, Tel: 0181 743 9792
Pastel 3, Hi Performance Systems, Tel: 01293 522241
Pegasus Senior, Pegasus Software, Tel: 01536 410044
QuickBooks, Intuit, Tel: 0181 990 5500
Sage Sovereign/Sterling, The Sage Group, Tel: 0191 201 3000
Simply Accounting, Computer Associates, Tel: 01753 577733
Sure Accounts Plus, Sure Computing, Tel: 0161 860 7821
Tetra 2000, TETRA, Tel: 01628 770378

QuickBooks contains over 50 standard reports covering profit and loss statement, balance sheet, VAT analysis, aged debtor and aged creditor reports, sales analysis by customer, by item or by rep. You can customize each of them with a report-writer then use the Quickzoom feature to drill down from any report total to display the underlying transactions in full detail.

For the service company or the company that does jobs and recharges costs to customer QuickBooks is excellent. For the business that buys things and resells them, it is less good. It holds a selling price but not a cost price for each stock item. Therefore, it can neither work out profit margins nor maintain an accurate cost of sales figure within the Profit and Loss account.

Intuit say that QuickBooks is 'designed for time-pressured business people, not trained book-keepers'. Being a Windows product, data entry is awkward and slippery compared with DOS. QuickBooks is therefore ideal for the owner–manager of a service or jobbing company who is already a keen user of products such as Excel or Ami Pro.

See Section 4 for further information on this subject.

Recommended reading

- *Financial Management for the Small Business: The Daily Telegraph Guide* by Colin Barrow, published by Kogan Page in 1990, revised edition.
- *A Guide to Accounting Software,* published by Kogan Page in association with the Institute of Chartered Accountants of Scotland.
- The clearing banks all produce packs with pro-forma accounts and tips on book-keeping.

7 | *Business and the law*

Everyone is affected in some way or another by the law, and ignorance does not form the basis of a satisfactory defence. Businesses are also subject to specific laws, and a particular responsibility rests on those who own or manage them. Although an indication of some of the main legal implications is given here, there is no substitute for specific professional advice.

A lawyer will probably know the way in which your particular business will be affected by the laws mentioned here and other laws. In the area of taxation an accountant can earn his fee several times over. Other organizations and professionals who can advise you are listed at the end of each sub-section. Most of the organizations in the first section of this book will be able to give you some guidance in this field.

This section identifies and outlines some 90 of the services or publications that can help you get a better understanding of business and the law.

Lawyers for Enterprise, which came into force in June 1988, is a scheme whereby lawyers will give a free initial interview, homing in on specific queries ticked by the client on a special leaflet obtainable from libraries, town halls, enterprise agencies and other small business organizations. Thereafter the client pays in the normal way. The leaflet also lists the 1,000+ solicitors who are part of the scheme. This scheme complements the efforts of the enterprise agency network, whose 300+ chain has 50 lawyers as board members (10 as chairmen). To send for a list of firms in your area, telephone 0171 405 9075 and give your name and address to the Law Society's reply service.

Two useful books that cover most of the field are *Law for the Small Business: The Daily Telegraph Guide* by Patricia Clayton, 7th edition 1991; price £10.95; and *Commercial Law* by R M Goode, published by Penguin in 1992; price £18.95.

■ CHOOSING THE LEGAL FORM OF THE BUSINESS

At the outset of your business venture you will have to decide what legal form your business will take. There are four main forms that a business can take, with a number of variations on two of these. The form that you choose will depend on a number of factors: commercial needs, financial risk and your tax position.

All play an important part. The tax position is looked at in more detail later, but a summary of the main pros and cons is set out later in this chapter.

Sole trader

If you have the facilities, cash and customers, you can start trading under your own name immediately. Unless you intend to register for VAT, there are no rules about the records you have to keep. There is no requirement for an external audit, or for financial information on your business to be filed at Companies House. You would be prudent to keep good books and to get professional advice, as you will have to declare your income to the Inland Revenue.

Without good records you will lose in any dispute over tax. You are personally liable for the debts of your business and, in the event of your business failing, your personal possessions can be sold to meet the debts.

A sole trader does not have access to equity capital, which has the attraction of being risk-free to the business. He must rely on loans from banks or individuals and any other non-equity source of finance.

Partnership

There are very few restrictions to setting up in business with another person (or persons) in partnership. Many partnerships are entered into without legal formalities and sometimes without the parties themselves being aware that they have entered a partnership.

All that is needed is for two or more people to agree to carry on a business together, intending to share the profits. The law will then recognize the existence of a partnership.

Most of the points raised when considering sole tradership apply to partnerships. All the partners are personally liable for the debts of the partnership, even if those debts were incurred by one partner's mismanagement or dishonesty without the other partner's knowledge. Even death may not release a partner from his obligations, and in some circumstances his estate can remain liable. Unless you take 'public' leave of your partnership by notifying your business contacts, and advertising retirement in The *London Gazette,* you will remain liable indefinitely. So it is vital before entering a partnership to be absolutely sure of your partner and to take legal advice in drawing up a partnership contract.

The contract should cover the following points:
- *Profit sharing, responsibilities and duration* This should specify how profit and losses are to be shared, and who is to carry out which tasks. It should also set limits on partners' monthly drawings, and on how long the partnership itself is to last (either a specific period of years or indefinitely, with a cancellation period of, say, three months).
- *Voting rights and policy decisions* Unless otherwise stated, all the partners have equal voting rights. It is advisable to get a definition of what is a

policy or voting decision, and how such decisions are to be made. You must also decide how to expel or admit a new partner.

■ *Time off* Every partner is entitled to his share of the profits even when ill or on holiday. You will need some guidelines on the length and frequency of holidays, and on what to do if someone is absent for a long period for any other reason.

■ *Withdrawing capital* You have to decide how each partner's share of the capital of the business will be valued in the event of either partner leaving or the partnership being dissolved.

■ *Accountancy procedure* You do not have either to file accounts or to have accounts audited. However, it may be prudent to agree a satisfactory standard of accounting and have a firm of accountants to carry out that work. Sleeping partners may well insist on it.

Sleeping partners A partner who has put up capital but does not intend to take an active part in running the business can protect himself against risk by having his partnership registered as a limited partnership.

Limited company

The main distinction between a limited company and either of the two forms of business already discussed is that it has a legal identity of its own separate from the people who own it. This means that, in the event of liquidation, creditors' claims are restricted to the assets of the company. The shareholders are not liable as individuals for the business debts beyond the paid-up value of their shares. This applies even if the shareholders are working directors, unless the company has been trading fraudulently or wrongfully.

The Insolvency Act, 1986, among other things brings into effect the notion that limited liability is a privilege rather than a right. Under these new rules incompetent as well as fraudulent directors may incur a measure of personal liability for debts incurred in the face of looming insolvency. Directors found unfit to manage can also be disqualified from holding office elsewhere.

Other advantages for limited companies include the freedom to raise capital by selling shares and certain tax advantages.

The disadvantages include the legal requirements for the company's accounts to be audited by a chartered or certified accountant, and for certain records of the business trading activities to be filed annually at Companies House. (See later for size-related exceptions to this rule.)

In practice, the ability to limit liability is severely restricted by the requirements of potential lenders. They often insist on personal guarantees from directors when small, new or troubled companies look for loans or credits. The personal guarantee usually takes the form of a charge on the family house. Since the Boland case, in 1980, unless a wife specifically agreed to a charge on the house, by signing a Deed of Postponement, then no lender can take possession in the case of default.

A limited company can be formed by two shareholders, one of whom must be a director. A company secretary must also be appointed, who can be a shareholder, director, or an outside person such as an accountant.

The company can be bought 'off the shelf' from a registration agent, then adapted to suit your own purposes. This will involve changing the name, shareholders and articles of association. Alternatively, you can form your own company, using your solicitor or accountant. The cost either way will be in the low hundreds of pounds.

Public limited company (PLC or plc)

This is not necessarily a company quoted on the stock exchange. Anyone prepared to back a venture to the tune of £50,000 worth of nominal shares can form a plc. The title adds a certain cachet above and beyond that of a plain limited company.

& Co

This title is one often used by partnerships and sole traders. The term '& Co' indicates unlimited liability, unless suffixed by the term, 'Limited'.

Co-operative

There is an alternative form of business for people whose primary concern is to create a democratic work environment, sharing profits and control. If you want to control or substantially influence your own destiny, and make as large a capital gain out of your life's work as possible, then a co-operative is not for you.

The membership of the co-operative is the legal body that controls the business, and members must work in the business. Each member has one vote, and the co-operative must be registered under the Industrial and Provident Societies Act, 1965, with the Chief Registrar of Friendly Societies (see also Co-operatives, Section 3).

Forms of business: pros and cons

Sole trader
Advantages
- Start trading immediately
- Minimum formalities
- No set-up costs
- No audit fees
- No public disclosure of trading information
- Pay Schedule 'D' tax
- Profits or losses in one trade can be set off against profits or losses in any other area
- Past PAYE can be clawed back to help with trading losses

Disadvantages
- Unlimited personal liability for trading debts
- No access to equity capital
- Low status public image
- When you die, so does the business

Partnership
Advantages
- No audit required, though your partner may insist on one
- No public disclosure of trading information
- Pay Schedule 'D' tax

Disadvantages
- Unlimited personal liability for your own and your partners' trading debts (except sleeping partners)
- Partnership contracts can be complex and costly to prepare
- Limited access to equity capital
- Death of a partner usually causes partnership to be dissolved

Limited company
Advantages
- Shareholders' liabilities restricted to nominal value of shares
- It is possible to raise equity capital
- High status public image
- The business has a life of its own and continues with or without the founder

Disadvantages
- Directors are on PAYE
- Full audit required if your turnover exceeds £350,000. (No audit up to £90,000 and a simplified report is required between £90,000 and £350,000.) Exemptions are automatic provided a company has assets of less than £1.4m and approval from 90% of its shareholders. Trading information must be disclosed
- Suppliers, landlords and banks will probably insist on personal guarantees from directors (except for government loan guarantee scheme)
- You cannot start trading until you have a certificate of incorporation

Sources of further information
Accountancy bodies are listed, together with their services (see Section 6).

Organizations
The Chief Registrar of Friendly Societies, 15/17 Great Marlborough Street, London W1V 2AZ (Tel: 0171 437 9992).
The Companies Registration Office, Crown Way, Maindy, Cardiff CF4 3UZ (Tel:

01222 388588) and for Scotland: 102 George Street, Edinburgh EH2 (Tel: 0131 225 5774). Both provide information and guidance on registering a limited company.

The Law Society, 113 Chancery Lane, London WC2 (Tel: 0171 242 1222; Fax: 0171 405 9522). Their Legal Aid Department publishes booklets which give the name, address and telephone number of solicitors in each area, indicating their area(s) of specialization, e.g. consumer law, landlord/tenant problems, employment or business problems generally, including tax and insolvency. They are available at libraries or Citizens' Advice Bureaux, and are solely concerned with solicitors willing to undertake legal aid work.

Alternatively, the society will simply give you the names of some firms of solicitors in your area.

Publications

Forming a Limited Company by Patricia Clayton, published by Kogan Page in 1992 (3rd edition); price £10.95. The major accounting firms have free publications on the Companies Act, the role and responsibilities of directors etc.

Being a Director, prepared by Coopers and Lybrand and published by GEC in 1994 (3rd edition); price £18.00. Available from GEC, Freepost, London E14 9BR or telephone 0800 289520.

■ THE BUSINESS NAME

The main consideration in choosing a business name is its commercial usefulness. You want one that will let people know as much about your business, its products and services as possible. Since 26 February 1982, when the provisions of the Companies Act, 1981, came into effect, there have been some new rules that could influence your choice of name.

Firstly, anyone wanting to use a 'controlled' name will have to get permission. There are some 100 or so controlled names that include words such as 'International', 'Bank', 'Royal' and 'University'. This is simply to prevent a business implying that it is something that it is not. Such names are controlled by the Secretary of State for Trade and Industry. The use of some other words are covered by other legislation where the Department of Trade and Industry may seek guidance from the relevant body before allowing their use. Architect, Dentist, Optician and Gymnast are some words controlled in this way.

Secondly, all businesses that intend to trade under names other than those of their owner(s) must state who does own the business and how the owner can be contacted. So, if you are a sole trader or partnership and you only use surnames with or without forenames or initials, you are not affected. Companies are also not affected if they simply use their full corporate name.

If any name other than the 'true' name is to be used, then you must disclose the name of the owner(s) and an address in the UK to which business documents can be sent. This information has to be shown on all business letters, on orders for goods and services, invoices and receipts, and statements and demands for business debts. Also, a copy has to be displayed prominently on all business premises. The purpose of the Act is simply to make it easier to 'see' who you are doing business with.

Choosing a name

There is no central register of business names in the United Kingdom. As so many new businesses have been established – over 3.9 million are now in operation – it has become increasingly difficult to find a name for your business that has not already been taken up.

But equally it is important to make sure you avoid being sued for 'passing off' as another business. In one famous recent case someone called their business 'Harrods' and was pursued and prevented from continuing by Harrods' then owners, the House of Fraser.

Some actions you can take to make sure that the name you choose is available include the following.

- Check the relevant telephone directories and yellow pages. These are available in all major reference libraries.
- Make a search of the trade marks registry. This however will only uncover trade names and service marks registered since 1986.
- Search for trade names in use using directories such as *Kompass* – also in major reference libraries.
- Search at Companies House, or via a CD-ROM data base such as FAME, to see if any limited company has already taken up that name.

■ PROTECTING YOUR IDEAS

Patent law can give you temporary protection for technological inventions. The registration of a design can protect the appearance or shape of a commercial product; copyright protects literary, artistic or musical creations and, more recently, computer programs; trade marks protect symbols, logos and pictures.

The period of the protection which these laws can give varies from five years, for the initial registration of the design, to 50 years after your death, for the copyright on an 'artistic' work. The level and scope of protection varies considerably, and is in the process of change. A flurry of activity in the late 70s set UK patent law on a course to harmonize it with EC law. So, for example, it is now possible with a single patent application made in the UK to secure a whole series of protections throughout Europe. The Patent Co-operation Treaty will eventually extend that protection to the USA, USSR and Japan.

In practice, however, defending 'intellectual' property is an expensive and complex process for a new or small business. If you have a unique business idea, you should investigate the four categories of protection: patenting, which protects technological and other inventions; design registration, which protects the shape or appearance of a commercial product; copyright, which protects literary, artistic and musical works; and trade mark registration, which protects symbols, logos and pictures.

Some products may be covered by two or more categories, e.g. the mechanism of a clock may be patented while its appearance may be design-registered.

Each category requires a different set of procedures, offers a different level of protection and extends for a different period of time. They all have one thing in common, though; in the event of any infringement your only redress is through the courts, and going to law can be wasteful of time and money, whether you win or lose.

Patents

A patent can be regarded as a contract between an inventor and the state. The state agrees with the inventor that if he/she is prepared to publish details of his/her invention in a set form and if it appears that he/she has made a real advance, the state will then grant him/her a 'monopoly' on his/her invention for 20 years: 'protection in return for disclosure'. The inventor uses the monopoly period to manufacture and sell his/her innovation; competitors can read the published specifications and glean ideas for their research, or they can approach the inventor and offer to help to develop his/her idea under licence.

However, the granting of a patent doesn't mean the proprietor is automatically free to make, use or sell the invention himself/herself, since to do so might involve infringing an earlier patent which has not yet expired.

A patent really only allows the inventor to stop another person using the particular device which forms the subject of his/her patent. The state does not guarantee validity of a patent either, so it is not uncommon for patents to be challenged through the courts.

Which inventions can you patent? The basic rules are that an invention must be new, must involve an inventive step and must be capable of industrial exploitation.

You can't patent scientific/mathematical theories or mental processes, computer programs or ideas which might encourage offensive, immoral, or anti-social behaviour. New medicines are patentable but not medical methods of treatment. Neither can you have just rediscovered a long-forgotten idea (knowingly or unknowingly).

If you want to apply for a patent, it is essential not to disclose your idea in non-confidential circumstances. If you do, your invention is already 'published' in the eyes of the law, and this could well invalidate your application.

There are two distinct stages in the patenting process:

■ from filing an application up to publication of the patent;
■ from publication to grant of the patent.

Two fees are payable for the first part of the process and a further fee for the second part. The whole process takes some two and a half years. Relevant forms and details of how to patent are available free of charge from the Patent Office.

It is possible – and cheaper – to make your own patent application but this is not really recommended. Drafting a specification to give you as wide a monopoly as you think you can get away with is the essence of patenting and this is the skill of professional patent agents. They also know the tricks of the trade for each stage of the patenting procedure. A list of patent agents is available from the Chartered Institute of Patent Agents.

What can you do with your idea? If you have dreamt up an inspired invention but don't have the resources, skill, time or inclination to produce it yourself, you can take one out of three courses once the idea is patented.

Outright sale. You can sell the rights and title of your patent to an individual or company. The payment you ask should be based on a sound evaluation of the market.

Sale and royalty. You can enter into an agreement whereby you assign the title and rights to produce to another party for cash but under which you get a royalty on each sold unit.

Licensing. You keep the rights and title but sell a licence for manufacturing and marketing the product to someone else. The contract between you and the licensee should contain a performance clause requiring the licensee to sell a minimum number of units each year or the licence will be revoked.

Whichever option you select, you need a good patent agent/lawyer on your side.

Trade marks

A trade mark is the symbol by which the goods of a particular manufacturer or trader can be identified. Trade marks can be a word, a signature, a monogram, a picture, a logo or a combination of these.

To qualify for registration the trade mark must be distinctive, must not be deceptive and must not be capable of confusion with marks already registered. Excluded are misleading marks, national flags, royal crests, insignia of the armed forces. A trade mark can only apply to tangible goods, not services (although pressure is mounting for this to be changed).

The Trade Marks Act of 1938 offers protection of great commercial value since, unlike other forms of protection, your sole rights to use the trade mark continue indefinitely. To register a trade mark you or your agent should first conduct preliminary searches at the Trade Marks Branch of the Patent Office to check there are no conflicting marks already in existence. You then apply for registration on the official trade mark form and pay a fee (currently £42).

Your application is then advertised in the weekly *Trade Marks Journal* to allow any objections to be raised. If there are none, your trade mark will be officially registered and you pay a further fee (currently £53).

Registration is initially for seven years. After this, it can be renewed for periods of 14 years at a time, with no upper time limit. It is mandatory to register a trade mark.

If an unregistered trade mark has been used for some time and could be construed as closely associated with the product by customers, it will have acquired a 'reputation' which will give it some protection legally, but registration makes it much simpler for the owner to have recourse against any person who infringes the mark.

Design registration

You can register the shape, design or decorative features of a commercial product if it is new, original, never published before or – if already known – never before applied to the product you have in mind. Protection is intended to apply to industrial articles to be produced in quantities of more than 50. Design registration only applies to features which appeal to the eye – not to the way the article functions.

To register a design, you should apply to the Design Registry and send a specimen or photograph of the design plus a registration fee (currently £44). This is examined to see whether it is new or original and complies with other requirements of the Registered Designs Act 1949. If it does, a certificate of registration is issued which gives you, the proprietor, the sole right to manufacture, sell or use in business articles of that design.

Protection lasts for five years but can be renewed for two further five-year periods. You can handle the design registration yourself but, again, it might be preferable to let a specialist do it for you. There is no register of design but most patent agents are well versed in design law.

Copyright

Copyright is a complex field and since it is unlikely to be relevant to most business start-ups we only touch on it lightly.

Basically the Copyright Act 1956 gives protection against the unlicensed copying of original artistic and creative works – articles, books, paintings, films, plays, songs, music, engineering drawings. To claim copyright the item in question should carry this symbol © with the author's name and date. You can take the further step of recording the date on which the work was completed (plus a £23 fee) with the Registrar at Stationers Hall. This, though, is an unusual precaution to take and probably only necessary if you anticipate any infringement.

Copyright is infringed only if more than a 'substantial' part of your work is reproduced (i.e. issued for sale to the public) without your permission, but since there is no formal registration of copyright the question of whether or not your work is protected usually has to be decided in a court of law.

Sources of further information

The British Technology Group, 101 Newington Causeway, London SE1 6BU (Tel: 0171 403 6666), Publicity Department. They can help you with the exploitation and development of your invention. They have financial, technological and commercial resources and expertise.

The Chartered Institute of Patent Agents, Staple Inn Buildings, High Holborn, London WC1V 7PX (Tel: 0171 405 9450). Not an advisory service but it will put you in contact with a patent agent in your area. Publishes a Register of Patent Agents which lists names and business addresses of all patent agents qualified to practise before the Patent Office.

Design Registry, Patent Office, Concept House, Cardiff Road, Newport, Gwent NP9 1RH (Tel: 01633 812078). Publishes free of charge guides to registering designs.

Institute of Information Scientists, 44/45 Museum Street, London WC1A 1LY (Tel: 0171 831 8003). Formed in 1978, it represents the interest of searchers, and has a register of searchers who will carry out literature searches in the patent field.

The Institute of Inventors, 19/23 Fosse Way, Ealing, London W13 0BZ (Tel: 0181 998 3540). £40 per annum membership (£120 to register). Provides help, support and advice to inventors.

Institute of Patentees and Inventors, Suite 505A, Triumph House, 189 Regent Street, London W1R 7WF (Tel: 0171 242 7812). A membership organization (membership costs £30 p.a.). Looks after the interests of patent holders and inventors. Can provide useful advice and guidance on almost every aspect of intellectual property from idea conception to innovation and development. Publishes quarterly journal and *New Patents Bulletin*. The latter acts as liaison with industry, bringing members' inventions to the notice of specialized manufacturing firms.

Institute of Trade Mark Agents, 4th Floor, Canterbury House, 2–6 Sydenham Road, Croydon, Surrey CR0 9XE (Tel: 0181 686 2052). Can put you in contact with a trade mark agent in your area and give general advice. Produces a register of trade mark agents.

Legal Protection Group, Marshalls Court, Sutton, Surrey SM1 4DU (Tel: 0181 652 1313). Can provide insurance at Lloyds, to cover some of the cost of fighting a patent infringer. The worst infringers of small inventors' ideas are international companies who bank on the little man being too poor to embark on a costly legal action, so this £250,000 (approx) a year insurance policy could be worth while.

Patent Office, State House, 66–71 High Holborn, London WC1R 4TP (Tel: 0171 438 4700); open to public Monday to Friday, 10 a.m. to 4 p.m.). Publishes the following pamphlets: *Applying for a patent, Introducing patents – a guide for inventors, How to prepare a UK patent application*.

Science Reference Library, 25 Southampton Buildings, Chancery Lane, London WC2A 1AW (Tel: 0171 323 7919). The Library houses all patent details, and is open 9.30 a.m. to 9 p.m., Monday to Friday, and on Saturday 10 a.m. to 1 p.m. More details of this library are given in the section on specialist libraries (Section 5).

Stationers Hall, Ave Maria Lane, Ludgate Hill, London EC4M 7DD (Tel: 0171 248 2934); open Monday to Friday, 10 a.m. to 4 p.m., for registration of copyright. Provides details and forms for registration.

Trade Marks Registry, 25 Southampton Buildings, Chancery Lane, London WC2A 1AY (Tel: 0171 438 4701); open Monday to Friday, 10 a.m. to 4 p.m. Publishes *Applying for a trade mark* (free of charge), *Trade Marks Journal* (£9.25 every Wednesday).

Provincial libraries – see Section 5.

Publication

Copyrights, Patents and Trade Marks, protecting your rights worldwide by Hoyt L Barber, published by McGraw Hill in 1994; price £14.95.

■ PREMISES

Buying or leasing business premises entails a number of important and often complex laws affecting your decisions. To some extent these laws go beyond the scope of the physical premises, into areas such as opening hours and health and safety.

Working from home

If you plan to work from home you need to check that you are not prohibited from doing so by the house deeds or the terms of your mortgage. Clearly if your business activity is noisy, dangerous or operates over anti-social hours your neighbours will be unhappy and may take action to curb your behaviour.

You will also have to notify your insurance company, as they will certainly view this change as a material fact. That said, tens of thousands of people work unhindered from their spare room. With the growth of telecommuting this trend is likely to grow. Many major public enterprises started out on the kitchen table.

Planning permission

An important first step is to make sure that the premises you have in mind can be used for what you want to do. There are nearly a score of different 'use classes', and each property should have a certificate showing which has been approved. The classes include retail, offices, light industrial, general industrial, warehousing and various special classes.

Certain changes of class do not need planning permission – for example, from general industrial to light industrial. Also, changes of use within a class – say, from one type of shop to another – may not need planning permission.

In August 1985 a booklet was issued by the Department of the Environment called *The Small Firm and the Planners*. The circular stated, among other things, that if a business premises was put to a 'non-conforming' use, that was not in itself sufficient reason for taking enforcement action or refusing planning permission. Permission should only be refused where the business would cause a nuisance or a safety or health hazard. This in effect means that running a business from home does not necessarily require planning permission.

Once you have taken on a premises, then the responsibilities for 'conforming' fall on your shoulders, so take advice.

Building regulations

Even if you have planning permission, you will still have to conform to building regulations. These apply to the materials, structure and building methods used, in either making or altering the premises. So if you plan any alterations you may need a special approval.

The lease

Before taking on a lease, look carefully at the factors below.

Restrictions

If you are taking on a leasehold property, then you must find out if there are any restrictions in the lease on the use of the property. Often shop leases have restrictions protecting neighbouring businesses. The lease will often stipulate that the landlord cannot 'unreasonably' withhold consent to a change in use. He may, however, insist on the premises being returned to its original shape before you leave.

Repairs

Most leases require the tenant to take on either internal repairing liability or full repairing leases. Resist the latter if at all possible, particularly if the property is old. If you have to accept a full repairing lease, then it is essential to get a Schedule of Condition. This is an accurate record of the condition of the premises when you take it over. It is carried out by your own and the landlord's surveyor. It is one expense you may be tempted to forgo – don't.

Rent reviews

However long (or short) your lease is, it is likely that a rent review clause allowing rent reviews every three to seven years will be included. Look very carefully at the formulas used to calculate future rents.

Security of tenure

The Landlord and Tenant Act, 1954, protects occupiers of business premises. When your lease ends you can stay on at the same rent until the steps laid down in the Act are taken. These steps are fairly precise, and you would be well advised to read the Act and take legal advice.

You will get plenty of warning, as the landlord must give you six months' notice in writing, even if you pay rent weekly. The landlord cannot just ask you to leave. There are a number of statutory grounds for repossession. The two main types of grounds are, firstly, that you are an unsatisfactory tenant, an allegation you can put to the test in court; or secondly, that the landlord wants the premises for other purposes. In that case you must be offered alternative suitable premises. These are obviously matters for negotiation, and you should take advice as soon as possible.

Unified Business Rate

From 1990, with a transition period of up to ten years for small businesses, a new and possibly more expensive form of business rates are coming into force. You should certainly be aware of the likely implications for your premises of the Local Government Finance Bill, as the law changing these rates is known.

Health and safety at work

Whatever legal form your business takes (if you are a sole trader for instance, or a limited company) you will be responsible for the working conditions of all your premises. Your responsibility extends to people who work on those premises, to visitors and to the public. If you have more than five employees, you will have to prepare a statement of policy on health, and let everyone who is working for you know what that policy is. You may also be required to keep records of such events as the testing of fire alarms and accidents.

The main laws concerned are the Health and Safety at Work Act (1974), the Offices, Shops and Railway Premises Act (1963) and the Factories Act (1961). Employers' liability is based on the common law, and your responsibilities can be extensive. A catalogue listing more than 2,000 relevant publications covering health and safety legislation is available from HMSO.

The Acts cover, among other matters, fire precautions and certificates; general cleanliness and hygiene; means of access and escape; machine and equipment safety; workspace; temperature; noise; welfare; catering arrangements; security of employees' property; toilet and washing facilities; protective clothing; the appointment of safety representatives and committees; and minimum insurance cover.

Special trades

Restaurants and all places serving food, hotels, pubs, off-licences, employment agencies, nursing agencies, pet shops and kennels, mini cabs, taxis, betting shops, auction sale rooms, cinemas and hairdressers are among the special trades that have separate additional regulations or licensing requirements.

Your local authority Planning Department will be able to advise you on the regulations that apply specifically to your trade. It would be as well to confirm the position whatever you planned to do. They can also tell you if any local by-laws are in force which could affect you.

Opening hours

Sunday trading and opening hours may be the subject of local restrictions. Once again, your local authority Planning Department will be able to advise you whether or not special local rules apply.

Advertising signs

There are some restrictions on the size and form that the name or advertising hoarding on your premises can take. A look around the neighbourhood will give you an idea of what is acceptable. If in doubt, or if you are going to spend a lot of money, take advice.

Sources of further information

The Building Centre, 26 Store Street, London WC1E 7BT (Tel: 0171 637 1022). This has the most extensive library and information service on the whole building field, including building regulations and sources of professional advice. Their free information service (Tel: 0171 637 8361) will provide answers to almost any building problem.

The Environmental Health Department will be able to advise you on particular problems related to using premises for service or producing food or drink.

Health and Safety Executive, 1 Long Lane, London SE1 4PG (Tel: 0171 407 8911). Apart from supplying pamphlets and reference materials on the various regulations, they can put you in contact with the nearest of their 21 area office information services. In each of these offices there are groups of inspectors specializing in the specific local industries and their problems.

Local authorities. Each has a Planning Department, which can give information and opinions on planning application and other matters relating to your premises; a Building Control Department, covering building regulation; an Environmental Health Department, covering health and safety at work; and an Industrial Liaison Department, giving general advice to encourage industrial development.

Publications

Land Law, in the Nutshell series, by W. Howarth, published by Sweet and Maxwell, South Quay Plaza, 183 Marsh Wall, London E14 9FT (Tel: 0171 538 8686). Regularly updated; price £4.95.

Selwyn's Law of Employment; Butterworths Bookshop, 35 Chancery Lane, London WC2A 1EL (Tel: 0171 405 6900); price £20.95.

Planning Permission: A Free Guide for Industry from the Department of the Environment, 2 Marsham Street, London SW1P 3EB (Tel: 0171 276 0900). Explains the planning control systems to help businesses submit a successful application.

■ TRADING LAWS

Once you start trading, whatever the legal form of your business, you will have certain obligations to your customers. These are contained in a number of legal acts and some of these are outlined below.

Contract law

All business life is affected by contracts. Almost everything done in business, whether it be for the supply of raw materials, the sale of goods and services or the hire of a fax machine, is executed under contract law. This is true whether the contract is in writing or whether it is verbal – or even merely implied. Only contracts for the sale of land, hire purchase and some insurance contracts have to be in writing to be enforceable.

To make life even more complicated, a contract can be part written and part oral. So statements made at the time of signing a written contract can legally form part of that contract.

For a contract to exist three events must take place:

- There must be an offer.
- There must be an acceptance.
- There must be a consideration – some form of payment.

By mail order or post, the contract starts when the supplier posts an acceptance letter, a confirmation or the goods themselves – whichever comes first. For credit purchases which do not take place on trade premises the purchasers have a five-day 'cooling off' period, during which they are not bound by the contract and can withdraw.

Standard terms and conditions

Certain standards have to be met by law for the supply of goods and services. Over and above these you will need your own terms and conditions, if you are not to enter into 'contracts' you did not intend. You will need help to devise these terms.

The following four basic propositions will govern your conditions.

- The conditions must be brought to the other party's attention before he makes the contract.
- The last terms and conditions specified before acceptance of an offer apply.
- If there is any ambiguity or uncertainty in the contract terms they will be interpreted against the person who inserted them.
- The terms may be interpreted as unreasonably unenforceable being in breach of various Acts of Parliament.

Check list for standard terms and conditions

General
Do they exclude any variation unless this is written and signed by a director of the company or the proprietor of the business or a partner?

Quotations
How long are these open for? 30 days, 60 days etc? Do different prices apply to exports?

Price
- Can the seller increase the price? If so, under what conditions?
- Is the price ex works exclusive of VAT? Does it include carriage, insurance or freight?

Terms of payment
- What time is given to pay? Is there a prompt payment discount?
- If it is an export contract, in what currency is payment made?
- Is interest due on unpaid invoices? If so, at what rate and from when is it charged?

Delivery
- Who delivers?
- Are delivery dates estimates only?

Risk and property
- When does the buyer take the risk of damage to or loss of the goods (i.e. need to insure them)?
- Does the seller reserve title in the goods until paid for?
- Is the buyer obliged to store the goods separately and mark them as being the property of the seller?

Warranties
- Does the seller seek to limit his obligations as to merchantable quality, fitness for purpose, or correspondence with samples under the Sale of Goods Act or the equivalent obligations in respect of services?
- Does the seller seek to limit his liability for any losses arising under the contract so that his liability for negligence, delay, consequential loss, etc is limited, e.g. to the value of the goods sold?
- Does the seller need a force majeure clause, i.e. one which prevents him being liable for any loss caused by his failure to fulfil his obligations under the contract for reasons beyond his control, e.g. fire, bad weather, strikes, destruction of premises?

Arbitration
- Should disputes be referred to an expert arbitrator rather than being left to the courts? This only applies to business contracts. Arbitration clauses in consumer contracts which automatically refer disputes to arbitration rather than to the courts are banned by the Consumer Arbitration Agreements Act 1988.
- If arbitration is necessary, who is to appoint the arbitrator? And bear in mind that, although arbitration is secret and often quicker, it is often more expensive than going to court as the arbitrator has to be paid as well. The £60 writ fee (High Court) or £43 summons (County Court) pays for the judge and the courtroom. Of course you will still have legal fees, either way.

Termination
How is the contract to be ended if it is more than a one-off agreement? What notice should be given? What happens if there is a breach of contract by one party? Does that automatically give the other the right to terminate?

Governing law

Does the contract stipulate which legal system is to regulate any disputes? This is very important, as otherwise large sums can be spent just deciding which legal system applies. This is relevant even for trading within the United Kingdom as English and Scottish law differs.

Sale of Goods Act, 1979 (and Supply of Services Act 1982)

This Act states that the seller has three obligations. Firstly, the goods sold must be of merchantable quality – that is, reasonably fit for their normal purpose. Secondly, those goods must also be fit for any particular purpose made known to the seller. This makes you responsible for your advice, if, for example, your customer asks you whether or not a product will perform a particular job. Thirdly, the goods sold must be as described. This would include the colour or size of the goods concerned.

The Food and Drugs Act, 1955

This Act makes it a criminal offence to sell unfit food; to describe food falsely; or to mislead people about its nature, substance or quality. This regulation covers food wherever it is sold, manufactured, packed, processed or stored for sale.

Prices Act, 1974

The Prices Act enables the Government to require prices to be displayed and to control how they are displayed. This requires restaurants, pubs, cafés and petrol stations to display their prices.

Consumer Credit Act, 1974

This Act took eleven years to implement throughout the whole range of credit provided to consumers, but as of 19 May 1985, the final sections came into force. It covers every aspect of trader relationships with customers who buy on credit.

Trade Descriptions Acts, 1968 and 1972

The Acts make it a criminal offence for a trader to describe his goods falsely. They cover such areas as declared car mileage on second-hand cars and statement of the country of manufacture on jeans.

Unsolicited Goods and Services Act, 1971

The Act makes it an offence to send goods without a customer's order, in the hope that they will then buy them.

Weights and Measures Act, 1985

The Act makes it an offence not to mark the quantity (weight, volume or, in a few cases, the number) on the contents of most packaged grocery items and many other items.

Unfair Contract Terms Act, 1977

The Act prevents firms from escaping their responsibilities by using 'exclusion clauses' or disclaimers, such as statements saying 'articles left at owner's risk'. The onus is on the trader to prove that his exclusions are fair and reasonable in the circumstances. The notice itself is not enough.

Consumer Protection Act, 1987

This Act safeguards consumers from products that do not reach a reasonable level of safety. Before this Act those injured had to prove a manufacturer negligent before they could successfully sue for damages. While a customer could already sue a supplier without proof of negligence, under the Sale of Goods law, this Act provides the same rights to anyone injured by a defective product whether or not the product was sold to them.

This Act provides an incentive, where one was not yet present, for businesses to ensure that their products provide the safety that users, or those affected, can reasonably expect.

For manufacturers, the UK national standard for quality assurance systems laid down in BS 5750 is now compulsory reading.

Sources of further information

Advertising Standards Authority, 2/16 Torrington Place, London WC1E 7HN (Tel: 0171 580 5555). Will put you right on your legal responsibilities if you advertise your goods for sale.

British Standards Institute: A scheme to 'demystify' the controversial BS 5750 quality management standard and help small businesses achieve registration more easily and cost effectively has been launched by the British Standards Institution. There is a reduction in fees, a payment spreading system, a helpline and a guidance document to the implementation process. BSI: 01908 220022.

Environmental Health Departments of the local authority will be able to provide advice on all matters to do with food, drink and hygiene.

Lloyd's Register Quality Assurance (LRQA), a subsidiary of Lloyd's Register of Shipping and one of the bigger certification bodies, has brought out a 'plain English, common-sense' scheme aimed at helping small businesses achieve the BS 5750 quality standard. It follows a British Standards Institution policy committee call that achieving BS 5750 should be made easier for small firms.

Many certification bodies are introducing simpler schemes and LRQA suggests small businesses should shop around for the best deal. Total costs for the first year in some cases can be established only by adding up several cost elements, LRQA said.

As well as the main expense of an initial assessment, during the first year there can also be an additional surveillance visit to pay for. LRQA quotes a single total cost for the first year and estimates that a quality management system can be approved for as little as £1,600. The scheme is open to businesses employing fewer than 30 people. Details: LRQA, Norfolk House, Wellesley Road, Croydon, Surrey CR9 2DT (Tel: 0181 688 6883).

Office of Fair Trading, Fields House, Breams Building, London EC4A 1PR (Tel: 0171 242 2858). The office provides useful booklets on most aspects of trading law from the consumer's point of view.

The Small Claims Procedure is a useful low-cost way to collect money owed to you. Small debts of up to around £1,000 can be sued for with the minimum of formalities. All County Courts keep a stock of an invaluable book, *Small Claims in the County Court,* written in layman's language. A companion volume, *Enforcing Judgements in the County Court,* is also available.

The Trading Standards Department of the local authority can also give you advice on acceptable trading behaviour.

Publications

Consumer Law, in the Nutshell series, by Sandra Silberstein, published in 1994 by Sweet and Maxwell, South Quay Plaza, 183 Marsh Wall, London E14 9FT (Tel: 0171 538 8686); price £4.95.

The Unsafe Product, a Manager's Guide to the Consumer Protection Act 1987 by Derrick Owles, published in 1988 by Kogan Page, 120 Pentonville Road, London N1 9JB (Tel: 0171 278 0433); price £18.95.

■ EMPLOYING PEOPLE

Apart from the problems of finding the right people to work in your business, and making sure that the conditions under which they will have to work are satisfactory, you may have other responsibilities. Examples are given below.

Terms of employment

Within 13 weeks of them starting to work for you, you have to give people a written set of terms of employment. These terms will cover pay, holidays, sick pay, overtime commitments, job title, pensions, discipline and notice.

Notice of lay-offs

Once an employee has worked for you for over four weeks, they are entitled to at least one week's notice of dismissal. They are also entitled to guaranteed pay up to five days in any three months if you decide either to lay them off or to put them on short time.

Discrimination

You cannot discriminate against anyone on the basis of their sex or on colour or racial grounds. The same protection applies to married people. There are some exceptions to these rules – for example if sex or race or nationality is a genuine occupational qualification (e.g. an Italian waiter for an Italian restaurant).

Criminal records

Under the Rehabilitation of Offenders Act certain convictions become 'spent' after a certain time. For example if someone had been to prison for no more than 2½ years, after ten years that conviction would not normally have to be disclosed to a potential employer. For a probation order the offence would be invisible after only one year.

In certain cases, if the applicant is asked, all past offences have to be revealed to a potential employer. These include: prison staff; teachers; doctors; dentists; solicitors and other professionals. Only if a person with an 'unspent' conviction fails to disclose this when asked, could he or she subsequently be fairly dismissed if the conviction is discovered.

Disabled staff

Employers with more than 20 staff have to see that their workforce contains at least 3% registered disabled persons. No vacancy can be legally filled with an able-bodied employee unless at that date the employer already employs the appropriate number of registered disabled people.

Maternity – Statutory Maternity Pay (SMP)

To qualify for SMP, a woman must be employed full time (16 hours plus per week), have been with her employer over two years, work until at least eleven weeks prior to the birth and give at least three weeks' notice that she intends to stop work because she is pregnant.

Once these conditions are met, a woman is entitled to about 90% of her normal pay for six weeks. The employer can offset the SMP against his National Insurance contribution, or claim a refund from the Department of Social Security if that is insufficient.

A woman also has the right to return to work if she gives notice of that intention within three weeks of leaving to give birth and returns within 29 weeks.

Dismissal

You can only dismiss employees by giving them the notice laid down in the contract. The exception to this rule is if an employee has been guilty of gross misconduct – e.g. theft, violence or serious breaches of discipline.

Wrongful dismissal

Clearly you need to take care that you are behaving correctly when dismissing staff and do not leave yourself open to a claim for unfair or wrongful dismissal. Despite all the publicity surrounding this matter only a third of applications for unfair dismissal succeed, and the average award is under £2,000.

You may find it useful to join an organization such as the Institute of Personnel Management or the Industrial Society, who can give you timely and cost-effective advice in this field. Such organizations keep absolutely up to date with all the many changes in this field of legislation, a task beyond the resources of most small firms with other, more pressing, problems.

Sources of further information

Advisory, Conciliation and Arbitration Service (ACAS), 27 Wilton Street, London SW1X 2AZ (Tel: 0171 210 3000). Although you mainly hear of ACAS in big public disputes between unions and their management, a large part of their work is concerned with preventing disputes and dispensing information. Nearly a quarter of their 12,500+ (p.a.) advisory visits are to firms with fewer than 50 employees.

They offer advice on recruitment and selection, payment systems and incentive schemes, manpower planning, communications and consultations, collective bargaining and so on. They also produce free advisory booklets on job evaluation, introduction to payment systems, personnel records, labour turnover, absence, recruitment and selection and introduction of new employees.

Their regional offices are as follows.
London: Clifton House, 83/117 Euston Road, London NW1 2RB (Tel: 0171 388 5100).
Merseyside Office: Cressington House, 249 St Mary's Road, Garston, Liverpool L19 0NF (Tel: 0151 427 8881).
Midlands (Northamptonshire (except Corby), Shropshire, Staffordshire (except Burton-on-Trent), West Midlands, Hereford and Worcester, Warwickshire): Alpha Tower, Suffolk Street, Queensway, Birmingham B1 1TZ (Tel: 0121 631 3434).
Midlands (Derbyshire (except High Peak District), Nottinghamshire, Leicestershire, Corby, Lincolnshire, Burton-on-Trent): Nottingham Office, 66/72 Houndsgate, Nottingham NG1 6BA (Tel: 0115 9415450).
North (Cumbria, Tyne and Wear, Cleveland, Northumberland, Durham): Westgate House, Westgate Road, Newcastle-upon-Tyne NE1 1TJ (Tel: 0191 261 2191).
North West (Lancashire, Cheshire, High Peak District of Derbyshire, Greater Manchester): Boulton House, 17/21 Chorlton Street, Manchester M1 3HY (Tel: 0161 228 3222).
South East (Cambridgeshire, Norfolk, Suffolk, Oxfordshire, Buckinghamshire, Bedfordshire, Hertfordshire, Essex, Berkshire, Surrey, Kent, Hampshire (except Ringwood), Isle of Wight, East Sussex, West Sussex): Westminster House, Fleet Road, Fleet, Hampshire GU13 8PD (Tel: 01252 811868).
South West (Gloucestershire, Avon, Wiltshire, Cornwall, Devon, Somerset, Dorset, Ringwood): Regent House, 27a Regent Street, Clifton, Bristol BS8 4HR (Tel: 0117 9744066).
Yorkshire and Humberside (North Yorkshire, South Yorkshire, Humberside, West Yorkshire): Commerce House, St Albans Place, Leeds LS2 8HH (Tel: 0113 2431371).

Scotland: Franborough House, 123/157 Bothwell Street, Glasgow G2 7JR (Tel: 0141 204 2677).
Wales: Phase 1, Ty-Glas Road, Llanishen, Cardiff CF4 5PH (Tel: 01222 762636).

The Industrial Society, Peter Runge House, 3 Carlton House Terrace, London SW1Y 5DG (Tel: 0171 839 4300). The society campaigns for the involvement of people at work and argues that increased involvement means greater efficiency and productivity.

Annual membership costs between £130 and £265 for companies with up to 200 employees, and this gives access to an extensive range of services and publications. Their Information and Personnel Advisory Services department will answer enquiries from members on any subject in the field of personnel management and industrial relations. Most enquiries are dealt with the same day, though complicated questions that have to be referred to their legal advisers or the medical advisory panel may take about ten days. Of particular interest to small business is the Personnel Advisory Service, which can, in effect, provide you with all the services of a professional personnel manager, from recruitment to redundancy.

Institute of Personnel Management, IPM House, 35 Camp Road, Wimbledon SW19 4UW (Tel: 0181 946 9100). The Institute has over 30,000 individual members, and has extended its service to businesses through its Company Membership Service. The cost of membership for a company employing up to 75 people would be £220 plus VAT per annum. This would give access to the Institute's library, publications, conferences and seminars, and, more importantly, it would allow use of the Information and Advisory Service. This service is staffed by a small team of multi-discipline specialists, including a legal adviser who is a barrister at law. They can answer or find answers to most problems in this field.

Enquiries can be made by letter, telephone or a personal visit between 9 a.m. and 5 p.m. daily, Monday to Friday.

Interestingly enough, of the 800 or so enquiries they handle each month, pay and conditions of employment account for half, followed by employment law, employee relations and then training.

Legal Protection Group, Marshalls Court, Sutton, Surrey SM1 4DU (Tel: 0181 652 1313). They provide an employer's legal protection package. They also undertake commercial legal proceedings insurance, provide legal fees for the protection of patents, copyright, registered designs and trade marks, and in respect of 'passing off' actions.

See also National Federation of Self Employed and Small Business.

Publications
Croner's Guide to Fair Dismissal, 3rd edition, 1988; price £7.95.
Employing and Managing People by L Lanz, published by Pitmans in 1991; price £11.99.

■ INSURANCE

Insurance forms a guarantee against loss. You must weigh up to what extent your business assets are exposed to risk and what effect such events could have on the business if they occurred. Insurance is an overhead, producing no benefit until a calamity occurs. It is therefore a commercial decision as to how much to carry, and it is a temptation to minimize cover. You must carry some cover, either by employment law, or as an obligation imposed by a mortgager.

You will have to establish your needs by discussing your business plans with an insurance broker. Make sure you know exactly what insurance you are buying; and, as insurance is a competitive business, get at least three quotations before making up your mind.

Employer's liability

You must carry at least £2 million cover to meet your legal liabilities for death or bodily injury incurred by any employee during the course of business. In practice, this cover is usually unlimited, with the premiums directly related to your wage bill.

Personal accident

Employer's liability only covers those accidents in which the employer is held to be legally responsible. You may feel a moral responsibility to extend that cover to anyone carrying out an especially hazardous task. You may also have to cover your own financial security, particularly if the business depends on your being fit.

Product liability insurance

Obligations are placed on producers or importers of certain types of goods under both the Consumer Protection Act 1987 and the Sale of Goods Act 1979. In addition the Common Law rules of negligence also apply. In a partnership, for example, with unlimited liability, it would be quite possible to be personally bankrupted in a law suit concerning product liability. Even if the business was carried out through a limited company, although the directors may escape personal bankruptcy the company would not.

If you believe the risks associated with your product are real, then you need to consider taking out product liability insurance.

Director's and officer's liability insurance

Risks insured under this heading include: negligent performance of duties; breach of the Companies Acts – particularly the Insolvency Act, which can hold directors personally liable to a company's creditors.

Public liability

This protects employers against legal liability for death or injury to a third party on their property. These events can occur through defects in your premises, negligent acts by your employees or from liabilities arising from the product that you market.

Professional liability

Solicitors, accountants and management and computer consultants are obvious examples. Anyone involved in giving professional advice should consider their possible liability arising from wrongful advice and negligence to their client.

Business premises, plant and equipment

These obviously need cover. There are, however, a number of ways of covering them. 'Reinstatement' provides for full replacement cost, while 'indemnity' meets only the current market value of your asset, which means taking depreciation off first. There are other things to consider too. Removal of debris, architect's fee, employees' effects and (potentially the most expensive of all) local authorities sometimes insist that replacement buildings must meet much higher standards than the ones they replace.

Stock

From raw materials through to finished goods, stock is as exposed as your buildings and plant in the event of fire or another hazard. Since 1982 theft from commercial property has exceeded £50 million per annum.

Consequential loss

Meeting the replacement costs of buildings, plant, equipment and stock will not compensate you for the loss of business and profit arising out of a fire or other disaster. Your overheads, employees' wages, etc, may have to continue during the period of interruption.

You may incur expenses such as getting sub-contracted work done. Insurance for consequential loss is intended to restore your business's finance to the position it was in before the interruption occurred.

Goods in transit

Until your goods reach your customer and he accepts them, they are still at your risk. You may need to protect yourself from loss or damage in transit.

Commercial vehicle policy

Although you may have adequate private-use cover for your present vehicle, this is unlikely to be satisfactory once you start to use the vehicle for business purposes. That and any other vehicles used in the business should be covered by a commercial-use policy.

Fidelity guarantee and other thefts

Once in business you can expect threats from within and without. A fidelity guarantee can be taken to protect you from fraud or dishonesty on the part of key employees. Normal theft cover can be taken to protect your business premises and its contents.

Key-man insurance

You may be required by anyone putting money into your business to have key-man insurance. This will provide a substantial cash cushion in the event of your death or incapacity. This is particularly important in small and new firms where one person is disproportionately vital in the early stages. Partners may also consider this a prudent protection.

Sources of further information

Write to **Witherby** at 32–36 Aylesbury Street, London EC1R 0ET, for its comprehensive list of insurance publications and related subjects, or to the **Chartered Insurance Institute Library** at 20 Aldermanbury, London EC2V 7HY, for its insurance reading list. The Chartered Insurance Institute (same address) also publishes a very comprehensive range of books in conjunction with its tuition service, which is separately available and recommended.

The Insurance Industry Training Council, 90 Kippington Road, Sevenoaks, Kent TN13 2LL, publishes a series of 'Brief Guides to Principles and Practice' of the most common forms of insurance. These provide useful introductions.

Association of British Insurers, 51 Gresham Street, London EC2V 7HQ (Tel: 0171 600 3333).

Association of Consulting Actuaries, PO Box 144, Norfolk House, Wellesley Road, Croydon, Surrey CR9 3EB (Tel: 0181 668 8040).

British Insurance and Investment Brokers' Association, 14 Bevis Marks, London EC3A 7NT (Tel: 0171 623 9043).

Chartered Insurance Institute, 20 Aldermanbury, London EC2V 7HY (Tel: 0171 606 3835).

Fire Protection Association, 140 Aldersgate Street, London EC1A 4HX (Tel: 0171 606 3757). This is the UK national fire safety organization. Backed by insurers, it provides advice and literature on fire safety and loss prevention.

Insurance Industry Training Council, 90 Kippington Road, Sevenoaks, Kent TN13 2LL (Tel: 01732 450801).

Society of Pension Consultants, Ludgate House, Ludgate Circus, London EC4A 2AB (Tel: 0171 353 1688).

■ NATIONAL INSURANCE, PAYE, TAX, VAT AND PENSIONS

This is one field where good professional advice at the outset will more than pay for itself. Although considerable publicity is given to the 'Black Economy', there are also many people paying more tax than they need. However, you will get the best of your professional adviser if you understand the basics yourself.

Taxation and Value Added Tax (VAT)

There are two areas where taxation affects the small business – VAT (although this is not strictly speaking a tax, in that it is run by the Customs and Excise, not the Inland Revenue) and either income tax (if you are a sole trader or partnership) or corporate tax (if your business is being run as a limited company).

Value Added Tax (VAT)

VAT is a complicated tax. Essentially, you must register if your taxable turnover, i.e. sales (not profit), exceeds £45,000 (as at 1994) in any twelve-month period. The general rule is that all supplies of goods and services are taxable at the standard rate (17.5%) unless they are specifically stated by the law to be zero-rated or exempt. In deciding whether your turnover exceeds the limit you have to include the zero-rated sales (things like most foods, books and children's clothing) as they are technically taxable – it's just that the rate of tax is 0%. You leave out exempt items. There are three free booklets issued by the Customs and Excise: a simple introductory booklet called 'Should you be registered for VAT?' and two more detailed booklets called 'General Guide' and 'Scope and Coverage'. If in doubt (and the language is not easy to understand) ask your accountant or the local branch of the Customs and Excise; after all, they would rather help you get it right in the first place than have to sort it out later when you have made a mess of it.

Each quarter, you will have to complete a return which shows your purchases and the VAT you paid on them, and your sales and the VAT you collected on them. The VAT paid and collected are offset against each other and the balance sent to the Customs and Excise. If you have paid more VAT in any quarter than you have collected you will get a refund. For this reason it sometimes pays to register even if you don't have to – if you are selling mostly zero-rated items for example; also being registered for VAT may make your business look more workmanlike and less amateurish to your potential customers.

Here's a simple example: You buy goods with a selling price of £100. On this you have to pay VAT at 17.5% so you actually write a cheque for £117.50. You then sell these goods at basic price of £150, on which you have to charge VAT, so you will actually receive £150 + £26.25 = £176.25. You have paid VAT of £17.50; you have collected VAT of £25.25 so you send the difference of £8.75 to the Customs and Excise. You should note that this has absolutely no effect on your profit margins. If VAT did not exist your profit would have been £150-£100 = £50. Allowing for VAT you have paid out £117.50 + £8.75 = £126.25 but you have received £176.25, so the difference is still £50. In other words, VAT has no effect on registered traders except to involve them in more detailed and tedious record-keeping than they might otherwise require. In fact, if you sell for cash, thereby collecting your VAT immediately, but buy on credit, you may derive a cash-flow advantage through not have to pay over till the end of the quarter.

Warning! The Customs and Excise started out as a body of men recruited to stop smuggling and other such criminal activities. To enable them to carry out their duties they have powers of search, entry etc which are sometimes said to be the envy of the fraud squad, so you would be well advised not to upset, deceive or otherwise get on the wrong side of them. Remember, ignorance of the law is no excuse. You may also need proof of your inputs and outputs; you should keep invoices etc for at least three years.

The basis of taxation

It must be emphasized that taxation is an extremely complicated area, and one that changes very rapidly, so this section can give only a very broad outline of the main considerations.

Business profits (whether sole traders/partnerships or limited companies) are taxed according to the rules of Schedule D Case I or II. (I relates to profits from a trade, II to income from a profession or vocation – there are no important differences.) Your taxable profit is computed by taking your profit according to the accounts and adjusting it. The adjustment is necessary because the normal rules for preparing a set of accounts are not the same as those in tax law, which means that your accounting profit will often bear very little relation to your taxable profit. An accountant's help is vital here if you do not wish to pay more tax than you legally must.

You are allowed to set an expense against your income if it is:

■ incurred wholly and exclusively for the purposes of trade;
■ properly charged against income (not, for example, purchase of a property lease, which is capital);
■ not specifically disallowed by statute (for example, you cannot set entertainment of customers against your tax, although it is a perfectly legitimate accounting expense).

It is beyond the scope of this book to detail all the expenses which are not allowable. The following points should, however, be noted carefully:

■ If you do some of your work at home you can normally set a proportion of your rent, rates, light, heat, and telephone bills etc against your business income.
■ If you are a married man and your wife cannot work outside the home (perhaps because there are young children) she can be an employee and be paid up to £3449 a year (1992/93) which will be deducted from your profits but will not be taxable on her. It is necessary to convince the Inspector of Taxes that she does actually do work for the business to this value, and that it is paid to her.

If you are a sole trader or partnership your tax is assessed effectively a year in arrears, except in the first two or three years, when the profits earned in the first year or 18 months determine the liability. For this reason it is vital that your taxable profits in this first period should be as low as legally possible (a loss is preferable) as this will affect your tax payable for three years. Note: this does not apply to limited companies.

Choose your accounting date carefully. Deciding when your business started trading is rarely a clear-cut decision. Often business expenses were incurred months and even years before the first cash came in. Left to their own devices, most people prepare their first accounts for a 12-month period, based either on the calendar or tax year. They mistakenly think that administrative tidiness or convenience are the only factors to consider. This is not so. There is an opportunity to influence the timing of cash flow in the business's favour. This sort of advantage can often mean the difference between success and failure in the first year. Look at the two cases below:

Business A decides on 31 March 1990 as the end of its first financial year. Half of the tax on the profits is due on 1 January 1991 and the balance on 1 July 1991, so tax is paid an average of 12 months after the profits have been made. (31 March 1990 to 1 January 1991 = 9 months; 31 March 1990 to 1 July 1991 = 15 months; (9 + 15) ÷ 2 = 12 months.)

Business B, however, decides to have 30 April 1990 as the end of its financial year, as this is after the end of the Inland Revenue's tax year, which ended on 5 April 1990, so tax is not due until 1992. Half is paid on 1 January 1992 and the balance on 1 July 1992. This means an average of 23 months elapses before tax is paid, giving an extra 11 months' interest-free credit.

This cash-flow benefit is created by the simple expedient of choosing the best first year end for a particular business. This example is something of an over-simplification and other factors will come into play. It will not, for example, apply to new limited companies who all have to pay tax a flat nine months after the year end, whatever that date is, but it does serve to illustrate the potential benefits to be gained by using professional advice.

The biggest difference in treatment between sole traders and limited companies as far as tax is concerned relates to the treatment of losses. If you are a sole trader (or partnership) your income from the business is just one of your sources of income, and is added to any other income you may have. Similarly, as it is your aggregate income which is important, any business losses can be set against your other income.

So if you earn £8,000 a year as a part-time teacher and have had PAYE deducted of (say) £1,800 and your business makes a loss of £4,000, then, assuming you have no other income, the two will be netted off and you will have an income of only £4,000 against which you will set your personal allowance, and so you will be able to reclaim some of the PAYE. The relief in the opening years is even more generous – if you make a tax loss in any of the first four years of the business, you may reclaim some or all of the tax you have paid in the preceding three years. Neither of these loss reliefs applies to limited companies; a limited company is a separate legal person, so the profits belong to the company, the company has its own tax liability, and most important, the losses are 'locked' into the company; you cannot set company losses against your own other income. This is the other side of the coin of limited liability – if you wish to take advantage of the protection provided for your personal assets by operating the business through a separate legal entity, you cannot also treat that entity's losses as your own and benefit from them.

If you are a limited company you will take remuneration as director's remuneration. As you are technically an employee of your company, tax should be paid under PAYE, and also National Insurance Class I contributions are due – both employer's (the company) and employee's (yourself). This can prove very much more expensive than the classes 2 and 4 paid by a sole trader.

Unless you take out the entire profits as director's remuneration, the balance will be taxed at corporation tax rate of 25% on profits up to £250,000 rising to 34% on profits up to £1.25 million. The rate of corporation tax is fixed annually by Parliament in the Finance Act for the proceeding financial year.

Expenditure on plant and machinery qualifies for writing down allowances on a 25% reducing balance basis. It may therefore make more sense in some circumstances to lease than to buy outright (the cost of leasing can be set against tax). Do not let the tax tail wag the commercial dog! In other words, you are in business primarily to make profits, not to avoid paying tax. Your primary concern should be with the business; do not make decisions purely to save tax.

Purely from a tax point of view, most businesses are better off starting as sole traders or partnerships for the cash-flow reasons mentioned earlier. It is also much simpler to start off as a sole trader or partnership and to incorporate when necessary than to try to do the procedure in reverse.

Despite the tax advantages to beginning as a sole trader, particularly at low levels of profit, you may feel that the protection of your private assets by operating as a limited company is well worth the tax disadvantages – much depends on your personal circumstances and your attitude to taking risks.

Finally, it should be realized that in revenue law the onus of disclosure and proof is on the taxpayer. In criminal law you are innocent until proved guilty, but for tax purposes you are liable until you prove otherwise. Moreover, it is your responsibility to notify the Inland Revenue of taxable income, not for the Inspector to ask (though he eventually will). Remember, ignorance of the law is no excuse.

The position on leased assets is somewhat different. You do not own the asset, the lessor does. He/she therefore, is entitled to claim the writing down allowances and this benefit to him/her is reflected in the lower rental figure that he/she can then charge. Whether outright purchase or leasing is beneficial will depend on the individual business and the anticipated profits. If finance is not available, however, there may be no choice but to lease. One point to note is that if there is an option to purchase the asset after a certain period, the Inland Revenue may not regard the transaction as a genuine leasing arrangement, but as a form of credit sale. Again, this is not necessarily a disadvantage; it all depends on the pattern of profits and professional advice should be sought.

Tax system changes

The whole basis of business taxation is under review, at the time of writing.

New tax systems for the self-employed

The Inland Revenue is calling for comments from the public following the recent publication of a consultative paper into the way Britain's 3.5m self-employed are taxed.

At the moment, self-employed people pay tax under Schedule D. As we all know, this is an unwieldy process involving a mass of paperwork, time and expense and usually requiring an accountant. Also, liability for the current year is assessed in the previous year's earnings, which in the present economic climate may work against small businesses.

The main proposal is a plan to replace the current system of paying tax in one year based on the previous year's profits. The first option suggested by the papers is that tax would be calculated on same-year profits and paid in instalments. The second, more complex, proposal suggests a move to an accounting period basis. This would involve larger businesses making their accounts up to their chosen date and then paying tax on the income for the whole accounting period, rather than the tax year. Tax could still be paid in instalments, but they would work on the accounting period year-end, not the end of the tax year. Smaller businesses would use the same systems but, instead of electing a year-end, would use the tax year as their accounting period.

Tax bills would be based on assessments provided by the tax payers, using simpler return forms. Reforms in the taxation system for the self-employed will come into place in 1995/6, and not all the proposals look like making life easier. For example, it is proposed that each partner in a partnership firm will have to make a return. In a partnership of 50, this would mean 50 returns instead of one – making more rather than less work.

A Simpler System for the Self-Employed costs £4 including postage and is available from the Inland Revenue, Schedule D Review, Room 3, New Wing, Somerset House, London WC2R 1LB.

New tax systems for companies

From 1992, the country's 900,000-plus companies came under a new and revolutionary tax system called Pay and File.

Under Pay and File, a company will be expected to make and pay its own estimate of its corporation tax liability by the normal due date, nine months after the end of the accounting period. The liability will arise automatically and the company will not have the scope to defer settlement, as now. There will be no need to wait for the inspector's assessment, nor will the liability have to be agreed with him or her.

The Pay and File system will bring plenty of anguish in the early years. People have never had to take absolute decisions on the extent of their tax liabilities. The traditional approach is dilatory and people have not had to comply with strict deadlines. At the moment, providing you pay a certain amount of tax on the due date, you can carry on for years before finally agreeing liability.

Pay As You Earn (PAYE)

Employers are required to deduct income tax from the pay and other emoluments of employees. This not only applies to wages and salaries but also to certain benefits in kind.

General instructions on the operation of PAYE are sent to employers before the start of each tax year. Comprehensive information is contained in explanatory booklets available from any tax office. (Selected examples are listed at the end of this section.) The amount of tax to be deducted will be determined by the employee's tax code applied to the appropriate tax tables which are supplied by the Inland Revenue.

For PAYE purposes 'pay' includes salaries, wages, overtime payments, bonuses, fees, commission, and pensions. Holiday pay, payment during sickness or other absence from work and various payments in kind are also classified as 'pay' for these purposes. Although there may be a few exceptions, any payment made or benefit provided to an employee can normally be considered as taxable.

As an employer you are accountable to the Inland Revenue for the PAYE tax on the wages and salaries of your employees. Tax deducted from employees' earnings is accounted for monthly – up to the 5th of each month – and must be remitted to the Collector of Taxes within 14 days of that date. If you fail to meet this requirement it will be you who is considered liable.

National Insurance contributions

The National Insurance contributions you are required to pay will depend upon the legal form of your business. A sole trader or partner is classified as self-employed and pays contributions in class 2, which is a weekly sum – currently £5.35 per week – and in class 4 based on annual profits.

You can pay your class 2 contributions by direct debit through your bank or National Giro account. Leaflet NI 41 provides specific information on contributions and can be obtained from the local office of the Department of Social Security (DSS).

It may be possible to arrange for a deferment of payment of contributions until your exact liability is known. You should enquire about this at your DSS office.

A company director pays contributions as an employee and the company pays as an employer. You can therefore end up paying considerably more than if you had chosen to operate as a sole trader or partnership.

Employers must make NI contributions for each employee according to salary level and whether or not they have contracted out of the state scheme.

Pensions

Once you are working for yourself, you will have to make your own pension provision (and perhaps provision for those working for you). Fortunately for people in profitable self-employment, there are now a large number of highly tax-efficient pension schemes. By selecting the right scheme you can get tax relief at your highest income tax rate, and so get the Inland Revenue to contribute up to 40% of your pension.

Currently you can contribute between 17½ % and 40% of your earnings into an approved pension scheme. It is also possible, under certain circumstances, to use the funds in a self-administered pension fund to finance investments in your own business.

Sources of further information

National Association of Pension Funds, 12/18 Grosvenor Gardens, London SW1W 6DH (Tel: 0171 730 0585).
Society of Pension Consultants, Ludgate House, Ludgate Circus, London EC4A 2AB (Tel: 0171 353 1688).

Tax and National Insurance
A number of very useful pamphlets, etc are available free of charge from the Inland Revenue and the DSS. Ask for the New Employers Starter Pack P4. Also useful are:

IR28 – *Starting in Business*
IR57 – *Thinking of Working for Yourself?*
IR53 – *Thinking of Taking Someone On?*
IR34 – *PAYE*
IR71 – *PAYE Inspection of Employers' Records*
IR69 – *Expenses Forms P11D*
IR56/IR39 – *Employed or Self-Employed*
IR480 – *Notes on Expenses, Payments and Benefits for Directors and Certain Employees*
N135 – *Directors' Earnings*
N1274 – *Directors' National Insurance*

Value Added Tax
There are a large number of free publications available from the VAT office, for example:

Should I Be Registered for VAT?
The VAT Guide
VAT Publications – This sets out a list of particular pamphlets on VAT which may be of relevance to you in your business.

Board of Inland Revenue, Press Office, Somerset House, Strand, London WC2R 1LB.
Institute of Chartered Accountants in England and Wales, PO Box 433, Chartered Accountants Hall, Moorgate Place, London EC2P 2BJ (Tel: 0171 628 7070).

The major accountancy firms, the clearing banks and some newspapers provide annual guides to tax, VAT, National Insurance and pensions.

■ DATA PROTECTION

The Data Protection Act was passed in 1984 and grew out of public concern about personal privacy in the face of rapidly developing computer technology. However, even at the time it was passed it was virtually inconceivable that computers would permeate every sector of business and society to the extent to which they now have.

The Act was also passed to enable the United Kingdom to ratify the Council of Europe Convention on Data Protection, allowing data to flow freely between the United Kingdom and other European countries with similar laws, preventing damage to the economy and international trade which might otherwise have occurred.

The maximum penalty for non-registration is £5,000 plus costs in the Magistrates' Court and an unlimited fine in the Higher Courts.

What does the Act cover?

The Act is concerned with 'personal data' which is 'automatically processed'.

- **Personal data** is information about living, identifiable individuals. This need not be particularly sensitive information and can be as little as a name and address.
- **Automatically processed** means, broadly speaking, information which is processed by computer. It does not cover information which is held and processed manually, i.e. in ordinary paper files.

The Act works in two ways – giving individuals (data subjects) certain rights while requiring those who record and use personal information on computer (data users) to be open about their use of that information and to follow sound and proper practices (the Data Protection principles).

- **Data users** are those who control the contents and use of a collection of personal data. This can be any type of company or organization, large or small, within the public or private sector. A data user can also be a sole trader, partnership, or an individual. A data user need not necessarily own a computer.
- **Data subjects** are the individuals to whom the personal data relate.

Who needs to register?

Do I need to register? This is the question which interests small-business people most! The answer is fairly straightforward: if you hold personal information about living individuals on computer or have such information processed on computer by others (for example, by a computer bureau or your accountant), yes – you probably do need to register under the Data Protection Act.

Exemptions from registration

There are a number of exemptions from registration under the requirements of the Act for individuals and organizations which make only very limited use of personal data.

There is no procedure for officially claiming an exemption and data users are not obliged to notify the Registrar that they are relying on one. However, you should be aware that you may need to defend your decision to rely on an exemption in the criminal or civil courts. You may be surprised to see that the exemptions look much the same as some of the purposes on the registration application form. This is because exemptions can easily be lost if you use information in many of the normal ways you would want to in running a business, for instance, using pay and pensions records for other personnel purposes.

Often data users find it easier to proceed as though an exemption were not available rather than to continually monitor their compliance with its terms. Bear in mind also that although an exemption may cover you now, your circumstances may change later. It is also important to realize that two exemptions cannot be claimed at the same time for the same data. In other words, it is often safer to register.

The payroll, pensions and accounts exemption

The payroll and pensions purpose involves the use of personal data for the calculation and payment of wages and pensions. The accounts purpose consists of the keeping of accounts, records of purchases, sales and other transactions in the course of a data user's normal business activities for the purpose of ensuring that the requisite payments are made. These data may also be used for the purpose of making financial forecasts. In order to rely upon the exemption personal data must be held only for these purposes, and personal data must only be disclosed in very limited circumstances, including:

- for the purpose of audit;
- at the request of the individual to whom the personal data relates;
- when it is required by a court of law, the prevention of crime or national security;
- to prevent injury or damage to health of any person.

This exemption can easily be lost if, for instance:

- payment records include records of time keeping or trade union membership, or
- accounts records are used for marketing, or checking the credit-worthiness of customers, or
- accounts records are passed to debt collecting agencies – not simply to enable the agency to collect debts but also so that it can be used to build up credit reference information.

The mailing list exemption

Personal data held only for distributing, or recording the distribution of, articles and information to individuals fall within the scope of this exemption. However, in the business world this exemption is very difficult to apply. Personal data must only be used for the purpose of mailings and the personal data that may be held are restricted to names and addresses and any other information needed for making the distribution such as fax numbers. Moreover, all the individuals must be asked if they object to personal data being held about them.

Text preparation

Although not technically an exemption, small businesses may wish to note that they do not become data users merely by using the editing facilities provided by a simple word processor for the sole purpose of producing a letter, report or other document, even though that document, when printed, may contain information about a living individual. Further information on this subject is available in the *Registrar's Guideline 2: The Definitions*.

Further information

As the above information gives only a general idea of the scope of the exemptions, you are strongly advised, if you wish to rely upon one or more exemptions, to consult a copy of the Registrar's *Guideline 6: The Exemptions* which gives a full explanation of all the exemptions from registration and other provisions of the Act.

How to register

The application forms

There are two different forms available for registration: the full (DPR1) registration form, and a special shortened registration form (DPR4) which provides a shorter and simpler means of registration and covers the four main purposes for which most small businesses need to register (personnel/employee administration; marketing and selling; purchase/supplier administration; customer/client administration).

Should you need to register any further purposes, you may do so on the Part B form. Notes are included in the DPR4 form but if you require further explanation of the codes listed under various sections of the Part B form, you should telephone the enquiries number (Tel: 01625 535777, 9 a.m. to 5 p.m.) and ask to be sent a copy of the booklet 'Notes to help you apply for registration on Form DPR1'.

Registration application forms are generally only available from the Registrar's office (though your trade association, solicitor or accountant may possibly keep supplies).

The fee

All applications for registration must be accompanied by the standard fee (£75 in April 1993) – which covers a three-year period. As registration applications cannot be accepted without the correct fee, you are advised to telephone the Registrar's enquiries number, above, to check the current fee amount before you submit your application.

What do I register?

Before you can complete your registration application form you will need to do two things:

- Carefully read the notes which accompany the form so that you fully understand exactly what information is required of you.

- Carry out an audit of all your planned and present computing activities so that you are fully aware of all the categories of data, sources of information and uses and disclosures of data which your register entry will need to cover.

Once you've done all this you'll need to set aside an hour or so to actually complete the forms and check that the information you've given covers everything that you do. (On average, the forms take about 40 minutes to complete.) Remember, at this stage you're not completely on your own. If, having read the notes and considered your computing activities you're still unsure of how you should register some or all of the information, you can ring the enquiry line, given above, where they'll be happy to advise you.

Similarly, you may wish to consider contacting your trade association (if you have one) to see if they issue any guidance on data protection registration or any other information on complying with the Act.

Computer bureaux

It is important to realize that you don't necessarily need to own a computer to be liable for registration. The qualifying factor is who controls a collection of data. If the answer is you then you will need to register as a data user even if the data is actually processed on someone else's computer – for example, a computer owned by your accountant or a computer bureau.

If, however, you process data for others on your computer, you may need to register as a data user and computer bureau, or, if you do not control the content of any of the data, as a computer bureau only. In either case, registration still costs the same amount and is made on the same forms as application for registration as a data user.

What if I don't register?

If you've considered your computing activities and have decided that you don't need to register you will have to ensure that your computing activities do not transgress the exemption or exemptions you are claiming. Two exemptions cannot be claimed at the same time for the same data. If, however, you now know you should be registered, you should put in your application without delay. Failure to register is a criminal offence for which the Registrar does not hesitate to prosecute. Fines of up to £5,000 plus costs may be imposed in the Magistrates' Courts, or unlimited fines in the higher courts.

What happens next?

Some weeks after you've submitted your registration application form and fee, you should receive confirmation of your acceptance on to the register. At this time you'll also be sent a copy of the information pack 'Now You're Registered – A guide to your obligations under the Data Protection Act'.

This gives you an outline of your continuing obligations under the Act, covering:

- the eight data protection principles
- subject access requests
- renewals, removals and alterations to your register entry
- general information about good practice

It also tells you how to obtain further information on all aspects of data protection should you require it.

Remember:

- The size of your business is immaterial.
- The nature of your business is unimportant.
- The amount of personal data you hold is irrelevant.
- The sensitivity of the data is immaterial.
- You needn't even own a computer!

If you hold and process personal data on computer, you probably need to register under the Data Protection Act.

The contact details for obtaining the pack, or any other information or guidance about the Data Protection Act, is:

Information Services Dept, Data Protection Registrar, Wycliffe House, Water Lane, Wilmslow, Cheshire SK9 5AF (Tel: 01625 535777; Fax: 01625 524510).

■ BUSINESS FAILURE

Hundreds of thousands of businesses close down each year. Most do so because the proprietor(s) wishes to retire, has sold up, or moved on to do something else.

Several tens of thousands of small businesses are forced to close down each year for financial reasons. The issues that surround business failure are as follows:

- bankruptcy – if you are a sole trader or partnership;
- receivership – for limited companies;
- winding up and liquidation – for limited companies;
- administration – for limited companies;
- wrongful trading, fraudulent trading and the disqualification of directors – for limited companies;
- sheltering personal assets.

Bankruptcy

Bankruptcy is a way of dealing with your financial affairs if you cannot pay your debts. While it is not a criminal offence to get into debt, becoming a bankrupt has serious implications. You can be made bankrupt if you own £750 or more and fail to pay it within three weeks of receipt of a statutory demand; or if you fail to satisfy a judgement debt.

Under these circumstances a creditor can apply to the court for an order of bankruptcy, or the debtor can apply himself. If the debtor has paid the bill(s) in question, or the court feels he has made a reasonable offer to his creditors which has been unreasonably refused, then a bankruptcy order will not be made.

As soon as the bankruptcy order is made, the debtor becomes an undischarged bankrupt. With the exception of the tools of the bankrupt's trade, clothing, bedding, and household equipment – all of a basic nature – all of the bankrupt's personal and business assets come under the control of the official receiver, who becomes his trustee in bankruptcy.

A bankrupt cannot act as a director or be involved in the management of a company; be an MP, counsellor or JP; obtain credit of more than £250 without revealing he is an undischarged bankrupt; engage directly or indirectly in any business other than in the name he was adjudged bankrupt without disclosing his bankruptcy. Any money a bankrupt earns belongs to his trustee in bankruptcy, less anything the trustee feels is necessary to maintain or motivate him. The trustee uses all the bankrupt's assets to pay off, first, the secured creditors (the bank), then the preferential creditors (PAYE, VAT, National Insurance and wages) and then everyone else.

On the bright side, bankruptcy frees the debtor from financial worry and allows him to make a fresh start. And unless the bankrupt makes a habit of this offence the stigma is short-lived. If the debts are less than £20,000 the bankrupt is automatically discharged after two years. In all other cases a bankrupt will be discharged after three years.

These conditions only apply to people who have not been bankrupted before in the last 15 years. These will have to wait five years or longer for their discharge.

Voluntary Arrangements

These were brought into being by the Insolvency Act 1986. Until then it was not possible for a debtor to make a legally binding compromise with all his creditors. Any single creditor could scupper the plan.

Now a debtor can make a proposal to his creditors to pay all or part of the debts over a period of time. The mechanics are simple. The debtor applies to the court for an interim order stating that he intends to make a proposal naming a qualified insolvency practitioner who will be advising him. The position is then frozen, preventing bankruptcy proceedings until the insolvency practitioner reports back to the court.

A creditors' meeting will be called notifying all creditors and if the proposal is approved by more than 75% by value of the creditors' meeting, it will be binding on all creditors.

This course of action avoids all the less attractive features of bankruptcy – but it will only work if you have something credible to offer your creditors.

Receivership

This occurs when a borrower (a company) fails to meet its obligations to a mortgagee. The most usual scenario is where a company gives a charge over assets (such as property or equipment) to its bankers. This in turn allows the banker to advance funds to the company.

In these circumstances, if the company fails to meet its obligations to its bankers, for example by not repaying money when due, then the bank can appoint a receiver. The receiver has wide powers to step in and run the business or sell off its assets for the benefit of the person who appointed him. The existing director's authority will be suspended and existing contracts with the company only have to be carried out by the receiver if he believes it worthwhile to do so.

Money generated by the receiver first goes to paying the costs of selling assets (auctioneers' fees), then to paying the receiver's own fees. Only then will the person appointing the receiver get his debt paid. Once that too has been discharged, others further down the pecking order, such as preferential debts (see earlier), may get paid.

Winding up and liquidation

This is to limited companies what bankruptcy is to sole traders and partnerships. A limited company is considered to be unable to pay its debts if a creditor leaves a demand for a debt of £750 or more, in a certain prescribed form at its registered office and that debt is not paid within 21 days. Once this position is reached an application can be made for the company to be wound up. The company itself can ask to be wound up as can any creditor, or in some circumstances various government officials can so ask.

Before a winding up order is made the court appoints a provisional liquidator – always called 'the official receiver'. Once the winding up order is made, all court proceedings against the company are stopped; all employees' contracts are terminated and its directors are dismissed.

The liquidator's job is to get in the company's assets and pay off the creditors. The order of payment is as shown under receivership.

Administration

The Insolvency Act 1986 introduced legislation to help companies in serious financial difficulties to trade their way back to financial health. The thinking here is similar to that behind that of Voluntary Arrangements, although Administration usually involves much more substantial sums.

While in Administration the company is protected from its creditors while an approved rescue plan is implemented. Administration orders will only be made where the court is satisfied that the company has cash available from either shareholders or lenders to finance the rescue plan. It follows that not many Administrations are granted – and not many are successful.

Wrongful trading

Wrongful trading can apply if, after a company goes into insolvent liquidation, the liquidator believes that the directors (or those acting as such) ought to have concluded earlier that the company had no realistic chance of survival. In these circumstances the courts can remove the shelter of limited liabilities and make directors personally liable for the company's debts.

Fraudulent trading

This is rather more serious than wrongful trading. Here the proposition is that the director(s) were knowingly party to fraud on their creditors. The full shelter of Limited Liability can be removed in these circumstances.

Disqualification of directors

Former directors of insolvent companies can be banned from holding office for periods up to 15 years. Fraud, fraudulent trading, wrongful trading or a failure to comply with company law, for example filing your annual accounts, may result in disqualification.

Breaches of a disqualification order can lead to imprisonment and/or fines. Also you can be made personally liable for the debts and liabilities of any company in which you are involved. Neither can you issue your orders through others, having them act as a director in your place. This will leave them personally liable themselves.

Sheltering personal assets

Only by trading through a limited company, giving no personal guarantees, and having never fallen foul of the fraudulent or wrongful trading laws, can you be confident your personal assets are safe.

If you are a sole trader, a partner or have given personal guarantees to support a limited company, then your personal assets are at some risk.

It is possible, if you gave your assets away five years before going bankrupt, to save them from your creditors. This calls for extraordinary foresight – and even then things can go wrong.

Firstly the person you 'give' the assets to could make off with them. After all, over a third of marriages end in divorce.

Secondly anyone making a claim against you can ask the court to set aside any gift however long ago it was made, if they can prove it was your intention at the time to put those assets beyond their reach.

Clearly you can take steps to protect personal assets – but it is not a simple matter.

Sources of further information

The Bankruptcy Association of Great Britain and Ireland, 4 Johnson Close,

Abraham Heights, Lancaster LA1 5EU (Tel: 01524 64305; Fax: 01524 844001). Founded in 1983 and run by John McQueen, the Society has 2,500 members – mostly bankrupts or near bankrupts. They provide assistance, advice and publications. Particularly useful is *Bankruptcy: Reality and the Law*.

■ LITIGATION

It is a sad fact of business life that you will be unlikely to survive many years in business without having cause to consider taking legal action against someone.

Unsurprisingly, getting customers to pay up is the foremost legal issue for many small firms. There are three important measures you can take to make sure you get paid after all your hard work.

Firstly do get the conditions under which you propose to do business put on your invoices, or at any rate sent to your clients (see earlier in this section for Standard Terms of Business).

Secondly send bills out promptly and follow up with a statement as soon as payment is due. So if your terms are net monthly and your bill goes out on 1 May, send a statement on 1 June. Follow this up with a polite phone call later that week.

It really pays to be firm from the outset and so get your customers into good habits.

Finally consider legal action.

Except for the most simple of cases you will always need legal advice. In some cases you might consider doing it yourself.

Whichever route you take to recover money owed or to remedy a wrong, it is important to establish whether or not those you are about to sue have the means to pay up. If your debtor is adept at moving around or is penniless there is little a court can do to help, even if you do get judgement in your favour.

The main steps in DIY litigation are as follows:

- **The Letter Before Action** should state clearly how much is due, since what date and that you are giving the defendant 14 days within which to settle the debt, otherwise you will start proceedings in the County Court for its recovery. This should be sent by recorded delivery.

- **Particulars of Claim** sets out the particulars of your claim; including your name and address and also the defendant's; a brief statement of the circumstances and the amount involved; any interest you are seeking on the money owed.

- **Lodging your Action.** Sadly, as the innocent party, you are the one put to maximum inconvenience. You cannot use the county court most convenient to you. You have to sue either where your defendant carries on his business or in the area where the cause of the action arose. In any event the defendant has the right to have the case transferred to his local county court.

- **Starting Off.** The particulars of your claim can now be sent or taken to the appropriate county court. You will need form N201, 'Request for Default Summons' – available free from the county court; two copies of the particulars of your claim; the court fee in cash or crossed postal orders (cheques are not accepted); and an envelope addressed to yourself.

■ **The Next Step.** One of three things can now happen. If, by 14 days after the summons was served, the defendant has done nothing, you are entitled to ask the court for a 'judgement in default' against them. To do this you send form N30, available free from the county court. The court will then issue judgement in your favour. Don't get too excited yet as you still have to 'enforce' it.

Alternatively the defendant could 'admit the claim' but seek time to pay. He must then answer questions as to his financial circumstances and make you an offer. The court will advise you of the offer and you have 14 days to accept. If you do not accept the terms, the court will fix a date for the registrar to decide how the debt is to be paid. The registrar will err on the side of being generous to the defendant in the hope that he will pay up without further need for court action.

Finally the defendant can deny the claim and offer a defence and counter-claim.

The case is the next stage and this itself is split into two parts. The pre-trial review is an informal meeting at court to sort out the facts of the case. You should take everything with you – paperwork, invoices etc – to prove your case. If the defendant does not turn up you can apply for a judgement in default then and there, and you may get it on the spot.

If the defendant does appear the registrar will check both plaintiff's and defendant's papers, and if he feels more information is needed he can order it to be produced. Then comes the trial. A date is set and you and your witnesses give your evidence first, in open court. The defendant can cross- examine you and your witnesses. Then the roles are reversed. Both yourself and the defendant can make a closing speech. The judge will then give judgement. If the claim is for over £500 the winner can claim for costs.

Small claims

If this all sounds too stressful, and your claim is for under £1,000, there is a much less threatening procedure for recovering small claims in the county court.

The proceedings start much as set out above. If both you and your defendant agree, an arbitrator can make a decision based on the written submissions alone. If you do wish to appear in person, the hearing is informal, in private and seated around a table.

The arbitrator will run the hearing as he thinks convenient, and will usually make a decision on the spot – unless he feels the need to consult an expert.

Four excellent leaflets in genuine plain English cover the whole small claims procedure:

■ What is a small claim?

- How do I make a small claim in the county court?
- No reply to my summons – what should I do?
- The defendant admits my claim – what must I do?

All available from any county court.

Enforcing the judgement

Whichever route you take to court, getting judgement in your favour is only half the battle. The other half is getting paid.

If the debtor does not comply with the court order you have three major options as a business. You can send in the bailiff – form N4(1) is the procedure here. Bailiffs cannot break into domestic premises and can only seize property identified as belonging to the debtor. This has obvious limitations.

You can get a charging order against any land, property or investments that a debtor may have. You need to swear an affidavit – and a solicitor is really needed to draft this. Still, if there are any assets worth pursuing, you should eventually get paid.

Where the person you are pursuing is a private individual in employment, it could be possible to get an attachment of earnings. In this way the debt is paid by regular deductions from salary or wages.

Further information

The Institute of Credit Management, The Water Mill, Station Road, South Luffenham, Oakham, Leicestershire LE15 8NB (Tel: 01780 721888).

8 | *Training for small business*

There are now many opportunities for education and training, at every level, in the business and management field. No formal academic qualifications are required for most of the courses and costs are generally modest. In certain cases, participants may be eligible for grants or subsidized training.

The bulk of the activities are concentrated in universities and colleges throughout the whole of the UK. However, there are a growing number of opportunities for the less mobile to take up some form of home study in the business field in general, and small-business opportunities in particular. There is now some reliable evidence to show that people attending small courses can significantly improve their chances of success.

■ COURSES AT UNIVERSITIES, COLLEGES AND OTHER INSTITUTIONS

Our survey has divided the courses on offer into the following main categories.

Start-up courses

For people considering starting up a business. These are usually of short duration, charging a modest fee. They concentrate on giving an introduction on how to start your own business. As well as providing lectures, the courses give an opportunity for those who have recently started up in business to talk about their experiences.

The demand for these courses is high. Various estimates suggest that upwards of 100,000 people attended such courses during 1993/94. This certainly forms the most cost-effective method of finding out very quickly a lot about what is going on in the 'new and small business world'. These courses are frequently run at weekends and sometimes on evenings during the week.

Topic courses

These are usually run over a few days or weeks, for those already in business. They cover topics such as financial management, marketing, book-keeping, exporting, computers, employing people and strategy/business growth. Also, after the budget, some colleges hold tax update courses.

Business growth

These programmes are aimed at people who already have their business up and running and are actively seeking ways to expand profitably. The Cranfield Business Growth Programme, launched in 1988, is one of the pioneers in this sector. Some 200 entrepreneurs have been through their programme and many have achieved substantial growth. One company going through the 1990 programme has grown from £8 million turnover to £50 million in 1994 and plans to reach £250 million by the year 2000. It will have gone public before that date.

Business growth programmes usually start with a comprehensive review of company strategy, analysing strengths and weaknesses; go on to review the business opportunities and threats ahead; set goals, objectives and business strategy; and culminate in business and action plans to show how growth will be achieved. Classroom sessions focus on real issues in participants' companies, and are often led by successful entrepreneurs with exciting stories to tell. As well as classroom sessions, each participant will have a personal counsellor, whose task is to help that individual prepare their plans.

Often participants are themselves the main benefit – there being so few forums where owner–managers can debate and discuss their ideas with a peer group whose views they can fully respect.

Where to find a course

The results of our 1994 survey of the small-business education provisions are set out below. In the case of topic courses the legend corresponds to the initials of the subject covered. So financial management is (FM), marketing is (M), bookkeeping is (B), exporting is (E), computers is (C), employing people is (P), strategy/business growth is (S). We have also identified where advice and consultancy are available, and research activities are under way.

Business Club is the name often given to the regular meetings of smallbusiness people for discussions or seminars. These are often hosted by colleges and we have shown those that do. Finally, we have listed whether or not the institution has a full-time commitment to the small-business field. Very often the task of teaching in this field is divided up among people with other important and time-consuming commitments.

Key to columns
1 Start-up courses
2 Topic courses
3 Business growth
4 Consultancy & advisory
   services
5 Research activity
6 Business Club
7 Special small-business unit

Key to initials
FM = Financial management
M = Marketing
B   = Book-keeping
E   = Exporting
C   = Computers
P   = Employing people/
      management
S   = Strategy

	1	2	3	4	5	6	7
England							
Aston Business School, Management Development Programme, Aston University, Aston Triangle, Birmingham B4 7ET Tel: 0121 359 3011; Fax: 0121 333 5774. Contact: Dr Andrea Taylor	–	S M FM P	–	∎	∎	–	–
Bedford College, Cauldwell Street, Bedford MK42 9AH Tel: 01234 345151; Fax: 01234 342674. Contact: C Kenyon	–	FM M B C P	–	–	–	–	–
Birmingham University, Department of Commerce, Ashley Building, Birmingham B15 2TT Tel: 0121 414 6692; Fax: 0121 414 6707. Contact: N J Kavanagh	∎	–	–	–	–	–	–
Bolton Institute, Bolton Business School, Deane Road, Bolton BL3 5AB Tel: 01204 28851; Fax: 01204 399074. Contact: Alan Turner	∎	FM M C P S	∎	∎	∎	∎	∎

	1	2	3	4	5	6	7
University of Bradford, Management Centre, Emm Lane, Bradford BD9 4JL Tel: 01274 384336; Fax: 01274 546866. Contact: Dr S Hogarth-Scott	■	FM M P S	■	–	■	–	■
University of Bristol, Business Development Centre, Wills Memorial Building, Queens Road, Bristol BS7 1HR Tel: 0117 9303614; Fax: 0117 9254975. Contact: Claude Lambshead	–	M P S	■	■	■	–	■
Broxtowe College, School of Business Management and Tourism, High Road, Chilwell, Nottingham NG9 4AH Tel: 00115 9228161; Fax: 00115 9257658. Contact: Nick Hammond	■	FM M B C P	■	■	■	–	–
Brunel University, The Brunel Management Programme, Uxbridge, Middlesex UB8 3PH Tel: 01895 256461; Fax: 01895 811737. Contact: Irene Williams	–	P S	–	–	–	–	–
Bucks College Business School, Newland Park, Chalfont St Giles, Bucks HP8 4AD Tel: 01494 874441; Fax: 01494 874230. Contact: S Halliday	■	–	–	–	■	–	–
Business Creation Interface Ltd, Stockwell Chapel, East Stockwell St, Colchester, Essex CO1 1ST Tel: 01206 561700; Fax: 01206 46338. Contact: Stuart Beckwith	■	FM M B P S	■	■	■	■	■

	1	2	3	4	5	6	7
Business Development Centre, Stafford Park 4, Telford, TF3 3BA Tel: 01952 290751; Fax: 01952 290752. Contact: David Chiva	■	–		–	–	–	–
Business Enterprise Consultants, Fillebrook House, 24 Fillebrook Ave, Enfield, Middlesex EN1 3BB Tel: 0181 363 4011; Fax: 0181 366 0797. Contact: B Englebright	■	FM M B E C P S	■	■	■	■	■
Centre for Business Research, University of Cambridge, Department of Applied Economics, Sidgwick Avenue, Cambridge CB3 9DE Tel: 01223 335249; Fax: 01223 335768. Contact: Dr David Keeble	–	–		–	–	■	–	■
University of Central England, Business School, Management and Business Development Centre, Perry Barr, Birmingham B42 2SU Tel: 0121 331 5202; Fax: 0121 331 6366. Contact: Dr Upkar Pardesi	■	FM M E P S	■	■	■	–	■
City University, Courses for Adults, Northampton Square, London EC1V 0HB Tel: 0171 477 8268; Fax: 0171 477 8256. Contact: Search Line	■	–		–	–	–	–	–

	1	2	3	4	5	6	7
Coombe Cliff Adult Education Centre Enterprise Training Unit, Coombe Road, Croydon, Surrey CRO 5SP Tel: 0181 688 3113; Fax: 0181 667 0078. Contact: Beryl Osborne	■	FM M E P S	–	–	–	–	–
Cornwall College, Trevendon House Management Centre, Pool, Redruth, Cornwall TR15 3RD Tel: 01209 612828; Fax: 01209 612828. Contact: David Paveling	–	FM M C P S	■	■	■	■	■
Cranfield University, School of Management, Cranfield, Beds MK43 0AL Tel: 01234 751122; Fax: 01234 751806. Contact: Colin Barrow	–	FM M B E C P S	■	■	■	■	■
De Montford University, Business Solutions, Leicester Business School, The Gateway, Leicester LE1 9BH Tel: 0116 2577222; Fax: 0116 2577264. Contact: D M Williams	■	FM M E C P	■	■	■	■	–
University of Derby, School of Management, Kedleston Road, Derby DE3 1GB Tel: 01332 622211; Fax: 01332 385991. Contact: Ted Knight	■	FM M E P S	–	■	■	–	–
Durham University Business School, Mill Hill Lane, Durham DH1 3LB Tel: 0191 3742227; Fax: 0191 3744748. Contact: Ruth Ratcliffe	■	FM M E C P S	■	■	■	–	■

	1	2	3	4	5	6	7
University of East London, Duncan House, High Street, Stratford, London E15 2JB Tel: 0181 590 7722; Fax: 0181 534 4168. Contact: Ivan Rush	–	FM M B P	–	–	–	–	–
East Surrey College, Redhill Business School, Claremont Road, Gatton Point, Redhill, Surrey RH1 2JX Tel: 01737 770348; Fax: 01737 768641. Contact: Ian Elliott	■	M B C P	■	■	–	■	–
The Enterprise Partnership Ltd, 15 Park House, 140 Battersea Park Road, London SW11 4NB Tel: 0171 627 4991; Fax: 0171 978 1208. Contact: Sarah Healy	–	FM M E P S	–	–	–	–	–
The Essex Business Centre, Chelmer Court, Church Street, Chelmsford, Essex CM1 1NH Tel: 01245 283030; Fax: 01245 492486. Contact: David Wood	■	FM M B E C P S	■	■	–	■	■
University of Exeter, Continuing Education and Training, Cotley, Streatham Rise, Exeter EX4 4PE Tel: 01392 411906. Contact: Clive Nicholas	■	FM M B E C P S	■	■	■	■	■
GEC Management College, Rugby Road, Dunchurch, Rugby, Warwickshire CV22 6QW Tel: 01788 810656; Fax: 01788 522657. Contact: John Amos	–	FM M E P	–	■	–	–	–

	1	2	3	4	5	6	7
Gloucestershire Centre for Management, Faculty of Business and Social Studies, Fullwood Park, Suffolk Square, Cheltenham, Glos GL50 2EB Tel: 01242 543586; Fax: 01242 543568. Contact: June Simms	–	FM M C P S	■	■	■	■	–
University of Greenwich, Wellington Street, Woolwich, London SE18 6PF Tel: 0181 316 8590; Fax: 0181 316 8145. Contact: Course Enquiry Unit	–	FM M B E C P S	–	–	–	–	–
Hammersmith and West London College, Giddon Road, Barons Court, London W14 9BL Tel: 0181 563 0063. Contact: Admissions Office	–	FM M B E C P S	–	–	–	–	–
Institute of Management, Management House, Cottingham Road, Corby, Northants NN17 1TT Tel: 01536 204222; Fax: 01536 201651. Contact: Management Information Centre	■	M P S	–	■	–	–	–
The Isle of Wight College, Newport, Isle of Wight PO30 5TA Tel: 01983 526631; Fax: 01983 521707. Contact: John Peck	■	FM B C P	–	■	–	–	■
Kensington College of Business, 52a Waltham Grove, Fulham, London SW6 1QR Tel: 0171 381 6360; Fax: 0171 386 9650. Contact: Registrar	–	FM M B P	–	–	–	–	–

	1	2	3	4	5	6	7
Kidderminster College, Management Development Centre, Hoo Road, Kidderminster, Worcs DY10 1LX Tel: 01562 820811; Fax: 01562 748504. Contact: Roy Bishop	■	FM M B C P	–	–	–	–	–
Kingston University, Small Business Research Centre, Kingston Hill, Surrey KT2 7LB Tel: 0181 547 7218; Fax: 0181 547 7029. Contact: Professor James Curran	■	FM P S	–	–	■	–	■
Knowsley Community College, Rupert Road, Huyton, Merseyside L36 9TD Tel: 0151 443 5400; Fax: 0151 443 4319. Contact: J Fisher	■	FM M B E C P	–	■	–	■	–
Lambeth Business Training Centre, Knights Hill, West Norwood, London SE27 0TX Tel: 0171 501 5750. Contact: Admissions Office	–	FM M B E C P S	–	–	–	–	–
Lancaster University, CETAD, Charlotte Mason College, Ambleside, Cumbria LA22 9BB Tel: 015394 30253; Fax: 015394 30305. Contact: Sue Nutter	–	P S M	–	–	–	–	–
Leeds Metropolitan University, PO Box 152, Leeds LS3 1TL Tel: 0113 2832600; Fax: 0113 2833227. Contact: Martyn Robertson	–	FM M E C P S	■	■	■	–	–

	1	2	3	4	5	6	7
Lewes Tertiary College, Mountfield Road, Lewes, East Sussex BN7 2XH Tel: 01273 483188; Fax: 01273 478561. Contact: Jan Adams	■	M B C P E	■	■	–	–	–
London Business School, Sussex Place, Regent's Park, London NW1 4SA Tel: 0171 262 5050; Fax: 0171 724 7875. Contact: Dean of Executive Education	–	–	–	–	■	–	–
London Guildhall University, Short Course Unit, 84 Moorgate, London EC2M 6SQ Tel: 0171 320 1430; Fax: 0171 320 1439. Contact: Rosemary Royds	■	FM M B C P	■	■	–	–	■
London School of Small Business, 86 Old Brompton Road, South Kensington, London SW7 3LQ Tel: 0171 823 7282; Fax: 0171 584 2637. Contact: John Dalton	–	FM M B E C P S	–	–	–	–	–
Loughborough University, Business School, Ashby Road, Loughborough, Leics LE11 3TU Tel: 01509 263171; Fax: 01509 869332. Contact: Chris McEvoy/ David Cooper	–	–	–	■	–	–	■
University of Luton, Putteridge Bury, Faculty of Management, Hitchin Road, Luton LU2 8LE Tel: 01582 482555; Fax: 01582 482689. Contact: Andy Moore	■	FM P S	■	■	■	–	■

	1	2	3	4	5	6	7
	■	FM M P S	■	■	■	■	■

University of Manchester,
Manchester Business School,
Booth Street West, Manchester
M15 6PB Tel: 0161 275 6537;
Fax 0161 275 6542.
Contact: Professor Ray Oakey

	–	FM M C P S	–	■	■	–	■

**Middlesex University Business
School,** The Burroughs,
Hendon, London NW4 4BT
Tel: 0181 362 6166;
Fax: 0181 362 5822.
Contact: Joanna Mills

	■	M B C P S	■	■	–	■	–

**Milton Keynes Business
Venture,** Medina House, 314
Silbury Boulevard, Milton
Keynes MK9 2AE
Tel: 01908 660044;
Fax: 01908 233087.
Contact: Alan J Wade

	■	FM M B C P S	–	■	■	–	–

Nelson and Colne College,
Scotland Rd, Nelson, Lancs
BB9 7YT Tel: 01282 603151.
Contact: Eileen Sutcliffe

	–	FM M B C P	–	–	–	–	–

Nene College,
Sunley Management Centre,
Moulton Park, Northampton
NN2 7AL Tel: 01604 719531;
Fax: 01604 712413.
Contact: Sue Laste

	■	FM M B E C P S	■	■	■	■	■

Northbrook College,
Northbrook Business Centre,
Littlehampton Road, Goring by
Sea, Worthing, Sussex BN12
6NV Tel: 01903 830057;
Fax: 01903 265303.
Contact: Chris Ellis

■

	1	2	3	4	5	6	7
North East Surrey College of Technology, Reigate Road, Ewell, Epsom, Surrey KT17 3DS Tel: 0181 394 3038 Contact: Course Enquiries Desk	–	FM M B E C P S	–	–	–	–	–
North Tyneside College, Embleton Ave, Wallsend, Tyne and Wear NE28 9NL Tel: 0191 230 1061; Fax: 0191 295 0301. Contact: Norman Moore	■	M B E C FM	–	–	–	–	–
The College of North West London, Kilburn Centre, Priory Park Road, London NW6 7UJ Tel: 0181 208 5050. Contact: Information Hotline	–	FM	–	–	–	–	–
University of Northumbria, Centre for Enterprise and Management Development, Newcastle Technopole, Kings Manor, Newcastle upon Tyne NE1 6PA Tel: 0191 2274189; Fax: 0191 2274193. Contact: Richard Gay	■	FM M B E C P S	■	■	–	■	–
University of Nottingham, University Park, Nottingham NG7 2RD Tel: 0115 9515273; Fax 0115 9514159. Contact: Dr Martin Binks	–	FM	–	–	■	–	–
Open University, Open Business School, Walton Hall, Milton Keynes MK7 6AA Tel: 01908 655831; Fax: 01908 655898. Contact: Colin Gray	■	FM M B E C P S	■	–	■	■	■

	1	2	3	4	5	6	7
Oxford College of Further Education, Small Business Centre, Cricket Road Centre, Cricket Road, Oxford OX4 3DW Tel: 01865 716171; Fax: 01865 772910. Contact: Sue Brough	■	FM C P	–	■	–	–	–
Park Lane College, Park Lane, Leeds LS3 1AA Tel: 0113 2443011; Fax: 0113 2446372. Contact: Chris Staveley	■	FM M B C P	–	–	–	–	–
University of Plymouth, Plymouth Business School, Drake Circus, Plymouth PL4 8AA Tel: 01752 232810; Fax: 01752 232853. Contact: Ian Chaston	–	FM M E P S	–	–	■	–	■
University of Portsmouth, Business School, Locksway Road, Milton, Southsea, Hants PO4 8JF Tel: 01705 844059; Fax 01705 844059. Contact: Dr Alan Hankinson	■	FM M E P S	–	■	■	–	■
Professional Training Centre, Colchester Institute, Sheepen Road, Colchester, Essex CO3 3LL Tel: 01206 718978; Fax: 01206 763041. Contact: Helen Dyer	■	FM M B E C P S	■	■	■	■	■
Quantum Training and Consultancy, Thornton House, Cemetery Road, Shelton, Stoke on Trent ST4 2DL Tel: 01782 202366; Fax: 01782 279290. Contact: B Trowers	■	FM M B C P S	–	■	–	–	–

	1	2	3	4	5	6	7
Rother Valley College, Doe Quarry Road Dinnington, Sheffield S31 7NH Tel: 01909 560973; Fax: 01909 550504. Contact: John Line	■	–	–	–	–	–	–
St Helens College, School of Management, Water Street, St Helens, Merseyside WA10 1PZ Tel: 01744 33766; Fax: 01744 28873. Contact: Raymond Murphy	■	FM M B C P S	■	■	■	■	■
Sheffield Business School, The Old Hall, Totley Hall Lane, Totley, Sheffield S17 4AB Tel: 0114 2532839/6; Fax: 0114 2532870. Contact: Professor Colin Gilligan	–	FM M C P S	■	■	■	–	■
Sheffield University, Management School, 9 Mappin Street, Sheffield S1 4DT Tel: 0114 2768555; Fax: 0114 2725103. Contact: Dr Everett M Jacobs	■	M S FM	–	■	■	–	–
Small Business Bureau, Curzon Street, Church Road, Windlesham, Surrey GU20 6BH Tel: 01276 452010; Fax: 01276 451602. Contact: Jacqueline Russell-Lowe	–	–	–	–	–	–	■
South Bank University, 103 Borough Road, London SE1 0AA Tel: 0171 815 8158; Fax: 0171 815 6199. Contact: Admissions	■	–	–	–	–	–	–

	1	2	3	4	5	6	7
Stockport College of Further and Higher Education, Wellington Road South, Stockport SK1 3UQ Tel: 0161 958 3100; Fax: 0161 480 6636. Contact: H Bennett	–	FM M C S P	■	■	–	–	■
Stroud College, South Cotswold Training, Stratford Road, Stroud, Glos GL5 4AH Tel: 01453 761168. Contact: John Edwards	■	FM M B C P P S	■	■	–	–	–
University of Surrey, Research Park Office, The Surrey Research Park, 30 Frederick Sanger Road, Guildford, Surrey GU7 1QB Tel: 01483 579693; Fax: 01483 68946. Contact: Dr Malcolm Perry	–	–	–	–	■	■	–
Teesside Small Business Club Ltd, Unit 8b Royce Avenue, Cowpen Industrial Estate, Billingham, Cleveland TS28 4BX Tel: 01642 370094; Fax: 01642 563813. Contact: Brian H Whitfield	–	–	–	–	–	■	–
Thames Valley University, Walpole House, 18–22 Bond Street, Ealing, London W5 5AA Tel: 0181 579 5000. Contact: Janet Parsons	–	FM M B E C P S	–	–	–	–	–
URBED Enterprise Development, 3 Stamford Street, London SE17 2NP Tel: 0171 401 2099; Fax: 0171 261 1015. Contact: Brenda Gorman	■	FM M B P S	■	■	■	■	■

	1	2	3	4	5	6	7
Wigan and Leigh College, PO Box 53, Parsons Walk, Wigan, Lancs WN1 1BS Tel: 01942 501501. Contact: Anne Wolley	■	FM M B E C P S	■	■	■	■	–
Wirral Management Centre, 8th Floor, Tower Block, Carlett Park, Eastham, Wirral L62 0AY Tel: 0151 327 4331; Fax: 0151 327 6271. Contact: Eric Brown	■	FM M B E C P S	■	■	■	–	■
Northern Ireland **Castlereagh College,** Montgomery Road, Belfast BT6 9JD Tel: 01232 797144; Fax: 01232 401820. Contact: John Baird	–	M B FM E	–	–	–	–	–
Newry College of Further Education, Patrick Street, Newry, Co. Down BT35 8DN Tel: 01693 61071; Fax: 01693 60684. Contact: J B E Lannon	■	FM M B C P S	■	■	–	■	■
Training and Employment Agency, Business Support Division, Swinson House, Glenmount Road, Newtownabbey BT36 7LH Tel: 01232 365171; Fax: 01232 862912. Contact: Product Manager	–	FM M P S	■	–	–	–	–
University of Ulster, NISBI (The Small Business Institute), BP Enterprise Centre, Ulster Business School, Newtownabbey BT37 0QB Tel: 01232 365060; Fax: 01232 365117. Contact: Michael Brennan	■	–	–	–	–	–	–

		1	2	3	4	5	6	7
Scotland								
The Barony College, Parkgate, Dumfries DG1 3NE Tel: 01387 86251; Fax: 01387 86395. Contact: Neil Wood		■	P	–	■	–	–	–
Borders College, Melrose Road, Galashiels, Selkirkshire TD1 2AF Tel: 01896 57755. Contact: M Turner		■	FM M B C P S	■	■	–	–	–
Duncan of Jordanstone College, School of Food and Accommodation Management, 13 Perth Road, Dundee, Tayside DD1 4HT Tel: 01382 23261; Fax: 01382 27304. Contact: Dr T G Vickers		–	–	–	■	–	–	■
Edinburgh's Telford College, Crewe Toll, Edinburgh EH 4 2NZ Tel: 0131 332 2491; Fax: 0131 343 1218. Contact: N Wilson		■	FM M B C P	–	■	–	–	–
Elmwood Business Training, Elmwood House, Cupar KY15 4JB Tel: 01334 56500; Fax: 01334 56795. Contact: Tom Black		–	FM M B C P	–	■	–	–	–
Fife College, St Brycedale Avenue, Kirkcaldy, Fife KY1 1EX Tel: 01592 268591; Fax 01592 640225. Contact: M Gallacher		■	FM M B C P S	–	–	–	–	–

	1	2	3	4	5	6	7
Kilmarnock College, Molehouse Road, Kilmarnock, Ayrshire KA3 7AT Tel: 01563 23501. Contact: Angus Redpath	■	FM M B C P	■	■	–	■	–
Motherwell College, Dalzell Drive, Motherwell, Lanarkshire ML1 2DD Tel: 01698 259641; Fax: 01698 275430. Contact: Martin Milligan	■	FM M B E C P	■	■	–	–	■
Napier University, Department of Business Studies, Sighthill Court, Edinburgh EH54 8PW Tel: 0131 455 3336; Fax: 0131 458 5089. Contact: A Morrison	–	–	■	■	■	–	■
University of Paisley, Department of Economics and Management, High Street, Paisley PA1 2BE Tel: 0141 848 3399; Fax: 0141 848 3395. Contact: Professor George Blazyca	–	FM M P S	■	■	■	■	■
Queen Margaret College, Development Centre, Drumsheugh House, 38b Drumsheugh Gardens, Edinburgh EH3 7SW Tel: 0131 539 7095; Fax: 031 539 7096. Contact: Jock Anderson	■	FM M B E C P S	■	■	■	–	–
University of Stirling, Women's Enterprise Unit, Stirling FK9 4LA Tel: 01786 467353; Fax: 01786 450201. Contact: Christina Hartshorn	■	FM M B E P S	■	■	■	■	■

	1	2	3	4	5	6	7
Thurso College, Ormlie Road, Thurso, Caithness KW14 7EE Tel: 01847 66161; Fax: 01847 63872. Contact: D Macbeath	∎	FM M B C P S	∎	∎	–	–	–
Wales **Barry College,** Colcott Road,Barry, South Glamorgan CF62 8YJ Tel: 01446 743519; Fax: 01446 732667. Contact: B Clark	∎	FM M B C P	∎	∎	–	–	∎
Gorseinon College, Business Centre Belgrave Road, Gorseinon, Swansea, West Glamorgan SA4 2RF Tel: 01792 898283; Fax: 01792 898729. Contact: Lesley Grove	∎	FM M B E C P S	∎	∎	∎	∎	∎
Llandrillo College, Llandudno Road, Rhos-on-Sea, Colwyn Bay, Clwyd LL28 4HZ Tel: 01492 546666; Fax: 01492 543052. Contact: E J Cupitt	–	FM M B C P S	–	–	–	–	–
Swansea Institute of Higher Education, Mount Pleasant, Swansea, West Glamorgan SA1 6ED Tel: 01792 481195. Contact: Clive Norling	∎	FM M B P S	∎	–	∎	–	–
University of Wales: Lampeter, College Street, Lampeter, Dyfed SA48 7ED Tel: 01570 423532; Fax: 01570 423423. Contact: Dr I Roffe	–	FM M C P S	∎	∎	∎	–	–

■ OTHER USEFUL INFORMATION

Association of British Correspondence Colleges, 6 Francis Grove, London SW19 4DT (Tel: 0181 544 9559).

They keep a register of correspondence colleges and courses that they teach. Relevant subjects include book-keeping, computer appreciation, cost accountancy, market research, marketing, sales management and salesmanship. If you telephone them they will forward details on the topic of your choice.

Career Development Loans

A recent series of improvements to the Career Development Loans system means:

- course lengths eligible for support are doubled to two years;
- the maximum loan is increased from £5,000 to £8,000;
- a new option for people registered as unemployed at the end of training, to extend deferment of repayment to up to six months.

The changes, which came into effect in April 1994, were being implemented at the end of a year in which more than 12,000 people took advantage of CDLs to pay for training of their choice.

Since 1988, CDLs have helped nearly 50,000 people to pay for training which they would not otherwise have been able to afford, with loans worth well over £128 million. Many of them set up their own businesses.

Further information from: Barclays, Clydesdale and Cooperative Banks.

The Industrial Society

The Society runs some 150 courses itself, the largest offering in the country. Its quarterly survey, *Training Trends*, gives a strategic overview and regional and industry-wide comparisons. Industrial Society offices:

Thames West/Thames East Business Group, Peter Runge House, 3 Carlton House Terrace, London SW1Y 5DG (Tel: 0171 839 4300; Fax: 0171 839 3898).

Southern Business Group, Robert Hyde House, 48 Bryanston Square, London W1H 7LN (Tel: 0171 262 2401; Fax: 0171 706 1096).

Central England, West and Wales Business Group, Quadrant Court, 49 Calthorpe Road, Edgbaston, Birmingham B15 1TH (Tel: 0121 454 6769; Fax: 0121 456 2715).

Northern Business Group, Wira House, Clayton Wood Rise, Leeds LS16 6RE (Tel: 0113 2780521; Fax: 0113 2786127).

Scotland Business Group, 4 West Regent Street, Glasgow G2 1RW (Tel: 0141 332 2827; Fax: 0141 332 9096).

Northern Ireland Business Group, 4th Floor, Philip House, 123 York Street, Belfast BT15 1AB (Tel: 01232 330674; Fax: 01232 313631).

Members' Information Service: Tel: 0171 262 2401.

Direct Members' Line, to book courses: Tel: 0121 452 1030.

The National Training Index, founded in 1968, provides comprehensive information and advice on business training courses, correspondence courses, training films and training packages. The Index provides:

- detailed information (dates, duration, location, cost and syllabus summaries) on more than 12,000 business courses in the UK;
- comprehensive listings of in-company training schemes, course organizers, correspondence courses, training films and packages;
- a thorough but easy-to-use classification system which lists all courses and other training aids under 124 different subject headings;
- a quarterly information update and newsletter;
- an assessment of the quality of courses and training films listed in the Index, based on constant reports (more than 10,000 a year) sent in by members.

The Lecturers' Index maintains cards on 9,600 lecturers who have spoken at training courses, external and internal, during the past decade. Advice on suitable external speakers can also be given to members planning to run their own in-company training programmes.

The Conference Location Guide maintains files on hotels and conference centres with facilities for courses and conferences. Members who let them know the location, size and audio-visual requirements of any external course planned, will be supplied promptly with names and addresses of suitable venues.

Contact: Stuart Macnair, Manager, National Training Index, 1st floor, 25/6 Poland Street, London W1V 3DB (Tel: 0171 494 0596; Fax: 0171 494 1268). Two directories contain all the information, backed up by a telephone advisory service. Price £800.

Pick-up

Pick-up – professional, industrial and commercial updating – is a programme designed by the Department of Education and Science to encourage educational institutions to help businessmen and their employees to keep up with the latest technology and skills.

The Pick-up scheme is operated in colleges, universities and polytechnics and can take any form – one-to-one tutorials, distance learning, small group work, and form lectures.

Teaching can take place at an education centre, at the workplace or at home, and at different times of the day, week or year. For small firms the scheme can offer individual teaching or can bring together several businesses with the same or similar needs. Pick-up provision can cover any facet of general business, or it can be tailored to the needs of a particular industry or employer.

Each course comprises four days' full-time tuition for a group of ten students, spread over a period of six weeks. Courses are not free – they have to cover their costs – and the DES says that owner–managers should expect to pay a realistic price for training. More details of courses and costs are available from the Pick-up agents.

Guides to Pick-up services are available free on request. To order, contact: Adult Training Promotions, Department of Education, Sanctuary Buildings, Great Smith Street, London SW1P 3BT (Tel: 0171 925 5010).

Rapid Results College, Tuition House, 27/37 St George's Road, London SW19 4DS (Tel: 0181 947 2211; Fax: 0181 946 7584).

Jointly developed with the Midland Bank and the London Enterprise Agency. The Business Start-Up Programme was launched in 1988. This open learning course aims at helping anyone going into business, or who is currently in a start-up position. The main features of the programme include:

- comprehensive and easy to follow material covering all major start-up issues, from assessing personal strengths and weaknesses to raising finance, marketing, selling and preparing a detailed business plan;
- expert business counselling support service by telephone and in writing to help participants work through their own business ideas and plans;
- numerous practical activities, case studies, check-lists and assignments to help participants apply the material to their own business situations.

Fees are £159.

Training loans

Loans of up to £125,000 for training are being offered by the government to help businesses with up to 50 employees. The loans are available for education and training courses directly linked to the business and the development of employees as well as the cost of training consultancy. But each loan application must be endorsed by a Training and Enterprise Council which will be paid £500 for every successful application approved by the banks involved in the scheme.

Around £30m is available for loans each year. The Employment Department estimates the funding should benefit 3,000 businesses and 15,000 employees. The loans range from £500 to £125,000 and carry an interest-free element since repayments are deferred for up to 13 months. They are available for up to 90% of the course fee and the full cost of books, materials and other training-linked expenses up to an overall average of £5,000 per trainee.

Up to 90% of the cost of hiring training consultants can be covered by the scheme, up to a maximum of £5,000. The cost of cover for workers undergoing training may also be covered by the scheme.

The Employment Department has drawn up an agreement in partnership with three banks, Barclays, Clydesdale and the Co-operative Bank. Contact your local TEC (see Section 2) for further details.

Publications

The Business Growth Handbook by Colin Barrow, Robert Brown and Liz Clarke, published by Kogan Page in 1992; price £25.

Small firms tend to stall when their staff level reaches twenty. This can be avoided by taking appropriate action to stimulate growth, successfully handling the transition from an owner-managed business to team-management and delegation. This book explains the phases of growth and provides a framework for nursing the business through each delicate stage until it becomes substantial and secure. Tried and tested in the Growth Programme at Cranfield University, School of Management, the assessment forms for doing a company 'health check' include:

- diagnosing your organization
- marketing options
- financing growth
- visionary leadership
- managing change
- a new business plan
- exit routes

Each section is illustrated with case studies, tables and drawings. Assignments enable owners to check their businesses' position and base their future on a sound plan for growth.

The Business Plan Workbook by Colin Barrow, Paul Barrow and Robert Brown, published by Kogan Page in 1994 (2nd revised edition); price £10.95.

Based on the Enterprise Programme at Cranfield University School of Management, this book describes in detail how to find and prepare the material you need to write a business plan from scratch, for a new venture.

A business plan provides a blueprint for the future of a company. It sets out the company's aims and how it proposes to achieve them. A bank or venture capital house also needs to see a business plan before it will consider a loan for start-up or expansion.

This class-tested workbook is particularly valuable for students of business and management as well as for practising businessmen and women. It takes different business subjects – such as marketing, finance and the law – and shows how they relate to your business plan. There are 20 assignments, with worksheets, examples from actual business plans, and lists of reading material for self-study.

Directory of Computer Based Training, available from LOGOS Information Services, Clarendon Buildings, 25 Horsell Road, London N5 1XI (Tel/Fax: 0171 607 5086).

The *Directory* is designed to give you instant access to a wealth of information about computer based training products; updated twice-yearly; helpline available. Annual subscription £59.95 (DOS version) or £55.95 (Windows version). Subject areas include:

General management	Finance
Sales	Marketing
Project management	Business development
Banking	Communication skills
Self-development	Time management
Customer relations	Industrial relations
Business simulations	Stress management
Public sector training	Small business training
Languages for business	Health and safety
Typing skills	Hotel and catering

Directory of Multimedia Training, available from LOGOS Information Services (address above). Similar to the *Directory of Computer Based Training.*

Working for Yourself Series, published by Kogan Page.

Running Your Own Boarding Kennels by Sheila Zabawa, 1992 (2nd edition); price £8.99.

Running Your Own Catering Company by Judy Ridgway, 1992 (2nd edition); price £8.99.

Running Your Own Hairdressing Salon by C Harvey and H Steadman, 1986; price £6.99.

Running Your Own Mail Order Business by Malcolm Breckman, 1992 (revised edition); price £9.99.

Running Your Own Market Stall by Dave J Hardwick, 1992; price £6.99.

Running Your Own Photographic Business by J Rose and L Hankin, 1989 (2nd edition); price £8.99.

Running Your Own Playgroup or Nursery by Jenny Wilson, 1992 (2nd edition); price £8.99.

Running Your Own Pub by Elven Money, 1992 (2nd edition); price £8.99.

Running Your Own Shop by Roger Cox, 1989 (2nd edition); price £8.99.

Running Your Own Small Hotel by Joy Lennick, 1989 (2nd edition); price £6.99.

9 | *Youth opportunities for self-employment*

■ OPPORTUNITIES FOR YOUNG PEOPLE TO START UP A BUSINESS

There is a growing recognition that young people have been neglected in the major initiatives intended to help people to get a business started. There are signs that a major push is under way to redress this imbalance. As well as the initiatives briefly described below, most of the small-business courses listed in Section 8 are open to young people, and the Enterprise Agencies in Section 2 can also help.

Graduate Associate Programme (GAP)

If you are a young graduate who does not want to start a small business yet, but would like to find out at first hand what it is like to work in one, then this programme could be for you.

GAP's main aim is to boost the regional economy by encouraging small companies to employ graduates while providing both companies and graduates with support from a Business School.

More specifically, GAP:

- gives small/medium-sized companies the chance to employ a graduate who will receive training from a business school;
- reduces the cost to companies of the first year of employing a graduate by providing a subsidy;
- encourages graduates to take up careers in local small/medium-sized companies and provides them with a relevant and stimulating package.

Customers

GAP is targeted at:

- small/medium-sized businesses which do not normally recruit graduates or wish to employ a graduate in a new role;
- graduates of any age who have graduated in the last year or so.

The GAP formula

The companies select suitable graduates (of any university) from candidates initially attracted and vetted by the business school and take them on as employees in early September. They pay a privately negotiated salary of around £10,500, receiving a subsidy of £3,500 paid in three instalments during the first year.

The business school starts the training of graduates in late September with an initial two-week residential course followed by a long weekend each month until May. Overall, the graduates receive about 40 days' training during their first year of employment. It covers essential aspects of business such as accounts, marketing, production and IT and focuses especially on developing the personal and team-working skills needed by managers of small businesses.

As part of their normal job, the graduates carry out three work-related projects on topics chosen by their employers, such as finance, marketing and technical issues. They complete a case study and a dissertation, make a formal presentation and take an examination. The emphasis on projects and case studies helps stop the graduates being side-tracked into fire-fighting activities and ensures that they get a broad involvement in the business.

A tutor is assigned to each company who visits the graduate and other company staff at least once per term and is available for consultation. Company personnel are also involved in workshops.

Results

The results speak for themselves:

- 70% of the graduates make 'a major contribution' to the business (as assessed by the owner/MD);
- 42% stay with the business for at least six months after GAP involvement ends;
- 79% keep working in small businesses.

Contacts

Both the Teaching Company Directorate (TCD) and Durham University Business School (DUBS) have been commissioned by the Department of Trade and Industry to promote the adoption of arrangements similar to the University's GAP throughout the UK.

TCD is part of Cranfield University and has extensive experience of managing national schemes which link firms with higher education. It employs regional consultants who can assist the formation of consortia to fund and deliver initiatives similar to GAP.

Graduate Association Programme, Teaching Company Directorate, Hillside House, 79 London Street, Faringdon, Oxfordshire SN7 8AA (Tel: 01367 242822; Fax: 01367 242831).

Durham University Business School, Mill Hill Lane, Durham City DH1 3LB (Tel: 0191 374 3385; Fax: 0191 374 7482).

Head Start in Business

This began in 1983 as the collaborative brainchild of the Industrial Society and the then chairman of the Abbey National Building Society, Clive Thornton, following the Brixton riots when an initiative to help unemployed people was launched.

Head Start in Business is a business skills course designed for people wanting to set up on their own in a small business or as freelance. The course provides practical training on various subjects which are essential to the successful running of a business enterprise, such as tax, cash flow, simple bookkeeping methods, health and safety etc.

At the end of the course a business plan will have been prepared and presented to a panel of experts. This business plan can be presented and assessed for a City and Guilds certificate. Although this may sound a little daunting, experience has proved that the course provides the knowledge and builds the confidence which enables people to plan thoroughly and communicate their ideas effectively. The course provides:

- practical training for people who are wanting to establish their own business;
- part-time courses for 6–8 weeks, during which benefits may continue to be drawn;
- people from the local business community as tutors and as business mates, ensuring that the programme is always relevant and up to date. This practice forges valuable local links;
- many locations throughout the country run by the Industrial Society or by other agencies in the enterprise network. A continuous rolling programme of specialist courses is operating in London.

Contact: Elaine Bennett, The Pepperell Dept, The Industrial Society, 48 Bryanston Square, London W1H 7LN (Tel: 0171 262 2401; Fax: 0171 706 1096).

Livewire

The purpose of Livewire is to develop, manage and share quality programmes which improve opportunities for young people to realize their potential through the creation and development of business enterprises. Such programmes will contribute towards a more buoyant economy and a community of more fulfilled individuals.

Origins

Livewire was originally launched in Strathclyde by Shell UK Ltd in 1982. It had become a national scheme by 1984. Project North East was given the management contract in 1986. Shell's commitment currently extends to the end of 1996, at least.

Objectives

The stated objectives of Livewire are to:

- promote awareness of the importance of 'enterprise' among young people and those who work with them;
- promote generally the importance of young people starting and growing businesses;
- assist young people interested in starting their own business to do so;
- help young people established in business to expand;
- prepare and distribute appropriate and useful materials for youth enterprise;
- set an example to encourage the continual raising of standards among those working in youth enterprise.

Activities

Livewire seeks to achieve its purpose and objectives through three distinct programmes.

First, the enquiry service.

- The aim of the enquiry service is to act as a gateway to youth enterprise support.
- The service provides any 16–25-year-old in the UK who wants to start up their own business with a link to free, local advice and support.
- Each enquirer receives by return post an 'Unlock Your Potential' or 'Could This Be You?' booklet. This helps them to understand what starting a business involves and shows how to take the first steps towards turning their idea into reality.
- Through a network of local co-ordinators, a suitable adviser is appointed, if requested.
- The Livewire adviser has a free Business Plan Guideline for every enquirer. It has been specifically designed in a loose-leaf format so that sections can be issued as appropriate.
- Advisers are supported by the provision of 'Adviser Guidelines' and access to support materials.

Secondly, Business Start-Up Awards.

- These awards have been the most constant feature in a rapidly changing youth enterprise scene. They provide an annual celebration of the nation's most promising young business people.
- Over 80 awards presentations take place each year at county, regional and national levels, leading the winners to the Livewire UK final. Entrants to the competition must be 16–25 years of age and submit a start-up business plan to their local co-ordinator. Independent judging panels assess the people and their plans using Livewire judging guidelines.

Awards of over £175,000 and support 'in kind' are presented at the awards ceremonies. These events provide an opportunity for young businesses, sponsors, advisers, and other providers of enterprise services, to meet and learn from one another. A major cash award is presented to the most promising young business at the UK awards ceremony in London.

Thirdly, Business Growth Challenge. A major challenge facing the enterprise support network in the 1990s is how to help businesses grow.

- Business Growth Challenge offers individual owners the opportunity to experience a programme of personal, management and business development activities with other entrepreneurs who are at a similar stage of development.
- It is designed for those employing up to about four staff, who have been trading for over 18 months and who are looking to the next stage in developing their business.

To apply for the programme, the owner–manager is sent brief guidelines which help to identify their personal and business development needs, and to indicate how BGC might help them to address those needs.

Following discussions with a local co-ordinator, applicants are offered the chance to take part in a residential weekend. This combines a series of individual and team-based challenges which are specifically designed to test and develop business management skills and personal abilities.

Review sessions follow the activities. They help owners relate experiences to the way they can improve the running of their business.

Livewire believes that taking a short time out of the business to experience an intensive programme of management challenges in an invigorating outdoor setting, and working with others who run their own companies, helps small-business owners to see their personal and business needs with greater clarity and provides them with the opportunity to test and improve their management skills. The experience of working with, talking with and learning from others in similar situations is seen by Livewire to be an important feature of the Challenge.

After the training programme the owner–manager is provided with encouragement and help to put what they have learned as a result of the experience into practice in their business operation. They are also encouraged to produce a plan for the development of their business and can be linked into further advice or training they require.

Finance

The major sponsor of Livewire is Shell UK Ltd. British Railways Board also provides substantial sponsorship each year. In Northern Ireland, Northern Ireland Electricity are co-sponsors with Shell. LEDU and the International Fund for Ireland also provide support. In Wales, Kimberly-Clark is joint sponsor. Livewire is also supported in cash or in kind by some 200 other local sponsors throughout the UK.

Structure

Livewire employs a total of 17 staff. Programme and policy decisions are made by an executive team which is chaired by the Livewire UK director.

The four national directors on the executive team are responsible for implementing the team's decisions in their areas. The UK office, based in Newcastle upon Tyne, provides services to the four national offices.

Livewire co-ordinators

A UK network of over 80 co-ordinators is appointed by Livewire to undertake the management of programmes in each county. They have all been identified as a focal point for youth enterprise development and have demonstrated an enthusiasm to utilize Livewire to enhance the service they can offer to young people in their area.

■ The co-ordinator draws upon a range of local people and organizations to provide a service through which advice, training, finance, premises and other support can be accessed easily by young businesses.

■ The Livewire UK office and national offices provide resources and consultancy support to co-ordinators. Regular meetings of co-ordinator groups are held to discuss Livewire programmes and related enterprise issues.

Livewire Advisers

The Livewire Adviser network combines the resources of over 2,000 professionals and volunteers from advice organizations such as enterprise agencies, TECs and LECs and local authorities, dedicated volunteers from business and the professions, and retired business people.

Performance

In any one year, Livewire registers over 8,000 business start-up enquiries, from over 9,600 individuals aged 16–25 years. Since its inception in 1982, Livewire has provided advice and support to over 55,000 people, between the ages of 16 and 25, who have decided to pursue the self-employment option.

Future

In the 1990s the key emphasis for all businesses is delivering a higher quality service or product. Livewire wants to be able to do that while also being able to respond faster and more flexibly. This can best be achieved by devolving responsibility and authority as far down the organization as possible.

Business Growth Challenge will develop to provide better training, more closely aligned to the needs of entrepreneurs who wish to develop their business. Livewire hopes to expand the number of training places available by encouraging others such as TECs, LECs and local authorities to fund local events.

Regional offices

Livewire UK Office, Hawthorn House, Forth Banks, Newcastle upon Tyne NE1 3SG (Tel: 0191 2615584; Fax: 0191 2611910).

Livewire England, The Fishergate Centre, 4 Fishergate, York YO1 4AB (Tel: 01904 620105; Fax: 01904 651260).

Livewire Scotland, PO Box 2, Penicuik EH26 0NR (Tel: 01968 679915; Fax: 01968 679915).

Livewire Wales–Cymru, Greenfield Business Centre, Greenfield, Holywell, Clwyd CH8 7QB (Tel: 01352 710199; Fax: 01352 715210).

Livewire Northern Ireland, Young Business Centre, 103–107 York Street, Belfast BT15 1AB (Tel: 01232 328000; Fax: 01232 439666).

Livewire co-ordinator network
England

Avon: CSV Enterprise Centre,
56 Baldwin Street, Bristol, Avon
BS1 1QN (Tel: 0117 9225555).
Contact: Maurice Husbands.
Bedfordshire: TLC Associates,
33a St Peter's Street, Bedford
MK40 2PN (Tel: 01234 270290).
Contact: Ethel Buck.
Berkshire: Berkshire Enterprise
Agency, Suite 2, The Old Town Hall,
Market Place, Newbury RG14 5ES
(Tel: 01635 523472).
Contact: Diana New.
Birmingham: South Birmingham
Enterprise Centre, 249 Ladypool
Road, Sparkbrook, Birmingham
B12 8LF (Tel: 0121 4464215).
Contact: Bryany Whiteley.
Black Country: Sandwell Business
Advice Centre, Victoria Street, West
Bromwich B70 8ET
(Tel: 0121 5005412/3).
Contact: Tim Moore.
Buckinghamshire: Milton Keynes
Business Venture, Medina House,
314 Silbury Boulevard, Milton Keynes
MK9 2AE (Tel: 01908 660044).
Contact: Alan Wade.
Cambridgeshire: Cambridgeshire
County Council, Room 202, Shire
Hall, Castle Hill, Cambridge
CB3 0AP (Tel: 01223 317662).
Contact: Steve Bridges.
Channel Isles: Livewire England,
The Fishergate Centre, 4 Fishergate,
York YO1 4AB (Tel: 01904 620105).
Contact: c/o Sandy Whittle.
Cheshire: Youth Enterprise
Programme, Unit 4, Ground Floor,
Mill Lane, The Riveracre Business
Centre, Great Sutton, South Wirral
L66 3TH (Tel: 0151 3481163).
Contact: Sally Gosmore.
Cleveland: City Centre Training, 74
Skinner Street, Stockton, Cleveland
TS18 1EG (Tel: 01642 607231).
Contact: Val Pringle.
Cornwall: West Cornwall Enterprise
Trust, Pearl Assurance House, 8–10
Market Place, Penzance, Cornwall
TR18 2JA (Tel: 01736 330336).
Contact: Mike Penn.
Coventry: UDAP, Coventry
Polytechnic, Priory Street, Coventry
CV1 5FB (Tel: 01203 838508).
Contact: Derek Woods and
Minal Sodha.
Cumbria: Special Projects Manager,
PYBT, NORWEB plc, Castle Green,
Kendal, Cumbria LA9 6BH
(Tel: 01539 721301).
Contact: Ian Stephen.
Derbyshire: North Derbyshire
Enterprise Agency, 123 Saltergate,
Chesterfield, Derbyshire S40 1NH
(Tel: 01246 207379).
Contact: Bernard Eyre.
Devon: Enterprise Plymouth Ltd,
Computer Complex, Somerset Place,
Stoke, Plymouth PL3 4BB
(Tel: 01752 569211).
Contact: Geoffrey Clouder.
Dorset: Dorset Enterprise,
1 Britannia Road, Lower Parkstone,
Poole BH14 8AZ (Tel: 01202 748333).
Contact: Val Moore.
Durham: Durham County Council,
County Hall, Durham, Co. Durham
DH1 5UF (Tel: 0191 3834348).
Contact: Greg Johnson.
Essex: Essex YEC, 33 Nobel Square,
Basildon, Essex SS13 1LT
(Tel: 01268 728078).
Contact: Tony Woollett.
Gloucestershire: Gloucester
Enterprise Agency, 19/21 Brunswick
Road, Gloucester GL1 1HG
(Tel: 01452 501411).
Contact: Errol Bryan.

Hampshire: Southampton Enterprise Agency, Solent Business Centre, Millbrook Road West, Southampton SO1 0HW (Tel: 01703 788088). Contact: Ian Cole.
Hereford/Worcester: Youth Enterprise Office, County Careers Centre, County Buildings, St Mary's Street, Worcester WR1 1TW (Tel: 01905 763763). Contact: Margaret Gray.
Hertfordshire: Herts Youth Enterprise Service, Popefield, Hatfield Road, Smallford, St Albans, Herts AL4 0HW (Tel: 01707 261161; Fax: 01707 276140). Contact: Karrie Musson.
Humberside: AIMS, Unit 6, Acorn Business Park, Moss Road, Grimsby DN32 0LW (Tel: 01472 344000). Contact: Barbara Harbinson.
Isle of Man: Enterprise in Man, c/o Manx Water Authority, Drill Hall, Douglas, Isle of Man (Tel: 01624 626393). Contact: Alf Stokes.
Isle of Wight: Isle of Wight Enterprise Agency, 6/7 Town Lane, Newport, Isle of Wight PO30 1JU (Tel: 01983 529120). Contact: Elizabeth Tappenden.
Kent: Kent YEC, Firmstart Medway, 256 Lower Twydall Lane, Rainham, Gillingham ME8 6QP (Tel: 01634 387419). Contact: Karen Heavey.
Lancashire East: Hyndburn Enterprise Trust, Suites 4, 5, 6 Arcade Offices, Church Street, Accrington BB5 2EH (Tel: 01254 390000). Contact: Linda Kirkman.
Lancashire West: Morecambe Youth Business Centre, 83 Euston Road, Morecambe, Lancashire LA4 5JY (Tel: 01524 831721). Contact: Brian Moore.

Leicestershire: Leicestershire County Council EDU, County Hall, Glenfield, Leicester LE3 8RJ (Tel: 0116 2657313; Fax: 0116 2657176). Contact: Pam Ellis.
Lincolnshire: Lincs CC Education, 2nd Floor, Wigford House, Brayford Wharf East, Lincs LN5 7AY (Tel: 01522 553165). Contact: Helen Rawsthorn.
London: Greater London
Central: Portobello Business Development Agency, Portobello Business Advice Centre, 14 Conlan Street, London W10 5AR (Tel: 0181 969 4562). Contact: Robert Austin.
City: LENTA, 4 Snow Hill, London EC1A 2BS (Tel: 0171 236 3000). Contact: Delaney Brown.
East: Stratford Biz Centre, Room 3, Essex House, 375 High Street, Stratford, London E15 4QZ (Tel: 0181 503 1666; Fax: 1081 519 4052). Contact: Sandra Brouet.
North: Barfield Enterprise Ltd, Enterprise Hse, St Wilfreds Road, East Barnet, Hertfordshire EN4 9SB (Tel: 0181 447 1000). Contact: Sheila Boad.
North West: North West London TEC, Kirkfield House, 118–120 Station Road, Harrow HA1 2RL (Tel: 0181 424 8866). Contact: Wendy Schultz.
South: Bromley Enterprise Agency Trust, 7 Palace Grove, Bromley BR1 3HA (Tel: 0181 290 6568). Contact: David Pollard.
South Thames: Downham Young People's Business Centre, 5 Oakridge Road, Downham, Bromley, Kent BR1 5QW (Tel: 0181 698 3464). Contact: Ailbhe Harrington.

Manchester: Greater Manchester
Bolton: c/o Bolton Business
Ventures, 46 Lower Bridgeman Street,
Bolton BL2 1DG (Tel: 01204 391400).
Contact: Livewire Co-ordinator.
Bury: The Bury Partnership, Unit 17,
Bury Business Centre, Kay Street, Bury
BL9 6BU (Tel: 0161 7051878).
Contact: Jeff Walker.
Oldham: Oldham Enterprise Agency,
The Meridian Centre, King Street,
Oldham OL8 1EZ
(Tel: 0161 6651225).
Contact: Ed Stacey.
Rochdale: Rochdale Enterprise
Generation Centre, Dane Street,
Rochdale OL12 6XB
(Tel: 01706 356250).
Contact: Shabir Khan.
Salford: Manchester Business Link,
Churchgate House, 56 Oxford Street,
Manchester M60 7HJ
(Tel: 0161 2374030).
Contact: Linda Mickleburgh.
Stockport: Stockport Business
Venture, Errwood Park House,
Crossley Road, Heaton Chapel,
Stockport SK4 5BH
(Tel: 0161 4323770).
Contact: Diane Payne.
Tameside: as Salford.
Trafford: as Salford.
Wigan: The Fishergate Centre,
4 Fishergate, York YO1 4AB
(Tel: 01904 620105).
Contact: c/o Helen Symmonds.
Merseyside: Livewire England,
The Fishergate Centre, 4 Fishergate,
York YO1 4AB (Tel: 01904 620105).
Contact: c/o Helen Symmonds.
Norfolk: Norfolk CC, County Hall,
Martineau Lane, Norwich NR1 2DH
(Tel: 01603 222726).
Contact: Pat Holtom.
Northamptonshire: c/o NCDA, 36a
Milton Street, Northampton NN2 7JF

(Tel: 01604 791990).
Contact: Jenny Coleman.
Northumberland: Northumberland
TEC, 2 Craster Court, Manor Walks,
Cramlington NE23 6XX
(Tel: 01670 713303).
Contact: Brian Rothery.
Nottinghamshire: The Fishergate
Centre, 4 Fishergate, York, North
Yorkshire YO1 4AB
(Tel: 01904 620105).
Contact: c/o Helen Symmonds.
Nottinghamshire North: MSK Enter-
prise Partnership, The Old Town Hall,
Market Place, Mansfield,
Nottinghamshire NG18 1HY
(Tel: 01623 422010).
Contact: Bernard Wale.
Oxfordshire: Thames Business Advice
Centre, 3rd Floor, Seacourt Tower,
West Way, Oxford OX2 OJP
(Tel: 01865 249279).
Contact: Kim Hills Spedding.
Shropshire: Economic Development
and Employment Dept, The Shire
Hall, Abbey Foregate, Shrewsbury SY2
6ND (Tel: 01743 252259).
Contact: Bill Webster.
Somerset: Livewire Somerset, 10
Burton Place, Taunton, Somerset TA1
4HD (Tel: 01823 252089). Contact:
Charles Minall.
Staffordshire: Staffs Development
Association, The Business Advice
Centre, Shire Hall, Market Street,
Stafford ST16 2LQ
(Tel: 01785 277370).
Contact: Mary Bloomer.
Suffolk: Suffolk Enterprise Centre,
3 Coachman's Court, Old Cattle
Market, Ipswich IP4 1DX
(Tel: 01473 289500).
Contact: Chris Baber.
Surrey: Self Start, The Old
Firestation, Queen Street,
Godalming, Surrey GU7 1BD

(Tel: 01483 427247).
Contact: Rita Kelly.
Sussex East: East Sussex County
Council, Careers Service, County Hall,
Lewes BN7 1SG (Tel: 01273 481000).
Contact: Andrea Marshall Wright.
Sussex West: West Sussex Area
Enterprise Centre, 69a Chapel Road,
Worthing, West Sussex BN11 1BU
(Tel: 01903 231499).
Contact: Brenda McCurdie.
Tyneside: Project North East, 1 Pink
Lane, Newcastle upon Tyne
NE1 5DW (Tel: 0191 2616009).
Contact: Denise Ormston.
Warwickshire: Warks CC Careers
Service, 22 Northgate Street, Warwick
CV34 4SR (Tel: 01926 410410).
Contact: David Haines.
Wearside: Sunderland Enterprise
Centre, 1–2 John Street, Sunderland,
Tyne and Wear SR1 1HT
(Tel: 0191 5109191).
Contact: Jacqui Kerry.
Wiltshire: Community Council for
Wiltshire, 64 St Edmund's Church
Street, Salisbury, Wiltshire SP1 1EQ
(Tel: 01722 329863).
Contact: John Lakeman.
Yorkshire North: North Yorks County
Careers, County Hall, Northallerton,
North Yorkshire DL7 8AE
(Tel: 01609 780780).
Contact: Jayne Rawlins.
Yorkshire South
Barnsley: Thurnscoe Managed
Workshop, Princess Drive,
Thurnscoe, Rotherham SG3 9PG
(Tel: 01709 881951).
Contact: Austin Carr.
Doncaster: Business Link Doncaster,
White Rose Way, Doncaster N4 5ND
(Tel: 01302 761000).
Contact: Karen Hornsby.
Rotherham: Treeton Youth Enterprise
Centre, Old School Buildings, Front

Street, Treeton, Rotherham S60 5QP
(Tel: 0114 2695053).
Contact: Janet Beecher.
Sheffield: SENTA, 23 Shepherd Street,
Sheffield, South Yorkshire S13 7BA
(Tel: 0114 2755721).
Contact: Paul Suter.
Yorkshire West
Bradford: Bradford Economic
Development Unit, Britannia House,
Broadway, Bradford BD1 1JF
(Tel: 01274 754566).
Contact: Jean Hamer.
Halifax: Calderdale Business Advice
Centre, Croftmill, West Parade,
Halifax HX1 2EQ
(Tel: 01422 343898).
Contact: Jane Greenwood.
Huddersfield: Kirklees Enterprise
Agency, 1 Lord Street, Huddersfield
HD1 1QA (Tel: 01484 427212).
Contact: Shirley Woolham.
Leeds: Chel Business Centre, 26
Rounday Road, Leeds
(Tel: 0113 2425996).
Contact: Alan Sandy.
Wakefield: Wakefield Enterprise
Agency, 147 Westgate, Wakefield
WF2 9RY (Tel: 01924 201343).
Contact: Robert Seery.

Wales
Clwyd: Greenfield Business Centre,
Greenfield, Holywell, Clwyd CH8
7QB (Tel: 01352 711747).
Contact: Kate Catherall.
Dyfed: Foothold, Unit 4B, New Dock
Industrial Park, Llanelli, Dyfed SA15
2EL (Tel: 01554 775579).
Contact: Georgina Runnalls.
Mid Glamorgan: Mid Glamorgan
County Council, Business Develop-
ment Team, Greyfriars Road, Cardiff
CF1 3LG (Tel: 01222 820770).
Contact: Jayne Elliot.
South Glamorgan: Cardiff and Vale

Enterprise, 159 Holton Road, Barry, South Glamorgan CF63 4HP (Tel: 01446 739799). Contact: Lynn Wilson

West Glamorgan: Pontardulais Workshops, Tyn-y-Bonau Industrial Estate, Tyn-y-Bonau Road, Pontardulais, Swansea SA4 1RS (Tel: 01792 885197). Contact: Tony Morgan.

Gwent: Newport Enterprise, Enterprise Way, Newport, Gwent NP9 2AQ (Tel: 01633 254041). Contact: Ray Bulpin and Tony Utting.

Gwynedd: TARGED, Llys Britania, Parc Menai, Bangor, Gwynedd LL57 4BN (Tel: 01248 670627). Contact: Vanessa Fricker.

Powys

Montgomery District: Montgomeryshire Business Centre, 42 Broad Street, Welshpool, Powys SY21 7JE (Tel: 01938 554000). Contact: Judy Bennett.

Radnorsire District: Heart of Wales Business Centre, The Old Town Hall, Temple Street, Llandridnod Wells LD1 5DL (Tel: 01597 824777). Contact: Cathy Boore.

Brecknock Borough: Brecon Business Centre, Ynyscedwyn Industrial Estate, Gorof Road, Ystradgynlais, Powys SA9 1DX (Tel: 01874 624141). Contact: Clive Pritchard.

Scotland

Ayr/Renfrew: Renfrewshire Enterprise, 27 Causeyside Street, Paisley PA1 1UL (Tel: 0141 8423567). Contact: Cathy McCreadie.

Borders: Scottish Borders Enterprise Ltd, Wheatlands Road, Galashiels TD1 21SW (Tel: 01896 58991). Contact: Tom Harley.

Central: 8 Station Road, Killearn, Glasgow G63 9NS (Tel: 01360 50310). Contact: Bob Ballantyne.

Dumfries and Galloway: Dumfries and Galloway College of Technology, Business Development Centre, George Street Annexe, George Street, Dumfries DG1 1EA (Tel: 01387 67450). Contact: Ruth McNaught.

Fife: South Fife Enterprise Trust Ltd, 6 Main Street, Crossgates, Fife KY4 8AJ (Tel: 01383 515053). Contact: Linda Fitzsimmons.

Glasgow/Eastwood: Glasgow Opportunities, 7 West George Street, Glasgow G2 1EQ (Tel: 0141 2210955). Contact: Jacqueline Lauder.

Grampian: Aberdeen Enterprise Trust, 6 Albyn Grove, Aberdeen AB1 6SQ (Tel: 01224 582599). Contact: Leigh Coyle.

Highland/Islands: Highland Opportunity Ltd, Development Dept, Highland Regional Council, Glenurquhart Road, Inverness IV3 5NX (Tel: 01463 702000). Contact: David Knight.

Lothian: Capital Enterprise Trust, Allander House, 141 Leith Walk, Edinburgh EH6 8NQ (Tel: 0131 5535566). Contact: Frank Riddell.

Orkney Islands: Orkney Islands Office, Council Offices, School Place, Kirkwall, Orkney KW15 1NY (Tel: 01856 3535). Contact: Jeremy Baster and Shona Croy.

Strathclyde

Argyll: Livewire Scotland, PO Box 2, Penicuik EH26 0NR (Tel: 01968 679915). Contact: c/o Colin Wilson.

Dumbarton: Dumbarton District Enterprise Trust, Block 2/2, Vale of Leven Industrial Estate, Dumbarton G82 3PD (Tel: 01389 50005).

Contact: Jean Atkinson.

Lanark: c/o Motherwell Enterprise Trust, 2 Belhaven Road, Wishaw ML2 7NZ (Tel: 01698 359499). Contact: Bill McGilliard.

Strathkelvin: Strathkelvin Enterprise Trust, Southbank House, Southbank Business Park, Kirkintilloch, Glasgow G66 1XQ (Tel: 0141 7777171). Contact: Grace Macdonald.

Tayside: Dundee Enterprise Trust, Dudhope Castle, Barrack Road, Dundee DD3 6HF (Tel: 01382 26002). Contact: Ron Kelly.

Western Isles: Western Isles Council, Sandwick Road, Stornoway, Outer Hebrides, PA87 2BW (Tel: 01851 703773 ext. 421). Contact: Ken Kennedy, Principal Development Officer.

Northern Ireland

Carrickfergus/Larne: Young Business Centre, ARC House, 103–107 York Street, Belfast BT15 1AB (Tel: 01232 328000). Contact: Joy Allen.

East (Belfast): as Carrickfergus/Larne. Contact: Gerry Ford.

North/West: Livewire, NI Electricity Plc, 30 Deverney Road, Ormagh, Co. Tyrone (Tel: 01662 245411). Contact: Deirdre Timoney.

South/West: NI Electricity, Craigavon Area Office, Carn Industrial Estate, Portadown BT63 5QJ (Tel: 01762 356221). Contact: Michelle McCaughley.

The Prince's Youth Business Trust

The Prince's Youth Business Trust (PYBT) has as its president the Prince of Wales. The PYBT has now helped 20,000 young people – over 17,500 businesses have been set up or expanded with help from the Trust. Each year they budget to spend £2,500,000 on bursaries (grants) and £6,000,000 on loans and help some 3,000 young people.

Nearly half the unemployed people in Britain are under 30, the numbers having risen 150% in two years. The loss of potential and opportunity is colossal, as is the disillusionment engendered. The Trust wants to respond to this increased need by helping more young unemployed people. This means more support for existing businesses and more advice each year for up to ten times the number backed financially.

Aims

The PYBT's object is to change the lives of those who have no hope by providing a means to fulfilment and self-respect. You could say that they are 'growing' people, not just businesses.

The PYBT has established a track record of delivering probably the cheapest package of support to young people; transferring them from the demoralizing condition of long-term unemployment to constructive self-employment and an active contribution to the economy. The net cost of around £2,500 for each business established is achieved because three-quarters of the package of support is made up of volunteer effort.

How the PYBT works

The whole of England, Wales and Northern Ireland is now served by the PYBT, while north of the border there is a separate Prince's Scottish Youth Business Trust. The work of the PYBT is carried on through 38 regional boards. Each board is made up of local people and has one or more full-time regional managers. They are mostly men and women seconded by industry and commerce for two years to run the day-to-day work of the Trust in the regions. It is to them that young people apply for financial support and the support of industry and commerce in providing them is essential to their work.

Who the PYBT helps

They now help 18- to 29-year-olds who are out of work, are finding life tough for one of a number of reasons and/or are a member of their target groups (ex-offender, disabled people, member of ethnic minorities). Those living in deprived areas singled out for government or EC support are also of special concern, as are those with limited formal education, those living in bad housing conditions, those from single-parent families, with unemployed parents or no family support. In the case of disabled applicants, the age limit is 30. They must all have a viable idea for starting up their own business and indicate that they have the necessary initiative and commitment to make a go of it, but cannot obtain money from other sources.

How the PYBT helps

They give grants of up to £1,500 to individuals or up to £3,000 for groups of people wanting to start a business. This may be used for tools, equipment, transport, fees, insurance and training, but not for working capital, rent, rates, raw materials or stock. (This is for tax reasons.)

They also give loans of up to £5,000 (average £2,000) to those in the same age group setting up or expanding a business. A loan may be used for stock, equipment or for working capital. No interest is charged in the first year; 3% in the second and 8% in the third. Interest rates are calculated on the outstanding balance at the end of each month, not the total sum. No repayment of capital is made for the first six months, thereafter capital repayments are made monthly by direct debit. Where possible, they naturally prefer to give loans rather than grants to conserve funds.

Since 1991, they have been able to give second loans of not more than £5,000 to people under the age of 30 who have already had a loan or a grant. This is purely for expansion.

Advisers

They also give on-going help and advice to every PYBT-supported business. Each one starting up has his own adviser – a volunteer bank manager or other person with a suitable experience who keeps a friendly eye on the business for a couple of years or more and can call in other expert help if necessary. They have some 4,567 advisers and at least 2,000 new volunteers are needed each year. Marketing experts are particularly in demand.

In March 1994, HRH the Prince of Wales wrote to each adviser asking him or her to help to find another volunteer so that the numbers could be doubled to cope with the increase in PYBT-supported businesses.

Success rate

They are the largest business consultancy in the world which pays its consultants nothing. It has been estimated that the PYBT gives £5m of advice free each year to the supported businesses.

An independent survey of the PYBT carried out on behalf of the Employment Department – a great supporter of the Trust – showed that two-thirds of the businesses are still trading after two to three years. This is a strong performance against any criteria, but especially taking into account the age and background of those helped. Of those who are not still going, another half decided that self-employment was not for them, but got a job – often for the first time in their lives and usually as a result of their PYBT-supported experience. (In a few instances where their intervention has resulted in finance from other sources, they give advice but not funds.)

Minority communities

The PYBT sets out to encourage a greater proportion of young people from the minority communities to apply to the Trust for help in setting up their own businesses.

A Community Affairs section was set up in 1990 and, as a result of this initiative, there has been a greater awareness of what the Trust can and does do to help these communities. Not only have more young people come forward to apply for help but more businesses led by members of these communities have become loyal and generous supporters of the PYBT.

Field workers from these communities are employed in key areas and more and more men and women are coming forward to act as advisers to the young people.

A leaflet has been printed in Urdu, Bengali, Hindi, Punjabi and Gujarati. A new leaflet has also been printed in Welsh. It is hoped that in future it will be possible to help an increasing number of young people from the minority communities. At the moment 12% of those young people helped by PYBT are from minority communities.

The Trust is also particularly concerned to help disabled would-be entrepreneurs and have been at some pains to make their organization better known among organizations dealing with disabled people.

Staff/Secondees

Some 103 members of the present staff – full and part-time – are paid by the Trust with 118 seconded to the PYBT by government, industry and big business.

They need to attract at least 40 new secondees a year in a programme that yields real benefits to the individuals, the seconding companies and the Trust.

Types of businesses supported

Businesses helped range from fashion concerns to a swingboat operation in fairgrounds, those in the world of electronics to handmade pottery, a whole host of mobile businesses (farriers, hairdressers, etc) to dry-stone wallers and repair firms of every sort dealing with everything from golf clubs to musical instruments, ceramics to gilding. There are carpet concerns, humane rat-catchers, cake-makers, photographers taking aerial pictures from the ground by way of a camera mounted on a mast, a stick-insect breeder, pet-food delivery services, a milk-testing service with a £6m turnover – their most successful business – a lighting designer and manufacturer with a £300,000 turnover ... the list goes on.

They have some unusual businesses, e.g. a cow chiropodist (who was in fact the 10,000th person to be helped). There are charcoal burners, incense importers and a firm that tracks underground pipes and cables. They have just set up a hypnotist. There are falconers and there's a highwire motor-cycling, fire-eating jouster. One PYBT-supported business gives chess tuition. The 20,000th business was that of a girl in Sheffield who has set up a Shiatsu practice. A young man who uses a wheelchair himself couldn't find a lightweight, inexpensive model, so started a business to make them himself. He's now on line for a £200,000 turnover.

One young business generally considered likely to be among their first millionaires is a Kenyan-born Asian running a garage in Peterborough. His expected turnover for the year is £650,000. He has been appointed as a member of his regional board to help others.

Another very successful business is run by Karen Dowling who provides tools and fixings for the building trade. She has a £1 million-plus turnover and in 1991 was the winner of an annual *Reader's Digest*/PYBT award for the best recently started business. She has now become a PYBT business adviser helping others.

The *Reader's Digest* 1993 award winners were Yolande and Stephen Humphreys from Bridgend, Mid Glamorgan, who run YC Plastics, a firm making vacuum formers in which to pack items as well as producing plastic printed circuit board trays for use by manufacturers of larger equipment. They won £5,000 plus another £500 for being a finalist, and an additional £500 for being the regional winner for South East Wales. The success stories are endless.

PYBT contact list
Head Office: 5th Floor, 5 Cleveland Place, London SW1Y 6JJ
(Tel: 0171 925 2900; Fax: 0171 839 6494; Minicom: 0171 925 2900).

England
Bedfordshire/Hertfordshire/Buckinghamshire
PYBT, Popefield, Hatfield Road, Smallford, St Albans, Herts AL4 0HW
(Tel: 01707 271474; Fax: 01707 276140; Mobile: 01860 793694).
Contact: R F Kirkby.

Berkshire/Oxfordshire
PYBT, Berkshire Enterprise Agency, Office Suite 2, Old Town Hall, Mansion House Street, Newbury, Berkshire RG14 5ES (Tel: 01635 523472 – Weds only). Contact: Jack Williams (Berkshire); Michael McGuire (Oxfordshire).

Bristol
PYBT, The Coach House, 2 Upper York Street, St Paul's, Bristol BS2 8QN (Tel: 0117 9445555). Contact: Neil Saddington.

Cambridgeshire
PYBT, Montagu House, 81 High Street, Huntingdon, Cambs PE18 6EQ (Tel: 01480 456168; Fax: 01480 431200). Contact: Peter Quest.

Cheshire
PYBT, c/o Business Link Ltd, 62 Church Street, Runcorn, Cheshire WA7 1LD (Tel: 01928 563037; Fax: 01928 580711). Contact: Liz Wake, David Thornley.

Cumbria
PYBT, Ingwell Hall, Westlakes Science and Technology Park, Moor Row, Cumbria CA24 3JZ (Tel: 01946 592677). Contact: Alan Hurst.

Derbyshire
PYBT, Derven House, 32 Friar Gate, Derby DE1 1DA (Tel: 01332 384483; Fax: 01332 290880). Contact: Catherine Rylance.

Devon and Cornwall
PYBT, The OPUS Suite, 6th Floor, Inter-City House, North Road Station, Plymouth, Devon PL4 6AA (Tel: 01752 251051; Fax: 01752 251768). Contact: Andrew Smy.

Dorset
PYBT, c/o Southern Electric, 25 Bourne Valley Road, Branksome, Poole, Dorset BH12 1HH (Tel: 01202 768027; Fax: 01202 784244; Mobile: 01851 614595). Contact: Chris Mulford.

Essex
PYBT, c/o Essex Young Enterprise Centre, 33 Nobel Square, Basildon, Essex SS13 1LT (Tel: 01268 728078; Fax: 01268 590005). Contact: Eddie Cornwell.

Gloucestershire
PYBT, Enterprise House, 19/21 Brunswick Road, Gloucester G11 1HG (Tel: 01452 307028; Fax: 01452 305664). Contact: John Harper.

Hampshire/Isle of Wight
PYBT, c/o Coopers & Lybrand, 1 Port Way, Port Solent, Portsmouth PO6 4TY (Tel: 01705 200916; Fax: 01705 201818). Contact: John Le Riche.

Hereford and Worcester
PYBT, c/o Hereford and Worcester County Council, County Buildings, St Mary's Street, Worcester WR1 1TW (Tel: direct line 01905 765489; 01905 763763 ext 5489; Fax: 01905 765527). Contact: Brenda Howson.

Humberside
PYBT, Spacehire (Goole) Ltd, Rawcliffe Road, Goole, North Humberside DN14 8JW (Tel: 01405 768229; Fax: 01405 765441). Contact: Derek Stevenson.
PYBT, Hull Business Development Centre, 34–38 Beverley Road, Hull HU3 1YE (Tel: 01482 215500; Fax: 01482 581555; Mobile: 01860 574402). Contact: Peter Moores.

Kent
PYBT, County Hall, Maidstone, Kent ME14 1XQ (Tel: 01622 694280;
Fax: 01622 694383). Contact: Ron Dunham.

Lancashire
PYBT, Norweb plc, Mid-Lancashire Area, Hartington Road, Preston PR1 8LE
(Tel: direct line 01772 848289 or 01772 848338; Fax: 01772 848636). Contact:
Jim Lawrenson, John Ollerton.

Leicestershire
PYBT, Beaumont Enterprise Centre, Boston Road, Leicester LE4 1HB (Tel: 0116
2341222; Fax: 0116 2351844). Contact: Laurie Anderson.

Lincolnshire
PYBT, Unit 10, Innovation Centre, West Yard, Ropewalk, Lincoln LN6 7DQ
(Tel: 01522 531264). Contact: Terry Gibbon.

London East
PYBT, 32 Cheshire Street, London E2 6EH (Tel: 0171 613 1413;
Fax: 0171 613 1413). Contact: Gill Daly.

London North
PYBT, The Park Business Centre, Kilburn Park Road, London NW6 5LF
(Tel: 0171 625 8008/9; Fax: 0171 372 4801). Contact: Sally Crombie,
Terry Crimmings.

London South
PYBT Centre, 5 The Pavement, London SW4 0HY (Tel: 0171 498 2774;
Fax: 0171 498 8097). Contact: Tim Lyon, Gary Rigden.

Manchester
PYBT, Howard House, Fitzwarren Street, Salford, Manchester M6 5RS
(Tel: 0161 737 0999). Contact: Jim Carr, Margaret Watson.

Merseyside
PYBT, Bedford House, Oxford Street, PO Box 147, Liverpool University,
Liverpool L69 3BX (Tel: 0151 794 3197; Fax: 0151 794 3318).
Contact: Don Dunbavin, Allan Cooper, Kevin Smullen.

Norfolk
PYBT, c/o Norwich and Norfolk Chamber of Commerce and Industry, 112
Barrack Street, Norwich NR3 1UB (Tel: 01603 625977 ext. 230; Fax: 01603
633032 [Fax is property of N&NCC – use only in an emergency!!]).
Contact: Anne Lavery.

North East
PYBT, c/o Thorn Lighting Ltd, Spennymoor, County Durham DL16 7HA (Tel:
01388 420042 ext. 2504 Tue/Thur; 01388 605265 Mon/Wed/Fri;
Fax: 01388 812556). Contact: Eddie Doole.
PYBT, c/o St Mary's Training and Enterprise Centre, Oystershell Lane,
Newcastle-upon-Tyne NE4 5QS (Tel: 0191 230 1997; Fax: 0191 233 0775).
Contact: Sandra Kennedy.

Northamptonshire
PYBT, The Northamptonshire Training and Enterprise Council, Royal Pavilion,
Summerhouse Pavilions, Moulton Park, Northampton NN3 1WD
(Tel: 01604 671200; Fax: 01604 670362). Contact: Brian Lawrence.

Nottinghamshire
PYBT, 3 The Broadway, The Lace Market, Nottingham NG1 1PR (Tel: 0115 9484619; Fax: 0115 9410334). Contact: Vince Baker.

Shropshire
PYBT, c/o Shropshire TEC, Hazeldine House, Centre Square, Telford, Shropshire TF3 4JJ (Tel: 01952 291471 ext 316; Freephone (for applicants): 01800 252972; Fax: 01952 291437). Contact: Clive Hopkins.

Staffordshire
PYBT, The Close, Lichfield, Staffs WS13 7LD (Tel: 01543 253622; Fax: 01543 414660). Contact: Steve Clutterbuck.

Suffolk
PYBT, 3 Coachman's Court, Old Cattlemarket, Ipswich, Suffolk IP4 1CX (Tel: 01473 289500; Fax: 01473 288863). Contact: Christopher Baber.

Surrey
PYBT, c/o Self Start, 1 Balfour Road, Weybridge, Surrey KT13 8HE (Tel: 01932 820241). Contact: Maureen Tory.

Sussex
PYBT, TSB Central Banking Operation, Trustcard House, 1–9 Gloucester Place, Brighton BN1 4BE (Tel: 01273 745433; Fax: 01273 745356). Contact: John Waskett.

West Midlands
PYBT, 85/87 Vittoria Street, Hockley, Birmingham B1 3NU (Tel: 0121 236 5095; 0121 236 3902; 0121 236 5081 Wed/Thurs; Fax: 0121 233 4820). Contact: Kathy Williams, Jack Curtin, Gerry Scott, Ted Gray.

Yorkshire North
PYBT Court Business Centre, off Skipton Road, Harrogate HG1 4BA (Tel: 01423 525100). Contact: Angelika Sumpton.

Yorkshire South
PYBT, 50 Christ Church Road, Doncaster, South Yorkshire DN1 2QN (Tel: 01302 367100/367102; Fax: 01302 769120). Contact: David Houghton, Doreen Jenner.
PYBT, Portacabin, Meadowbank House, Meadowbank Road, Rotherham S61 2DY (Tel: 01709 559923; Fax: 01709 559924).

Yorkshire West
PYBT, Suites 8–11, Union Business Centre, 288 Harrogate Road, Bradford BD2 3SP (Tel: 01274 626414; Fax: 01274 626401). Contact: Pauline Seddon.

Wales
North
PYBT, Greenfield Business Centre, Greenfield, Holywell, Clwyd CH8 7QB (Tel: 01352 710751). Contact: Bob Haynes.

South/Central
(West Glamorgan, Mid Glamorgan (West of A470) South Powys)
PYBT c/o MADE, Gadlys Enterprise Centre, Depot Road, Gadlys, Aberdare, Mid Glamorgan CF44 8DL (Tel: 01685 882515; Fax: 01685 882806). Contact: Allan Pritchard.

South/East
(South Glamorgan, Mid Glamorgan (East of A470), Gwent)
PYBT, 4th Floor, Empire House, Mount Stuart Square, Cardiff CF1 6DN (Tel: 01222 495875; Fax: 01222 482086).
Contact: Nayland Anderson.
West
PYBT, 2 Coleshill Terrace, Llanelli, Dyfed SA15 3DB (Tel: 01554 758956; Fax: 01554 774693). Contact: Jill James.

Northern Ireland
PYBT, 103–107 York Street, Belfast BT15 1AB (Tel: 01232 328000; Fax: 01232 439666). Contact: Jim Toal.

Scotland
The Prince's Scottish Youth Business Trust (PSYBT), Mercantile Chambers, 6th Floor, 53 Bothwell Street, Glasgow G2 6TS (Tel: 0141 248 4999; Fax: 0141 248 4836). Contact: Fiona O'Hare.

10 | *Starting up overseas*

Interest in going overseas to work has been widespread in the UK for a long time. A more recent activity has been for entrepreneurs to both 'emigrate' and set up a business.

The relaxation of exchange controls by the first Thatcher Government has played its part in making this a more viable option. And of course our membership of the newly enlarged EEC has made the environment in those countries less hostile.

The risks inherent in starting up a business in a completely new environment are clearly greater. But both the rewards and the incentives can be greater too. Many countries positively discriminate in favour of the incoming entrepreneur, and have programmes of commercial and industrial support – Canada and Australia for example.

The commercial attaché at the UK Embassy or High Commission of the country you are interested in starting up in may be able to help you. But the organizations listed in this section will be a source of direct help.

■ EUROPEAN COMMUNITY BUSINESS AND INNOVATION CENTRES (EC–BIC)

The network was created in 1984 on the initiative of the European Commission with the objective of encouraging the creation and development of new entrepreneurial and innovative small and medium-sized enterprises.

The network has now spread well beyond Europe and by 1994 over a 100 BICs were in operation from Brazil to Slovenia, and Japan to South Africa.

Via a BIC, the entrepreneur is helped to draw up a comprehensive business plan; to develop and improve their managerial skills; and to get practical assistance with premises, incubation units, funding, technology, marketing and other essential services.

Even where a project does not meet EC–BIC's criteria of innovativeness they will redirect entrepreneurs towards appropriate local agencies. This makes them an ideal point of contact for anyone wishing to set up in business in their country.

The list below mainly comprises EC–BICs, by country. However, certain organizations with a broadly similar role have been included. Such organizations are shown in italics.

Belgium

Amalinvest Consultants: M. Vincent J. Derudder, Avenue Louise, 512, B – 1050 Bruxelles. Tel: (32) 2/640 74 18; Fax: (32) 2/648 16 91.

AMASCO: M. Pierre Scokaert, Avenue de Tervuren, 32, B – 1040 Bruxelles. Tel: (32) 2/7322826; Fax: (32) 2/7320295.

BEPN – Bureau Economique de la Province de Namur: M. Jean Bouvry, Avenue Sergent Vrithoff, 2, B – 5000 Namur. Tel: (32) 81/735209; Fax: (32) 81/742945.

Biotech – Biological Technology: M. Henry Francart, Zevenbronnenstraat, 111, B – 1653 Dworp. Tel: (32) 2/3810304; Fax: (32) 2/2158308.

Bruxelles Technopôle: M. Jacques Evrard, Rue de la Fusée, 64, B – 1130 Bruxelles. Tel: (32) 2/2159200; Fax: (32) 2/2158308.

CEEI '3E': M. Philippe Chevremont, Avenue Général Michel, 1E, B – 6000 Charleroi. Tel: (32) 71/320474–272815; Fax: (32) 71/316735.

Centre de Développement de Projets (CDP): M. Daniel Gheza, Avenue Nothomb, 8, B – 6700 Arlon. Tel: (32) 63/219948; Fax: (32) 63/226584.

Centre de Technologie et de Gestion des Affaires: M. Jean-Claude Ettinger, Rue de l'Industrie, 20, B – 1400 Nivelles. Tel: (32) 67883611 – 02/650 41 61; Fax: (32) 67/883688 – 02/650 40 50.

CIME SA: M. Olivier Delbrouck, Avenue de Tervuren, 252–254 – Boite 1, B – 1150 Bruxelles. Tel: (32) 2/7710175; Fax: (32) 2/7711087.

EEBIC: M. Lucien Pary, Avenue Joseph Wybran, 40, B – 1070 Bruxelles. Tel: (32) 2/5295811; Fax: (32) 2/5295911.

ERIDO: Prof. M J de Meirleir, Leopoldstraat, 95, B – 2800 Mechelen. Tel: (32) 15/423820; Fax: (32) 15/423619.

EVCA: M. William Stevens, Keibergpark, Minervastraat, 6 – Bus 6, B – 1930 Zaventem. Tel: (32) 2/7206010; Fax: (32) 2/7253036.

Fonds Léon A. Bekaert: M. Christian Mayne, Rue de la Loi, 26 – Boite 12, B – 1040 Bruxelles. Tel: (32) 2/230 45 70; Fax: (32) 2/512 36 97.

Générale de Banque: M. Etienne Colin, Montagne du Parc, 3 (B–64), B – 1000 Bruxelles. Tel: (32) 2/518 20 20; Fax: (32) 2/518 47 44.

Innotek: M. Luc Peeters, BIC Kempen, Kleinhoefstraat, 5, B – 2440 Geel. Tel: (32) 14/570057; Fax: (32) 14/581325.

Interface Enterprises Université: M. René van Daele, Place du XX Août, 7 (A 1), B – 4000 Liège. Tel: (32) 41/665293; Fax: (32) 41/665703.

Managetic: M. Jean-Pierre Leenen, Blvd Henri Rolin, 5b, B – 1410 Waterloo. Tel: (32) 2/3510099; Fax: (32) 2/3510195.

Socran SA: M. Robert Frédéric, Parc ind. du Sart-Tilman, Avenue Pré Aily, B – 4031 Angleur. Tel: (32) 41/678311; Fax: (32) 41/678300.

SPI: M. André Lacroix, Rue Lonhienne, 14, B – 4000 Liège. Tel: (32) 41/223083–232137; Fax: (32) 41/232184.

Brazil

Quickchip: M. João C Chaves, Av. Brig. Faria Lima, 1664 – cj. 728, São Paulo 10452. Tel: (55) 11/8143601; Fax: (55) 11/8143586.

Cyprus

Proplan Ltd: Dr Yannis Fessas, Industrial Engineering Consultants, 2, Dem Severis Avenue, PO Box 5672, Nicosia. Tel: (357) 2/458440; Fax: (357) 2/458138.

Czech Republic

BIC Brno: M. Jaroslav Chaloupka, Marianske nam. 1, CZ – 61700 Brno. Tel: (42) 5/43216014; Fax: (42) 5/43216015.
BIC Plzen: M. Jan Vratnik, Riegrova 1 – PO Box 325, CZ – 30625 Plzen. Tel: (42) 19/221805; Fax: (42) 19/35320.
BIC Prague: M. Pavel Komarek, Plzenska 221/130, CZ – 15000 Prague 5. Tel: (42) 2/558812 (Komarek); Fax: (42) 2/524330.

Denmark

Storstroms Erhvervscenter: Herr Kristian Primdal, Marienbergvej, 80, DK – 4760 Vordingborg. Tel: (45) 55/34 01 55; Fax: (45) 55/34 03 55.

Egypt

Arab Foundation for Enterprise Development (AFED): Ahmed Mohamed Abou El Yazeid, 7 Al Andalus Street, Flat 18, Behind the Merry Lane, Roxy, Cairo. *Tel: (20) 2 4544467; Fax: (20) 2 2470181.*
Small Business Services: Ali Abdelaziz Mikhtar, Center for Development Services, 4 Ahmed Pasha Street, City Bank Building (6th Floor), Garden City, Cairo. Tel: (20) 2 3546599; Fax: (20) 2 3552946.

France

AIDA, Agence pour l'Industrialisation et le Développement de l'Ardèche: M. Michel Cahen, Z.I. Le Lac, Avenue de l'Industrie – BP 429, F – 07004 Privas Cedex. Tel: (33) 75 64 45 10; Fax: (33) 75 64 73 43.
ANCE: M. Michel Hervé, Rue Delambre 14, F – 75682 Paris Cedex 14. Tel: (33) 1/42 18 58 58; Fax: (33) 1/42 18 58 00.
Association du Technopôle de Brest-Iroise: M. Jacques Jestin, Rue Jim Sevellec, 40 – B.P. 4, F – 29608 Brest Cedex. Tel: (33) 98 05 44 51; Fax: (33) 98 05 47 67.
ASTEC – Aire de Services et de Transfert de Technologie: M. Louis Bordeaux, Avenue des Martyrs, 15 – 85X, F – 38042 Grenoble Cedex. Tel: (33) 76 88 30 45;

Fax: (33) 76 88 36 89.

Bordeaux Technopolis: M. Georges Capurro, Immeuble Croix du Palais, Terrasse du Général Koenig, F – 33081 Bordeaux Cedex. Tel: (33) 56 99 33 07; Fax: (33) 56 96 19 10.

Cap Alpha: M. Jean-Claude Monnier, Avenue de l'Europe – Clapiers, F – 34940 Montpellier Cedex 9. Tel: (33) 67 59 30 00; Fax: (33) 67 59 30 10.

Carrefour Enterprise Sarthe: M. Joel Bruneau, 75 Bd Alexandre Oyon, F – 72100 Le Mans. Tel: (33) 43 57 72 72; Fax: (33) 43 87 01 02.

CEEI d'Ile et Vilaine (CREAT'IV), M. Jean-Luc Hannequin, Espace Performance, F – 35042 St-Grégoire. Tel: (33) 99 23 79 00; Fax: (33) 99 23 78 11.

CEEI Multipolaire des Bouches-du-Rhône: M. Luc Sollier-Bresset, Domaine du Petit-Arbois – BP 88, F – 13762 Aix-les-Milles Cedex. Tel: (33) 42 24 59 59; Fax: (33) 42 24 59 60.

CEEI de Nîmes: M. Frederic Escojido, Rue de la République 12, F 6 30000 Nîmes. Tel: (33) 66 76 33 87; Fax: (33) 66 76 24 60.

CEEI de Toulon: M. Jean-Noel Loiseau, Place G. Pompidou, Quartier Mayol, F – 83000 Toulon. Tel: (33) 94 03 89 01; Fax: (33) 94 03 89 14.

CEEI d'Evry – 'Le Magellan': Mme Puezellout, Rue Montespan, 7, F – 91000 Evry Cedex 06. Tel: (33) 1/69 47 60 00; Fax: (33) 1/69 47 60 70.

CEPAC: M. P. Dehollain, Rue de l'Echelle du Temple, 7, F – 02200 Soissons. Tel: (33) 23 53 37 78; Fax: (33) 23 59 51 33.

Commissariat à l'Energie Atomique: M. Albert Teboul, Délégation à l'Essaimage, Direction des Technologies Avancées, Centre d'Etudes de Saclay, F – 91191 Gif-sur-Yvette Cedex. Tel: (33) 1/69 08 83 42; Fax: (33) 1/69 08 24 04.

Ergo Sarl: M. John Michel Gibb, Allée du Berger, 13, F – 06130 St Jacques de Grasse. Tel: (33) 93 70 79 19; Fax: (33) 93 70 06 12.

IMT: M. Christian Rey, Technopôle de Château-Gombert, F – 13451 Marseille Cedex 13. Tel: (33) 91 05 44 38; Fax: (33) 91 05 43 67.

IRPSIMMEC – Institution de Retraite ARRCO du Groupe Malakoff: Mme Jacqueline Renauld, Avenue du Centre, 15, F – 78281 Saint-Quentin-en-Yvelines. Tel: (33) 1/30 44 45 11; Fax: (33) 1/30 44 48 88.

Izarbel – Technopôle de la Côte Basque: M. Joel Thevenin, Avenue Foch, 15, F - 64100 Bayonne. Tel: (33) 59 44 72 72; Fax: (33) 59 44 72 99.

La Lettre du Business: M. Olivier Réal, Sud-Est Economie Aménagement, Rue de Rome, 89, B.P. 2353, F – 13006 Marseille. Tel: (33) 91 55 66 58; Fax: (33) 91 55 66 75.

Nancy Brabois Innovation: M. Bernard Guerrier de Dumast, Espace Corbin, 10, Rue Poirel, B.P. 516, F – 54008 Nancy Cedex. Tel: (33) 83 17 42 03; Fax: (33) 83 17 42 30.

PA Consulting Group: M. Francis Willigsecker, Rue des Graviers 3-5, F – 92521 Neuilly-s-Seine Cedex. Tel: (33) 40 88 79 79; Fax: (33) 47 45 48 65.

Pépinière d'Entreprises Henri Farmen: M. Olivier Fiquet, Allée Albert Caquot, 2, F – 51100 Reims. Tel: (33) 26 89 50 00; Fax: (33) 96 89 50 50.

Pôle Européen de Plasturgie: M. Raphael Favier, Rue Pierre et Marie Curie 2, F –

01810 Bellignat. Tel: (33) 74 81 92 60; Fax: (33) 74 81 92 61.
Préface Ordimega: M. Patrick Senicourt, Avenue de Wagram, 89, F – 75017 Paris. Tel: (33) 1/42 67 52 56; Fax: (33) 1/46 22 80 32.
Promotech Nancy: M. Jacky Chef, Allée Pelletier Doisy, 6, F – 54600 Villers les Nancy. Tel: (33) 83 50 44 44; Fax: (33) 83 44 04 82.
Régie Departementale des Ruches d'Enterprises: M. François-Louis Billon, 6 Rue Gauthier de Chatillon, F – 59800 Lille. Tel: (33) 20 63 57 59;
Fax: (33) 20 63 58 85.
Service Création d'Enterprises Industrielles et Innovantes de la CCI de Lyon: M. Eric Salvat, Rue de la Bourse, 20, F – 69289 Lyon Cedex 02.
Tel: (33) 72 40 57 15; Fax: (33) 72 40 58 33.
Synergie: M. Hubert Trost, Place de Chambre 29, F – 57000 Metz.
Tel: (33) 87 76 36 36; Fax: (33) 87 76 23 03/87 76 30 43.
Théogone SA: M. Daniel Blonde, Route de Mondavezan, F – 31220 Martres-Tolosane. Tel: (33) 61 98 85 00; Fax: (33) 61 28 56 00.
TSD: M. Peter Lindholm, Espace Beethoven, Route des Lucioles – BP 63, F – 06902 Sophia Antipolis Cedex. Tel: (33) 93653830; Fax: (33) 93654135.
Yonne Développement: M. Gilles Groneau, Place du Maréchal Leclerc, 9, F – 89000 Auxerre. Tel: (33) 86 52 89 90; Fax: (33) 86 51 67 89.

Germany

ADT – Arbeitsgemeinschaft Deutscher Technologie – und Grunderzentren e.V.: Herr Bernd Gross, Gustav-Meyer-Allee, 25, D – 13355 Berlin.
Tel: (49) 30/4694157; Fax: (49) 30/4633095.
BIC Stendal Innovations – und Grunderzaentrum Altmark: Dr Christian Krause, Technologiepark, Arneburger Strasse 24, D – 39576 Stendal.
Tel: (49) 3931/216840 – 216862; Fax: (49) 3931/216884.
BIC Zwickau GmbH: Herr Hans-Jurgen Uhlmann, Lessingstrasse, 4, D – 08058 Zwickau. Tel: (49) 375/54 10; Fax: (49) 375/54 13 00.
BIG – Berliner Innovations-und Grunderzentrum: Dr Dieter Pagel, Gustav-Meyer-Allee 25, Geb. 12, D – 13355 Berlin. Tel: (49) 30/469 46 66;
Fax: (49) 30/469 46 49.
Dr Peschke & Partner: Dr Bernhard Peschke, Kirdorfer Strasse 5, D – 61350 Bad Hamburg v.d.H. Tel: (49) 61/7286061; Fax: (49) 61/7283591.
Experconsult GmbH: International Business Development: Herr Erg Lennardt, Heinrich-Hertz-Strasse 4, D – 44227 Dortmund.
Tel: (49) 231/75 443 230-232; Fax: (49) 231/75 443 27.
Frankfurt BIC: Ing. Uwe Hoppe, Im Technologie park 1, D – 15236 Frankfurt (Oder). Tel: (49) 335/557 1100; Fax: (49) 335/557 1110.
Gesellschaft für Wirtschafts-Foerderung im Landkreis Cloppenburg mbH: Herr Dietmar Schulze, Eschstrasse, 29, D – 49661 Cloppenburg.
Tel: (49) 4471/15/275; Fax: (49) 4471/79 03.
Technologie-und-Innovationspark Jena GmbH: Herr Hans-Georg Seifarth, Wildenbruchstrasse 15, D – 07745 Jena. Tel: (49) 3641/675 100;
Fax: (49) 3641/675111.

Greece

BIC Larissa: Mr Dimitrios Stylopoulos, Papakiriazi Street 44, GR – 41222 Larissa.
Tel: (30) 41/534 917/918; Fax: (30) 41/534919.
BIC Patras: Mr Evangelos Floratos, Michalakopoulou Street 58, GR – 26221
Patras. Tel: (30) 61/277830; Fax: (30) 61/276519.
KTESME – Centre of Technical Consulting for SMEs Co Ltd: Ms Flora
Kontomarinos, 5 Stournari St, GR – 106 83 Athens.
Tel: (30) 1/361 04 27 – 364 36 62; Fax: (30) 1/363 22 25.
Serres EC–BIC: Mr Nikolaos Karanasios, Solomou 12, GR – 621 22 Serres. Tel:
(30) 321/56 030; Fax: (30) 321/56 031.

Hungary

Hungarian Foundation for Enterprise Promotion: Mr Lajos Kustos, Etele ut 68,
H – 1115 Budapest. Tel: (36) 1/185 2711; Fax: (36) 1/161 1813.
Innotech: Mr Laszlo Racz, Technical University Innovation Park Ltd, 1119
Budapest XI Andor u. 60, Hungary. Tel: (36) 1/181 01 57;
Fax: (36) 1/181 29 59.

India

*Entrepreneurship Development Institute of India: V G Patel, Ahmedabad (near
Village Bhat, via Ahmedabad Airport and Indira Bridge), PO Box Chandkheda 382
424, Gujaret. Tel: (91) 272 811331; Fax: (91) 272 815367.*
*National Institute of Entrepreneurship and Small Business Development:
Mrs Rita Sengupta, NSIC–PDTC Campus, Okhla, New Delhi 110 020.
Tel: (91) 11 6830199.*

Indonesia

Indonesia BIC: c/o Mr Ahmad Faris Rasyid, Build Palmulang Inda C 13/1,
Jakarta 15470. Tel: office (62) 21/720 01 52, home (62) 21/749 20 33;
Fax: (62) 21/749 15 60.

Ireland

Dublin Business Innovation Centre: Mr Desmond C W Fahey, IDA Enterprise
Centre, Pearse Street, IRL – Dublin 2. Tel: (353) 1/671 31 11;
Fax: (353) 1/671 33 30.
Innovation and Management Centre Ltd: Mr Joe Greaney, Hardiman House,
Eyre Square, IRL – Galway. Tel: (353) 91/679 75; Fax: (353) 91/679 80.
Innovation Centre Limerick: Mrs Alice Morgan, Plassey Technological Park, IRL
– Limerick. Tel: (353) 61/33 81 77; Fax: (353) 61/33 80 65.
Southwest Business and Technology Centre: Mr Cathal O'Connor, IDA
Enterprise Centre, North Mall, Cork. Tel: (353) 21/39 77 11;
Fax: (353) 21/30 21 31.

Israel

International Trade and Innovation Institute: Dr Ilan Bijaoui, PO Box 48068, 9 Shoshana Parsitz, ISR – Tel-Aviv. Tel: (972) 3/6990449-6990447; Fax: (972) 3/6990460.

Italy

BIC Basilicata Sarl: Dott. Raffaele Ricciuti, CEII Systema, Via Pretoria, 77, I – 85100 Potenza. Tel: (39) 971/35836; Fax: (39) 971/410266.

BIC Calabria SpA: Dott. Francesco Morelli, Via Santa Teresa, 7, I – 87100 Cosenza. Tel: (39) 984/77715; Fax: (39) 984/77716.

BIC Lazio SpA: Dott. Paolo Palomba, Viale Parioli, 39/B, I – 00197 Roma. Tel: (39) 6/8587159; Fax: (39) 6/8078839.

BIC Liguria SpA: Dott. Paolo Corradi, Via Greto di Cornigliano, 6, I – 16152 Genova. Tel: (39) 10/6512273; Fax: (39) 10/6518752.

BIC Livorno/Piombino SpA: Dott. Giorgio Starnini, Scali degli Olandesi, 42, I – 57125 Livorno. Tel: (39) 586/880568 (Livorno), (39) 565/276606 (Piombino); Fax: (39) 586/887413 (Livorno), (39) 565/276615 (Piombino).

BIC Marche Srl: Dott. Tulio Piersantelli, Via Cimabue, 21 – Z.I. P.I.P., I – 60019 Senigallia (Ancona). Tel: (39) 71/6608537/8/9; Fax: (39) 71/6609581.

BIC Puglia Sprind SpA: Dott. Cosimo del Vecchio, Via A. Gioia, 131, I – 70054 Giovinazzo (BA). Tel: (39) 80/8943499; Fax: (39) 80/8943795–80/232546.

BIC Sardegna SpA: Dott. Giuseppe Matolo, Via Maddalena 14, I – 09124 Cagliari. Tel: (39) 70/663634/660545; Fax: (39) 70/659273.

BIC Sicilia Occidentale SpA: Ing. Giorgio Chimenti, Centro Europeo di Impresa e Innovazione, Via Magg. Toselli, 87 B, I - 90143 Palermo. Tel: (39) 91/6250626-27; Fax: (39) 91/6250620.

BIC Trieste SpA: Dott. Francesco Zacchigna, Via Flavia, 23/1, I – 34148 Trieste. Tel: (39) 40/8992270; Fax: (39) 40/8992257.

Centro Europeo di Impresa e di Innovazione Toscana Sud Srl: Sr Franco Bartali, Via San Gimignano, 69/71, I – 53036 Poggibonsi (Siena). Tel: (39) 577/938227; Fax: (39) 577/983219.

Centro Techofin Servizi SpA: Ing. Vittorio Menghini, Via Fortunato Zeni, 8, I – 38068 Rovereto. Tel: (39) 464/443111; Fax: (39) 464/443112.

CII Pistoia: Arch. Francesco Baicchi, Via Panciatichi 24, I – 51 100 Pistoia. Tel: (39) 573/33693; Fax: (39) 573/33943.

CISI Catania SpA: Dott. G. Nicotra, Piazza Roma, 9, I – 95100 Catania. Tel: (39) 95/504676; Fax: (39) 95/504677.

CISI Napoli SpA: Dott. Claudio Azzolini, Centro Direzionale Lotto G/7, Via G. Porzio, 4, I – 80143 Napoli. Tel: (39) 81/7877511; Fax: (39) 81/7877222.

CISI Taranto SpA: Dott. Francesco Ruggieri, C. de 'Carmine', Quartiere Paolo VI – C.P. 100, I – 74100 Taranto. Tel: (39) 99/4730444; Fax: (39) 99/4730433.

Consorzio Bologna Innovazione: Dr Antonio Speranza, Via Lame 24, I – 40122 Bologna. Tel: (39) 51/6347472; Fax: (39) 51/6347770.

EC–BIC Piemonte SpA Finpiemonte: Dott. Giovanni Bertone, Via Curtatone, 5, I

– 10121 Torino. Tel: (39) 11/6602666; Fax: (39) 11/6603333.
Euro-BIC Abruzzo: Dott. Antonio Sutti, Via dei Frentani 191, I – 66013 Chieti Scalo. Tel: (39) 871/349271; Fax: (39) 871/331795.
Euro-BIC Piceno Aprutino: Sr Umberto Fanuzzi, Z.I. Marino del Tronto, Via Allessandria, 12, I – 63100 Ascoli Piceno. Tel: (39) 736/342160; Fax: (39) 736/342170.
Filse SpA: Dottssa Silvana Galante, Via Peschiera, 16, I – 16122 Genova. Tel: (39) 10/818891; Fax: (39) 10/814919.
Isvor-Fiat: Dott. G F Gambigliani Zoccoli: Corso Dante, 103, I – 10126 Torino. Tel: (39) 11/6665111; Fax: (39) 11/6665568.
Omega Srl: Ing. Francesco di Pietrantonio, Via Monticelli, 291, I – 63100 Ascoli Piceno. Tel: (39) 736/341249; Fax: (39) 736/46994.
Quater SA: Sr Salvatore Coppola, Via Po' 43, I – 00198 Roma. Tel: (39) 6/8840255; Fax: (39) 6/8547443.
Società di Gestione e partecipazioni industriali SpA: Dott. Andrea Saraceno, Via del Serafico, 200, I – 00142 Roma. Tel: (39) 6/503981; Fax: (39) 6/5037426.
Società Finanziaria Industriale Rinascita Sardegna – SFIRS: Dott. Bruno Valenti, Via Santa Margherita, 4, I – 09124 Cagliari. Tel: (39) 70/668371-663534; Fax: (39) 70/663213.
Società Provinciale Insediamenti Produttive SpA – SOPRIP: Dott. Edoardo Terenziani, Strada della Repubblica, 45, I – 43100 Parma. Tel: (39) 521/282592 – 282833; Fax: (39) 521/235407.
SPI – Promozione e Sviluppo Imprenditoriale – Gruppo IRI: Dott. Romualdo VOLPI, Via Guglielmo Saliceto, 5, I – 00161 Roma. Tel: (39) 6/854541; Fax: (39) 6/85454359-75
Tecnopolis Csata Novus Ortus: Sperimentazione del Programma Tecnopolis: Dottssa Anna Maria Annicchiarico, Strada per Casamassima Km 3, I – 70010 Valenzano (BA). Tel: (39) 80/8770321 – 8770531; Fax: (39) 80/8770595.
VILA srl Valorizzazione dell'Imprenditorialita e del Lavoro Associato: Dott. Renato Paravia, Via Michele Conforti 1, I – 84124 Salerno. Tel: (39) 89/22 66 35; Fax: (39) 89/22 66 10.

Japan

Institute for Industrial Interchange Inc: Mr Akiyoshi Kokubu, 3-59-12 Wakaba-cho, Tachikawa, JP – Tokyo 190. Tel: (81) 425/342061; Fax: (81) 425/342062.

Kenya

Small Enterprises Finance Co Ltd: Mr W K Kiiru, PO Box 34045, Nairobi. Tel: (254) 2 726026.
The ILO: Julius M Mutio, Improve Your Business Project, PO Box 40304, Nairobi. Tel: (254) 2 20283/4.

Luxemburg

TII: Mr Christopher Hull, Rue des Capucins, 3, L – 1313 Luxembourg.
Tel: (352) 463035; Fax: (352) 462185.

The Netherlands

BIC Brabant: De heer Heert Jan Dokter, Van Limburg Stirumlaan, 6, PO Box 454, NL – 5000 Al Tilburg. Tel: (31) 13/635400; Fax: (31) 13/676664.
BIC Twente: De heer Roelant Lawerman, Postbus 545, NL – 7500 AM Enschede. Tel: (31) 53/885333; Fax: (31) 53/324555.
Europees Bedrijven Centrum Heerlen bv: De heer Th. G. Hommels, PO Box 2541, NL – 6401 DA Heerlen. Tel: (31) 45/237373; Fax: (31) 45/218326.
Technologisch Opleidings-Centrum – SBK Beheer bv: De heer Jacques Pronk, Gasthuisstraat, 102, NL – 5708 HP Helmond. Tel: (31) 4920/52067; Fax: (31) 4920/28983.

Norway

Forksniningsparken As: Herr Svenning Torp, Gaudstadalleen 21, NW 0371 Oslo. Tel: (47) 22/95.85.00; Fax: (47) 22/60.44.27.

Poland

BSC Lodz: M. Bartlomiej Walas, Al Pilsudzkiego, 8, PL – 91334 Lodz.
Tel: (48) 42/362881/362892; Fax: (48) 42/362892.

Portugal

AITEC – Tecnologias de Informação SA: Sr Francisco P Soares, Avenida Duque d'Avila 23 – 1, P – 1000 Lisboa. Tel: (351) 1/3520665; Fax: (351) 1/3526314.
Banco do Fomento Exterior: Sr F Roque de Oliveira, Avda Casal Ribeiro 59, P – 1000 Lisboa. Tel: (351) 1/562021-561071; Fax: (351) 1/548571.
CEISET – Centro de Empresa e de Inovação de Setubal: Sr Vasco Lemos Vieira, Av. Alianca Provo MFA, Apartado 217 – Cova da Piedade, P – 2806 Almada Codex. Tel: (351) 1/274.50.84/274.51.25; Fax: (351) 1/2766971.
CIEA – Centro de Inovação Empresarial do Alentejo: Sr Luis Sotto Mayor, Horta do Bispo – Apartado 479, P – 7005 Evora Codex. Tel: (351) 66/744272/3; Fax: (351) 66/744274.
CPIN – Centro Promotor de Inovação e Negocios: Sr Jose Faria do Amaral, Av. Almirante Reis, 178-r/c, P – 1000 Lisboa.
Tel: (351) 1/8476884 – 8477895 – 8477896; Fax: (351) 1/8475893.
GAPTEC – Gabinete de Apoio de Universidade Tecnica de Lisboa:
Sr A F Tovar de Lemos, Alameda De Santo Antonio dos Capuchos, 1, P – 1100 Lisboa. Tel: (351) 1/573984; Fax: (351) 1/3556472.
IAPMEI – Instituto de Apoio as Pequenas e Medias Empresas e ao Investimento:
Sr Manuel Regalado, Rua Rodrigo da Fonseca, 73, P – 1297 Lisboa Codex. Tel:

(351) 1/3559333; Fax: (351) 1/3863161.
NET SA – Novas Empresas Tecnologias: Sr Jorge Monteiro, Rua dos Salazares, 842, P – 4100 Porto. Tel: (351) 2/6170579-6179851; Fax: (351) 2/6177662.

Slovak Republic

BIC Bratislava: Mr Roman Linczelyi, Nevadzova, 5, SL – 82101 Bratislava. Tel: (42) 7/237666; Fax: (42) 7/2907417.
The National Agency for the Development of SMEs: Mr Jozef Brhel, Nevadzova 5, SL – Fax: (42) 7/222.434.

Slovenia

Chamber of Economy of Slovenia: Mrs Tanja Loncar, Information System Center, Slovenska C. 41, SLO – 61/150122; Fax: (38) 61/219536.

South Africa

Institute for Business Innovation (IMI): Dr D J Venter, PO Box 8912, Hennopsmeer 0046, Pretoria. Tel: (27) 12/667.25.46; Fax: 12/667.28.37.
Small Enterprise Foundation: Mr John De Witt, PO Box 212, Tzaneen 0850. Tel: (27) 1523 22 823.

Spain

Barcelona Activa SA: Sr Juan Oller, Llacuna, 162–166, E – 08018 Barcelona. Tel: (34) 3/4019703 – 4019777; Fax: (34) 3/3009015 – 3009654.
Beaz SA: Sr D. Francisco J Maqueda Lafuente, Alameda Recalde, 18 6, E – 48009 Bilbao. Tel: (34) 4/4239228 – 4237548; Fax: (34) 4/4231013.
BIC Euronova SA: Sr D. Alvaro Simon de Blas, Parque Tecnologico de Andalucia en Malaga, Apdo. de Correos 81, E – 29590 Campanillas (Malaga). Tel: (34) 5/261 91 27; Fax: (34) 5/261 91 28.
BIC Extremadura: Sr D. Manuel del Hoyo Macias, Dr Maranon, 2, E – 10002 Caceres. Tel: (34) 27/215950; Fax: (34) 27/215989.
BIC Galicia: Sr D. Santiago Gonzalez-Babe, Avda Alcalde Portanet 37–2, E – 36210 Vigo. Tel: (34) 86/209849; Fax: (34) 86/207882.
BIC Henares: Sr Ignacio Gamboa Maier, Plaza de la Victoria, 1, E – 28807 Alcala de Henares. Tel: (34) 1/8827707; Fax: (34) 1/8824143.
CEEI Alcoy: Sr Jordi Segui Roma, Plaza Emilio Sala 1, E – 03801 Alcoy. Tel: (34) 6/554.16.66; Fax: (34) 6/554.40.85.
CEEI Cantabria: Sr Ricardo La Porte Rios, Isabel II, 24, E – 39002 Santander (Cantabria). Tel: (34) 42/31.15.53; Fax: (34) 42/31.16.53.
CEEI Elche: Sr Joaquin Alcazar Cano, Ronda Vall d'Uxo, 125 Pol. Carrus, E – 03205 Elche (Alicante). Tel: (34) 6/666.10.17; Fax: (34) 6/666.10.40.
CEEI de Aragon: Sr D. Javier Sanchez Asin, C/Maria de Luna 11 (Pol. Actur), E –

50015 Zaragoza. Tel: (34) 76/733500; Fax: (34) 76/763719.

CEEI de Cartagena: Sr D. Ramón Gomez Perez, Poligono Industrial Cabezo Beaza, C/ Berlin, Parcela 3-F, E – 30395 Cartagena (Murcia). Tel: (34) 68/521017; Fax: (34) 68/527989.

CEEI de Castilia y Leon SA: Sr D. Ramón Bocos Munoz, Parque Tecnologico de Boecillo, E – 47151 Boecillo (Valladolid). Tel: (34) 983/552211; Fax: (34) 983/552369.

CEEI de Navarra SA: Sra D. Celia Oiz Gil, Carretera Estacion, s/n, Poligono Industrial Elorz, E – 31110 Noain (Navarra). Tel: (34) 48/106000 – 106001; Fax: (34) 48/106010.

CEEI de Valencia: Sr D. Jesus Casanova Paya, Calle 3 – Sector Oeste, Parque Tecnologico de Paterna, E – 46980 Paterna (Valencia). Tel: (34) 6/1994200; Fax: (34) 6/1994220.

Centre d'Empreses de Noves Tecnologies: Sr D. Javier Garriga Fortuño, Parc Tecnologic del Valles, E – 08290 Cerdanyola (Barcelona). Tel: (34) 3/5820200; Fax: (34) 3/5801354.

Centro de Empresas e Innovación de Alava SA: Sr Luis Del Teso, Castro Urdiales 10, E – 01006 Vitoria-Gasteiz. Tel: (34) 45/14.63.78; Fax: (34) 45/14.67.52.

Diputación Foral de Bizcaia: Sr Jose Antonio Bikandi, Gran Via, 25, E – 48009 Bilbao. Tel: (34) 4/415 32 00; Fax: (34) 4/415 48 75.

Diputación Foral de Guipuzcoa: Sr D. Miguel Ibanez San Roman, Plaza de Guipuzcoa, s/n, E – 20004 San Sebastian. Tel: (34) 43/423511 ext. 235; Fax: (34) 43/421024.

Eurocel, Centro Europeo de Empresas e Innovación, SA: Sr Enrique Piriz, Autovia Sevilla-Coria, s/n, Apartado de Correos 76, E – 41920 San Juan de Aznalfarache (Sevilla). Tel: (34) 5/4170517 / 4170527; Fax: (34) 5/4171117 / 4170512.

Impi – Instituto de la Pequeña y Mediana Empresa Industrial: Sr D. Jose Maria Ivanez Gimeno, Paseo de la Castellana, 141, E – 28046 Madrid. Tel: (34) 1/582 93 00; Fax: (34) 1/571 28 31.

Parque Tecnologico de Madrid: Sr D. Salvador Justel Moriche, Edificio Centro de Encuentros, Isaac Newton, s/n, E 28760 Tres Cantos (Madrid). Tel: (34) 1/8037244; Fax: (34) 1/8038668.

SOCEX – Sociedad de Cooperación Exterior: Sr Roberto Padrón, Avenida Ramón y Cajal 9, Edif. Proa, 7 A, E – 41005 Sevilla. Tel: (34) 5/463 67 32; Fax: (34) 5/463 67 32.

Sweden

Nutek: Herr Bjorn Sandstrom, Liljeholmsvagen 32, S – 11786 Stockholm. Tel: (46) 8/6819446-6819100; Fax: (46) 8/6453795.

Utvecklingsfonden Jamtlands Lan: Herr Erik Akerlund, PO Box 656, S – 63/13 36 89.

Switzerland

RET SA (Recherches Economiques et Techniques): M. Claude Bobillier, Z.I. – Allée du Quartz 1, CH – 2300 La Chaux-De-Fonds. Tel: (41) 39/252155.

USA

National Business Incubation Association – NBIA: Mrs Dinah Adkins, One President Street, Athens, Ohio 45701. Tel: (1) 614/5934331; Fax: (1) 614/5931996.

West Indies

BIDC – Small Business and New Enterprise Development Centre: 'Pelican House', P.O.Box 1250, Princess Alice Highway, St Michael, Barbados. Tel: (WI) 427 5350; Fax: (WI) 426 7802.

∎ THE FAST TRACK OVERSEAS

If you have a successful track record in business, or have in excess of £240,000 to invest abroad, then some countries will make you particularly welcome.

For example, in the United States, there is a fast-track immigration policy for businessmen and women who can offer £660,000 and guarantee to employ 10 people. Six hundred millionaires emigrated to America in 1993.

A similar scheme has begun in Australia, not that it really needs one. It has always attracted millionaire investors because of a points system – taking into account age, qualifications and connections with the country – that makes provisions for the wealthy.

Canada also uses a points system that encourages those with more than £250,000 to settle, providing they have a proven business record. New Zealand's strict measures for all potential immigrants are waived if the immigrant invests £240,000.

If you have a particular country in mind for your overseas venture, contact the relevant embassy for details.

Australia

Victoria: Small Business Development Corporation, 9th Floor, 100 Exhibition Street, Melbourne, Victoria 3000. Tel: 03 655 8934; Fax: 03 655 9500.
Queensland: Small Business Development, 545 Queen Street, Brisbane, Queensland 4000. Tel: 07 834 6789.
Western Australia: Small Business Development Corporation, NZI Securities Building, 553 Hay Street, Perth 6000. Tel: 09 325 3388; Fax: 09 220 0222.
South Australia: Small Business Corporation of South Australia, 74 South Terrace, Adelaide 5000. Business Advice and Education: Tel: 08 212 5344; **Business Licence Information:** Tel: 08 211 8599. Tasmania: Small Business Service Enquiry, 22 Elizabeth Street, Hobart 7000. Tel: 022 20 6712.

Australian Capital Territory: ACT Small Business Bureau, Level 5, ACT Administration Centre, Cnr London Circuit and Constitution Avenue, Canberra City ACT 2601. Tel: 062 75 8888.
Northern Territory: Small Business Advisory Services, Development House, The Esplanade, Darwin 0800. Tel: 089 89 7914).

Belgium

Brussels: Office for Foreign Investments, Ministry of Brussels Capital Region, Rue du Champ de Mars 25, 1050 Brussels. Tel: (32) 2/513 97 00; Fax: 2/511 52 55 (M. J C Moureau, Administrateur-général).
Flanders: Flanders Investment Office – FIOC, Ministry of Flanders Region, Markiesstraat 1, 1000 Brussels. Tel: 2/507 38 52; Fax: 2/507 38 51 (Mme J Mercken, Managing Director).
Wallonia: Ministry for Foreign Investors – OFI, Ministry of Wallonia Region, Avenue Prince de Liège 7, 5100 Namur. Tel: 81/32 16 17; Fax: 81/30 64 00 (M. J M Agarkow, Deputy General Manager).

Canada

Alberta: Canada Place, #540, 9700 Jasper Ave, Edmonton AB T5J 4C3. Tel: 403/495-4782; Fax: 403/494-4507 (Glen Fields, Executive Director).
British Columbia: Scotia Tower, #900, 650 West Georgia St, PO Box 11610, Vancouver BC V6B 5H8. Tel: 604/666-0434; Fax: 604/666-8330 (L M Russell, Executive Director),
Manitoba: 330 Portage Ave, PO Box 981, Winnipeg MB R3C 2V2. Tel: 204/983-2300; Fax: 204/983-2187 (Rainer Anderson, Executive Director).
New Brunswick: Assumption Place, 770 Main St, PO Box 1210, Moncton NB E1C 8P9. Tel: 506/851-6412; Fax: 506/851-6429 (Yvon Lavallee, Executive Director).
Newfoundland: Atlantic Place, #504, 215 Water St, St John's NF A1B 3R9. Tel: 709/772-4866; Fax: 709/772-2373 (Frank Nolan, Executive Director).
NWT: PO Box 6100, Yellowknife NT X1A 2R3. Tel: 403/920-8578; Fax: 403/873-6228 (Glen Fields, Executive Director).
Nova Scotia: 1801 Hollis St, 5th Floor, PO Box 940, Stn M, Halifax NS B3J 2V9. Tel: 902/426-3458; Fax: 902/426-2624 (Robert Russell, Executive Director).
Ontario: Dominion Public Building, 1 Front St West, 4th Floor, Toronto ON M5J 1A4. Tel: 416/973-5000; Fax: 416/973-8161 (William Cram, Executive Director).
Prince Edward Island: Confederation Court Tower, #400, 134 Kent St, PO Box 1115, Charlottetown PE C1A 7M8. Tel: 902/566-7400; Fax: 902/566-7450 (Richard Young, Director).
Quebec: #3800, Stock Exchange Tower, 800, Place Victoria, CP 247, Montreal PQ H4Z 1E8. Tel: 514/283-5938; Fax: 514/283-3302 (Anne-Marie Willis, Executive Director).

Saskatchewan: Canada Building, #401, 119 – 4 Ave South, Saskatoon
SK S7K 5X2. Tel: 306/975-4318; Fax: 306/975-5334 (William Reid, Executive
Director).
Yukon: #210, 300 Main St, Whitehorse YT Y1A 2B5. Tel: 403/667-3921;
Fax: 403/668-5003 (Lyle Russell, Executive Director).

Denmark

Information on specific investment questions including location of new indus-
tries and assistance in establishing contact with local authorities is provided by:
Information Office for Foreign Investment in Denmark: 25 Sondergade,
DK-8600 Silkeborg, Denmark. Tel: +45 6 82 56 55.
Ministry of Industry: Slotsholmsgade, DK-1216 Copenhagen K, Denmark.
Tel: +45 1 12 11 97.

The following organizations will be pleased to mail further information:
Danish Bankers Association, 7 Amaliegade, DK-1256 Copenhagen K, Denmark.
Tel: +45 1 12 01 00.
The Association of State-Authorized Public Accountants, 8 Kronprinsessgade,
DK-1306 Copenhagen K, Denmark. Tel: +45 1 13 91 91.
Federation of Danish Industries, 18 H C Andersens Boulevard, DK-1596
Copenhagen V, Denmark. Tel: +45 1 15 22 33.

France

**Agence Nationale pour la Création et le Développement des Nouvelles
Entreprises (ANCE),** 142 Rue du Bac, 75341 Paris Cedex 07. Tel: 1 44 39 58 58.
Direction de l'Action Régionale et de la Petite et Moyenne Industrie (DARPMI),
84 Rue de Grenelle, 75353 Paris Cedex 07. Tel: 1 43 19 36 36.
**Ministère de l'Economie, des Finances et du Budget, Direction du Commerce
Intérieur,** 207 Rue de Bercy, 75012 Paris. Tel: 1 44 87 17 17.

Germany

German–British Chamber of Industry and Commerce, Mecklenburg House, 16
Buckingham Gate, London SW1E 6LB. Tel: 071 233 5656;
Fax: 071 233 7835.

Greece

Ministry of National Economy, Department of Private Investment Promotion
and Evaluation, Platia Syntagmatos, Athens. Tel: (30) 333 2228;
Fax: (30) 333 2311.
Hellenic Organization of Small and Medium Sized Industries and Handicrafts,
16 Xenias Str, 115 28 Athens, Greece. Tel: (30) 333 2315.

Holland

Institute of Small and Medium Businesses, Nettogendoylean 49, Werden, Holland.

Republic of Ireland

Industrial Development Authority of Ireland (IDA), Wilton Park House, Wilton Place, Dublin 2, Ireland. Tel: 0001 686633 (Contact: Colm Regan).

Italy

Confederazione Italiana, Piccola Industria, Via Colonna Antonina 52, 00186, Roma.
Ministero Industrie e Commercio, D G Produzione Industriale, Via Vittorio Veneto 33, 00100, Roma.

Luxemburg

Ministère de l'Economie, 19–21 Boulevard Royal, L-2914 Luxembourg. Tel: (352) 4794 312; Fax: (352) 46 04 48 (Contact: Claude Lanners).

The Netherlands

Central Institute for Medium and Small Sized Businesses, Dalsteindreef 9, 1112 XC Diemen, The Netherlands.
Co-ordinating Foundation for Maintaining Service-Supply Centres for Small Businesses: address as above.
Economic Institute for Medium and Small Sized Businesses, Italielaan 33, 2711 CA Zoetermeer.

New Zealand

The Small Business Agency, PO Box 11-012 (Manners St), 14th Floor, Databank House, 175 The Terrace, Wellington. Tel: (4) 472 3141; Fax: (4) 499 5545 (Contact: Bruce Harris).

South Africa

Small Business Development Corporation Ltd, PO Box 7780, Johannesburg 2000. Tel: (11) 643 7351/9; Fax: (11) 642 2791.
Small Business Advisory Bureau, Potchefstroom University, PO Box 1880, Potchefstroom 2520. Tel: (148) 991002; Fax: (148) 991394.

USA

Small Business Administration, Washington Office Center (WOC), 409 3rd Street, SW, Washington DC 20416. Tel: (202) 205-6600. Advisory Services Hotline: (202) 566-4423.

Small Business Administration, Professional Building (PRO1), 2100 K Street, NW, Washington DC 20416. Tel: (202) 653-7735 (Contact: John Barnett).

11 | *Preparing the business plan*

So far this book has covered sources of help, advice and information. With all the appropriate information gathered and analysed, the entrepreneur's next step is to organize it into a business plan. The business plan has two functions:

- It will be required by the bank or whichever financial institution you intend to approach for investment.
- It will be a vital strategic planning tool for your own use. Large businesses recognize that they must have a planning strategy, both for the short and the long term. Small businesses need them too, but all too often entrepreneurs fail to realize this. Financiers and business now regard a thorough and coherent business plan as an essential sign of business maturity. And the events of the last decade have proved that a business with a planning strategy is more likely to survive.

Table 11.1 Age of firms with a business plan

Source: Cranfield Survey 1990

Age of business (years)	Percentage with current business plan
0–1	20
1–3	40
3–5	60
5 +	80

From the figures given in Table 11.1, it is clear that over the period when small businesses are at their most vulnerable, most have no plan to guide or determine their actions. Yet the construction of a business plan is probably the most important step in launching any new venture or expanding an existing one. Such a plan must include goals for the enterprise, both short and long term; a description of the products or services on offer and the market opportunities anticipated for them; finally, an explanation of the resources and means to be employed to achieve goals in the face of likely competition.

Preparing a comprehensive business plan along these lines takes time and effort. Once completed, it will serve as a blueprint to follow which, like any map, improves the user's chances of reaching the destination.

■ THE BENEFITS

There are a number of other important benefits that can be anticipated from preparing a business plan. These include:

■ Few businesses can grow without additional finance. While it would be an exaggeration to say a business plan is a passport to sources of finance, without it a business will not really know how much money is needed to finance growth, and few organizations will lend or invest in a business without a plan.

■ A systematic approach to planning enables mistakes to be made on paper, rather than in the market-place. One potential entrepreneur, while gathering data for his business plan, discovered that the local competitor he thought was a one-man band was in fact the pilot operation for a proposed national chain of franchised outlets. This had a profound effect on his marketing strategy!

Another entrepreneur found out that, at the price he proposed charging for a new product, he would never recover his overheads or break even. Indeed 'overheads' and 'break even' were themselves alien terms before he embarked on preparing a business plan. This naive perspective on costs is by no means unusual.

■ A business plan will make the management team and others involved in the venture more confident that they can achieve the strategic goals set. They will then be better able to communicate the company's strategy to others. This will give you management 'in depth' which is absolutely essential for organizations with ambitions to grow.

■ Preparing a business plan will give you an insight into the planning process. It is this process itself that is important to the long-term health of a business, and not simply the plan that comes out of it. Businesses are dynamic, as are the commercial and competitive environments in which they operate. No one expects every event as recorded on a business plan to occur as predicted, but the understanding and knowledge created by the process of business planning will prepare the business for any changes that it may face, and so enable it to adjust quickly.

Despite these many valuable benefits, thousands of would-be entrepreneurs still attempt to start without a business plan. The most common among these are businesses that either appear to need little or no capital at the outset, or whose founders have funds of their own; in both cases it is believed unnecessary to expose the project to harsh financial appraisal.

This belief is usually based on the easily exploded myth that customers will all pay cash on the nail – they will not. Moreover, suppliers are often thinner on the ground than optimistic entrepreneurs think: leading to higher prices and supply problems. Things tend to go wrong in two ways: either the product or service on offer fails to sell like hot cakes and mountains of unpaid stocks build up, all of which eventually have to be financed; or it does sell like hot cakes and more financially robust entrepreneurs are attracted into the market. Without the staying power that adequate financing provides, these new competitors will rapidly kill the original business off.

Those would-be entrepreneurs with funds of their own, or borrowed from friends and relatives, tend to think that the time spent in preparing a business plan could be more usefully (and enjoyably) spent looking for premises, buying a new car, or installing a micro-computer. In short, anything that inhibits them from immediate action is viewed as time-wasting.

Jumping in at the deep end is risky – and unnecessarily so. Flaws in your idea can often be discovered cheaply and in advance when preparing a business plan; they are always discovered in the market-place, invariably at a much higher and usually fatal cost.

■ THE INGREDIENTS OF A BUSINESS PLAN

A well constructed and presented business plan needs these five ingredients:
- packaging
- layout and content
- writing and editing
- focus on the recipient
- the oral presentation.

Packaging

Every product is enhanced by appropriate packaging and a business plan is no exception. Most experts prefer a simple spiral binding with a plastic cover on the front and back. This makes it easy for the reader to move from section to section, and it ensures the plan will survive frequent handling. Stapled copies and leatherbound tomes are viewed as undesirable extremes.

A near letter quality (NLQ) printer will produce a satisfactory type finish which, together with wide margins and double spacing, will result in a pleasing and easy-to-read document.

Layout and content

There is no such thing as a universal business plan format. That being said, experience has taught us that certain layouts and contents have gone down better than others. These are our guidelines to producing an attractive business plan which tries to cover both management requirements and the investors' point of view. Not every sub-heading will be relevant to every type of business, but the general format can be followed, with emphasis given as appropriate.

First, the cover should show the name of the company, its address and phone number and the date on which this version of the plan was prepared. It should confirm that this is the company's latest view on its position and financing needs. If your business plan is to be targeted at specific sources of finance, it's highly likely that you will need to assemble slightly different business plans, highlighting areas of concern to lenders as opposed to investors, for example.

Second, the title page, immediately behind the front cover, should repeat the above information and also give the founder's name, address and phone number. A home number can be helpful for investors, who often work irregular hours – rather as you probably do. Someone reading the business plan may want to talk over some aspects of the proposal before arranging a meeting.

The executive summary

Ideally one but certainly no longer than two pages, this should follow immediately behind the title page.

Writing up the executive summary is not easy but it is the most important single part of the business plan; it will probably do more to influence whether or not the plan is reviewed in its entirety than anything else you do. It can also make the reader favourably disposed towards a venture at the outset – which is no bad thing. These two pages must explain:

- The current state of the company with respect to product/service readiness for market, trading position and past successes if already running, and key staff on board.
- The products or services to be sold and to whom they will be sold, including details on competitive advantage.
- The reasons customers need this product or service, together with some indication of market size and growth.
- The company's aims and objectives in both the short and longer term, and an indication of the strategies to be employed in getting there.
- A summary of forecasts, sales, profits and cash flow.
- How much money is needed, and how and when the investor or lender will benefit from providing the funds.

Obviously, the executive summary can be written only after the business plan itself has been completed.

The table of contents

After the executive summary follows a table of contents. This is the map that will guide the new reader through your business proposal and on to the conclusion that they should put up the funds. If a map is obscure, muddled or even missing, then the chances are you will end up with lost or irritated readers unable to find their way around your proposal.

Each of the main sections of the business plan should be listed and the pages within that section indicated. There are two valid schools of thought on page numbering. One favours a straightforward sequential numbering of each page: 1, 2, 3 ... 9, 10, for example. This seems to us to be perfectly adequate for short, simple plans, dealing with uncomplicated issues and seeking modest levels of finance.

Most proposals should be numbered by section. In the example that follows, the section headed 'The Business and Its Management' is Section 1, and the pages that follow are listed from 1.1 to 1.7 in the table of contents, so identifying each page as belonging within that specific section. This numbering method also allows you to insert new material without upsetting the entire pagination during preparation. Tables and figures should also be similarly numbered.

Individual paragraph numbering, much in favour with government and civil service departments, is considered something of an overkill in a business plan and is to be discouraged, except perhaps if you are looking for a large amount of government grant.

The table of contents which follows shows both the layout and content which in our experience is most in favour with financial institutions. It is, however, a guide only. Not many start-up investors would have need for each and every heading.

Sample table of contents

Appendices should include:
- management team biographies
- names and details of professional advisers
- technical data and drawings
- details of patents, copyright, designs
- audited accounts (if already trading)
- consultants' reports or other published data on products, markets etc
- orders on hand and enquiry status
- detailed market research methods and findings
- organization charts

Writing and editing

The entrepreneurs and their colleagues should write the first draft of the business plan themselves. The niceties of grammar and style can be resolved later. Different people in the team may have been responsible for carrying out the various research needed, and writing up the section(s) of the business plan for which they are most responsible. This information should be circulated to ensure that:
- everyone is still heading in the same direction;
- nothing important has been missed out.

A 'prospectus', such as a business plan seeking finance from investors, can take on a legal status, turning any claims you may make for sales and profits (for example) into a 'contract'. Your accountant and legal adviser will be able to help you with the appropriate language that can convey your projections without giving them contractual status.

This would be a good time to talk over the proposal with a friendly banker or venture capitalist. They can give an insider's view as to the strengths and weaknesses of your proposal.

When the first draft has been revised, then comes the task of editing. Here the grammar, spelling and language must be carefully checked to ensure that your business plan is crisp, correct, clear and complete – and not too long. If writing is not your trade then once again this is an area in which to seek help.

Your local college or librarian will know of someone who can produce 'attention-capturing' prose, if you yourself don't.

However much help an entrepreneur gets with writing up their business plan it is still just that – their plan. So the responsibility for the final proofreading before it goes out must rest with them. Spelling mistakes and typing errors can have a disproportionate influence on the way your business plan is received.

The other purpose of editing is to reduce the business plan to around twenty pages. However complex or sizeable the venture, outsiders won't have time to read it if it is longer – and it will give the impression of muddled thinking. If your plan includes volumes of data, tables, graphs etc, then refer to them in the text, but confine them to an appendix.

The text (not the table or appendices) of your final business plan should be eminently readable if you want to stay out of the reject pile in lenders' and investors' offices. The Fog Index can help you make sure the business plan is readable.

Research into the subject has shown that two things make life hard for readers: long sentences and long words. Back in 1952 Robert Gunning, a business language expert, devised a formula to measure just how tough a letter, report or article is to read. Called the 'Fog Index', it takes four simple steps to arrive at.

1. Find the average number of words per sentence. Use a sample one hundred words long. Divide total number of words by number of sentences. This gives you average sentence length.
2. Count the number of words of three syllables or more per one hundred words. Don't count words that are capitalized, combinations of short easy words like 'book-keeper', or verbs that are made up to three syllables by adding 'ed' or 'es' – like 'created' or 'trespasses'.
3. Add the two factors above and multiply by 0.4. This will give you the Fog Index. It corresponds roughly with the number of years of schooling a person would require to read a passage with ease and understanding.
4. Check the results against scale:
   - 4 and below: very easy – perhaps childish.
   - 5: fairly easy – tabloid press, hard sales letters.
   - 7 or 8: standard – *Daily Mail*, most business letters.
   - 9 to 11: fairly difficult – *Times*, good product literature.
   - 12 to 15: difficult – *Economist*, technical literature.
   - 17 or above: very difficult – *New Scientist*; no business use, except to bamboozle.

The Fog Index might be useful in honing your executive summary, but be wary of applying it too rigorously. A complex business idea requires sophisticated business language to explain it. Aim for clarity, not blandness.

Focus on the recipient

Clearly a business plan will be more effective if it is written with the reader in mind.

This will involve some research into the particular interests, foibles and idiosyncrasies of financial institutions. If you are interested only in raising debt capital, the field is narrowed to the clearing banks for the main part. If you are looking for someone to share the risk with you then you must review the much wider field of venture capital. Here, some institutions will look only at proposals over a certain capital sum, such as £250,000, or will invest only in certain technologies.

It is a good idea to carry out this research before the final editing of your business plan, as you should incorporate something of this knowledge into the way your business plan is presented. You may find that slightly different versions of Section 9.4, 'The deal on offer', have to be made for each different source of finance to which you send your business plan.

Don't be disheartened if the first batch of financiers you contact don't sign you up. One Cranfield Enterprise Programme participant had to approach twenty-six leading institutions, ten of them different branches of the same organization, before getting the funds she wanted. One piece of information she brought back from every interview was the reason for the refusal. This eventually led to a refined proposal that won through.

However, financial institutions are far from infallible, so you may have to widen your audience to other contacts.

Anita Roddick, the Body Shop founder, was turned down flat by the banks in 1976, and had to raise £4,000 from a local Sussex garage owner. This, together with £4,000 of her own funds, allowed the first shop to open in Brighton. Today there are 100 outlets in the UK and a further 250 abroad. The company has a full listing on the Stock Exchange, Ms Roddick is a millionaire many times over – and one Sussex bank manager at least must be feeling a little silly!

Finally, how long will it all take? This also depends on whether you are raising debt or equity, the institution you approach and the complexity of the deal on offer. A secured bank loan, for example, can take from a few days to a few weeks to arrange.

Investment from a venture capital house will rarely take less than three months to arrange, and will more usually take six or even up to nine months. Two entrepreneurs, Richard Meredith of Holcott Press and Robert Segeser of Dairyborn Products, raised substantial six-figure sums during the 1991 recession and took eleven and thirteen months respectively from first approach to getting the cheques in the bank! Although the deal itself may be struck early on, the lawyers will pore over the detail for weeks. Every exchange of letters can add a fortnight to the wait. The 'due diligence' process in which every detail of your business plan is checked out will also take time – so this will have to be allowed for in your projections.

The oral presentation

If getting someone interested in your business plan is half the battle in raising funds, the other half is the oral presentation. Any organization financing a venture will insist on seeing the team involved presenting and defending their plans – in person. They know that they are backing people every bit as much as the idea. You can be sure that any financier you are presenting to will be well prepared. Remember that they see hundreds of proposals every year, and either have or know of investments in many different sectors of the economy. If this is not your first business venture they may even have taken the trouble to find out something of your past financial history.

Keep these points in mind when preparing for the presentation of your business plan:

- Be well prepared, with one person (you) orchestrating individual inputs. Nevertheless, you must also come across as a team.
- Use visual aids and rehearse beforehand.
- Explain and, where appropriate, defend your business concept.
- Listen to the comments and criticisms made and acknowledge them politely. You need to appear receptive without implying you have too many areas of ignorance in your plans.
- Appear business-like, demonstrating your grasp of the competitive market forces at work in your industry, the realistic profits that can be achieved, and the cash required to implement your strategies.
- Demonstrate the product if at all possible – or offer to take the financiers to see it in operation elsewhere. One entrepreneur arranged to have his new product, a computer-controlled camera system for monitoring product quality in engineering processes, on free loan to Fords for the three months he was looking for money. Not only did this help financiers to understand the application of a complex product, but the benefit of seeing it at work in a prestigious major company was incalculable.
- What empathy is there between the financiers and the entrepreneurs? You may not be able to change your personality but you could take a few tips on public speaking. Eye contact, tone of speech, enthusiasm and body language all play their part in making the interview go well, so read up on this – and rehearse the presentation before an audience.

■ WHAT FINANCIERS LOOK FOR IN A BUSINESS PLAN

Successful entrepreneurs with a proven track record can have as many problems raising finance for their ventures as the relative novice.

The late Bob Payton, who founded the Chicago Pizza Pie Factory in the late 1970s, related a story making exactly this point to an enterprise programme at Cranfield in 1990.

I now have a ten-year track record in the hospitality business. My company had a turnover of £10 million this year, and made a profit of £1 million. But the one constant problem I have had for the past ten years has been raising finance to put my ideas into practice. Getting the £4.5 million for my latest venture, Stapleford Park, a country house hotel in Leicestershire, will, by the time it opens in May, have taken three years. It has been as diffi-cult and as gut-wrenching as trying to raise £35,000 for my first place, the Chicago Pizza Pie Factory.

Originally EMI had agreed to back my first venture. We'd shaken hands on the deal and I had ordered the ovens and gone off to the States to learn how to make pizza. When I came back I got a 'Dear John' letter. They'd decided, on reflection, not to go ahead. I have that letter, framed and hanging on the wall in my office. After a lot of trouble I finally raised the money elsewhere and went ahead. EMI were subsequently proved to be wrong.

So if you need finance then, as well as the operation benefits of preparing a business plan, examine what financiers expect from you, if you are to succeed in raising those funds.

It is often said that there is no shortage of money for new and growing businesses – the only scarce commodities are good ideas and people with the ability to exploit them. From the potential entrepreneur's position this is often hard to believe. One major venture capital firm alone receives several thousand business plans a year. Only five hundred or so are examined in any detail, fewer than twenty-five are pursued to the negotiating stage, and only six of those are invested in.

The business plan is the ticket of admission giving the entrepreneur a first and often only chance to impress prospective sources of finance with the quality of the proposal.

Try to think yourself into the position of those financiers and make sure you tell them all the things they will want to know.

In our experience at Cranfield the plans that succeed meet all of the following requirements.

Evidence of market orientation and focus

David Stapleton, who took his company Pinneys from sales of £100,000 per annum in 1977 to over £30 million in 1987, learnt the lesson of market orientation the hard way. He started out aiming to sell lamb, beef, venison and grouse, all products close to hand to his Scottish Borders home, to overseas markets. Full of enthusiasm, he made a sales trip to the Far East, and went into the Peninsular Hotel in Hong Kong carrying a side of lamb of his back. But they didn't want to know about anything – except smoked salmon. He made a loss of £14,000 on that trip but he did discover what customers wanted. On the strength of that he raised £20,000 and bought out his smoked salmon supplier; his company now makes £1 million per annum profit.

Entrepreneurs must demonstrate that they have recognized the needs of potential customers, rather than simply being infatuated with an innovative idea. Business plans that occupy more space with product description and technical explanations than with explaining how the product will be sold and to whom, usually get cold-shouldered by financiers. They rightly suspect that these companies are more of an ego trip than an enterprise.

But market orientation is not in itself enough. Financiers want to sense that the entrepreneur knows the one or two things their business can do best – and that they are prepared to concentrate on exploiting these opportunities.

case STUDY

Two friends who eventually made it to an enterprise programme – and to founding a successful company – had great difficulty in getting backing at first. They were exceptionally talented designers and makers of clothes. They started out making ballgowns, wedding dresses, children's clothes – anything the market wanted. Only when they focused on designing and marketing fashionable clothes for pregnant women was it obvious they had a winning concept. That strategy built on their strength as designers and their experiences of pregnancy, and exploited a clear market opportunity neglected at that time by the main player in the market-place – Mothercare.

From that point their company, Blooming Marvellous, grew from turning over a couple of hundred pounds a year into the several-million-pound league.

Evidence of customer acceptance

Financiers like to know that your new product or service will sell and is being used, even if only on a trial or demonstration basis. The founder of Solicitec, a company selling software to solicitors to enable them to process relatively standard documents such as wills, had little trouble getting support for his house conveyancing package once his product had been tried and approved by a leading building society for their panel of solicitors.

If you are only at the prototype stage then, as well as having to assess your chances of succeeding with technology, financiers want an immediate indication that, once made, your product will appeal to the market. Under these circumstances you have to show that the 'problem' your innovation seeks to solve is a substantial one that a large number of people will pay for.

One inventor from the Royal College of Art came up with a revolutionary toilet system design which, as well as being extremely thin, used 30% of water per flush of the conventional product, and had half the number of moving parts – all for no increase in price. Although he had only drawings to show, it was clear that with domestic metered water for all households a distinct possibility, and a UK market for a half a million new units per annum, a sizeable acceptance was reasonably certain.

As well as evidence of customer acceptance, entrepreneurs need to demonstrate that they know how and to whom their new product or service must be sold, and that they have a financially viable means of selling it.

Proprietary position

Exclusive rights to a product through patents, copyright, trademark protection or a licence helps to reduce the apparent riskiness of a venture in the financiers' eyes as these can limit competition – for a while at least.

One participant on a Cranfield enterprise programme held patents on a revolutionary folding bicycle he had designed at college. While no financial institution was prepared to back him in manufacturing the bicycle, funds were readily available to enable him to make production prototypes and then license established bicycle makers throughout the world.

However well protected legally a product is, marketability and marketing know-how generally outweigh 'patentability' in the success equation. A salutary observation made by an American Professor of Entrepreneurship revealed that less than 0.5% of the best ideas contained in the *US Patent Gazette* in the last five years have returned a dime to the inventors.

Financiers' needs

People lending money to or investing in a venture will expect the entrepreneur to have given some thought to their needs, and to have explained how they can be accommodated in the business plan.

Bankers, and indeed any other sources of debt capital, are looking for asset security to back their loan and the near certainty of getting their money back. They will also charge an interest rate which reflects current market conditions and their view of the risk level of the proposal.

Depending on the nature of the business in question and the purpose for which the money is being used, bankers will take a five- to fifteen-year view.

As with a mortgage repayment, bankers will usually expect a business to start repaying the loan and the interest on a monthly or quarterly basis immediately the loan has been granted. In some cases a capital 'holiday' for up to two years can be negotiated, but in the early stages of any loan the interest charges make up the lion's share of payments.

Bankers hope the business will succeed so that they can lend more money in the future and provide more banking services such as insurance and tax advice to a loyal customer.

It follows from this appreciation of lenders' needs that they are less interested in rapid growth and the consequent capital gain than they are in a steady stream of earnings almost from the outset. As most new or fast-growing businesses generally do not make immediate profits, money for such enterprise must come from elsewhere. Risk or equity capital, as other types of funds are called, comes from venture capital houses, as well as being put in by founders, their families and friends.

Because the inherent risks involved in investing in relatively young or rapidly expanding ventures are greater than for investing in established companies, venture capital fund managers have to offer their investors the chance of larger overall returns. To do that, fund managers must not only keep failures to a minimum; they have to pick some big winners too – ventures with annual compound growth rates above 50% – to offset the inevitable mediocre performers.

case

Debbie Moore's Pineapple dance studios was one such company. Introduced to the Unlisted Securities Market (USM) in 1982 by its venture capital providers, its shares quickly went to an 85% premium. Profits rose by 50% in 1983, as forecast, and the company raised a further £1.5 million via a rights issue. Ms Moore was even given the coveted Businesswoman of the Year Award.

But this time the backers were not so fortunate. In 1985 aerobics began to lose its popular appeal as health experts cast doubts on its efficacy. By May the company was in a nosedive, showing half-year losses of £197,000. In the latter half of 1985 Peter Bain, a new boardroom recruit, evolved a strategy to run the company into a marketing services group. After several acquisitions and a total change of direction, Pineapple reported profits of £1.25 million in 1986.

But the dance studios clearly couldn't be made to work. 'It soon became obvious,' to quote Ms Moore, 'that it was difficult to deliver the kind of money the City wanted out of dance.' She resigned from the Pineapple Group in December 1987, taking the loss-making dance studios with her for a nominal sum, leaving the rest of the group to pursue its new strategy.

Typically, a fund manager would expect from any ten investments: one star, seven also-rans, and two flops. It is important to remember that despite this outcome, venture capital fund managers are only looking for winners, so unless you are projecting high capital growth, the chances of getting venture capital are against you.

Not only are venture capitalists looking for winners, they are also looking for a substantial shareholding in your business. There are no simple rules for what constitutes a fair split, but *Venture Capital Report*, a UK monthly publication of investment opportunities, suggests the following starting point:

For the idea:	33%
For the management:	33%
For the money:	34%

It all comes down to how much you need the money, how risky the venture is, how much money could be made – and your skills as a negotiator.

However, it is salutary to remember that 100% of nothing is still nothing. So all parties to the deal have to be satisfied it is to succeed.

Venture capital firms may also want to put a non-executive director on the board of your company to look after their interests. You will have at your disposal a talented financial brain so be prepared to make use of it, as these services won't be free – you'll either pay up front the fee for raising the capital, or you'll pay an annual management charge.

As fast-growing companies typically have no cash available to pay dividends, investors can profit only by selling their holdings. With this in mind the venture capitalist needs to have an exit route such as the Stock Exchange or a potential corporate buyer in view at the outset.

Unlike many entrepreneurs (and some lending bankers) who see their ventures as life-long commitments to success and growth, venture capitalists have a relatively short time horizon. Typically, they are looking to liquidate small company investment within three to seven years, allowing them to pay out individual investors and to have funds available for tomorrow's winners.

So to be successful, your business must be targeted at the needs of these two sources of finance, and in particular at the balance between the two. Lending bankers ideally look for a ratio of £1 of debt to £1 of equity, but have been known to go up to £4–5. Venture capital providers will almost always encourage entrepreneurs to take on new debt capital to match the level of equity funding.

If you plan to raise money from friends and relatives, their needs must also be taken into account in your business plan. Their funds can be in the form of debt or equity, but they may also seek some management role for themselves. Unless they have an important contribution to make, by virtue of being an accountant or marketing expert or respected public figure, for example, it is always best to confine their role to that of a shareholder. In that capacity they can give you advice or pass on their contacts and so enhance the worth of their (and your) shareholding, but they won't hold down a post that would be better filled by someone else. Alternatively, make them non-executive directors, which may flatter them and can't harm your business. Clearly, you must use common sense in this area.

One final point on the needs of financial institutions: they will expect your business plan to include a description of how performance will be monitored and controlled. One entrepreneur blew an otherwise impeccable performance at a bankers' panel by replying, when asked how he would control his venture: 'I'm only concerned with raising finance and getting my new strategy under way at the moment – once that's over I'll think about bean counting.' He had clearly forgotten who owned the beans!

Believable forecasts

Entrepreneurs are naturally ebullient when explaining the future prospects for their businesses. They frequently believe that 'the sky's the limit' when it comes to growth, and money (or rather the lack of it) is the only thing that stands between them and their success.

It is true if you are looking for venture capital, that the providers are also looking for rapid growth. However, it's as well to remember that financiers are dealing with thousands of investment proposals each year, and already have money tied up in a hundred business sectors. It follows, therefore, that they already have a perception of what the accepted results and marketing approaches currently are, for any sector. Any company's business plan showing projections that are outside the ranges perceived as acceptable within an industry will raise questions in the investor's mind.

Make your growth forecasts believable: support them with hard facts where possible. If they are on the low side, then approach the more cautious lending banker, rather than venture capitalists. The former often see a modest forecast as a virtue, lending credibility to the business proposal as a whole.

Recommended reading

The Business Plan Workbook by Colin Barrow and Paul Barrow, published by Kogan Page in 1992 (2nd edition).

12 | *Glossary of key business terms*

This glossary gives a meaning to words that have either been used in the book (and may or may not have been explained in context) or that you are likely to meet early on in your business life.

Words in capitals in definitions refer to other entries.

Access time Time between asking a computer for information and the information being available.

Account(s) Usually annual financial records of a business.

Accrual An accounting concept that insists that income and expenses for the accounting period be included, whether for cash or credit.

Acoustic coupler A device enabling a computer to be attached to the telephone line and so communicate with another computer anywhere.

Added value The difference between sales revenue and material costs. See also VALUE ADDED.

Adoption curve A graphic representation of the classification of users or buyers of an innovation according to the time of adoption. These categories are as follows: innovators first 2.5%, early adopters next 13.5%, early majority next 34.0%, late majority next 34.0%, laggards last 16.0%. Research has shown that these adopter groups have different characteristics, i.e. social class, age, education and attitudes. Those launching new products or businesses have to pay particular attention to the characteristics and behaviour of the innovator group in order to identify the most likely early customers, and so focus initial marketing effort on them.

Advertising The central purpose of all advertising activity is to secure as many favourable buying decisions as possible. As a concept, advertising has been around too long for its origins to be precisely traced. As an institutionalized business it has existed in the UK since the 1700s, when newspapers began to feature advertisements. The UK's oldest advertising agency, Charles Baker, was founded in 1812. The most surprising fact about advertising is not how much money is spent on doing it (although that is quite surprising) but in how much money is misspent. Lord Leverhulme is reputed to have said, 'Half the money I spend on advertising is wasted, but I can't find anyone to tell me which half!' For the smaller firm, leaflets and brochures consume the greater proportion of advertising expenditure. Answering these five questions before committing to any expenditure can usually ensure that this intangible activity has some concrete results:

1. What do you want to happen? (i.e. X people to buy Y quantity of produce Z)
2. How much is that worth?
3. What message will make it happen?
4. What media should be used?
5. How will the results be checked?

Advisory, Conciliation and Arbitration Service (ACAS) The name ACAS conjures up images of late-night sessions in smoke-filled rooms holding the ring between trade union bosses and company directors. The reality of their work is rather more prosaic, and is in the main concerned with preventing disputes before they can get to the public eye. They also offer advice on recruitment and selection, payment systems and incentive schemes, and manpower planning. It is in these areas that they can prove particularly helpful to new firms, and over a quarter of their 12,500+ advisory visits each year are to companies with fewer than 50 employees.

Angel Someone who puts up risk capital for a theatrical performance, show or film. A West End musical, for example, costs upwards of £500,000. *Starlight Express* cost over £2.2 million, so external funding is essential. These 'angels' must be prepared to lose their money, and many do. The rewards, however, can be spectacular. Investors who bought into *Evita* have recouped their cash six and a half times. Those who put up money for the smash hit musical *Me and My Girl* recouped their money and received their first profit within ten months. The term has now been taken over by the venture capital industry to mean any private investor.

Animal spirits A term coined by J Maynard Keynes to describe the effects of entrepreneurial zeal on the healthiness or otherwise of an economy. Surveys such as those conducted by the Confederation of British Industry and the Small Business Research Trust regularly attempt to monitor some aspects of these animal spirits.

Annual report See AUDIT.

Asset Something owned by the business which has a measurable cost.

Audit A process carried out by an accountant (auditor) on all companies each year, to check the accuracy of financial records. The auditor cannot be the company's own accountant. The result is the annual report.

Authorized capital The share capital of a company authorized by law. It does not have to be taken up. For example, a £1,000 company need only 'issue' two £1 shares. It can issue a further 998 £1 shares without recourse to law. After that sum it has to ask the permission of its shareholders.

Back-up Copies made of data and programs to be available in the event of originals being corrupted, damaged or lost.

Bad debts The amounts of money due in from customers that either have become or are expected to become uncollectable. The accounting principle of conservation requires that all reasonably likely losses be anticipated. So debts that are almost certainly uncollectable are deducted from the total;

debts which are reasonably likely to be uncollectable have a specific provision made against them; and in addition a general provision can be made against the rest of the debts, based on past experience. Thus was CREATIVE ACCOUNTING born.

Balance sheet A statement of assets owned by a business and the way in which they are financed, taken from both liabilities and owner's equity. This report does not indicate the market value of the business.

Bankruptcy Imposed by a court when someone cannot meet his bills. The bankrupt's property is managed by a court-appointed trustee, who must use it to pay off the creditors as fairly as possible.

Barriers to entry The way in which big businesses appear to pull up the drawbridge after them. The greater the barriers to entry the fewer the opportunities for new firms to enter a market. Such barriers include ECONOMIES OF SCALE, access to distribution channels, high capital requirements, high spending on research and development, short PRODUCT LIFE CYCLES, break-even pricing, high advertising expenditure and government policy.

Basic Beginners' All-purpose Symbolic Instruction Code. The most popular microcomputer language.

Bespoke software A computer program specially written by a software house to meet the unique requirements of the user.

Better mousetrap fallacy Coined by Geoffrey Timmons, Professor of Entrepreneurship at Northeastern University, to describe the often unwarranted faith put into a new product or invention by entrepreneurs, especially if it has been granted a patent. His thesis is that technological ideas must indeed be sound, but that marketability and marketing know-how generally outweigh technical elegance in the success equation. To illustrate this claim, Professor Timmons's research shows that less than 0.5% of the best ideas contained in the *US Patent Gazette* in the last five years have returned a dime to the inventors.

Bit A binary digit, usually represented by 'O' or '1', or 'off' or 'on'.

Black economy Usually refers to businesses run by the self-employed who illegally avoid tax and National Insurance. There is therefore no official record, and they are collectively referred to as the black economy.

Blue chip In gambling, the high chips are usually blue. In businesses, this refers to high-status companies and their shares. They are usually large companies with a long successful trading history.

Bolton Report (Cmd 4811 1971) This report fathered many of the government-sponsored initiatives in the small business field, including the Small Firms Service. Set up under the chairmanship of J E Bolton in July 1969, the committee was to 'consider the role of small firms in the national economy, the facilities available to them, and to make recommendations'. Small firms were further defined as those with fewer than 200 employees. The committee found this definition somewhat unhelpful and added some views of their own. They felt that the firm should have a relatively small share of its market, it should be run by its owner, and should be independent and not the subsidiary of a larger firm. The quantitative limits were set at 200 employees in manufacturing firms, an annual turnover of £50,000 per annum (1970 prices) in retailing and 25 employees in construction. A postal questionnaire to 3,500 firms revealed some interesting characteristics:

Proprietors

- The average age of owner–managers was 54.
- Few were professionally qualified, or had received higher education.
- Independence was their primary motivation.
- They were unwilling to accept help or advice from outsiders, including their accountants.
- They were generally weak in matters to do with financial planning, costing, pricing and control.

Performance

- Net output per person was up to 18% lower than in large firms, reflecting the lower capital intensity.
- Return on capital was markedly higher.
- They had good industrial relations despite paying lower wages.
- Mainly internally financed, and a larger number had never borrowed.
- They paid on average 2% points more than larger firms for credit financing.
- They were squeezed by larger firms, who forced prompt payment out of them, while delaying payment themselves.
- Average transaction costs varied inversely with the size of the firm so in this respect they were at a disadvantage.

Importance

- They contributed nearly a quarter of the GNP produced in the private sector.
- The sector had contracted since 1935, when its output share had been 41% (1969 was 25%).
- This was particularly true of the firms in manufacturing.
- They played an important role as specialist suppliers to larger firms.
- They were an essential competitive challenge to monopolistic larger producers.

Bolton came to the conclusion that small firms were ill-informed about sources of finance and were also poorly advised. He also noted that state procurement contracts tended to go to large producers. RED TAPE was a major problem, with legislation placing a disproportionate burden on small firms in terms of form-filling and unproductive administration of legislation. Lenders came in for some criticism too, and they were accused of a lack of knowledge of the affairs of small firms.

Book-keeping The recording of all business transactions in 'journals' in order to provide data for accounting reports.

Book value Usually the figure at which an asset appears in the accounts. This is not necessarily the market value.

Break-even point The volume of production at which revenues exactly match costs. After this point profit is made.

THE COMPLETE SMALL BUSINESS GUIDE

Business transfer agents Analogous to estate agents, they help bring buyers and sellers of small and usually retail businesses together.

Byte A sequence of eight 'bits', used to represent one character of information. A letter, digit, symbol or punctuation mark.

Cadillac syndrome This occurs when entrepreneurs brush aside the vital price–volume issue and its relationship to the BREAK-EVEN POINT, with the explanation that, 'We are the Cadillac of the field.' This leads to the setting of such an unreasonably high price that may imply a market so small as to sink the business. Although the theoretical profit margin on each unit sold is high in percentage terms, the volume sold is too low to even recover the investment. For many inventors financial failure is often of secondary importance to their 'artistic' success (unless it is their money at stake). The fact that their product is on the market is, in itself, sufficient success. Synonymous with the Rolls Royce syndrome.

Capital It has several meanings, but unprefixed it usually means all the assets of the business.

Cash The 'money' assets of a business, which include both cash in hand and cash at the bank.

Cash flow The difference between total cash coming in and going out of a business over a period of time.

Chairman (of the Board) The senior director of a company. In a small business this role is usually combined with that of MANAGING DIRECTOR. He is responsible for presenting the ANNUAL REPORT to the shareholders, along with his own comments on how the business is performing in the light of world affairs.

Company director A person elected by the shareholders of a limited company to control for them the day-to-day management of the business, and to decide on policy. The Companies Acts set out directors' duties and responsibilities. In most companies one third of the directors are required to retire from office each year. The directors who retire in any one year are those who have been longest in office since their last election. A retiring director can stand for re-election.

Company doctor Someone brought in to turn around an ailing venture. The term can also apply to someone who makes a habit of buying up loss-making ventures and returning them to profitability. Usually the measures taken by a company doctor in restoring a business to health include large-scale redundancies, closing down loss-making units, and the sale of any parts of the venture peripheral to its main trade. This may account for why such people are reticent to assume the title, but they are well known on the acquisition/merger circuit.

Company secretary Every limited company in the UK must have a company secretary. In public companies they must be professionally qualified and in a private company they must be 'suitable' but need not have professional qualifications. They are appointed by the board of directors to carry out the legal duties of the company such as keeping certain records, sending information to the Registrar of Companies, and generally to manage the administration of the company.

Computer-aided design (CAD) Software to produce two- and three-dimensional drawings on the screen and as hard copy.

Computer program Instructions telling a computer to carry out a specific task.

Corruption A distortion or elimination of data from the memory or disk, usually caused by electromagnetic impulses – e.g. when a disk is left near another electronic or magnetic device such as a loudspeaker.

Costs of goods sold The costs of goods actually sold in any period. It excludes the cost of the goods left unsold, and all overheads except manufacturing.

Crash What happens when a program refuses to continue. Usually the program has to be reloaded, with the loss of all work in progress – unless you have kept a back-up.

Creative accounting The term used to describe the rather elastic treatment of accounting rules and concepts, usually in an effort to create a picture that is favourable to the entrepreneur. In its more extreme forms it becomes fraud.

Current assets Assets normally realized in cash or used up in operations during the year. It includes such items as debtors and stock.

Current liability A liability due for payment in one trading period, usually a year.

Database An electronic filing program enabling data to be kept in an organized way for later retrieval and analysis.

Debenture Long-term loan with specific terms on interest, capital repayment and security.

Debug Computerese for 'trouble-shoot'.

Demand, Law of An economic theory that suggests, all other things being equal, the lower the price, the greater the demand. The concept is much misunderstood by new entrepreneurs who believe the only thing that has to be done to beat a competitor is to have a lower price. The theory was put to good effect by the late Sir Jack Cohen of Tesco's in his philosophy of 'stack it high and sell it cheap'. He understood the need for good promotion, a good range and mix of products and above all good location for his stores, as well as having competitive prices. Unfortunately (or perhaps not!), the demand for all products or services is not uniformly elastic – that is, the rate of change of price versus demand are not similarly and directly interlinked. Some products are actually price inelastic. For example, Jaguar and Rolls Royce would be unlikely to sell any more cars if they knocked 5% off the price – indeed by losing snob value they may sell less. So if they dropped their price they would simply lower profits. However, people would quite happily cross town to save 5p in the £1 on fresh vegetables and meat. This concept is closely allied to working out the BREAK-EVEN POINT.

Depreciation A way of measuring the cost of using a fixed asset. A set portion of the asset's cost is treated as an expense each period of its working life.

Direct costs Expenses, such as labour and materials, which vary 'directly' according to the number of items manufactured. Also called variable costs.

Director General of Fair Trading An office created by the Fair Trading Act, 1973.

His main functions are to keep under review and collect information on all commercial activities in the UK that are concerned with supplying goods or services to the general public; to ascertain whether any activity could adversely affect consumers' interests; to make recommendations to the government on measures to be taken to mitigate the adverse effects of particular trading practices; to investigate whether particular situations should be referred to the Monopolies and Mergers Commission and to assist that commission in its work. The Director General's department, the Office of Fair Trading, provides a booklet, *Fair Deal*, which gives a summary of the main laws affecting traders.

Disk (floppy, hard, Winchester) A circular magnetic disk on which data can be stored permanently and retrieved randomly without the need to sequentially search the whole disk.

Dot matrix printer A printer which forms its characters by impressing a pattern of dots on to the page, at high speed: typically 100–700 characters per second.

Downside risk Everyone who goes into a business venture does so with the expectation of making a profit. After the excitement of calculating the size of the prospective fortune to be made, the prudent entrepreneur also takes stock of the likely maximum to be lost if it all goes wrong. This is called the downside risk. The Midland Bank's association with Crocker in the USA shows that it's not just your original stake that can be at risk. Crocker's loans were in the main secured against farm land values, which was fine while prices were rising, but became a catastrophe when they started to fall as they did shortly after the Midland acquisition. Crocker's BAD DEBT provision had to be topped up with extra money from the UK parent.

Economies of scale The gain experienced by firms that can spread their costs over a large volume of output. Other advantages, such as more efficient buying, can accrue to big producers. It is one of the BARRIERS TO ENTRY, inhibiting new firms from entering certain markets successfully. However, achieving economies of scale carries some penalties. For example, it makes such businesses relatively inflexible and less responsive to change than their smaller cousins.

Ego trip A rather more accurate description of what many entrepreneurs are up to than the more prosaic term 'business'. The ego is only recognized by such entrepreneurs when it is bruised by BANKRUPTCY.

e-mail The modern alternative to telex and conventional paper-based mail, whereby computers are linked by MODEM either directly or via a commercial system (such as Telecom Gold), to send and receive information.

Entrepreneur An entrepreneur is someone who recognizes an opportunity, raising the money and other resources needed to exploit that opportunity, and bears some or all of the risk associated with executing the ensuing plans. Entrepreneurship can be more correctly viewed as a behaviour characteristic than a personality trait, which explains why the 'typical' entrepreneur is difficult to describe – or to detect in advance using questionnaires.

Equity The owner's claims against the business, sometimes called the shareholder's funds. This appears as a liability because it belongs to the shareholders and not to the business itself. It is represented by the share capital plus the cumulative retained profits over the business's life. The reward for equity investment is usually a dividend paid on profits made.

Experience curve A graphical description of what happens to costs as a business acquires a history of experience of producing a product. Typically for each doubling of experience, as represented by the absolute volume of output, unit costs can be expected to fall by 20–30%. This axiom poses at least one threat and one opportunity for entrepreneurs.

Extraordinary general meeting (EGM) Held within the rules laid down by company law and the company's own rules to deal with unusual events, such as responding to a takeover bid and changing the capital structure of a business.

Fair trading See DIRECTOR GENERAL OF FAIR TRADING.

Financial ratio The relationship between two money quantities, used to analyse business results.

Financial year A year's trading between dates agreed with the Inland Revenue. Not necessarily the fiscal year, which starts on 5 April.

Firmware Computer instructions stored in a read-only memory (ROM).

Fixed assets Assets such as land, building, equipment, cars, etc, acquired for long-term use in the business and not for stock in trade. Initially recorded in the balance sheet at cost.

Fixed cost Expenses that do not vary directly with the number of items produced. For example, a car has certain fixed costs, such as tax and insurance, whether it is driven or not.

Floating charge The security given by a borrower to a lender that floats over all his assets. So if the borrower fails to repay the loan the lender can lay claim to any and all of his assets up until the full sum due has been recovered. This contrasts with a fixed charge.

Forecast A statement of what is likely to happen in the future, based on careful judgement and analysis.

Funds Financial resources, not necessarily cash.

Gearing The ratio of a business's borrowings to its equity. For example, a 1:1 ratio would exist where a bank offered to match your investment pound for pound.

Going concern Simply an accounting concept, it assumes in all financial reports that the business will continue to trade indefinitely into the future unless there is specific evidence to the contrary – i.e. it has declared an intention to liquidate. It is not an indication of the current state of health of the business.

Goodwill Value of the name, reputation or intangible assets of a business. It is recorded in the accounts only when it is purchased. Its nature makes it a contentious subject.

Graphics Software to produce graphs, charts, presentation graphics and even high quality pictures.

Gross Total before deductions. For example, gross profit is the difference between sales income and costs of goods sold. The selling and administrative expenses have yet to be deducted. Then it becomes the net profit.

Growth vector matrix When planning for growth, entrepreneurs tend to be led by opportunity, which more often than not leads them to select diversification strategies at the outset. By their nature diversification strategies are the most risky as they build on neither the company's proven product nor market skills – it simply uses surplus cash or borrowings to back a hunch. Successful diversification calls for strong management skills, a commodity in short supply in most small firms. The growth vector matrix was developed in 1965 by Igo Ansoff to help companies to cluster and analyse their strategies for growth, and to assess their relative riskiness. The dimensions of the matrix are defined as product and market, each of which is defined in terms of the present position and the new position, resulting in four basic growth strategies: market penetration, market development, product development and diversification.

Hardware The physical part of a computer.

Income statement See PROFIT AND LOSS ACCOUNT.

Insolvency A situation in which a person or business cannot meet the bills. Differs from bankruptcy, as the insolvent may have assets that can be realized to meet those bills.

Interface Electronic device that links computer hardware together. For example, a printer or VDU to the computer itself.

Invisible hand The cornerstone of the theory of economist Adam Smith (1723–90) on the way the capitalist system works, as expounded in his book, *The Wealth of Nations* (1776). The book lends credibility to entrepreneurial activity by proposing that if all individuals act from self-interest, spurred on by the profit motive, then society as a whole prospers, with no apparent regulator at work. It is, wrote Smith, as if an 'invisible hand' guided the actions of individuals to combine for the common wealth. Governments are 'selective' in the ways in which they demonstrate their belief in this theory and their all too visible hand is seen in the creation of more and more RED TAPE that often seems only to inhibit enterprise.

Know-how agreement This is a promise to disclose information to a third party. If the disclosure is made for them to evaluate the usefulness of the know-how, the agreement is called a secrecy agreement. If the disclosure is made to allow commercial production, it is called a know-how licence.

Laser printer Uses technology similar to a photocopier to print both graphics and text at high speed with exceptional quality. Prints between 6 and 12 pages per minute.

Learning curve The improvement in the performance of a task as it is repeated and as more is learned about it.

Liabilities The claims against a business, such as loans and equity.

Liquidation The legal process of closing down a business and selling off its assets to meet outstanding debts.

Loan capital Finance lent to a business for a specific period of time at either a fixed or varied rate of interest. This interest must be paid irrespective of the performance of the business.

Love money Money put into a business by family, friends or successful business neighbours. It is a US term that has less to do with love than it has to do with tax. In the USA anyone investing in a new enterprise can do so out of pre-tax income and so have that investment effectively subsidized by their marginal tax rate.

Management buy-out (MBO) A growing phenomenon whereby the managers of a company become its owners. They do this by setting up a new company which buys either all, or more usually a part, of their old company. The money to do so is raised from banks, venture capital funds and from the managers themselves. The reason for the buy-out often stems from the desire of the parent company to pull out of a certain activity, or to de-merge from a previous amalgamation.

Management consultant 'Someone who borrows your watch to tell you the time – then charges you for the privilege.' A rather disparaging description, but one that is instantly recognizable by anyone that has used a consulting firm. Management consultants sell professional advice on most aspects of business, including financial management, marketing, market research, strategy formulation and manpower planning. They have come into their own in the information technology area and in all aspects of managing change in organizations. Management consultants are much in evidence after takeovers where they are used to help the victor make sure of the spoils. In the UK there are about 5,000 management consultants, with 2,800 belonging to the Institute of Management Consultants, their professional body.

Managing director A company director holding special powers to manage the day-to-day affairs of a company. Next in importance to the chairman.

Marginal cost The extra cost incurred in making one more unit of production.

Market segment A group of buyers who can be identified as being especially interested in a particular variant of the product. For example, a cheap day return ticket for a train is a variant of a rail fare, especially attractive to people who do not have to get to their destination early, perhaps to work.

Market share The ratio of a firm's sales of a product, in a specified market, during a period, to the total sales of that product in the same period in the same market.

Marketing mix The combination of methods used by a business to market its products. For example, it can vary its price; the type and quantity of advertising; the distribution channels can be altered; finally, the product itself can either be enhanced or reduced in quality.

Marketing strategy Philip Kotler, the US marketing theorist, identified four basic competitive marketing strategies. While strategy is classically a big business concept, there is no reason why small businessmen should not profit by using the same principles. Indeed, there is much evidence to suggest they are more likely to succeed if they do.

Megabyte (Mb) One million bytes.

Memorandum of Association A legal document drawn up as a part of the registration of a company in the UK. The memorandum must state the company's name, its registered office, its purposes and its authorized share capital. The purpose of the business, as set out in the memorandum, is very broad, deliberately so, in order not to preclude any type of trade the company may choose to embark on in the future. The memorandum is sent to the Registrar of Companies, who must also be informed of any changes.

Memory Computers use their electronic memory to store and process data. There are two sorts of memory – ROM (read-only memory), which is a permanent store containing the computer's internal operating instructions; and RAM (random-access memory), which is a temporary store containing data and programs currently being used. When the power is turned off all data and programs in the RAM memory are lost.

Microcomputer A small computer using a microprocessor as its central processing unit.

Microfiche A sheet of photographic film on which a number of microcopy images have been recorded. You need a special viewer to look at the recorded information, which is very efficiently stored.

Microprocessor Electronic circuitry etched onto a silicon chip that can be used to manipulate information.

Modem A device that allows computers (and ancillary equipment) to communicate over telephone wires. The portable version is called an acoustic coupler.

Multi-tasking The ability for one or more users to have access to and use common programs and data at the same time.

National Insurance A state insurance scheme in the UK administered by the Department of Health and Social Security, by which every employer, employee and self-employed person makes weekly payments to provide insurance against accidents, sickness and unemployment, and towards a pension and other benefits. Since April 1975 the self-employed have had to pay an additional contribution ('Class 4'). This is in effect a tax on profits and is levied at between 6.3 and 8% on all profits from self-employment between about £4,000 and £14,000 per annum.

Networking Linking together several computers, either within one building (Local Area Network System, LANS) or over large distances (Wide Area Network Systems, WANS).

Non-disclosure agreement An agreement which allows you to reveal secret commercial information – for example, about an invention – to a third party, and which prevents them from making use of that information without your agreement.

Non-executive director A part-time director, who helps to plan and decide the policy of a company but who has no responsibility for carrying out such policies. Normally companies raising capital through merchant banks and other financial institutions will be 'encouraged' to have a nominee of theirs as a non-executive director. When Lonrho bought the *Observer* newspaper in 1983, guarantees of editorial independence were sought by the Office of Fair Trading. This was eventually secured by requiring six independent non-executive directors to sit on the newly constituted *Observer* board of directors.

'Off the shelf' company A company without a trading history that has been formed and held specifically for re-sale at a later date. Agencies keep a large stock of such companies in numerous categories of business. They cost around £130 each, and can be up and running in a day or so. An 'off the shelf' company may have an unsuitable name, but that can be changed later for a modest fee. A tailor-made company will cost more than an 'off the shelf' company, and it takes four to five weeks to set up. So if speed is of the essence the 'off the shelf' is the first choice.

One per cent syndrome (or the market research cop-out clause). This describes the situation in which a prospective business owner starts a venture on the premise that 'If we only sell 1% of the potential market, we'll be a great success.' This argument is then advanced so that no time is wasted in doing basic market research – after all, the business only has to sell to this tiny percentage of possible buyers! In fact, this type of thinking leads to more business failures than any other single factor. If the market is so huge as to make 1% of it very profitable, then inevitably there are large and established competitors. For a small firm to try to compete head-on in this situation is little short of suicidal. It can be done, but only if sound research has clearly identified a market niche; or if there is a particular industry 'lag' that would allow a new business to obtain a special place. However, more usually the idea itself is badly thought through – as are ideas that do not take the customers' viewpoint – and this causes the business to fail to gain even the magical 1%.

Opportunity cost The value of a course of action open to you but not taken. For example, keeping cash in an ordinary share account at a building society will attract about 2% less interest than a five-year term at the same society. So the opportunity cost of choosing not to tie up your money is 2%.

Overhead This is an expense which cannot be conveniently associated with a unit of production. Administration or selling expenses are usually overheads.

Overtrading Expanding sales and production without enough financial resources – in particular, working capital. The first signs are usually cash-flow problems.

Pareto principle The rule which states that 80% of effort goes into producing 20% of the results. For a new business this rule is usually observed first when it is seen that 20% of their customers produce 80% of sales by value. As this rule is close to impossible to change, it is only by widening the customer base and lowering the dependence on a few important customers that a new firm can hope to survive.

Peripheral Collective name for any piece of equipment, e.g. printers, disk drives, monitors, modems, plotters, which can be attached to a computer.

Piggy-backing Usually associated with firms that market other firms' products as well as their own, but the term can be used to describe any 'free riding' activity.

Pixel Dots on the screen produced by the computer to draw text or pictures. The greater the number of pixels on the screen the better the definition will be.

Plotter Device connected to a computer to draw graphs, charts, pictures etc in one or more colours.

Preference shares These usually give their holders the right to a fixed dividend and priority over ordinary shareholders in liquidation, and confer voting power only in matters concerning the varying of the shareholders' rights or in cases when dividends have not been paid. There are four types of preference share in the entrepreneurs' 'capital' armoury:

1. Cumulative preference shares, which give the right to payment of any past dividends not paid.
2. Redeemable preference shares, which are those that the company has agreed to repay on a specified date, often at a premium over issuing price.
3. Participatory preference shares, which, in addition to the right to a fixed dividend, allow further profit participation in good times.
4. Convertible preference shares, which have the right to be changed for ordinary shares at specified dates and prices.

Product life cycle A concept which states that every product (or service) passes through certain identifiable stages in its life. Understanding the implications of each of these stages for the company's CASH FLOW, PROFIT and MARKETING STRATEGY is an important element in successfully launching a new venture.

1. Pre-launch: All the work done to bring the product or service to market. This includes product development, market research, etc.
2. Introduction: Usually featured by low sales and no profits. Innovators (ADOPTION CURVE) are the main customers.
3. Growth: If all goes well and the product is accepted by the innovative customers, sales begin to grow, sharply at first.
4. Maturity: Sales growth stops, new competitors have probably arrived, and the original product is beginning to look a bit stale.
5. Decline: Unless the product is re-launched, by changing various elements in the MARKETING MIX, sales will decline.

Profit The excess of sales revenue over sales cost and expenses during an accounting period. It does not necessarily mean an increase in cash.

Profit and loss account A statement of sales, costs, expenses and profit (or loss) over an accounting period monthly, quarterly or annually. Also known as the income statement.

Pyramid selling A form of multi-level distributorship which typically involves the manufacture or sale by a company, under its own trade name, of a line of products through 'franchises' which appear to be regular franchise distributorships. The pyramid may include three to five levels of non-exclusive distributorships, and individuals may become 'franchisees' at any level by paying the company a fee, and agreeing to buy stock, based on the level of entry. Once in, the individual earns a commission by selling the company's products, but at higher levels in the pyramid it is made more attractive to introduce new members. This product is sold down the chain at progressively higher prices, until the final person has to sell to the public. Since most people make a profit by merely being a link in the chain, the emphasis is placed on recruiting more investors–distributors, rather than on selling to end customers. The schemes, like chain letters, are lucrative for those at the top of the pyramid. But inevitably the market becomes saturated, no further participants can be recruited and the system then collapses. Contrary to public opinion, pyramid selling is not illegal in the UK. It is, however, controlled by the Fair Trading Act, 1973 (section 118), and the provision of the Consumer Credit Act, 1971.

RAM Random-access memory is the space used for storing computer data as programs. It can be changed as new programs or data are called up.

Receiver Someone called in by a troubled company's creditors to try to sort out the company's financial problems. The receiver's aim is to get the company back on the straight and narrow without it going into liquidation.

Red tape The excessive use of or adherence to formalities. Despite protestations to the opposite, it would appear to describe accurately the relationship between Whitehall and enterprise. Research by the Forum of Private Business has shown that an entrepreneur wishing to set up a limited company as an electrician needed to make 18 telephone calls, travel 127 miles to collect papers, and spend 24 hours reading 269,200 words to understand government regulations.

- The average time spent by small businesses in complying with government regulations is 10½ hours per week at a cost of £2,000 per year.
- Failure to comply with regulations can result in prison sentences of up to 2½ years and/or fines of up to £2,000.
- At every pay day there are 34 clerical operations per employee to calculate tax and National Insurance contributions and to provide the pay slip.
- Customs and Excise requires a quarterly form, VAT 100, to be completed. But the VAT inspector will expect to see every VAT invoice and bill by way of confirmation.

With the seemingly endless encroachment of legislation it seems unlikely that government-inspired deregulation measures will be effective in the short run. The only hope in the foreseeable future is a microcomputer with the appropriate software – alas, as yet unwritten.

Registered office This need not necessarily be the same address as the business is conducted from. Quite frequently the address used for the registered office is that of the firm's solicitor or accountant. This is, however, the address where all official correspondence will go. EEC regulations now require the name of the company to be prominently displayed at the registered office address.

Reserves The name given to the accumulated and undistributed profits of the business. They belong to the ordinary shareholders. They are not necessarily available in cash, but are usually tied up in other business assets.

Revenue Usually from sales. Revenue is recognized in accounting terms when goods have been despatched (or services rendered) and the invoice sent. This means that revenue pounds are not necessarily cash pounds. A source of much confusion and frequent cash flow problems.

ROM Read-only memory.

Royalty The money paid to the owner of something valuable for the right to make use of it for a specified purpose. Examples include payments made to the owners of a copyright for permission to publish, or the owner of a patent for permission to use a patented design.

Schedule 'D' Cases I and II are the Inland Revenue rules that govern tax allowances for self-employed people.

Schedule 'E' Allowances for employed people.

Seasonality A regular event, usually one that causes sales to increase or decrease in an annual cycle. For example, the weather caused by the seasons or events associated with the seasons: Christmas, spring sales, summer holidays etc.

Secured creditor Someone lending money to a business whose debt is secured by linking a default in its repayment to a fixed asset, such as a freehold building.

Share capital The capital of the business subscribed for by the owners or shareholders.

Share option A facility that allows top managers and employees to have shares in the companies for which they work, on special terms. The most effective way to improve employees' attitudes, productivity and understanding of the company's position is by instituting a share option scheme. In this way they can participate in success (and failure) too. Half of all leading UK companies operate such schemes. Indeed, various Finance Acts from 1972 have relaxed the tax position in this area.

Six badges of trade The list drawn up by the Royal Commission on the Taxation of Profits and Income, 1955, to distinguish whether an activity constitutes trading (and is therefore taxable), or is simply a hobby (and is not). The list includes:
- the frequency of the activity
- the value added, or amount of work done
- the motive
- the nature of the transaction
- the circumstances
- the methodology

Sleeping partner Someone who has put up capital but does not intend to take an active part in running the business. They can protect themselves against the risk of unlimited liability by having the partnership registered as a limited partnership. The Limited Partnership Act of 1908 sets out the arrangements and relationships that apply in the absence of any formal agreement being reached by the various partners. In a company the 'sleeping partner' would normally be a shareholder and so limit his financial exposure in that way.

Software A computer term usually associated with programs and related documentation.

Spreadsheet Program designed to help financial planning. It can be used to perform repetitive numerical calculations and is sometimes referred to as a modelling tool. It comprises rows and columns into which numbers, formulae and text can be entered.

Strategy A general method of policy for achieving specified objectives. It describes the essential resources and their amounts, which are to be committed to achieving those objects. (See TACTICS.)

Sweat equity The value that accrues to a business by virtue of the time, energy and intellectual effort required to get to the immediate pre-launch phase. It is a notional concept applied by venture capitalists to assess the commitment the entrepreneur has to his business idea; it is a substitute for the commitment that hard cash would demonstrate in the event that a proprietor has no money to put up.

SWOT analysis An acronym for Strengths, Weaknesses, Opportunities and Threats, the four factors that have to be considered when developing a successful business STRATEGY.

Synergy A cooperative or combined activity which is more effective or valuable than the sum of its independent activities.

Tactics The method by which resources allocated to a strategic objective are used.

Tax avoidance Action taken to avoid having to pay tax unnecessarily, using legal means.

Tax evasion Using illegal means of avoiding payment of tax and making a false tax declaration. About 70,000 small businesses are investigated by the UK Inland Revenue department each year for irregularities in their tax affairs. Just short of £400 million in extra tax is recovered from these firms. Most proprietors who have gone through the experience of a tax investigation would be reluctant to do anything that might incur a repeat of the experience.

Tax loss A loss that has been manufactured specifically to reduce or eliminate taxable profits. Such action usually consists of bringing forward expenditure. That unfortunately has the usual effect of increasing profits in the next year. However, for sole traders it can be attractive to have a loss in their first trading period as this forms the reference base for future tax.

Trade cycle At times the economy appears to behave like a roller coaster, encouraging new ventures and expansion plans on the upswing, only to dash them on to the rocks a short time later when the downturn comes. This effect is known as the trade cycle. No one is quite sure why there is this regularity – or rather everyone is sure, but for different reasons.

True and fair An accounting concept that states that the business financial reports have been prepared using generally accepted accounting principles.

Turn key Usually refers to a client-commissioned system, accepted only when you can 'turn on a key' and are satisfied with the results, or output.

Unique selling proposition Coined in 1940 by Rosser Reeves, advertising copy-writer of the leading advertising agency, Ted Bates. His thesis was that from the launch of a product or service onwards you should always seek to identify and promote a unique selling proposition. This can be done by asking two questions: what is different about me, the seller, and what is different about our product or service? If nothing is different, why on earth should anyone want to buy from you? This is a particularly powerful concept at the outset of a new venture when a firm is short on market credibility.

User group Organization set up by computer users who have a common interest. This common interest may be a particular computer, some piece of software or some activity. Usually there is a free exchange of ideas, programs and tips and quite frequently a magazine is produced and circulated to members.

Value In accounting it has several meanings. For example, the 'value' of a fixed asset is its costs less its cumulative depreciation. A current asset, such as stock, is usually valued at cost or market value, whichever is the lower.

Value added The difference between sales revenue that a firm gets from selling its products (or services), and the cost to it of the materials used in making those products.

Variable costs See DIRECT COSTS.

Variance The difference between actual performance and the forecast (or budget or standard).

VDU Visual display unit – another term for monitor.

Word processor The essential element in word processing is the ability to enter text into a computer and manipulate it so that the desired final output is obtained, before the hard copy is printed.

Working capital Current assets less current liabilities, which represents the capital used in the day-to-day running of the business.

Working life The economically useful life of a fixed asset. Not necessarily its whole life. For example, technological development may render it obsolete very quickly.

Work in progress Goods in the process of being produced, which are valued at the lower end of manufacturing costs or market value.

Index